Conrad Veidt on Screen

Conrad Veidt on Screen

A Comprehensive Illustrated Filmography

JOHN T. SOISTER

Biography by PAT WILKS BATTLE
Afterword by HENRY NICOLELLA

McFarland & Company, Inc., Publishers
Jefferson, North Carolina, and London

ALSO BY JOHN T. SOISTER

Claude Rains: A Comprehensive Illustrated Reference to His Work in Film, Stage, Radio, Television and Recordings
(McFarland, 1999)

Of Gods and Monsters: A Critical Guide to Universal Studios' Science Fiction, Horror and Mystery Films, 1929–1939
(McFarland, 1998)

Frontispiece: Conrad Veidt as Jaffar, in *The Thief of Bagdad* (1940).

Library of Congress Cataloguing-in-Publication Data
Soister, John T., 1950–
Conrad Veidt on screen : a comprehensive illustrated filmography /
John T. Soister ; biography by Pat Wilks Battle ;
afterword by Henry Nicolella. 2002
p.   cm.
Includes bibliographical references and index.

ISBN 0-7864-1289-5 (illustrated case binding : 50# alkaline paper)

1. Veidt, Conrad, 1893–1943.   I. Battle, Pat Wilks.   II. Title.
PN2658.V37S65   2002   791.43'028'092 — dc21   2002006497

British Library cataloguing data are available

On the cover (clockwise from top left): Conrad Veidt as Cesare the Somnambulist in *Das Cabinet des Dr. Caligari*; as Matathias in *The Wandering Jew*; as Joseph Oppenheimer in *Jew Süss*; and as Ayan in *Das indische Grabmal*

Manufactured in the United States of America

McFarland & Company, Inc., Publishers
Box 611, Jefferson, North Carolina 28640
www.mcfarlandpub.com

For Mom and Dad

Acknowledgments

Data compilation can be viewed as either a necessary evil (to be endured, albeit deplored), or a challenge in terms of objective completion: achieving such-and-such *may* lead one to personal gratification. No matter how you view it, it is an arduous task, and not something that a normal person would seek to undertake alone. As I had no wish to push the envelope on normalcy, I immediately sought the assistance of the following folks. To these generous souls, and to the others — who may have forgotten to note their names on their contributions, or who chose to pass on my request for just that information — I am extremely grateful. If there's anything I can do for *you*, you have only to ask.

Stephan Eichenberg, Rolf Peter Stens, Dorothy L. Skeels, Corinne Malgouyard (Bibliothèque du Film), Brigitte Capitain (Deutsches Filminstitut), Adriano Apra and Elisabetta Bruscolini (Cineteca Nazionale), Olaf Brill, Geoffrey Wheeler (Archivist and Photographer), Barbara Peterson, Barrie Pattison, Robert G. Dickson (Aye!), April Dawson, Tracey Doyle, Paula Vitaris (for allowing me to quote from her splendid interview with film archivist David Shepard), Mika Raatikainen, Randolph Mann, Nostalgia Family Video, Phil Edwards, Alan Levine, Gary Pominville, Wendy Cunningham, Sandy Schweigert and Tara Wishkin (my three darlings from Staples), Mary Corliss (Movie Stills Archive; MOMA), Charles Silver (Film Study Center; MOMA), Richard Bojarski, John Parnum, JoAnna Wioskowski, Eileen Bowser, Hyde Flippo, Jeff Angelo, Coleen Ingalzo, Joyce Stripe, Howard and Ron Mandelbaum (Photofest), Madeline Matz (Library of Congress), Rubin Sherman, The Morris Everett Collection, Louise Bowers, Tom Mitchell (my friend of 20 years), Tessa Forbes and Ayesha Khan (The British Film Institute), Jeremy Soister (a wizard on the PC!), Bob Wallets, and Thomas Kuntz, who is both an extraordinary artist and a generous friend.

Elisabet Helge (of the Svenska Filminstitutet): I love you.

Table of Contents

Indented titles are parts of series

Preface

As much as I've always relished a good challenge, compiling what is hoped to be a solid reference on Conrad Veidt's film career has been a pip. In addition to the normal stumbling blocks that crop up during projects like this—contradictory information, divergent data, and unreliable sources—there are also variations of spelling or printing between/among languages, the ravages of two World Wars, and that grand abyss of time: Veidt's first picture was released just about 85 years ago. Film criticism was in its infancy during the teens, and while the film industry did quite well for itself during the Great War (no one could deny the important role it played in maintaining morale), personnel and resources that might otherwise have been directed toward *das Kino* were doubtless diverted toward *der Kaiser*.

The cinema of the late teens and early twenties sired the trend that kicked in again (albeit in reverse) during the eighties and has endured to the present day: the star as director. Erna Morena and Reinhold Schünzel (to name but two) joined Veidt in helming certain titles in their catalogue, in addition to gracing the screen. In some instances, however, a healthy skepticism confronts similar situations involving those who must now be considered lesser luminaries: which antique, widely disparate and conflicting credits list may be viewed as gospel, and which ought to be taken *cum grano salis*? (See: *Der Weg des Todes*, in Appendix.)

Does one strive to homogenize variations in spelling? Take Käte Oswald and Käte Waldeck-Oswald, and then toss "Käthe" into the hopper instead of "Käte." As different sources cite different versions, which does one choose as definitive? Some data always list certain actors as using "von" with their surnames; others omit the appellative preposition altogether; still others appear to choose capriciously. To umlaut, or not to umlaut? *Das ist die Frage.* Just don't look to existing documentation for an answer chiseled in granite.

If a piece of information comes directly from the prestigious Deutsches Filminstitut, does that give it the weight of Holy Scripture? Well, what if it is at odds with a corresponding bit of information from the no less prestigious Stiftung Deutsche Kinemathek? Whither goest thou from that point? And while the contemporary German film magazines (such as *Film-Kurier*) didn't fail to comment on thereto incomparable visions like *Das Cabinet des Dr. Caligari*, they were critically parsimonious on such now-lost productions as *Das Rätsel von Bangalor* and *Wenn Tote sprechen*. Were these oversights due (as I've suggested above) to wartime energies being directed elsewhere, or to (even then) perceptions that "lesser" efforts deserved little mention? Compounding the felony was the tendency to cite only the principal actors in reviews (such as they were); supporting and bit players may have had their following, but their fans would have been hard-pressed as to their heroes' identities had they had recourse only to studio publicity pieces or cast lists.

As the pièce de résistance, Berlin, the seat of the German film industry since its inception, was also the political capital of the country and, as such, was decimated by the Allied forces. This wholesale destruction devastated any well-ordered film archives and studio warehouses, and so it is only with the greatest luck that the minute fragments that accompany some titles in this book have survived at all.

The films collected herein represent the professional motion pictures in which Conrad Veidt personally took part. This means that no coverage will be afforded movies, TV shows, etc., wherein Veidt's saturnine presence is the result of the inclusion of archival footage. Hence, items such as *Rund um die Liebe* (1929), a compilation film consisting of love scenes appropriated from earlier features (and including Connie and Elizabeth Bergner from *Der Geiger von Florenz*), or West Germany's oddball *Das Gabs nur einmal* (1958) merit no mention other than this brief remark. Likewise, Richard Hirschfeld's 1924 documentary *Der Film im Film*— listed virtually everywhere as a legitimate entry in the Veidt canon — is noteworthy (per our focus) only for its inclusion of sequences from *Lucrezia Borgia*.

Research has disproved Veidt's involvement in some films with which he has been identified over the years. Connie just isn't to be found in Dimitri Buchowetzki's *Danton*, despite a profusion of ink to the contrary. Ditto with *Die Seeschlacht*, a 1917 Richard Oswald film that starred Werner Krauss. (Connie was in the eponymous play that inspired the film, however; he first met his future wife, Gussy Holl, after a matinee performance.) *König Richard III* and *Lord Byron* never got beyond the talking stages, that's Max Shreck (and not Connie) glaring out from the extant stills from *Der Richter von Zalamea*, and the Internet Movie Data Base apart, the Marquis de Sade was not impersonated by our man in Abel Gance's *Napoleon*, due to an inability of Herr Veidt and Monsieur Gance to come to financial terms. (A great deal of the picture's advance publicity was crafted prior to negotiations breaking down, though; hence, the display ad mentioning Veidt's name.) Hungarian film magazines from 1923–24 listed Veidt as set to portray the title role in an imminent production of *Faust* (along with Liane Haid as Margit, Werner Krauss as Mefiszto and Albert Bassermann as Wagner); when the picture was made (by F.W. Murnau in 1926), Swedish actor Gösta Ekman filled in for Connie, and Emil Jannings filled out the role of Mephisto. Other crapshoots of yore are either conspicuous by their absence herein or are tagged and displayed in the Appendix chapter of this book.

This winnowing of "chaff" has resulted in a film list which, at first glance, is rather significantly shorter than the half-dozen or so which may be found in print or on the Internet. The brevity of the tally is illusory, as both "halves" of sundry two-part film series have been logged in under one title. (Please see my note, below.)

Rather than sweeping notes and sources into a haphazard pile a page or two north of the index, I've interspersed them in the text itself. Most of the quoted

Apparently some of the advertising hit before all the contracts were signed. Veidt does NOT appear in *Napoleon*.

source material deals in opinion or theory, and while I don't necessarily agree with every author's every statement, I prefer not to commit sins of exclusion based solely on my own capacity to be swayed by giddy rhetoric. Even the masterworks of such heavy hitters as Lotte H. Eisner and Siegfried Kracauer have, over the last few years, been subject to scrutiny and reappraisal. In these cases, I've opted not to list these attendant revisionist reactions, mainly because this book is a filmography, not a doctoral dissertation, and I strongly suspect that the average reader would not choose this specific book while looking for either highly formulated debate on the philosophical applications of Expressionist art or a rabbinical parsing of related jargon. In any event, a meticulous appreciation for Expressionist trends and nuances is the prerequisite for appreciating most of the prose that takes Eisner and Kracauer to task, and the bibliography cites a number of examples of current Eisner/Kracauer reevaluation for those inclined to pursue the topic. If I hope to be true to my focus and format, that will have to suffice.

As a handful of Veidt's works—pictures like *Das Cabinet des Dr. Caligari*, *Anders als die Andern* and *Casablanca*— have, to date, received vast chapter-and-verse coverage, any attempt on my part to "compete" with them within the framework of this book would be foolhardy; rather, representative material on those pictures has been chosen for inclusion. And, given the encyclopedic bent of this volume, I have, for the most part, deferred to professional reviewers when the discussion turns to readily available films.

Obviously, it's exquisitely difficult to comment in situations where not only has the film been lost for years, but also where there is a dearth of contemporary critical literature upon which to draw. Entries on pictures such as these will of necessity be brief. There are some critiques that I've quoted that have survived the passage of time only as yellowed newspaper clippings, printed in "old" German typeset and missing both date of publication and the name of the paper in which they appeared. As I feel that their content more than compensates for the regrettable fact that circumstances have rendered them "unattributable," these bear the legend "unknown review" wherever they appear.

(Please bear in mind that a certain license had to be taken in translating these early pieces. Some of the then-contemporary phraseology was a trifle awkward even in those days, and that may safely be said without taking German word order into consideration. Exacerbating the situation is the feeling one gets that several of those critics purposefully wrote their commentaries in the most flowery fashion manageable, as if there were a direct relationship between one's personal genius and the degree to which his writing was convoluted. And then, as now, some of the reviewers tended to exaggerate the virtues of certain of their favorite actors or technicians, while turning the blindest of eyes to these same artists' vices. Finally, in addition to stylistic difficulties, in many instances the vocabulary itself underwent transformation: the meaning of some words changed, while other words/phrases became outmoded or obsolete. When all was said and done, it took a great deal of linguistic panning to get this gold into our hands.)

Stills from many of these films have likewise disappeared. Thus, in quite a few instances, the accompanying illustration will be taken from a contemporary program or postcard, rather than from a photograph printed specifically for publication.

For all this, in spite of an enormous collective effort, some of Connie's pictures remain woefully underdocumented. This volume, then, cannot claim to be either definitive or 100 percent comprehensive. It does, however, reflect years of research spanning four continents and the help of a small cadre of highly dedicated and canny Conrad Veidt aficionados, whose enthusiasm for Connie is both a testimony to the actor's genius and a tribute to the man's personal philosophy.

Vivienne Phillips may well have the most comprehensive collection of Conrad Veidt film memorabilia anywhere, and she kindly invited me to come to Golders Green and delve among her treasures. What's more, she allowed me — in reality, a complete stranger — to remove items and bring them to the States for the purpose of copying them for publication. I owe many thanks to this most generous woman.

I finally met Michaela Krause at the British Film Institute, where she joined my buddy, Tom Mitchell, and me in a couple of days of rather intense research. Prior (and subsequent) to that, Michaela was a juggernaut, mowing down any assignment tossed into her path. She provided rare reviews and publicity pieces, translated them upon request, tracked down hitherto unseen images in sundry German archives, and provided commentary and insight *in ictuoculi*. (Check out Michaela's website: www.conradveidt.de). I am forever in her debt, and I look forward to working with her again.

Berliner Werner Mohr sent a parcel stuffed with absolutely incredible information and graphics at the eleventh hour. Responding to my want list, Werner went to great expense to provide me with lasers of items that plugged some substantial holes in the project. I don't know whether he owns any shining armor, but Werner is first knight as far as I'm concerned.

The name Pat Wilks Battle immediately perks up the ears of any and all knowledgeable Veidt aficionados, and I was enormously pleased to have Pat agree to pen the biographical sketch that opens *Conrad Veidt on Screen*. Pat's three-part "Films in Review" piece on Connie was one of the anchors of the book you're holding now, and I little dreamed at the outset that its author would lend her knowledge and her renown in this fashion. Thanks a million, Pat.

Henry Nicolella is a film buff, par excellence, and it was he who first planted the Connie bug in my head. Henry's field of expertise is the silent and early talkie era, and his writings, opinions and reviews have graced the pages of not a few periodicals. I'm thankful for Henry's impetus and contributions, and I hope he's happy with the results of our mutual labor.

In the names of these extraordinary folk — and, of course, in my own — I present an encyclopedic accounting of a film career that encompassed most of the then-known cinematic genres while spanning four decades. *Six* decades following the man's abrupt death, a brace of websites (one maintained by the *Conrad Veidt Society*) demonstrates the impact his career and personality still have on today's movie lovers. As I write this, Ms. Battle is readying a new Veidt biography, one that promises to deliver the kind of goods 21st century film scholarship dictates and Connie's legions of fans deserve. Indeed, I'm grateful to her for providing a nutshell version of this with which to launch my filmography.

One last explanatory note: I've tried to arrange the films in order of release date, although — at least twice in the earliest period — this is professional speculation on my part. I find that most of my research leads me to agree with the order posited by Cinegraph, the Hamburg-based professional research association. Also: more than once, Connie participated in one or two parts of a multipicture series; in the interest of continuity, the relevant parts have been listed together, even if they had verifiably different release dates. Thus, both *Das gelbe Haus* and *Die sich verkaufen* are listed under *Die Prostitution*; *Das Tagebuch einer Verlorenen* includes both the eponymous first part and *Dida Ibsens Geschichte*; *Henriette Jacoby* may be found in *Jettchen Geberts Geschichte*; the essay on *Christian Wahnschaffe* deals with *Weltbrand* and *Die Flucht aus dem goldenen Kerker*; and *Sündige Mütter* is first up in the chapter on *Es werde Licht!*, even though it was the last "teil" to be released. In an effort to make this book as user-friendly as possible, I've noted all this reorganization in the table of contents.

John T. Soister
Orwigsburg, Pennsylvania
Summer 2002

Biography

by Pat Wilks Battle

When the tributes to Conrad Veidt started pouring in to the newspapers after his fatal heart attack on a Los Angeles golf course in the spring of 1943, one in particular stood out for its amusing insight into the contradictory nature of the actor and the man.

In the German-Jewish paper *Aufbau*, Hans Kafka recalled a dinner party thrown for Veidt shortly before his death by the well-known chanteuse Greta Keller. The party was a chance for Veidt to get together with some old friends from his Berlin days, while his wife, Lily, was away in New York visiting her mother. Toward the end of the evening, the guests started playing a parlor game called "Who am I?" in which a person, sent out of the room, returns to guess the identity of a figure the others have chosen in his absence. The point of the game is to show the difference between what a person says is his taste is in clothing, drinks, cities, etc., and what the person truly prefers. Although the mystery figure is usually a historical character, Conrad's friends thought it would be great fun to have him try to guess himself.

Conrad Veidt was unable to guess himself.

"What kind of period costume would the person in question like?" the actor queried. "Rococo," came the answer.

"What kind of shoes would the person wear?" he asked again. "Prussian officer's boots."

"What music would the person like?" "Chopin's piano music," his friends responded, certain that Conrad would guess this time around. But, no.

"If the person were to invite three historical personalities to dinner, whom would he choose?" Veidt asked. His friends thought it would be too obvious to name any of the historical figures Conrad had portrayed in his films, such as Rasputin or Ivan the Terrible, so they chose others he might like to have played, such as Landru, the murderer; Krishnamurti, the Buddha; and Beau Brummel.

"Now stop it!" Veidt cried at this point. "That's all nonsense and contradictory. Chopin and Prussian boots, Landru, a living Buddha and Beau Brummel — that can't cover one personality!" So the guests broke down and told him that *he* was the mystery figure.

In concluding his recollection, Kafka wrote:

The most elucidating hint about his nature was given outside the game by himself when he could not identify himself with those exact descriptions. Without knowing much about the brilliant facets of his private and artistic personality, he just lived and acted on, a kind-hearted man and a great virtuoso ["In Memoriam Conrad Veidt," Aufbau, 9 April 1943].

It was a fitting summation of a short but remarkable life that was a study in contrasts. Best remembered today as the Nazi Major Strasser in *Casablanca*, Conrad Veidt had actually fled Hitler's Germany with his Jewish wife. One of the cinema's longest-reigning villains— his breakout role was that of the homicidal sleepwalker in 1919's *Das Cabinet des Dr. Caligari*— Veidt took a lifelong stand against bigotry and intolerance. He participated in many social reform films (like *Kreuzzug des Weibes*, which called for the decriminalization of abortion), appeared in one of the earliest gay-rights films (*Anders als die Andern*) and was the eponymous lead in both *Jew Süss* and *The Wandering Jew*, a brace of British-made features that combatted anti–Semitism. He devoted his career to fighting oppression in general and Nazism in particular. It was this aspect of his extraordinary life that inspired the Conrad Veidt Society to adopt as its motto "Courage, Integrity, Humanity" (The Conrad Veidt Society was founded in 1990 by James H. Rathlesberger of California, whose winter 1992/93 newsletter stated that "Veidt was an actor, not a statesman, but the character he personified off the stage remains important, even more so than his giant contributions to film." The CVS can be contacted via Barbara Peterson, 2355 Fairview Avenue, Suite 154, Roseville MN 55113. E-mail inquiries may be sent to nocturne_cvs@yahoo.com).

One of the first international film stars whose career spanned three decades and twice as many countries, Hans Walter Conrad Veidt (pronounced "fight") was born in Berlin on the 22nd of January, 1893, to middle-class, Protestant, nontheatrical parents. Philipp Veidt, a deeply conservative civil servant and former sergeant in the Royal Artillery, would come to deplore his son's chosen profession. Mother Amalie, on the other hand, doted on her sensitive boy and would secretly encourage his theatrical bent.

As a child, though, Connie — as his intimates called him — had no such leanings; rather, he dreamed of becoming a surgeon. His only sibling, older brother Karl, died of scarlet fever at age nine, and two years later, his father fell gravely ill. A heart specialist performed the delicate and dangerous operation that saved Philipp Veidt's life and then, mindful that the family could not possibly afford his normal lofty fee, graciously charged only what the family could comfortably pay. Impressed by both the surgeon's kindness and skill, Connie vowed to "model my life on that of the man who had saved my father's life."

Connie's hopes for a medical career were dashed in high school, where, ranked 13th out of 13 pupils, he was discouraged by the sheer amount of study necessary for him to qualify for medical school. Fortunately, a new career path opened up to him during a school Christmas play in which he delivered a long prologue before the curtain rose. The play went off so badly that the audience was heard to mutter "Too bad the others didn't do as well as Veidt" while leaving the building. Connie was hooked.

The incipient thespian decided to study all the great actors he could and left school to pursue his new calling. "My father was very unhappy," he told a magazine many years later. "He said, 'An actor is a gypsy, an outcast.' For in 1912, actors were not normal to other people" ("Conrad Veidt Looks in the Mirror" by Gladys Hall. Silver Screen (magazine), September 1941).

To create a proper bohemian image,

Left: Connie's father, Philipp: conservative, regimented and aghast that his son wanted to be an actor. *Right:* Mother Veidt, Amalie, with baby Conrad.

Connie took to wearing a wide-brimmed, floppy hat, a black cape, a flowing cravat … and a monocle, set in an impressive black frame and fastened about his neck with a long, black silk ribbon. He was quite shortsighted in his right eye, but reasoned: "Whoever heard of an actor in spectacles?"

At the end of every performance, he loitered outside the theater, waiting for the actors and hoping to be mistaken for one himself. In later years, Veidt never failed to credit the theater porter with giving him his first break. The old man introduced the tall, thin, stage-struck young hopeful to a character actor, who agreed to coach him for free. A quick ten lessons later, Connie was ready to audition for Max Reinhardt — one of the greatest producers of Shakespearean theater of his day — himself. Veidt felt that nothing less than a major classic would do, so he announced that he would recite from Goethe's *Faust*. Rein-

hardt, Veidt later recalled, was so fascinated that he looked out the window the entire time. Nonetheless, apparently Connie did strike a chord with the legendary impresario; he was offered a contract as an extra for one season's work, from September 1913 to August 1914. The nouveau extra wasted no time in printing up business cards that read: "Conrad Veidt, Member of the Deutsches Theater." He found himself in stellar company with such fellow extras as Ernst Lubitsch and Friedrich Wilhelm Plumpe (who later forswore "Plumpe" in favor of "Murnau"), playing bit parts as spear carriers and soldiers. One member of the audience at almost every performance was Connie's proud mother, Amalie.

Veidt's contract with the Deutsches Theater was renewed for a second season, but now he faced an engagement of a different sort: the First World War. On December 28, 1914, he enlisted with the Army

Conrad Veidt, Member of the Deutsches Theater.

for him as a player of speaking parts at the Deutsches Theater. In the autumn of 1916, "Conrad Veidt, Member of the Deutsches Theater," returned to Berlin.

Nineteen seventeen was bittersweet for Connie. Although it was the year he both became a featured player for the illustrious Reinhardt company and embarked on a career in moving pictures, it was also the year Philipp Veidt died. It was a matter of endless sorrow that his father never knew what a success he had become. "It is still a deep regret to me that in choosing acting as my career, I was forced to hurt him," Veidt confessed in a newspaper interview years later. "He died too early to see that I had done the right, the only thing" ("Search: The Story of Conrad Veidt," Sunday Dispatch [London], 14 October 1934).

Motion pictures had been steadily growing more popular, and filmmakers, wanting to lure well-known stage artists into the fledgling industry, tempted the big names with big money. Many such artists had their doubts, however, and wondered whether a lengthy and fulfilling career could be had in films. The younger actors were torn between their great love for the "old" theater and the popular new medium of film.

Veidt, who had dismissed films as "low, low entertainment," had a change of heart when producers started coming around with lucrative offers. One agreed to pay him his $50 monthly salary *every day* if he would work in films. "That's how the movies got me," Connie later told a magazine. "After I signed the contract, I wondered if I was selling my soul, like Faust. I didn't know that I would find the

Service Corps and was shipped out to the eastern front, near Warsaw. It wasn't long, however, before the 6'3", 165-pound "walking cadaver" fell ill with jaundice and was sent back to a military hospital in East Prussia.

As both a shortage of talent and a need to boost the public morale prompted the army to grant leaves to actors who were wounded (or otherwise unable to perform their duties), Connie was furloughed soon after being declared unfit for further military service. Having perfected his craft at local (and front-line) theaters, Connie dispatched a letter to Edmund Reinhardt — the great man's brother and business manager — asking if there might now be a place

movies fascinating. Even if they did make a villain of me" ("Villain by Accident" by Betty Harris. Modern Screen [magazine], June 1941).

The title of the first "Conrad Veidt" film remains in dispute, but what is known is that he spent a good deal of 1917 playing sinister Hindus. (In fact, thanks to his angular features and exotic good looks, he would never completely get away from "turban parts," whether in Germany [*Furcht, Das indische Grabmal*] or in England [*Bella Donna, The Thief of Bagdad*].) One such film, *Das Rätsel von Bangalor*, was very successful financially. The script had been written by the film's set designer, Paul Leni, who would figure prominently in Veidt's film future.

Because films were shot during the day, Connie was free to fulfill his theatrical obligations at night. On January 17, 1918, a new five-act play by Georg Kaiser called *Die Koralle (The Coral)* opened at the Deutsches Theater. Veidt appeared only in the final act for a single short scene as a priest, but he caught the eye of Siegfried Jacobsohn, the distinguished critic for the Weltbühne. Jacobsohn pondered in print:

> Conrad Veidt ... is a strange-looking young man with a face you cannot forget... I hope his fate will not be to go on to films, but undoubtedly film producers will be rushing for his services.

Veidt memorized this review and never tired of quoting it to the press over the next 25 years.

The direct result of this notice was not an array of larger roles from Reinhardt, but rather an offer from producer Richard Oswald to appear in a series of *Aufklärungfilme* ("enlightenment" films), that purported to address the moral and social problems of the Weimar Republic. Dealing with such hefty subjects as prostitution and venereal disease — yet usually shot on a decidedly skimpy seven- to ten-day sche-

dule — the films were condemned by some critics for their "undeniable penchant for pornographic excursions" and for "indulging in a copious depiction of sexual debaucheries."

Still, some of these pictures managed to rise above the clouds of mere entertainment and aspire to social reform. The most significant of these was the aforementioned *Anders als die Andern*. Oswald's ostensible purpose for making this landmark film was to overturn paragraph 175 of the German penal code, which outlawed certain homosexual acts between consenting adults. To lend the film credibility, Oswald enlisted the services of Dr. Magnus Hirschfeld, a noted physician and gay rights advocate, to make the film's plea for tolerance and understanding.

Veidt starred as a gay concert violinist who falls in love with one of his pupils. After being blackmailed by a man he picks up at a dance, he eventually commits suicide. The picture created a box-office sensation, bringing Oswald a great deal of money and Veidt an avalanche of fan mail. It failed, however, to bring about a revision of paragraph 175. Right-wing extremists disrupted screenings with stink bombs, live mice and gunfire. After being attacked in the press as "A piece of rampant obscenity," *Anders als die Andern* was banned; later, during the heyday of Third Reich censorship, prints of it were burned. Although it was long feared completely lost, a 40-minute fragment of the original feature-length film was discovered and restored by the Munich Filmmuseum.

On March 3, 1918, Connie had a larger part than usual in the Deutsches Theater's *Seeschlacht (Sea Battle)*, Reinhard Göring's drama of a group of sailors aboard a WWI submarine. Besides Veidt, the cast included Emil Jannings, Werner Krauss and Paul Wegener as members of the crew. After the matinee performance, Connie was introduced to the famous cabaret artist Gussy Holl, who would become his first wife. The marriage was short-lived, though; Gussy would go on to marry Veidt's colleague Emil Jannings.

Like other actors who had achieved fame, Connie founded his own production company and directed himself in *Wahnsinn* and *Die Nacht auf Goldenhall*. Both pictures costarred Gussy Holl and both were unsuccessful; Veidt was content to remain in front of the camera for the rest of his film career.

Fortunately, at this time, Connie's old fellow extra from his very first season at the Deutsches Theater, F.W. Murnau, was embarking on his career as a director and engaged Connie for five pictures, most of which were studies in the macabre. *Der Januskopf* was an early version of the Jekyll and Hyde story, with Veidt essaying the dual role and Bela Lugosi appearing as his butler. Another Murnau-Veidt effort was *Der Gang in die Nacht*, wherein Connie portrayed a blind painter who falls in love with the wife of a surgeon. Murnau stripped Connie of all his flamboyance for the part of the painter and directed him to act in a slow, quiet manner with his eyes closed. Here, for the first time, Veidt displayed the almost spiritual intensity that he could choose to convey during highly emotional moments.

Although Connie worked with his share of "great" directors, it was his particular misfortune never to be in the right place at the right time. If he labored for a man whose reputation has swelled with the passage of time, he did so either in an early, "formative" period of that man's career (as he had with Murnau), or in some mediocre enterprise (like E.A. Dupont's German-language version of *Cape Forlorn*). Only once did Connie get to play a great part for a great director: when he starred as Gwynplaine in Paul Leni's *The Man Who Laughs*. For the most part, however, he played his most exciting and memorable roles for directors of second, third or even fourth rank.

During the 1919-1920 theater season, Veidt moved to the Lessing Theater, hoping that work for Victor Barnowsky — a technician of admittedly less genius than Max Reinhardt — would mean bigger and better parts. Connie's struggle to win acclaim on the stage persisted from the time of his return to Berlin after the war until his first departure for Hollywood in 1926 (although with waning frequency during the mid and late '20s). To be sure, certain of his colleagues did commend his stage work. Heinz Herald, who directed Veidt in a one-act play by Franz Werfel (*Der Besuch im Elysium [The Visit to Elysium]*) at the Deutsches Theater, recalled "He played the tragic role and … in a split second he was able to sense what I wanted, give it back, intensify it. One could play on him like a wonderful, old violin" (Aufbau, op. cit.).

Connie returned one last time to Reinhardt's theater for the debut of *Schöffer Martin (Chauffeur Martin)* by Hans J. Rehfisch, which lasted only four performances. The play dealt with manslaughter in an automobile accident and Veidt, with a crutch under his left shoulder, played a frenzied cripple. An even more striking role — as the Mandarin, Sang-Juen Wai, in *Der lasterhafter Herr Tschu (The Wicked Mr. Tschu)* — was to be had at the Lessing Theater, but Connie was somewhat overshadowed by the triumph of Elisabeth Bergner as a forlorn geisha girl. Years later, *Tschu* director Julius Berstl would write about Veidt: "Every word struck home. In his height alone, he was wonderful" (Odysee eines Theatermannes by Julius Berstl. Verlag Berlin-Grünwald, 1963; p. 151).

If Connie's increasingly irregular stage work brought him little satisfaction, his film career was taking off. Robert Wiene's Expressionist masterpiece *Das Cabinet des Dr. Caligari* proved to be a turning point, not only for Conrad Veidt, but also for filmmaking at large. In telling the story of a sideshow hypnotist and his murderous somnambulist, the camera became a subjective interpreter instead of a mere mechanical observer. Even *Caligari's* promotion was revolutionary: it was the first film to have a widely advertised catch phrase — "You Must Become Caligari!" It was echoed all over Germany, as Decla Film papered the streets with posters proclaiming just that. The message piqued curiosity, and soon the film was wending its way throughout Europe.

Lil Dagover, the only distaff member of the compact cast, wrote in her memoirs: "For the part, Veidt wore a horrifying costume, his lithe, reed-thin physique encased in narrow, black tights, moving about menacingly like a tiger." For all that, Dagover maintained that it was her co-star's eyes that affected her the most: "I still see how Veidt seems compelled to open the dead, black eyes; how the gleam fills the pupils, how the terror fills the eyes as the bloodless lips speak the words 'Until dawn'" (Ich war die Dame by Lil Dagover. Munich: Franz Schneekluth Verlag, 1979; pp. 82–83).

As for Connie's thoughts about the picture: "This film was the turning point in my career. Everything I had done up till now, on the stage and the films, was building me up, but *Caligari* established me, and made my Continental reputation" (Sunday Dispatch [London], 21 October 1934).

Although Veidt let his piercing, hypnotic eyes do the acting for him in some of his films (most notably, *The Man Who Laughs*), he repeatedly stressed that movement was the most profound expression of character. His artistry was not lost on critic Siegfried Kracauer, who maintained, "When Conrad Veidt's Cesare prowled along a wall, it was as if the wall had exuded him" (From Caligari to Hitler by Siegfried Kracauer. New Jersey: Princeton University press, 1947; p. 70).

Dagover agreed that "The scenes in the steep, dark, crooked alleyways … belonged to him." She also noted that Connie didn't just play a character, he became the character. "Even when he was not in front of the camera, he would prowl about the studio and startle us" (Dagover, op.cit., pp. 83–84).

Connie was finding his burgeoning reputation as the "Man with the Wicked Eyes" and "King of the Gooseflesh" a nuisance. "It is really glorious to be popular," he wrote at the time, "but the fact that God and the world see in me a quite different man from the one I am, that is something not at all pleasant." He complained that he couldn't walk into a restaurant without women gasping, "Look at him! What a demon he is!" When his wife tried to hire a maid, the woman balked: "What? I should work for this bloodthirsty man who slaughters women like hens?" ("Der Damon und meine Wenigheit" by Conrad Veidt. Revue des Monats, April 1927).

"My endlessly beloved mother, Mrs. Anna Veidt, born Göhtz, died unexpectedly after a brief illness at the age of 56. In unutterable pain, Conrad Veidt."

With his star on the rise, Conrad Veidt felt that 1922 would hold great promise. In January, though, his beloved mother, Amalie — whose encouragement and financial and moral support had helped make his success possible — died suddenly. Her death devastated him, and he would mourn her loss the rest of his life. As that year also saw the dissolution of his marriage to Gussy Holl, what had promised to be an *annus mirabilis* was rapidly becoming the worst period of his life. His personal fortune reversed one evening when he spotted the vivacious Felicitas Radke at a Charleston dance contest (which she won). Enraptured by the dark-haired, long-legged beauty, he invited her to lunch and a whirlwind courtship ensued. They married at Berlin's city hall on April 18, 1923.

Happy in his marriage, Connie also found himself embarking on a new stage of filmmaking. Thanks to the influence of Hollywood, the German studios were producing historical epics and big-budget spectacles, which stood in stark contrast to the modest productions and small sets that Veidt and other of his colleagues were used to. The first of these extravaganzas was *Das indische Grabmal*, written by Fritz Lang and his wife, Thea von Harbou, and based on Frau Lang's novel of the same name. Veidt played the disconsolate Maharajah of Bengal in the exotic adventure, which had been inspired by the building of the Taj Mahal. The 24-million-mark, two-part epic featured reconstructed temples, wild animals, and daring stunts. Per Siegfried Kracauer, it "outdid the serials in thrilling episodes" (Kracauer, op.cit., p. 56).

Veidt himself had never been so lavishly costumed or so flatteringly photographed.

With the huge commercial success of *Das indische Grabmal*, Veidt was now seen as a costume actor for superproductions, and Richard Oswald cast him in no fewer than three historical spectacles. *Lady Hamilton*, filmed on location in Italy, England and Germany, saw Veidt as the dashing, heroic Lord Nelson. American director D.W. Griffith, who knew a thing or two about epics himself, hailed the film as the best to come out of Europe at that time. Italy also served as the location for *Lucrezia Borgia*, wherein Veidt could be found as another Cesare — the brother of the titular heroine. For the first time in a film, Connie played opposite Albert Bassermann, one of his idols from his Deutsches Theater days. For his next period romance, *Carlos und Elisabeth*, Connie had the dual role of the Emperor Charles V and his grandson the Infante, Don Carlos.

Although its president had helmed only *Wahnsinn* and *Die Nacht auf Goldenhall*, Veidt's film company also produced *Paganini*, the last Veidt-Film to hit the screen. Connie's performance as the legendary violinist has been regarded by some as his greatest in any film. To critic Bela Balázs, for example, *Paganini* (1923) demonstrated the power of an audience's imagination — a feat that a "talkie" would be hard-pressed to duplicate. In describing how Paganini fiddles his way out of prison, Balázs wrote:

> His playing is bewitching — the enchanted turnkeys get out of his path and his violin paralyzes all resistance to his escape... In this film, the inaudible playing of a violin has a dramaturgical function, because it influenced the hero's fate, freed him from his prison. As a spectacle, it was a fine and convincing scene, precisely because it was silent! The great actor made us imagine violin playing so enchanting that hardened jailers dropped their weapons. It would have been necessary to hire a superb virtuoso on the violin in order to achieve this effect in a sound movie [The Theory of Film by Bela Balázs. London: Dennis Dobson, Ltd., 1953; pp. 200–01].

The "demonic" Conrad Veidt returned in a big way in Paul Leni's *Das*

Wachsfigurenkabinett (*Waxworks*, 1924). Like *Caligari*, *Waxworks* is set in a carnival tent, but it is the tales spun by the young poet (Wilhelm Dieterle) that bring alarmingly to life three tyrannical figures: Ivan the Terrible (Veidt), Jack the Ripper (Werner Krauss), and Oriental despot Haroun-al-Rashid (Emil Jannings), in the picture's three separate episodes. In the Russian sequence — which obviously bore great influence on Sergei Eisenstein's *Ivan the Terrible*— the czar places an hourglass before each of his poisoned victims so that he may anticipate the precise moment of death. When the Boyar prince discovers an hourglass labeled "Czar Ivan," he descends into madness and spends the rest of his days turning the glass over and over to thwart his fate. Veidt's stunning portrayal in this universally acclaimed masterpiece would prove to be his ticket to Hollywood three years later.

In the meantime, Connie appeared once again onstage in Karel Capek's *R.U.R.* at the Theater am Kurfürstendamm. It was the German premiere of a sensationally received new play concerning a rebellion at Rossum's Universal Robot factory. Connie's Mr. Alquist, the elderly head of the building department, was only a supporting role, but it was showy; he took center stage at the end of the third act, when the robots rebelled and spared his life. Veidt's Baron Kempelen, the robot inventor in the 1938 motion picture *Le Joueur d'échecs*, would not be so fortunate.

In 1924, Veidt traveled to Vienna to reteam with the director of *Caligari* for what would be the first of several screen versions of *The Hands of Orlac*. The psychological thriller concerned concert pianist Paul Orlac, who loses his hands in a train wreck, only to have the hands of an executed murderer grafted surgically in their place. Due to this, Orlac becomes obsessed with the idea that he is responsible for the stabbing death of his father. Expressionism had all but disappeared from films by this time, but Veidt was able to convey the agony of the sensitive artist through his stylized performance. As Lotte Eisner observed, "Conrad Veidt … dances a kind of Expressionistic ballet, bending and twisting extravagantly, simultaneously drawn and repelled by the murderous dagger held by hands which do not seem to belong to him" (The Haunted Screen by Lotte H. Eisner. Berkeley: University of California press, 1973; pp. 144–45).

In December of that same year, Connie signed a contract with director Mauritz Stiller to appear in the picture *The Odalisque from Smyrna* with Greta Garbo. Stiller's lovely young protégée was to star as a refugee from the Russian revolution who ends up in a Turkish harem; she eventually escapes to the Continent and becomes an actress. Stiller and Garbo preceded Veidt to Constantinople to set up for location shooting, but financing collapsed and the project was aborted. In comparing these two enigmatic actors, film historian William K. Everson noted that Veidt possessed "a literally beautiful rather than a handsome face that almost mirrored Garbo's. What a pity that they never had the chance to play together."

Financial constraints also appeared to be the reason why Veidt lost his chance to work with the great director Abel Gance on his epic picture *Napoleon*. Gance had offered Veidt the small (but plum!) role of the Marquis de Sade. The flurry of correspondence between the two men indicates that Connie was reluctant to travel to Paris to appear in what was essentially a cameo, while Gance appealed to him to "make a few concessions, one artist to another" (Veidt-Gance correspondence in the collection of the Cinematheque Francaise, Paris).

According to film historian Kevin Brownlow, who restored the 1927 masterpiece, a scene of the Marquis de Sade did appear in Gance's list of sequences in the long versions, but there is no evidence that the role was played by Veidt. None of the cast lists includes the role at all.

Veidt continued to vary his film roles, and he appeared opposite Elisabeth Bergner in her screen debut in *Nju*. Bergner was the title character, a woman who is neglected by her husband (Emil Jannings) and who subsequently falls in love with a poet (Veidt); she leaves her husband for him. The poet eventually tires of Nju and, when he orders her to return to her husband, she commits suicide. Bergner chose Veidt to appear with her in a second film (also directed by her husband, Paul Czinner), *Der Geiger von Florenz*. The actress, who made something of a career playing gamines, portrayed a girl who was jealous of the attention her father (Veidt) was paying toward her stepmother.

Felicitas and Viola

The role of loving father — unusual for Veidt — took on added significance when, on August 10, 1925, he received word that Felicitas had given birth to their daughter. Max Reinhardt sent a telegram to the newborn Vera Viola Maria Veidt, congratulating her on her choice of parents.

The "new" Conrad Veidt being forged by these roles dismayed both the public and the critics. Many of his female fans were left wondering what had become of their beloved demon. They needn't have worried, as Veidt's "procession of tyrants" resumed its march across the silver screen, both at home and abroad.

Nineteen twenty-five and 1926 were the last notable years of German cinematic ascendancy. The great silent pictures of the twenties, which had made German creativity the talk of world cinema circles, included *Variety*, *The Last Laugh*, *The Joyless Street*, *Faust*, and *Metropolis*. To this list must be added Henrik Galeen's *Der Student von Prag*, arguably Conrad Veidt's greatest starring vehicle of the silent era. If *Caligari* made him famous outside

Germany, *The Student of Prague* confirmed his status as an international star. The film also became one of Connie's personal favorites.

He played the role of Baldwin, a poor student in love with a highborn lady. In a desperate bid to win her away from her patrician fiancé, he sells his mirror image (his soul) to a Mephisthophelean character named Scapinelli (Werner Kraus) in return for riches and power. Inevitably, all turns out badly for Baldwin. Connie's powerful performance impressed the critic for the *National Board of Review Magazine*, who wrote:

> Conrad Veidt in the stellar role of Baldwin, the student, faces and overcomes the handicap of playing a dual role... To our mind it is his best performance of any picture shown in America. Certainly the final sequence of his vain flight from his ever-pursuing image and the life and death climax before the shattered mirror is one of the finest achievements of screen pantomime and camera magic" [National Board of Review Magazine, Vol. IV, No. 2 (February 1929)].

In the spring of 1926, a truly interesting stage role — Tom Prior, in the play *Outward Bound* — presented itself to Veidt. Sutton Vane's allegorical drama at the Trianon Theater featured Connie's long monologue as the drunkard who regrets his squandered life as he and his fellow passengers are ferried across the river Styx without their knowledge.

Connie ended his silent filmmaking days in Germany the same way he had begun them — with a call for social reform. *Kreuzzug des Weibes* was aimed at the criminal code outlawing abortion. Veidt played a district attorney who prosecutes a poor man for allowing his wife to have an abortion that proved fatal. The prosecutor then finds himself on the horns of a dilemma when his fiancée becomes pregnant after she is raped. The film was well-received except in heavily Catholic provinces such as Bavaria, where it was blacklisted. In reaction to *Kreuzzug des Weibes*, Kurt (Curtis) Bernhardt released *Babies' Souls Accuse*, which upheld the legitimacy of the criminal code and which was fully supported by the Catholic Church.

Connie's role as prosecutor wouldn't be the last time he was forced to choose between love and duty in a picture. Now Hollywood was asking him to make a major career decision, for, during the summer of 1926, a telegram had arrived:

> I saw your picture, *Waxworks*. You must play in my next picture. You must play King Louis XI. You know you are one of the most talented men in the film world. You don't know me, but I want you to come. I cannot make the picture without you.
> Yours sincerely, John Barrymore
> [Sunday Dispatch (London), 28 October 1934]

Flattered by the invitation, but reluctant to leave his wife and infant to travel to a strange country, Veidt hesitated. He then received a second, urgent telegram from Barrymore and decided to accept. With a one-picture contract, but without family, friends, or English, Conrad Veidt set sail for America on September 18, 1926.

When he arrived in Hollywood to appear in *The Beloved Rogue* opposite Barrymore (as the vagabond poet, François Villon), United Artists executives were not prepared for the fact that Connie stood six foot three. Studio historians insisted that King Louis was short and squat. What to do? UA came to the painful conclusion that Veidt would conceal his stature in long, full robes, and walk in a stooped fashion. It seemed as though Americans were more sticklers for detail than Germans, who hadn't seemed to mind that the lanky Veidt had portrayed the diminutive Lord Nelson without resorting to bended knees.

"Lon Chaney may soon have a real rival in Conrad Veidt," declared a fan magazine, reporting from the film's set. "Veidt gave the impression of being hunchbacked and stooped, and of a height not greater than four feet. With long, stringy black hair and a leering fantastical face, he looked like a first-class inducement for nightmares" (Picture Play [magazine], February 1927).

Critical reception of *The Beloved Rogue* was lukewarm, but Connie wasn't packing his bags just yet. With Lon Chaney a defector to MGM, Universal was looking for another "Man of a Thousand Faces," so Victor Hugo's *The Man Who Laughs*— which Carl Laemmle had bought for Chaney a few years earlier — was dusted off for Conrad Veidt. Signed to a $1500-a-week contract, Connie fetched wife and daughter from Berlin and then settled in Beverly Hills, where he ensconced his family in an Italianate mansion and entertained the fast-growing European film colony. While *The Man Who Laughs* was undergoing four different scenarios and as many directors, Universal tried to find another appropriate starring vehicle for their new property. After maneuvering Connie this way and that, studio and star agreed that *A Man's Past* would best serve as his eagerly awaited Universal debut. Veidt received good notices for his role as a physician imprisoned for practicing euthanasia, but the picture as a whole was unremarkable and holds the dubious distinction of being the actor's only "lost" American film.

Shooting on *The Man Who Laughs* finally got under way on September 1, 1927. It was a more successful venture than Connie's last film, due in part to the fact that director Paul Leni knew exactly what his star was capable of and could communicate nuances to him in their shared native tongue. The leading lady in the $1.5 million super-jewel was the petite Mary Philbin, who played Dea, the beautiful blind girl, to Veidt's Gwynplaine, the "Laughing Man" circus freak.

"Deprived of the use of his mouth, the German player employs but his eyes to portray the most heartbreaking tragedy," wrote a New York reviewer. "Here certainly is one of the grand portrayals of the cinema" (New York Herald Tribune, 28 April 1928). Comparisons to Lon Chaney were inevitable and favorable. "The picture is undoubtedly better than *The Hunchback of Notre Dame* ... and Mr. Conrad Veidt's impersonation of the laughing man is at least as good as anything Lon Chaney ever did with the aid of makeup," reported a trade paper (Moving Picture World & Exhibitor's Herald, 13 October 1928).

Despite good notices for Connie, the big-budget spectacle with its heavy German influences lacked popular appeal. Today, *The Man Who Laughs* is considered a classic of the genre and Veidt's greatest performance in an American silent film. The picture also has a legacy of sorts: Bob Kane, creator of the comic book "Batman," modeled his Joker character on Gwynplaine.

Connie's next film, *The Last Performance*, was aptly titled, as it would prove to be his swan song for Universal and his last silent film anywhere. He played Erik the Great, a stage magician obsessed with his lovely young assistant (Mary Philbin, again). In the midst of filming, Hollywood made the switch to sound, and the film was produced as a silent with dialogue added only to the last reel. In its review, Variety noted that the picture was released as a silent in Manhattan, "Dialogue reel apparently not standing up in opinion of U. heads" (Variety, 6 November 1929).

The language barrier made for a lost opportunity when Veidt chose to return to Berlin rather than portray Dracula for the talkies. Favored for the part by Universal

Left to right, Connie, Emil Jannings and Ernst Lubitsch: Hollywood, late 20s.

after Lon Chaney died of throat cancer, Connie decided the move was too risky, although "His appearance in *The Last Performance* was virtually a screen test for the role," wrote film historian, David J. Skal. "Judging from his many fine silent performances... Veidt might well have elevated the role of Dracula to pantheon status" (Hollywood Gothic by David J. Skal. New York: W.W. Norton & Company, 1990; p. 119).

Back home, Connie made his penultimate stage appearance in Franz Wedekind's five-act play, *The Marquis of Keith*, a special performance in memory of the late actor Albert Steinrück. The one-time benefit at the Staats-Theater featured an all-star cast in bit parts. For his final stage appearance, Connie had the title role in *He*, Alfred Savoir's comedy about an escapee from a mental institution who thinks he's God. The production opened at the Tribune Theater where it ran for two months before touring the provinces.

Although Conrad Veidt never did achieve the success he desired in the legitimate theater, his training made his voice perfectly suited for talkies, unlike many actors of the silent period. With the advent of sound, films were made in several different languages in order to maximize distribution, and in 1930 Veidt appeared in the German-language version of the British *Cape Forlorn*. Conversely, his first

English talkie was made in Germany: the internationally acclaimed *Congress Dances*. Connie, shining in the small but memorable role of the scheming Prince Metternich, also appeared in the German version.

Connie's hypnotic eyes were put to good use in the 1932 *Rasputin*, arguably his greatest performance in a German-language picture, and his personal favorite up to that time. His resemblance to the mad monk was startling, so much so that it moved Rasputin's daughter to confess to reporters gathered at the film's London premiere that she saw her father "in the flesh" in Veidt's impersonation. The picture demonstrates Connie's theory that a character's walk is key to expressing a character's essence. As one British paper observed, "He is transformed, not only facially, but in gesture and in the heavy gait, the swinging arms of the peasant" (Illustrated London News, 22 October 1932).

Gaumont-British production head Michael Balcon, an admirer of Veidt's work since *Caligari*, invited him to join the heady international cast of Britain's biggest film to date, *Rome Express*. The picture concerned a murder committed over a stolen painting that is restolen on the train from Paris to Rome. Veidt appeared as the desperate criminal, Zurta, in the critically acclaimed production that became the prototype for all subsequent train thrillers. Success in this picture won Connie the lead in *F.P. 1*, a science-fiction film about evil financiers who plot to destroy the first floating aerodrome. Connie starred in the English-language version of the film, which was based on the Curt Siodmak novel. Hans Albers took over the part in the German-language version, and Charles Boyer copped the honors for the French.

Veidt's second wife, Felicitas, divorced him in 1932. Connie reluctantly relinquished custody of Viola to her mother, since his work required him to be away from home for extended periods of time.

Concerned about the worsening political situation in Germany, the actor instinctively grabbed any opportunity to work abroad. When director Victor Saville offered him the part of the German commandant in the Gaumont-British film *I Was a Spy*, he gladly accepted. Before leaving for England, Connie married for the third and last time to the Jewish Lily Prager, whom he had met at the Berlin restaurant she ran that catered to actors and artists. When they left Germany in April 1933, he had to fill out a form asking his reasons for leaving the country. Connie, a gentile, scrawled the word "Jude" (Jew).

It was in *I Was a Spy*, while opposite Madeleine Carroll (in the title role), that Veidt established the screen persona he would forever be associated with: the monocled menace who will allow nothing — not even romance — to interfere with his duty. He developed a theory about the villains he was doomed to play for the rest of his life: "No human being is a villain just for villainy's sake. Something beyond his control relentlessly drives him. Always I have tried to get this across. To mingle a little sympathy with the audience's hate" ("Fascinating Villain" by Carol Craig. Motion Picture [magazine], September 1941).

Racial hatred was the target of a pair of pictures he starred in for British filmmakers in order to protest anti–Semitism. The first of these was *The Wandering Jew*, in which he played different characterizations in the four historical phases of the legendary figure's preternaturally extended life. Critics praised Connie's performance in the challenging role, but found the picture overlong and uninspired. A better and more political film was *Jew Süss*, taken from the Leon Füchtwanger novel about an 18th century German Jew who seeks power in order to help his people. In the denouement, he discovers that he is really a gentile.

Although his acceptance of the part meant he ought never set foot in Germany while Hitler was in power, Connie was obliged to return home to fulfill an existing contract with a sound remake of his 1923 *Wilhelm Tell*. When he did not report back to England in order to start *Jew Süss*, Michael Balcon received a letter from the actor in which he explained that illness prevented him from making the trip. His suspicions aroused, Balcon sent a physician to Germany. When Veidt was found to be in good health, strings had to be pulled to permit him to leave the Fatherland. Connie, who at the time was still a German citizen traveling on a German passport, had been detained by the authorities who did not want him to make *Jew Süss*. For all this, reviews of Gaumont-British's most expensive and ambitious production were mixed, stating that the picture had been hamstrung by inferior direction and ponderous production values. Once again, Veidt's performance was deemed superior to the overall film itself.

The Nazis, who were to make their own, virulently anti–Semitic version of the Füchtwanger novel, first denounced Veidt, then banned all his films from being shown in Germany. Connie never again returned to his homeland.

Moving from Gaumont-British to Alexander Korda, Connie was cast in a confusing spy picture, *Dark Journey*, opposite Vivien Leigh (in her first major role). The actor found that he was now a romantic lead. Still, with this first in a series of espionage films, Connie played a useful political role by reminding the public that the enemy could be clever, suave, ingenious, and worthy of respect.

With war approaching, Connie moved his daughter and her mother to safety in Geneva and, after six years in exile, he and Lily became British subjects in February 1939. At that time, he also embarked on what was probably the most successful period of his career, thanks to strong direction and superior scripts.

His first picture with the Michael Powell–Emeric Pressburger team was the hugely entertaining "Hitchcockian" thriller, *The Spy in Black*. Connie played a U-Boat captain who tries to sink the British fleet off Scotland during World War I, but is outfoxed by a double agent, portrayed by the cool, sophisticated Valerie Hobson. The chemistry of the teaming of Veidt and Hobson encouraged Powell to star them again in another wartime drama, *Contraband*. Connie was a Danish merchant captain this time around, chasing Nazi spies through an actual London blackout.

Veidt's greatest triumph in British cinema is undoubtedly the dazzling spectacle *The Thief of Bagdad*, his only color film. The role of Jaffar, the evil grand vizier, finally offered him the kind of demonic characterization that had made him a star in the first place. Restored to the turban parts of his youth, Connie looked resplendent in his flowing robes and silver bracelets as he pursued princess June Duprez. For the first and last time, audiences saw the color of his piercing blue eyes in startling closeups, as he hypnotized Duprez, blinded hero John Justin, and turned Sabu into a dog. The film won Oscars for color photography, art direction and special effects.

When war broke out, Veidt turned over his entire personal fortune to the British government, interest-free, and — to raise more money for his adopted country — he and Lily brought *Contraband* over to the United States in April 1940 to arrange for its American release. While in the States, he accepted an offer from MGM to replace Paul Lukas in the anti–Nazi picture *Escape*.

So began Veidt's procession of Nazi agents and other suspicious characters, culminating in his most famous role, the relatively minor one of the Nazi Major

Connie and Lily: The third time's the charm!

Strasser — a part originally intended for Otto Preminger — in *Casablanca*. Most of Veidt's scenes were with Claude Rains, who played Captain Louis Renault, the French Prefect of Police. A sort of bantering enmity between the two ran through the film: Veidt, determined to capture his prey (a heroic freedom fighter, enacted by Paul Henreid); Rains, just as determined to checkmate him. Since Connie was in such demand ("The line waiting for him forms to the right," quipped Louella Parsons), MGM charged $25,000 to loan him out to Warner Brothers, making Veidt the highest-paid actor in the Academy Award–winning film.

Connie at his studio bungalow: *King of the Damned.*

But Connie's finest role during his second Hollywood period was that of Joan Crawford's cruel lover in *A Woman's Face* (1941). Here, Veidt broke from his usual restraint to show flashes of the old demon and a sinister sensuality that caused a flood of letters from female admirers. The picture was popular enough to spawn a brace of radio versions with the German star, one with Bette Davis as Anna Holm, the other featuring Ida Lupino.

Radio provided another venue for Veidt to promote the Allied cause, whether for syndicated shows such as *Treasury Star Parade* ("Return to Berchtesgarden") or network programs such as *To the President*

Viola comes to visit her old dad on the set of *The Thief of Bagdad*.

("My Beloved Relatives"), *Plays for Americans* ("Hate"), and *Free World Theater* ("People March"). Connie continuously — and gladly — took to the airwaves to preach his anti–Nazi message.

Veidt and Joan Crawford appeared together again in what would be the actor's last film, *Above Suspicion*. The espionage drama was notable solely for Connie's unusual role as a good spy helping honeymooners Crawford and Fred MacMurray escape the evil clutches of Nazi menace Basil Rathbone.

Three months after the film wrapped, Connie died of a heart attack while playing golf at the Riviera Country Club in the Pacific Palisades on April 3, 1943. He was only 50 years old. "Connie was anxious to see the outcome of this second world struggle," wrote longtime colleague Reinhold Schünzel for a newspaper tribute. "He wanted to see peace and see his daughter again. Now he has peace. But not the kind of peace he was longing for" (*Aufbau*, op. cit.).

Conrad Veidt was laid to rest at Hollywood Cemetery, but when his widow, Lily, moved to New York in 1950, she had his ashes transferred to the Ferncliff Mausoleum in Hartsdale. She requested that, upon her death, her ashes be intermixed with his; this was done in 1980, and the couple's remains — along with all their worldly possessions — were bequeathed to Lily's nephew, actor Ivan Rado, who resided in Los Angeles.

Conrad Veidt: Actor — and human being — extraordinaire.

When this writer visited with Mr. Rado at his home in 1987, it was discovered that the Veidts' ashes had not yet received a proper burial. Mr. Rado said he was open to suggestions for an appropriate and permanent resting place. A decade later, unable to locate a satisfactory burial site, Mr. Rado turned over the ashes — and all the Veidt memorabilia — to James H. Rathlesberger, founder of the newly formed Conrad Veidt Society.

The society solicited ideas and donations for a proper resting place. Some members suggested Connie's native Germany, but that idea was rejected due to reports of increasing neo–Nazi activity. Member Vivienne Phillips of London proposed placing the ashes in Golders Green Cemetery, not far from the Veidts' former home in Hampstead. The society agreed and secured a ten-year lease on a niche in the columbarium.

On April 3, 1998 — the 55th anniversary of Conrad Veidt's death — the ashes were formally transferred in a ceremony attended by members of the Conrad Veidt Society and by fans and admirers of all ages and nationalities. After the ceremony, an anonymous donor secured the niche in perpetuity.

Conrad Veidt was laid to rest without an epitaph, but one had been written shortly after his death by his friend, producer Erich Pommer, who mused: "It is hard to say what was more to be admired in him, his artistry or his humanity" (Aufbau, op. cit.).

A Word About Censorship

It will be noted that virtually all of Connie's German-made films were subject, at one point or another, to government censorship, and the matter deserves explanation.

Before all else, it's necessary to remember that Max and Emil Skladanowsky had actually beaten the Lumières to the cinematic punch by almost two months when the brothers unveiled what they called their "*bioskop*" to Berliners at that city's Wintergarten music hall on the 1st of November 1895. While they technically were moving pictures, the Skladanowskys' rudimentary efforts were as primitive as the first shots taken by the French bothers, Thomas Alva Edison, or any of the others who laid claim to being the "inventor" of the medium. It wasn't long, however, before even their most memorable, seconds-long "*deutsche bioskop*" was supplanted by the prodigious output of Oskar Messter, who—a scant two years later—opened his own film studio on the Friedrichstrasse.

Messter—widely hailed as the "Father of German Cinema"–proceeded to turn out short films prodigiously. What they lacked in length—many unreeled in a minute or less—they more than made up for in terms of novelty, dealing as they did with the Kaiser's movements, isolated studies of natural beauty, humorous situations, and so forth. Out of the hundreds of short subjects Messter produced through his first decade in "the industry," a handful of titles from 1903 were the earliest still extant when Gerhard Lamprecht compiled his monumental Deutsche Stummfilme. Averaging 35 meters in length, these minimovies were more the rule than the exception, footagewise, for the then contemporary German cinema. (Messter's first *Grossfilm* [long film] hit screens in 1909; his *Andreas Hofer* is listed at 325 meters.)

Amid all this rudimentary sound and fury (Messter's was not the only film studio in Berlin by far) arose the first united effort at monitoring the output. Reacting to what they perceived to be a rash of *Schundfilme* (trash films), concerned teachers, clergymen and conservative cultural groups founded the *Kinematographische Reformpartei* (Cinematographic Reform Party) in 1905, and the police in a number of cities began instituting censorship a short time later. Berlin led the way, requiring that all films be submitted to the police for approval three days prior to screening; individual scenes could be excised or the entire work banned. Because pictures were regarded as more persuasive than words, the cinema was subject

27

to far more stringent controls than other media ["Cinema and Censorship in the Weimar Republic" by James D. Steakley. Film History (magazine), Volume 11, 1999; p. 188].

From that point on, motion pictures were open to being rated, edited or rejected outright, not via a national, uniform program, but by independent municipal groups. The tastes and opinions of one group need not have had the slightest semblance to the tastes and opinions of its counterpart in a neighboring city, and there were no guarantees that prints "making the rounds" would have their excised footage restored at any point in the circuit. (A similar, yet less well-organized — if such can be imagined — practice was occurring at the same time in the United States. Individual nickelodeon and theater owners were accustomed to snipping bits and pieces of prints they were to show, based solely on their own proclivities. Up until the mid 20s, many of the scraps of film that hit the projection room floor never made their way back into the print when the engagement was over, resulting in an ungodly number of motion pictures which survive nowadays only in severely truncated and/or bizarrely edited form.)

Things grew more structured as time went by, and these municipal boards gradually gave way to state boards. Just prior to the Great War, movies were forbidden fruit to children under six years of age, while youths between the ages of six and 14 could partake only in structured children's matinee performances. Ages 15 and up got to see what was left after the censors had done their work, which entailed the removal of material which could in any way be construed as morally or politically offensive, or which depicted either the commission of serious crimes, or the eluding of justice on the part of the more minor villains.

Conditions changed during the Great

War. The current *Kinematographische Reformpartei* pushed the envelope in the direction of the Reichstag, asking (among other things) that censorship become a matter of national concern. Alone, this issue would have spurred little debate; if nothing else, a uniform set of rules and standards would have freed up monies and manpower on the state and local levels. Unfortunately, the reform party also demanded that the government step in to seize the theaters and oversee all film production and distribution. As Germany's *Sitz im Leben* was not grounded in the nouveau Communism that was threatening Kaiser Wilhelm's Russian cousin, Nicholas, these suggestions that one's right to private property be abrogated provoked a great deal of discussion.

The discussion came and went, and so did the Great War. With the German government having to deal with the reorganization of the country and the reparation terms of the Versailles Treaty, it was felt that many of the responsibilities hitherto borne by it ought to be laid on other shoulders, if not forgotten altogether.

On 12 November 1918, the acting government — the "Council of People's Commissars" — promulgated its first decree, the third point of which read: "Censorship will not take place; theatre censorship is abolished." Philipp Scheidemann — later the first chancellor of the Weimar Republic — went on to say that all of Kaiser Wilhelm's regulations (dating back to 1906 and bolstered by special wartime restrictions) were annulled, and that a single, national standard was therewith created, thus eliminating with the stroke of a pen the crazy quilt of municipal and state ordinances and agencies created over the years ["Cinema and Censorship in the Weimar Republic" by James D. Steakley. Film History (magazine), Volume 11, 1999; p. 190].

Tabling artistic censorship in all forms made some noise, and The *New York Times* subsequently heard and reported on it:

At the present time no police censorship exists, and Plays [*sic*] of the most astounding impossibility are shown. No moral restrictions hold the producer in leash, and the offerings go the limit in frankness and realism. Sexual problems and medical topics are very definitely set forth on the screen — "to exert a moral influence over young people," as the programs put it. Naturally, pandering to the curious and the sensation-loving among the masses, such films have good box-office value and prove good investments for producers.

A markedly irresponsible strain characterizes scores of pictures of gay life which are being shown on the Berlin screens. Seldom is a great moral pointed as a deterrent to emulation of the ruinous and unholy existence depicted as being led by some of the leading figures in these plays. Contrasted to this class of drama, and offsetting some of its unhealthy effects, however, are many clean and interesting dramas based on the works of favorite authors ["Uncensored German Movies" by Margaret Forman. August 24, 1919].

The "offerings that go the limit in frankness and realism" were soon tagged *Aufklärungsfilme* ("enlightenment" or "clarification" films). These films provided elucidation — it was argued — on sexual and moral matters, thus allowing paying customers to learn of the dangers of prostitution, homosexuality, promiscuity, and a variety of other sexual milieu, and thus safely avoid them. Hype is hype, of course, and most folks realized that the well-publicized, lofty-sounding motivations were little more than attempts at justifying the production of the type of sensational films that a sizable chunk of the population would eagerly pay to see under any circumstances. Richard Oswald — along with *many* others — had taken advantage of the situation, and had produced numerous *Aufklärungsfilme*, among them, the groundbreaking and highly notorious exposé of society's inhuman prejudices against homosexuality, *Anders als die Andern* (1919). (Oswald had been mining this vein as early

as 1916 when — in cooperation with the *Deutsche Gesellschaft zur Bekämpfung der Geschlechtskrankheiten* [German Society to Combat Venereal Diseases] — he had filmed *Es werde Licht* [*Let There Be Light*], a "study" on the sort of behavior which usually resulted in syphilis.)

Well over a hundred enlightenment films saw the carbon arc before politicians, clergymen, and concerned citizens of all shapes and sizes took exception and moved that censorship be restored. With the emergence of the Weimar Republic, the procensorship forces had a new body to which they could appeal. On May 29, 1920, responding to the call for protection from filmed pornography, the National Assembly passed the Reich Film Act. As explained by Bruce Murray,

> In addition to prohibiting pornographic films, the law called for the censorship of films that endangered public order, Germany's reputation, or its relations with foreign countries. These broadly formulated guidelines enabled censors to mask political judgments as aesthetic judgments. Once the Weimar government moved to censor undesirable *Aufklärungsfilme*, efforts to nationalize the film industry ceased [Film and the German Left in the Weimar Republic. Austin (TX): University of Austin Press, 1990].

An interesting wrinkle followed, however, as almost any German-made film — no matter *when* produced or released — was now subject to the motion picture law, whether or not it had been scrutinized earlier by the Munich or Berlin bureaus of the Kinematographische Reformpartei, or by the state-led censorship boards in Bavaria, Prussia, Saxony or Baden-Württemberg. Thus, films that had already made their first visit to theaters were recalled, reassessed, possibly recut, and reclassified for consumption according to new norms. Occasionally, recensored prints were longer than they had been prior to submission, as outtakes, alternative shots, or previously excised material (if now deemed "acceptable") was inserted to preserve (and sanitize) the story line. In addition if a film was re-released subsequently or was picked up by a different distributor, it might very well be subject to recensorship once again.

This time around, children under the age of twelve were barred at the theater door, and adolescents (12–18 years of age) were restricted to limited fare (*Jungen*).

Hence, silent pictures listed herein may have more than one footage length or running time and more than one censorship notation: *Zensur* (or "original" censorship, for films either initially released before the abolition of theatrical and cinematic censorship on 12 November 1918, or after the Reich Film Act of 29 May 1920) or *Nachzensur* (or "subsequent" censorship — the scrutiny of any and all films first released between the two benchmark dates and which were being readied for reissue). Where applicable, sound films that were evaluated before or after release are annotated in English.

THE FILMS

Wenn Tote sprechen

[LOST] *If the Dead Speak*; Deutsche Bioscop GmbH, Berlin, 1917; Filmed at Bioscop-Atelier, Neubabelsberg; *Zensur*: June 1917 — 4 Acts, 1482 meters; World premiere: 27 July 1917 Tauentzien-Palast, Berlin

CAST: Conrad Veidt *Richard von Worth*; Maria Carmi *Maria von Brion/Leonore von Radowitz* [double role]; Carl [Karl] de Vogt *Edgar von Radowitz*

CREDITS: *Director* Robert Reinert (Robt. Dinesen); *Scenario* Robert Reinert; *Set Design* Robert A. Dietrich, Artur Günther

SYNOPSIS: Maria von Brion (Maria Carmi) finds her married sister, Countess Leonore von Radowitz (Maria Carmi), dead, and her brother-in-law, Edgar (Carl de Vogt), is strongly suspected of having murdered her. At night, the newly minted widower wanders restlessly through his castle, in his fist, a bundle of letters. Before being arrested, he hands the letters over to a faithful family retainer. The count is found innocent of the murder in court, and the letters are discovered to have come from the countess's lover, Richard von Worth (Conrad Veidt). Von Worth pursued not only the countess (who had committed suicide), but Maria as well, because of her great resemblance to her titled sister. Maria, who had always been fond of her brother-in-law, becomes his wife after he is released.

REVIEWS: "The four-act-long film by Robert Reinert (Deutsche Bioscop), *Wenn Tote sprechen*, deals with the happiness in love of two women.

"Like all of Reinert's films, [*Wenn Tote sprechen*] contains a great deal for the masses of picture-goers besides the literary side. [Reinert] knows his audiences and how to thrill them with high drama and how to move them with sentimentality. The plot leads off with convincing logic and skill; excellent acting and splendid sets add to it. The photography is good, as well.

"Maria Carmi, who may be the most important actress in film, plays the double role of the two sisters. Here again, this beautiful woman's mime is performed with deep artistic feeling. A great achievement. Karl de Vogt is her equal. The juvenile artist, in whose souls a storm seems to rage, promises to develop into an outstanding force within German film art."

Der Kinematograph (Düsseldorf),
1 August 1917

"Maria Carmi is the focal point of the picture, *Wenn Tote sprechen*. It is, as might be expected, a promising start to the 1917/1918 series. It is a combination of the

31

Original newspaper ad. (*Wenn Tote sprechen*)

criminal story and the society drama, and it makes the most of both genres. Carmi's splendid acting works well in a very sympathetic role. Love, envy, hate, and selfless devotion roil within the heart of the heroine... The great advantage of this picture is that it presents a complicated, true-to-life story in deeply real scenes. The backlit photography and shadow pictures in the first part are beautiful and show many fine, artistic moments."

> *Der Kinematograph* (Düsseldorf),
> 22 August 1917

NOTES AND QUOTES: As the principal cast is identical with *Der Weg des Todes* (see: Possibilities), and as the titles seem to refer to a common theme, this may be the second part of or a sequel to the earlier film.

Der Spion (In die Wolken verfolgt)

[LOST] *The Spy (Pursued Into the Clouds)*; Frankfurter Film-Compagnie GmbH, Frankfurt-am-Main, 1917; *Zensur*: September 1917 —

5 Acts, 1903 meters; *Zensur*: March 1918 — 5 Acts, 1838 meters; Forbidden to Adolescents

CAST: Conrad Veidt *Steinau*; Ferdinand Bonn *the Spy*, Bruno Lopinski *Director of the Cannon Factory*; with Leontine Kühnberg, Ellen Richter

CREDITS: *Director* Heinz Karl Heiland; *Asst. Director* Bruno Lopinski; *Photographed by* Bruno Lopinski

SYNOPSIS: Available information on the plot — which is scant — indicates that it concerned industrial, rather than political, espionage and that there were several memorable aerial sequences.

REVIEW: "The drama about the manufacture of cannon, *In die Wolken verfolgt* (Frankfurt Film Company), by Karl Heinz Heiland presents a clever combination of dramatic (in the pure theatrical sense of the word), sensational and propaganda moments. Dramatic, because of the development of the story, which is thrilling as it reveals in a peculiar fashion the traitorous career of a spy, until he is unmasked by the lady who loves him. Sensational, with scenes like the air-fight that make your blood race. Finally, propaganda. The events are set against a background that gives great insight into the cannon industry, that gives enlightenment without one's noticing; this is the most effective form of propaganda.

"All these elements are craftily combined here to show the success of a man of strong will, by means of ability, diligence, and imagination. The performances are good, unfolding against what is surely an unfamiliar background to the audience. This comes as no surprise, as the main roles are cast with Ferdinand Bonn, who as the spy pulls out all the stops with his innate theatrical skill; with Ellen Richter and Leontine Kühnberg, who compete both in looks and acting; and finally with the excellent Konrad Veidt.

"An interesting film which deserves the widest distribution."

> *Der Kinematograph* (Düsseldorf),
> No. 596; 5 June 1918

NOTES AND QUOTES: It has been suggested that the film was retitled *In die Wolken verfolgt*, as *Der Spion* may have led audiences to believe the picture concerned the Great War.

Furcht

Fear; Messter-Film GmbH, Berlin; 1917; Distributed by Hansa-Film-Verleih; Filmed at Messter-Film-Atelier, Blücherstrasse 32; *Nachzensur*: 17 January 1923 — 4 Acts, 1361 meters; Forbidden to adolescents

CAST: Conrad Veidt *the Indian*; Bruno de Carli *Count Greven*; Mechthildis Thein *the Lover*; Bernhard Goetzke *the Manservant*; Hermann Picha *the Vicar*

Top: The film was subsequently released as *In die Wolken verfolgt.* (*Der Spion*) *Bottom:* Bruno Lopinski (left) and Connie peruse the latest thing in cannon. (*Der Spion*)

CREDITS: *Producer* Oskar Messter; *Director* Robert Wiene; *Original Story*: Robert Wiene; *Set Designs* Ludwig Kainer

SYNOPSIS: Count Greven (Bruno de Carli) returns to his ancestral castle after spending several years touring the world. The servants note how the count has changed: he is now withdrawn and fearful. He orders that the doors to the castle be kept locked and no one admitted. A servant (Bernhard Goetzke) informs the vicar (Hermann Picha) about his master's melancholia, and the old man visits the castle, looking to help.

The count relates how, during his stay in India, he had heard of a statue of Buddha that was so beautiful that it made the sick well and the sad, joyous. Visiting the temple, he stole the figure and smuggled it back home. The count is aware that the temple priest swore a terrible revenge upon him for his sacrilege, and he has been living in mortal fear ever since.

One night, a turbaned figure does appear on the Greven grounds. The count demands that the Indian priest (Conrad Veidt) kill him then and there, but the man refuses. He warns that — from that very day — the count will have another seven years to live life to its fullest, after which he will die by the hand of the one who loves him most.

The count spends those years seeking out every joy life holds. He throws bacchanalias and hosts gambling parties, without finding satisfaction. He discovers a means of conquering world hunger, and then capriciously destroys it, all for his amusement. Still looking for fulfillment, for meaning, he becomes involved with a young woman (Mechthildis Thein) and revels in the experience of love. He and the young woman are wed.

Nevertheless, as the fateful day and hour approach, he becomes paranoid and terrified once again. Trusting no one — he even suspects that it will be his wife's hand

that will slay him — he shoots himself. The statue is carried back to India in the hands of the mysterious priest.

REVIEWS: These four acts ... are quite beyond the usual standard. One is really pleased, not only by the rich, deep thoughts, but also by the courage of a film factory to put aside thoughts of pure business for the sake of art, for the sake of refining taste... Wiene has crafted a great, soulful picture and he has proved that psychology — the most difficult subject for the screen, does not have to be excluded from the art of film..."

Der Kinematograph (Düsseldorf),
No. 561; 29 September 1917

NOTES AND QUOTES: "The main historical interest of [Oskar] Messter's features is that they provided the film debuts of performers like Henny Porten, Emil Jannings, Lil Dagover, and Conrad Veidt, who became major stars in the '20s" (David A. Cook. p. 107).

Messter, one of the true pioneers of German cinema, had progressed from the role of inventor (of the "Maltese Cross" method of advancing film through the projection gate) to producer of *Grossfilme* (feature films) before the new century's first decade had come to an end. In 1917 — the year of *Furcht*— Messter and a good number of his professional colleagues and competitors were subsumed by Universum Film Aktiengesellschaft (Ufa), a national film company that came to enjoy vast resources via government subsidies. Ironically, Conrad Veidt wouldn't "make the jump" to the giant conglomerate until 1925; a lengthy association with Richard Oswald, together with a penchant for the kind of offbeat themes that were almost exclusively the provenance of "independent" filmmakers, kept the actor away from Ufa's gates for almost a decade to come. In the interim, Messter-Film kept its hand in autonomous production and distribution,

The mysterious Indian in *Furcht:* Connie's first "turban" role. (*Furcht*)

and Connie appeared in both *Opfer der Gesellschaft* (1918) and *Schicksal* (1924), a Lucy-Doraine-Film which was released through Messter.

Furcht marked the first association Connie had with both Gdansk-born Bernhard Goetzke and Mechthildis Thein. Although Veidt wore the turban in this earliest of their features together, the Polish thesp donned the swathing for *Die Japanerin* (1918/19; wherein he was billed as "the *Arab* servant") and went the Indian mystic route as the yogi in *Das indische Grabmal* (1921). In the intervening *Das Geheimnis von Bombay*, another exercise in Oriental exotica a la the Weimar Republic, Goetzke also essayed a mysterious Indian (yclept *Hobbins!*). The actor garnered international recognition in the title role of Fritz Lang's *Der Müde Tod* (1924) and was castigated (along with the crème de la crème of the German film industry) by virtually everyone outside the Nazi yoke for participating in Veit Harlan's despicable rendition of *Jud Süss* (1940). Goetke, who died in Berlin in 1964, appeared with Veidt for the last time in 1930's *Rasputin*.

Mechthildis (Gretl) Thein's most enduring film credit was as Margot in Deutsche-Bioscop's fantasy serial *Homunculus*, which starred Olaf Fönss and Aud Egede Nissen (and which also featured future Veidt costars Lupu Pick and Theodor Loos). The serial, which owed a casual debt to Mary Shelley's *Frankenstein*, ran for only six chapters, but each was feature length. Following her rather brief role as "the lover" in *Furcht*, Thein would graduate to the title role in *Jettchen Geberts Geschichte* (and its sequel, *Henriette Jacoby*) in 1918.

A more important working relationship than that of Goetzke or Thein and Veidt was initiated by *Furcht*, however. The film was Connie's first with Robert Wiene, who went on to direct the lanky actor in what has come to be regarded as his international breakout role, Cesare in *Das Cabinet des Dr. Caligari* (1919), as well as in another of Germany's greatest psychological horror films, 1924's *Orlacs Hände*. (Wiene also served as the "artistic supervisor" for F.W. Murnau's *Satanas*, which starred Veidt.) Although the "demonic" Conrad Veidt was being celebrated at home even prior to *Caligari* (due to his roles in pictures like *Unheimliche Geschichten*, *Wahnsinn* and *Nachtgestalten* [all 1919]), it was the two Wiene thrillers (along with Paul Leni's triptych, *Das Wachsfigurenkabinett* [1924]) that caused American ticket buyers to speculate on Veidt the demon years before the arrival in Hollywood of Veidt the actor. Wiene was born in Breslau in April 1873. His script for *Die Waffen der Jugend* (1912) marked his industry debut; he soon made a name for himself writing and directing films starring Henny Porten. Wiene died in Paris in 1938.

Veidt hasn't much to do in *Furcht*, other than lurk about on the mansion's grounds and manage — mystically, of course — to find his way inside despite the count's numerous precautions. Still, Connie is given several brief opportunities to pause in front of the camera, and, in medium closeup, his not-quite-inscrutable Oriental expressions reflect an underlying menace interwoven with a sense of frustration and futility.

Das Rätsel von Bangalor

[LOST] *The Mystery of Bangalore*; Pax-Film, Berlin 1917; World premiere: January 1918 Lessing-Theater, Hamburg; Berlin Preview: 7 February 1918 U.T. Kurfürstendamm; *Nachzensur*: 18 October 1922 — 5 Acts, 1350 meters; Forbidden to adolescents

CAST: Conrad Veidt *Count Dinja*; Harry Liedtke *the Physician*; Gilda Langer *the Girl*

CREDITS: *Producer* Alexander von Antallfy; *Director* Paul Leni; *Screenplay* Rudolf Kurtz, Paul Leni; *Set Design* Paul Leni

SYNOPSIS: The beautiful daughter of the English viceroy is kidnapped by an Indian religious sect in retribution for perceived ill treatment by the British forces.

The girl (Gilda Langer) is brought before Lord Dinja (Conrad Veidt), who makes her his prisoner in his opulent castle.

Her fiancé, a Scottish physician (Harry Liedtke), succeeds in freeing her, and they flee. The sect pursues the couple no matter where they go, however, and they are soon caught and returned to India. Lord Dinja, lusting after the girl, tries to tempt the doctor to renounce her via every means at his disposal, but the Scot is unshaken in his love. Overwhelmed in the face of this fidelity, Lord Dinja sets the couple free and goes off to commit suicide.

REVIEW: "The dramatic story line of this film is very well developed... Here, German film art shows that it can compete on the international scene..."

Der Kinematograph, No. 580;
13 February 1918

NOTES AND QUOTES: I defer here to my colleague Pat Wilks Battle, whose comments on the film are succinct and resistant to improvement: "Veidt's first movie of any consequence was *Das Rätsel von Bangalor*, in which he appeared as a sinister Hindu. The picture was very successful financially and Veidt himself—thanks to his angular features and exotic look—never completely got away from turban parts for the rest of his life, whether in Germany (*Furcht, Indian Tomb*), or in England (*Bella Donna, The Thief of Bagdad*). The script was written and the sets designed by Paul Leni, who would figure prominently in Veidt's film future."

Paul Josef Leni was born on 8 July 1885 in Stuttgart and died of blood poisoning in Hollywood on 2 September 1929. An art director and set designer (he started in this capacity with Max Reinhardt in 1906) as well as an Expressionist director, Leni was most frequently associated with horror pictures by his American audiences. Prior to his achieving renown in this genre, he had made the famous *Hintertreppe* (aka *Backstairs*, 1922) along with Leopold Jessner (who was regarded as second only to Reinhardt in terms of his influence as a stage director); the film was considered one of the great *Kammerspiel** of all time.

Besides *Das Rätsel von Bangalor*, Leni worked with Veidt (in one capacity or another) on *Prinz Kuckuck* (1919), *Patience* (1920), *Lady Hamilton* (1921), *Das Wachsfigurenkabinett* (1924), and *The Man Who Laughs* (1928). Carl Laemmle brought Leni to Universal City in 1927, where the director embarked on a series of silent thrillers (including *The Cat and the Canary* and *The Chinese Parrot*, both 1927) that set the visual tone for many of the studios renowned horror films of the early thirties. Various film historians have recounted how the 1930 sound film *Dracula*—which paved the way for *Frankenstein* (1931) and an entire series of films based on grotesques found in literature and myth—was intended (by Carl Laemmle, Senior, at any rate) for the team of Leni and Veidt. Leni's death and the advent of sound saw Veidt to the door; he returned to Europe to confront talkies and the English language head on.

From trade advertising for *Das Rätsel von Bangalor*:

"Japanese teahouses and their mysteries as well as the splendor of the palaces of Indian princes are the wonderfully romantic setting of this magnificent Indian love-novel. Indian palaces alternate with

**Kammerspiel* was the name (derived, like so much else, from Max Reinhardt) given to pictures that were based on psychological themes, while boasting a minimum of actors and settings. These films follow the unities of time, place and action.

Heute URAUFFÜHRUNG
abends   8 Uhr

U.T

Das Rätsel von Bangalor

Phantastisches Abenteuer in 5 Akten

Personen:

Elles
die Tochter des Gouverneurs   **Gilda Langer**

Archie Douglas
ein schottischer Arzt.......   **Harry Liedtke**

Dinja ....   **Conrad Veith**

UNION-PALAST
Kurfürstendamm 26

Connie's name underwent a number of printed variations early in his career. (*Das Rätsel von Bangalor*)

Japanese landscapes. American skyscrapers impress because of their enormous size. The audience is guided across these three continents [*sic*] by steadily mounting tension.

From the Plot:

1st Part: A mysterious love-adventure of a Scottish physician in the Indian quarter of Bangalor.

2nd Part: Fanatics of love and hate.

3rd Part: The pursuit of love around the world.

4th Part: Mysteries of Japanese teahouses and their denizens.

5th Part: In the hands of the Japanese white slave traffic.

Place of Action:

1st and 2nd Parts: In the Indian quarter of Bangalor.

3rd Part: Beyond the Pacific.

4th and 5th Parts: Partly in Tokyo, partly in Ioshiwara, a Japanese garden-town."

Das Tagebuch einer Verlorenen

[LOST] *The Diary of a Lost Girl*; *1. Teil: Das Tagebuch einer Verlorenen*; Richard Oswald-Film GmbH, Berlin 1918; Submitted for censorship at 6 Acts, 2201 meters; *Zensur*: April 1918 — 5 Acts, 2114 meters; Later, 5 Acts, 2093 meters; Forbidden to adolescents; World premiere and press preview: 5 May 1918 U.T. Kurfürstendamm (Berlin); 29 November 1918 Berlin premiere: U.T. Kurfürstendamm *and* U.T. Nollendorfplatz; General release: 12 December 1918 Marmorhaus, Berlin; *Nachzensur*: 5 July 1922 — 6 Acts, 1934 meters; Forbidden to adolescents

CAST: Conrad Veidt *Doctor Julius*; Erna Morena *Thymian Gotteball*; Reinhold Schünzel *Count Kasimir Osdorff*; Paul Rehkopf *Gotteball, a Pharmacist*; Werner Krauss *Meinert, Gotteball's Assistant*; Max Laurence *The Old Count*; Marga Köhler *Lene Peters, Thymian's Stepmother*; Marie von Bülow *Miss Kindermann*; Clementine Plessner *Aunt Frieda*; Ilse Wejrmann *Elisabeth Woyens*

CREDITS: *Producer-Director* Richard Oswald; *Scenario* Richard Oswald; *Based on the eponymous novel by* Margarete Böhme; *Photographed by* Max Fassbender; *Production Design* August Rinaldi

SYNOPSIS: Thymian Gotteball (Erna Morena) finds life to be filled with mishaps and tragedies. She suffers when it is discovered that her governess and companion, Elisabeth (Ilse Wejrmann), is pregnant. She becomes worse when her father (Paul Rehkopf) throws Elisabeth out of the house, and is nearly beside herself when news that Elisabeth has been found drowned later reaches her ears. Things do not improve when, that very same day, a new governess—Miss Kindermann (Marie von Bülow)—is hired to replace the decedent.

Nestled between Count Osdorff (Reinhold Schünzel, left) and Dr. Julius (Connie), Thymian (Erna Morena) enjoys a brief respite from suffering. (*Das Tagebuch einer Verlorenen*)

Desperate for understanding, Thymian turns for comfort to Meinert (Werner Krauss), her father's assistant in the pharmacy. Soon, Thymian, too, is pregnant. When she refuses to accept Meinert's hand in marriage, her baby is seized shortly after birth and Thymian is shunted off to a reform school for girls.

A friend throughout all of this woe is Dr. Julius (Conrad Veidt), who tries to counsel the girl as best as he can. Also attracted to Thymian is Count Kasimir Osdorff (Reinhold Schünzel), who tries to reconcile the family members. He fails. Thymian escapes from the school and attempts to get her baby back. In the interim, the baby has died. After a while, the old count (Max Laurence) dies; so does pharmacist Gotteball. With no obstacles of caste or position in their way, Thymian and the count marry. She is, however,

never able to fully overcome the sadness she has experienced all her life.

REVIEWS: "It was one of those great, overwhelming successes... A sensation in the noblest sense of the word... The plot contains no real drama (hardly the smallest hints of it) and, as if Oswald wanted to emphasize this fact, he allowed the only scene with a dramatic core — the seducer meets the seduced after many years— to unfold unobtrusively, much tamer than it would have done so in reality. Nevertheless, although this tale reveals not the slightest bit of lyricism, it is not boring; it has the force of a real work of art...

"As for the acting ... the portrayal of Thymian is the heart of this picture. Erna Morena is the only German film artist who could manage it. Reinhold Schünzel presents a character study of almost elemental force ... and Werner Krauss, showing life at its most brutal, and Conrad Veidt, as the sensitive Dr. Julius..."

Der Kinematograph, No. 592;
8 May 1918

"Here we have a thrilling, well paced drama that shows in perfect detail the relentless consequences of a woman's fate. Even the most delicate aspects of this theme are revealed with such goodness and humanity that no impure notion intrudes. Along with all this we have Oswald's direction, which results in exemplary ensemble acting and strong, artistic performances that never waver while dealing thoroughly with this difficult subject...

"One ought to write a treatise about Werner Krauss, Conrad Veidt and the other actors. The title: 'New Methods of Film Acting Art.'"

B.Z. am Mittag, 6 May 1918

"Direction and acting shown perfection ... [Erna Morena's] partner was Conrad Veidt, an example of nobility, showing real, heartrending emotions..."

8 Uhr *Abendblatt*, 6 May 1918

"The film *Das Tagebuch einer Verlorenen*, much disputed by the censorship board, was adapted and directed by Richard Oswald, who has reached the apex of the art of direction with this film, which is being shown at the Union Theatre. We supported having this wonderful film go uncensored for artistic reasons... The public is quite happy with this work..."

Der Film, No. 49; 7 December 1918

NOTES AND QUOTES: The film's current title was forbidden in 1918 by the Berlin Board of Censors, which also ordered the film released (as *Das Tagebuch einer Toten*) without the prologue Oswald had shot. In November 1918, after the war ended and censorship was (temporarily) halted, the picture was restored to its original length and rereleased with the title by which it is presently known.

Das Tagebuch einer Verlorenen was one of Richard Oswald's many *Aufklärungsfilme* (see: "A Word About Censorship"), and Veidt was invited to participate on the strength of his presence in the stage drama *Die Koralle*. The fashion for these *Aufklärungsfilme* would wither within a few years—due mostly to outrage on the part of churchmen and canny politicians, and the reintroduction of an invigorated censorship program — but Oswald continued to churn them out as long as the practice remained profitable. Connie would go on to appear in more than 20 films that were produced or directed or both by this most prolific of artisans.

Das Tagebuch einer Verlorenen marked the screen debut of actress Clementine Plessner.

The film was remade (as a silent) in 1929 under the direction of Georg Wilhelm Pabst, who also produced. *Tagebuch* starred Louise Brooks, a stunning young actress from Wichita, Kansas, who— although she made but two films in Germany (the other, also with Pabst, was the near-mythic *Die Büchse der Pandora*)—would become something of an icon associated with Weimar film history.

Dida Ibsens Geschichte (Ein Finale zum "Tagebuch einer Verlorenen" von Margarete Böhme)

[LOST*] *2. Teil: Dida Ibsens Geschichte (Dida Ibsen's Story)*; Richard Oswald-Film GmbH, Berlin 1918; World premiere: 12 December 1918 Marmorhaus, Berlin; Submitted for censorship

---

*Karen Everson, an archivist-cataloguer in the film department of the George Eastman House in Rochester, New York, confirms that there is one 1600-foot reel of 16mm footage from *Dida Ibsens Geschichte* among the

at 5 Acts, 2114 meters; *Zensur*: November 1919 — 5 Acts, 2093 meters; Forbidden to adolescents; *Nachzensur*: 21 July 1922 — 5 Acts, 1890 meters (for rerelease by Nordstern Film Distributors); Forbidden

CAST: Conrad Veidt *Erik Knorrensen*; Anita Berber *Dida Ibsen*; Werner Krauss *Philipp von Galen*; Emil Lind *Dida's Father*; Clementine Plessner *His Wife*; Ernst Pittschau *Eken Kornils*; Eugen Rex *Lude Schnack*; Ilse von Tasso-Lind *Lady*; Maria Forescu *Servant*; Loni Nest *Dida's Daughter*

CREDITS: *Producer/Director* Richard Oswald; *Scenario* Richard Oswald; *Photographed by* Max Fassbender; *Set Design* August Rinaldi

SYNOPSIS: Dida Ibsen (Anita Berber) is told that she is to marry Eken Kornils (Ernst Pittschau), a man to whom her parents owe a large sum of money. She refuses and flees at the last minute to take up with Erik Knorrensen (Conrad Veidt), a man who means well but who cannot marry her, as his wife will not agree to a divorce. She opens a restaurant in town with Knorrensen's money and soon finds that she is pregnant with his child. Needing a husband if she is to maintain her respectability, Dida decides to marry Philipp von Galen (Werner Krauss), one of the regular customers at her restaurant. Von Galen, who has spent some time in the tropics, suffers from malaria. Dida soon finds her marriage insufferable, as her husband is a sadist who tortures her regularly. Her only friend and confidante is her servant (Maria Forescu), who is able to keep von Galen under control.

Although von Galen is cruel to Dida, he maintains that he loves her very much; thus, when his malaria worsens, he directs his wife to leave him. Dida attempts to make contact once again with Knorrensen, but he, too, is incurably ill; despondent, he shoots himself. Having no other choice, Dida returns to her parents' house. At first,

her mother (Clementine Plessner) refuses to take her in, but both parents quickly come to realize that their rigid attitudes have caused Dida's suffering.

(Note: A different source has Dida marrying Kornils after her father's death, and then returning to confront only her mother.)

REVIEWS: "This picture is clean, thrilling and will make its way, but it will find enemies as well. It has already found them at the premiere, in those who would deny the public need to see the sick, the unusual, and the untypical... Conrad Veidt, in tragic slimness [sic], is the classic, ever-noble human being and thrilling lover, right down to the smallest fiber."

Lichtbildbühne, No. 14;
December 1918

"These interesting, thrilling — but strange, throughout — five acts were adapted for the screen by Richard Oswald from the well known book, and were set up with the usual superior technique and care that mark that director's films as 'quality.' Conrad Veidt offers a wonderfully deep and balanced performance as Erik Norensen [sic]."

Der Film, No. 49; 7 December 1918

NOTES AND QUOTES: It was with the *Tagebuch* pictures that Connie first worked with Richard Oswald, the producer-director with whom he made more films than with any other visionary-technician, and the man who is generally acknowledged as having "discovered" him. Oswald was born Richard Ornstein (he took his professional name from a character in Ibsen's *Ghosts*) in Vienna on the 5 November 1880. His film output was prolific; some accounts note his having been involved in one capacity or another in over 200 feature films. Notes on

archival holdings. "There's no way of knowing — without physically inspecting the print — what the actual length is," advised Mrs. Everson. "It could be anything between 800 and 1600 feet." Hence, at least a fragment of the original motion picture still survives.

his *Aufklärungsfilme* can be found in the chapters on censorship and *Die Prostitution*, and there are sundry remarks on his later propensity for costume epics in the essay on *Carlos and Elisabeth* and *Lady Hamilton*. In addition to these genres, Oswald (and Veidt) teamed up for a variety of thrillers (like *Nachtgestalten*, 1919), thrilling comedies (*Kurfürstendamm*, 1920), and hybrid compilations (*Unheimliche Geschichten*, 1919). Biographical sketches (*Manolescus Memoiren*, 1920) and what can only be described — hype and patina aside — as "women's pictures" (*Der Reigen*, 1920) also proliferated. In all, Oswald made more than 20 silent features with Connie and would doubtless have made others, had the actor not moved to America at the invitation of John Barrymore and stayed (virtually until the end of the silent era) at the insistence of Carl Laemmle, Sr.

A Jew, Oswald fled to his native Vienna from Germany in May 1933, and thence to Paris. It was in the City of Lights that he directed his old colleague Connie Veidt (then a year from taking *British* citizenship himself) in 1938's *Tempête sur l'Asie*. In November of that year, it was Oswald's turn to make for California; his first U.S. picture —*Isle of Missing Men*— was directed for Monogram in 1942. One can't say for sure that his experiences at Monogram led the aging director to slow the hectic pace he had set during his youth (he went on to make only two more films during the decade), but he gradually turned his attentions to television. The father of director Gerd Oswald (*Brainwashed, Agent for H.A.R.M., Bunny O'Hare*), Richard Oswald died in Düsseldorf on September 11, 1963.

Reinhold Schünzel, Werner Krauss and Erna Morena likewise began rather lengthy associations with Veidt, courtesy of *Das Tagebuch einer Verlorenen*. Schünzel, who was born in Hamburg in either 1886 or 1888, was bitten by the acting bug only after trying his hand at journalism and commerce. The actor sparred with Connie in the course of a dozen silent films, the majority of which were Oswald-Filme. Occasionally Schünzel turned to screenwriting or directing himself; he did both (*and* played the titular character) in 1920's *Der Graf von Cagliostro*. Much as Connie had done the previous year with *Wahnsinn*, Schünzel set up his own production company. Schünzel was both director and screen author of *Viktor und Viktoria* (1933), the classic musical comedy that would later come to enjoy brief (and mild) notoriety in the hands of Blake Edwards. In 1938, he was off to Hollywood, under contract to MGM as a director; later, he returned to acting.

Schünzel was still in America (he returned to Germany in 1952) when Connie had his fatal heart attack, and a copy of his note of condolence to Lily Veidt has been published several times. "We became a well known team," Schünzel wrote to his friend's widow. "We had fun and never quarreled... With Conny a part of my life has gone."

Reinhold Schünzel died in Munich on November 11, 1954.

> There is no other actor of whom one is so ready to believe the worst when he glides onto the scene from the shadiest quarters of the big city. He brings a terrifyingly convincing realism to a milieu that does not really come alive until his entrance. So powerful is his presence that he seems to us to be sin incarnate, without equal in his cynical brutality, his devious eroticism, and his demonic cunning [Reinhold Schünzel. Hans-Michael Bock, Wolfgang Jacobsen, and Jörg Schöning, eds. Munich: 1989; p. 53].

If only for *Das Cabinet des Dr. Caligari*, Werner Krauss (born 23 June 1884 in Gestungshausen, Germany) would always be linked with Conrad Veidt, but the pair acted in nine other pictures together. For thriller aficionados, the silent psychological masterpieces *Das Wachsfigurenkabinett*

(1924) and *Der Student von Prag* (1926) strengthen the bond that *Caligari* forged. Krauss had made his film debut in the Paul Wegener film *Der Student von Prag* in 1913, and continued in the medium until 1955. His career as fecund as Veidt's, Krauss numbered among his accomplishments some of the most prestigious productions that the silent era had to offer.

Surprisingly, Krauss never traveled to America at the end of the '20s, as did large numbers of his German colleagues, although some sources maintain that he was never invited to do so. Along with Heinrich George, Paul Wegener, Erna Morena, and dozens of others, he elected to remain in Germany. Spirited debate can be had over whether these folk stayed because they agreed in spirit with the Nazi philosophy, or because they saw a narrowing of the professional field, as it were, and felt that it was better to rule in hell than share the wealth in heaven. Wherever the truth may ultimately lie, Werner Krauss eagerly embraced a leading role in *Jud Süss*, the Nazi-funded remake of Veidt's 1933 inspirational movie. (Felix Bucher [*Screen Series: Germany*. London: A. Zwemmer Limited; p. 101] could only tsk-tsk in his entry on Krauss: "Played some very vicious parts in purely Fascist films.")

Werner Krauss died in Vienna on 20 October 1959.

Like Schünzel and Krauss, Bavarian-born Erna Morena frequently shared screen space with Veidt, appearing in eight features with him by 1923. Equally adept at tragedy (*Der Gang in die Nacht*), comedy (*Kurfürstendamm*, both 1920), and everything in between (*Manolescus Memoiren* [1920], *Das indische Grabmal* [1921], *Wilhelm Tell* [1923]), Morena's career also spanned five decades. She, too, committed the personal and professional indiscretion of appearing in the 1940 *Jud Süss*. Erna Morena also passed away in Munich, on 21 July 1962; she was 70 years old.

Das Dreimäderlhaus (Schuberts Liebesroman)

[LOST] *The House of the Three Girls*; Richard Oswald-Film, GmbH, Berlin 1918; Filmed in Vienna, Austria; *Zensur*: July 1918 — 4 Acts, 1725 meters; World premiere: 22 September 1918 Tauentzien-Palast, Berlin (A "Sondervorführung" — A "Special Performance"); *Nachzensur*: 16 April 1921— 4 Acts, 1710 meters; Forbidden to adolescents

CAST: Conrad Veidt *Baron Schober*; Julius Spielmann *Franz Schubert*; Wilhelm Diegelmann *Schöll*; Sybille Binder *Hannerl*; Käthe Oswald *Heiderl*; Ruth Werner *Hederl*; Anita Berber *Grisi*; Bruno Eichgrün *Vogl*; Eynar Ingesson *Moritz von Schwind*; Raoul Lange *Nicolo Paganini*; Adolf Suchanek *Count Scharntorff*; Max Gülstorff *Novotny, a Confidante*

CREDITS: *Director/Producer* Richard Oswald; *Scenario* Richard Oswald; *Based on the musical by* A.M. Willner and Heinz Reichert; *Photographed by* Max Fassbender; *Musical Score for theaters* Hans Schindler; *Based on pieces by Franz Schubert*

SYNOPSIS: The film is based on the life and loves of Franz Schubert.

REVIEW: "This is not a picture in the common sense of the word. As opposed to the operetta, the film *Das Dreimäderlhaus* shows a row of lyric scenes that are crowned at the end with some strong and effective drama... Oswald knows how to avoid letting the lyric scenes become sentimental... He does not slavishly follow the settings of the operetta... Likewise, he approaches the plot freely and makes full use of poetic license... It runs through Schubert's life double time."

Der Kinematograph, No. 612;
25 September 1918

(It appears that Richard-Oswald-Film took exception to some of the reviews published in the aftermath of the "Special Performance" of *Das Dreimäderlhaus*, and a revised version of the critique printed below appeared the next evening, minus several of the offending lines. It is not known whether Oswald himself was aware of the problem. What is clear, though, is that the studio started a row with the newspaper, *Vossische Zeitung*, and was taken to court in a civil suit by the aggrieved party almost immediately.)

"Even so many years after his death, the pitiable Franz Schubert is not safe from being transformed into the saccharine hero from a cheap novel, being chased on- and offstage … like a figure from one of his own operettas, while bands, gramophones and hurdy-gurdies play his music, badly. Yesterday, you could see him in a special performance at the Tauentzien-Palast.

"The five acts presented by Richard Oswald are more authentic (in terms of location) than the *Dreimäderlhaus* operetta, as they were photographed at various historical sites in Vienna. What's more, the silence [of the film] is preferable [to the operetta] as the acting suits the capaciousness of the locations. On the other hand, the [photographic] effects are rough and the intertitles are barely competent.

"Schubert is played by Julius Spielmann, who boasts an admirable makeup, but who draws the maestro's clumsy shyness too broadly. Papa Schöll is Diegelmann, in a thoroughly splendid study, Grisi is Anita Berber, Novotny is Gülstorff. The 'gals' are played by three equally fascinating actresses. The picture, which seems determined to undermine the composer's already weak traits, still retains some [of the man's] charm, and, helped by those immortal Schubert melodies, hits the mark in the end."

Vossische Zeitung,
28 September 1918

Outside the titular house, the three gals ([left to right] Käthe Oswald, Sybille Binder, Ruth Warner) are all ears. That's Julius Spielmann (as Franz Schubert) second from right. Connie is third from right. (*Das Dreimäderlhaus*)

"Oswald would probably produce better films with her [Asta Nielsen] than he does now. His filmed *Dreimäderlhaus* is hardly an act of brilliance. Sure, the performances and technical quality are generally flawless, as are all of Oswald's works. But it must be pointedly written in capital letters that there are sections that desperately miss Oswald's erstwhile meticulous direction: the exaggerating Gülstorff as Novotny, for example. This grotesque clown figure is enormously annoying. Julius Spiegelmann, who duplicates 'Franzerl' in a perfect makeup, is far too foolishly clumsy. Why must he have his handkerchief constantly hanging out of his pocket like a disorderly office clerk? Why does he bow like a schoolmaster before inspection? Why does Hannerl fail? Then, there's this manuscript, almost devoid of mood. Has Oswald delivered so much good work that he can allow himself for once a less competent production? This can't have pleased him a great deal, or he wouldn't have exiled *Dreimäderlhaus* to the provinces."

Unknown review,
29 September 1918

NOTES AND QUOTES: A loose remake of the story was shot in West Germany in 1958. The color feature, directed by Ernst Marischka, starred Karlheinz Böhm and Eberhard Wächter; Rudolf Schock had Veidt's old role of Baron Schober.

Dresden-born Anita Berber would make only some two-dozen pictures in the course of her brief career (she died of tuberculosis at the age of 29 in 1928), but fully 40 percent of those found her on the screen with Conrad Veidt. *Das Dreimäderlhaus*'s Grisi was her debut role, and 1922's *Lucrezia Borgia* marked her last credit with Connie. Illness forced the beautiful young actress to retire following *Ein Walzer von Strauss* (fittingly produced in Austria) in 1925.

Es Werde Licht!

[LOST] *Let There Be Light!*; Richard Oswald-Film, 1917–18; This was a four-part release, with Veidt appearing in the last episode only, *Sündige Mütter*, in 1918; *Es Werde Licht! 4. Teil: Sündige Mütter (Strafgesetz § 218)*; *Guilty Mothers (Penal Law 218)*—1918; *Zensur*: July 1918—5 Acts, 1811 meters; Forbidden to adolescents; Premiere: October 1918 U.T. Lichtspiele Alte Promenade, Halle Berlin Premiere: 22 November 1918 Marmorhaus; *Nachzensur*: 1 December 1922—5 Acts, 1620 meters; Forbidden to adolescents

CAST: Conrad Veidt *Herr Kramer*; Alfred Abel *Sporck, a Bookkeeper*; Käte Waldeck-Oswald *his Daughter, Edith*; Reinhold Schünzel *Kallenbach, a Factory Owner*; Auguste Pünkösdy *Lene, Kramer's Wife*; Kurt Salden *Walter*; Emilie Unda *Therese Kallenbach*; Kissa von Sievers *the Woman*; Ilse Wehr *the Midwife*; with Kurt Vespermann

CREDITS: *Producer/Director* Richard Oswald; *Scenario* Richard Oswald, E.A. Dupont; *Photographed by* Max Fassbender; *Set Designs* August Rinaldi; *Technical Advisor* Dr. Magnus Hirschfeld

SYNOPSIS: Factory owner Kallenbach (Reinhold Schünzel) and his wife (Emilie Unda) find themselves unhappy in their later years because they have lost their only son. Frau Kellenbach hadn't wanted more than one child so that she would not lose her figure, and now that she yearns for more, it is too late.

The Kallenbachs' bookkeeper, Sporck (Alfred Abel), has a tragic fate awaiting him, as well. He loses both his wife and his daughter in the same way: both die while committing a crime against life. Sporck confesses that Mrs. Sporck went to a midwife (Ilse Wehr) for an abortion because they could not afford a second child. Disaster followed, and Mrs. Sporck did not return home alive.

Sporck has entrusted his daughter Edith (Käte Waldeck-Oswald)—a charming young woman who has grown without the guidance and care of a mother—to a woman of his acquaintance (Kissa von

SÜNDIGE MÜTTER

Fashionably dressed women + street corners = tragedy. (*Sündige Mütter*)

Pünkösdy) is always surrounded by her charming children. When she and her husband (Conrad Veidt) lose their oldest son in an accident, the two are able to stand strong in the face of their suffering because of the joy their children have brought them and will continue to bring.

REVIEW: "The premiere of Part IV of Richard Oswald's cultural film, *Es werde Licht!*, took place in the Marmorhaus. *Sündige Mütter* is the name chosen by Richard Oswald and E.A. Dupont, in collaboration with medical advisor, Magnus Hirschfeld. With an exceedingly thrilling plot, it shows offenses against § 218 and § 219 (crimes against the seed of new life) and the consequences of such sinful behavior in different social strata.

"That the film castigates the almost fashionable conditions [of abortion] in the strongest terms and shows its consequences almost brutally is of definite merit and serves the welfare of the individual as well as of our whole society. After the war and the hardships of peace our opponents will force upon us, we have to reconsider many things: May this film help us achieve a more noble, moral way of thinking about the topics discussed! (Another theme is shown as well in the film, although not so vividly: the care of unmarried mothers and the emancipation of illegitimate children.)

"Richard Oswald has done everything possible to increase the film's effectiveness. The spectator is thrilled as he follows the

Sievers). The hot-blooded and inexperienced girl is seduced by a lecher (a second account of the story has Kallenbach as the roué) and becomes pregnant; her "motherly friend" knows only that the shame must be averted and that Sporck must never know; the inevitable choice is the midwife. Edith follows her mother to the grave. (That second plot summary continues... Spork, embittered by these misfortunes, seeks out Kallenbach to exact a terrible revenge after many years.)

The good fortune of the Kramer family stands in contrast to this dismal account. The blonde Frau Kramer (Auguste

scenes of miserable families, unhappy through their own fault, and his heart enjoys the scenes showing the home of manager Kramer, whose wife has given him a dozen children. This contrast, that only film can present so effectively, will cause many to think. The audience, watching the decline of the Kallenbachs as opposed to the rise of the Kramers, will also ponder the fate of our German national family and recognize how every single citizen has to lead his family life to bring Germany back to its former state.

"Acting by Reinhold Schünzel, Alfred Abel, Emile Unda and Käte Oswald is very good. Fassbender's excellent photography makes the film a pleasure."

> *Die Filmwelt*, No. 47/48;
> 30 November 1918

NOTES AND QUOTES: While the plot summary given above is the result of the careful melding of two rather disparate extant accounts, James D. Steakley's comments on the film allude to still *other* plot wrinkles.

In consultation with the Deutsche Gesellschaft zur Bekämpfung Der Geschlectskrankheiten (German Society to Combat Venereal Diseases), [Richard Oswald] produced *Es Werde Licht!* A medical melodrama dealing with a syphilitic who transmits his infection to his wife and thence to his daughter, the film not only passed the censors but received praise from Reichstag delegates mindful of the salubrious effects it could have on the sexual hygiene of German soldiers, who were frequenting houses of prostitution maintained by the military command itself. Heartened by his success, Oswald produced, scripted and directed two sequels in 1917 and 1918, now with the support of the Ärztliche Gesellschaft für Sexualwissenschaft (Physicians' Society for Sexology) and the expertise of Dr. Iwan Bloch. Following Bloch's untimely death, Oswald collaborated for the first time with Magnus Herschfeld, who served as scientific advisor for the fourth part [of this saga], *Sündige Mütter*, that aimed to expose the danger of back-alley abortionists.

The common denominator of these so-called *Aufklärungsfilme* ("enlightenment," i.e. educational films) was the privileging of the discourse of sexual hygiene, personified in each case by a sage physician. Even before the end of the war, Oswald and Herschfeld had two even more daring projects in development: *Anders als die Andern* and *Die Prostitution*, the second of which argued that prostitutes were unjustly condemned by a hypocritical society ["Cinema and Censorship in the Weimar Republic" in *Film History* (magazine), Volume ll, 1999; p. 189].

Es Werde Licht! l. Teil — 1916/17; Press preview: 25 January 1917 — Tauentzien-Palast, Berlin; *Zensur*: February 1917 — 5 Acts, 2055 meters; Forbidden to adolescents; General Release: 2 March 1917 — Tauentzien-Palast, Berlin; *Nachzensur*: 11 March 1921 — 5 Acts, 1777 meters; Forbidden for adolescents

CAST: Bernd Aldor *Dr. Georg Mauthner*; Hugo Flink *Paul Mauthner, his Brother*; Nelly Lagarst *Assistant*; Ernst Ludwig *Councilman Kaufherr*; Leontine Kühnberg *Else, his Daughter*; Lupu Pick *Dr. Franzius*; Max Gülstorff *Patient*; Kurt Vespermann *Gerd*; Käte Oswald *Ingeborg*

CREDITS: *Producer/Director* Richard Oswald; *Scenario* Richard Oswald, Lupu Pick; *Based on an idea by* Lupu Pick; *Photographed by* Max Fassbender; *Set Design* Manfred Noa, August Rinaldi; *Released with* "the endorsement of the *Deutschen Gesellschaft zur Bekämpfung der Geschlechtskrankheiten* [the German Society to Combat Venereal Disease] under the leadership of Professor Blaschko."

Es Werde Licht! 2. Teil — 1917; Premiere: 25 January 1918 — Tauentzien-Palast, Berlin; *Zensur*: January 1918 — 5 Acts, 1697 meters; Forbidden to adolescents

CAST: Bernd Aldor *Dr. Erich Mautner*; Theodor Loos *Wolfgang Sandow, Scholar*; Rita Clermont *Ellen, his Sister*; Paul Hartmann *Ernst Hartwig*; Eva Speyer *Lilly Jensen*; Ernst Pittschau

CREDITS: *Producer/Director* Richard Oswald; *Scenario* Richard Oswald, Ewald André Dupont; *Set Design* Manfred Noa, Richard Dworsky; *Music (for theaters)* Kapellmeister Fischberg; *Photographed by* Max Fassbender; *Technical Advisor* Dr. Iwan Bloch; Released with "the endorsement of the Ärztlichen Gesellschaft für Sexualwissenschaft [the Medical Society for the Scientific Knowledge of

Sexuality] with the assistance of Dr. Iwan Bloch."

Es Werde Licht! 3. Teil—1918; Premiere: 24 March 1918—U.T. Friedrichstrasse, Berlin; *Zensur*: March 1918—5 Acts, 1915 meters; Forbidden to adolescents

CAST: Werner Krauss *Waldemar Gorsky, Gentleman Farmer*; Else Heims *Lisa, his Wife*; Theodor Loos *Hans*; Heinrich Schroth *Peter Osten, Gentleman Farmer*; Emil Lind *Older Servant*; Leo Connard *Country Doctor*; Gertrud Welcker *Peasant Girl*; Hugo Döblin *Bettler*; Guido Herzfeld *Physician*; Käte Oswald *Vilma*

CREDITS: *Producer/Director* Richard Oswald; *Scenario* Richard Oswald, Ewald André Dupont; *Photographed by* Max Fassbender; *Technical Advisor* Dr. Iwan Bloch.

Colomba

[LOST] (*An Exotic Novelette in 5 Acts*); Erna Morena-Film GmbH, Berlin—1918; Distributed by Hansa-Film-Verleih; World premiere: 8 November 1918 Tauentzien-Palast, Berlin; *Nachzensur*: 6 April 1921—5 Acts, 1348 meters; Forbidden to adolescents

CAST: Conrad Veidt *Henryk van Rhyn*; Erna Morena *Colomba*; Werner Krauss *Gonzales*; Alfred Abel *Juan, his Nephew*; Maria Forescu *Arjuna, a Negress*

CREDITS: *Producer* Erna Morena; *Director* Konrad von Wieder (Arzén von Cserépy); *Photography* Max Fassbender; *Based on the novel by* Emil Rameau; *Set Design* Ernst Stern

SYNOPSIS: Colomba (Erna Morena), a young girl for whom life is but a game, marries old Gonzales (Werner Krauss), the richest farmer near the Rio Grande, while spurning the passionate advances of his nephew, Juan (Alfred Abel). She soon discovers that her old, sickly husband cannot make her happy; Juan, aware of this, remains at the ready, waiting to be summoned. The unexpected occurs, however, when the young, elegant Henryk van Rhyn (Conrad Veidt) appears on the scene.

Henryk and Colomba spend a great deal of time together, arousing Juan's jealousy. The young man even attempts to kill Henryk, but he is foiled by Colomba's faithful servant, Arjuna (Maria Forescu). Gonzales falls ill. The doctor prescribes medicine, warning that an overdose would be fatal. When Gonzales dies shortly after having been ministered to by Colomba, Juan accuses the young woman of murdering his uncle so that she can be together with Henryk. He warns that Henryk will lose his love for her, just as she had lost her love for Gonzales. Colomba begs Henryk to take her away with him, and he does; the couple head for Holland, where they are married.

Unfortunately, Colomba still cannot find total happiness. She misses her carefree life on the prairie and, just as Juan has predicted, Henryk has become somewhat estranged from her. Juan has followed her, however, and he breaks into her bedroom one night, ready to carry her off. Colomba fights him off and threatens to call the police. Juan warns her that he will have his revenge in other ways, and promptly informs the local police that she has murdered his uncle. Henryk breaks the news of the accusation to Colomba, who is more fearful that her husband will abandon her to her fate than she is of the police. Henryk calms her down, and the two learn that the police need more evidence than the rantings of a jealous lover.

Colomba, though, cannot forget what she took to be a look of doubt in Henryk's eyes, and when Juan keeps harping on her guilt, she puts her husband to the test. She asks Henryk whether he would always love her. When he replies in the affirmative, she tells him she killed Gonzales; aghast, Henryk turns away. Distraught, Colomba leaves him and seeks out every diversion life has to offer. At last she writes to Henryk. She is innocent, she claims in the letter; she only claimed to kill Gonzales in order to test her husband's love for her, and he failed the test. No answer is forthcoming.

Colomba (Erna Morena) admires her reflection, while Henryk van Rhyn (Connie) admires the real McCoy. (*Colomba*)

Weary and resigned, Colomba returns to her homeland, where Juan awaits her; she is beyond hating him any longer. Only the hope that Henryk might return keeps her alive. As time goes by, her hope dies, and soon after, so does Colomba.

REVIEW: "This story has been brought to the screen with great skill and life on the Mexican prairie is simulated very well indeed. The most interesting and attractive [character] is the Colomba of Erna Morena, who used all her skill to create a figure rich in feelings and exotic appeal... Conrad Veidt is a calm and balanced Henryk. The settings by Ernst Stern are excellent and are shown to advantage by Fassbender's quite good photography."

Der Film, No. 46;
16 November 1918

Jettchen Geberts Geschichte

[LOST] *Jettchen Gebert's Story*; *1. Teil: Jettchen Gebert*; Richard Oswald-Film GmbH, Berlin — 1918; *Zensur*: September 1918 — 4 Acts, 1373 meters; Forbidden to adolescents; World premiere: October 1918 Schadow-Lichtspiele, Düsseldorf; Berlin premiere: 8 November 1918 U.T. Kurfürstendamm

CAST: Conrad Veidt *Dr. Friedrich Köstling*; Mechthildis Thein *Jettchen Gebert*; Leo Connard *Salomon Gebert*; Martin Kettner *Ferdinand Gebert*; Julius Spielmann *Jason Gebert*; Clementine Plessner *Rikchen, Salomon's Wife*; Else Bäck *Hannchen, Ferdinand's Wife*; Max Gülstorff *Uncle Eli*; Helene Rietz *Aunt Minchen*; Robert Koppel *Julius Jacoby*; Ilka Karen *Pinchen, His Sister*; Hugo Döblin *Uncle Naphthali*; with Fritz Richard

CREDITS: *Producer/Director* Richard Oswald; *Scenario* Richard Oswald; *Based on the novels* Jettchen Gebert and Henriette Jacoby *by* George Hermann Borchardt; *Photographed by* Max Fassbender

SYNOPSIS: The picture tells the story of the beautiful Jettchen Gebert (Mechthildis Thein), a young Jewish woman in Berlin in the 1830s. The fact that Jettchen is already in love does not matter to her family, which has arranged a marriage for her. These same relatives have helped the bridegroom obtain a divorce so that he will be free to wed Jettchen. When her wedding day comes, the despondent young woman realizes that she cannot live at the side of a man for whom she feels nothing.

REVIEWS: "The body of this picture doesn't do justice to the novel."

Der Kinematograph,
16 October 1918

"Cinematography is always looking for more and newer forms of expression and new artistic possibilities. A twentieth-century film director has the same great literary ambition as do his colleagues on the stage. Practically speaking, this leads to interesting offers and new sources of stimulation and enjoyment for cinema patrons...

"The Rheinische Lichtbild Aktiengesellschaft — a new concern in the west of the country — is set to prove that its pictures not only have artistic value, but also are milestones on the path to upward-development of the German art of the cinema. On first sight, *Jettchen Gebert*, the book by Georg Hermann [*sic*], with its atmospheric magic and subtle detail work, doesn't seem a candidate for film, as the author shows a preference for strong, pulsating interaction and sharp contrasts. But those of us who have been fortunate to see the picture are happily surprised by the solution that Richard Oswald has found. The oft-misused term 'cultfilm' is appropriate here, although not in the customary sense; rather, it refers to the understanding of culture through one's appreciation of contemporary art, one's lifestyle, and one's worldview.

"The tragic fate of beautiful Jettchen Gebert unfolds before us in episodic fashion. Because of pure happiness and pure

Lovely silhouette publicity piece from the Gebert saga. (*Jettchen Gebert/Henriette Jacoby*)

Dr. Köstling (Connie) and Jettchen (Mechthildis [Gretl] Thein) smile as Uncle Eli (Max Gül-storff, left) contemplates the eternal verities. (*Jettchen Geberts Geschichte*)

love, she doesn't recognize, until it's too late, the direction her life is taking. The story, which closely follows the widely read book, shouldn't be revealed in too much detail here. Certain players who have offered excellent performances, however, should be mentioned briefly. First of all, we must laud Mechthildis Thein, who was entrusted with the title role. Julius Spielmann plays Jason Gebert, while the two other brothers are performed by Leo Connard and Martin Kettner. Conrad Veidt imbues his character, Doctor Köstling, with his great talent.

"Richard Oswald is responsible for the direction. [Oswald] has created pictures genuinely reminiscent of the Biedermeier era in Berlin, and their beauty and magic have evoked an atmosphere [so touching] that even Georg Hermann with his delicate book could not arouse deeper or truer feelings. The premiere of this film, which is expected this month, can be anticipated with interest."

"Film in Berlin in Early March,"
unknown source, undated —
Alfred Rosenthal

NOTES AND QUOTES: *Jettchen* is a nickname for Henriette.

[LOST] *2. Teil: Henriette Jacoby*; Richard Oswald-Film GmbH, Berlin—1918; *Zensur*: September 1918—4 Acts, 1393 meters; Forbidden to Adolescents; Subsequently re-cut (date unknown) to 5 Acts; World premiere: October 1918 Schadow-Lichtspiele, Düsseldorf; Berlin premiere: 13 December 1918 U.T. Nollendorfplatz

CAST: Conrad Veidt *Dr. Friedrich Köstling*; Leo Connard *Salomon Gebert*; Mechthildis Thein *Jettchen Gebert*; Max Gülstorff *Uncle Eli*; Hugo Döblin *Uncle Naphthali*; Julius Spielmann *Jason Gebert*; with Fritz Richard

CREDITS: *Producer/Director* Richard Os-

Dr. Köstling encounters some resistance from Jason Gebert (Julius Spielmann). (*Henriette Jacoby*)

wald; *Scenario* Richard Oswald; *Based on the novels* Jettchen Gebert and Henriette Jacoby *by* Georg Hermann Borchardt; *Photographed by* Max Fassbender

SYNOPSIS: After the wedding, Jettchen Gebert is now Henriette Jacoby. Although she gamely tries to make the best of the situation, she feels she cannot live with things as they are, and moves to divorce her husband. Free again, she hopes to marry her first sweetheart, but circumstances conspire to foil her plans. She dies a suicide.

REVIEWS: "The great film that Richard Oswald crafted for the screen from Georg Hermann's novel has just been shown to eager German audiences for the first time. The premiere made a great impression on the cognoscenti and the numerous illustrious guests. The plot of the picture is very close to that of the novel. It depicts the fate of beautiful 'Jettchen Gebert' ... and the short, simple story fills two thick volumes in the novel... It's a great achievement for Richard Oswald, his being able to recapture this charm and grace on the screen, not only from a technical viewpoint — the photography is perfect — but also in a way that captures one's heart by storm...

"When one views the wonderfully composed interior scenes, or the terrific panoramic vistas at the end of the second part, one realizes how photographic art can add a dimension that audiences regard as sensational.

"In addition, there is the excellent acting. Mechthildis Thein is above everyone else, and Dr. Köstling, played by Conrad Veidt, and Jason Gebert — Julius Spielmann — adapt themselves to the spirit of the work. [If one were] extremely picky, one might wish that the first would try [to exercise] a bit more restraint, and the other, a bit more vigor. This is not to disparage the excellent work of these two actors, but one must judge this masterpiece by the highest standards, as, in both con-

ception and execution, it ranks well above other productions..."

Der Kinematograph, No. 615; 16 October 1918

"*Jettchen Geberts Geschichte* (Oswaldfilm), made from Richard Oswald's reworking specifically for the screen, went off just fine; [it was] gratefully received by the audience at the Unionpalast's silver screen. One has to admit that the film is much better than the play, thanks to the skillful adaptation and tactful direction of Richard Oswald. The story itself is quite well known, and the film is closer to the novel than to the stage play.

"The cast — great in every way — includes Leo Connard, Martin Kettner, Max Gülstorff, Clementine Plessner, and Hugo Döblin. Above them all is Mechthildis Thein, who seems to have found her [ideal] director in Oswald, and who shows real depth, truth and effectiveness. Her partner, Conrad Veidt, supports her soundly with calm and finesse.

"A wonderful picture that belongs among the best of them, both stylistically and dramatically."

Der Film (Berlin), No. 46; 16 November 1918

Peer Gynt

[LOST] *1. Teil: Peer Gynts Jugend* (*Peer Gynt's Youth*); Richard Oswald-Film GmbH, Berlin — 1918; *Zensur*: November 1918 — 4 Acts, 1864 meters; Forbidden to adolescents; Distributed by Martin Dentler; World premiere: 6 April 1919 Marmorhaus, Berlin (matinee); General release: 29 April 1919 Schöneberger Lichtspieltheater, Berlin

CAST: Heinz Salfner *Peer Gynt*; Ilka Grüning *Aase*; Lina Lossen *Solveig*; Hans Sternberg *Jon Gynt*; George John *Matz Moen*; Maria Forescu *The Woman in Green*; John Gottowt *Troll King*

CREDITS: *Producer* Richard Oswald; *Directors* Richard Oswald, Victor Barnowsky;

Scenario Victor Barnowsky; *Based on* Peer Gynt *by* Henrik Ibsen; *Photographed by* Max Fassbender

2. Teil: *Peer Gynts Wanderjahre und Tod* (*Peer Gynt's Journeyman Years and Death*); Richard Oswald-Film GmbH, Berlin—1918; *Zensur:* date unknown — 4 Acts, 1425 meters; Distributed by Martin Dentler; World premiere: 6 April 1919 Marmorhaus, Berlin (matinee); General release: 29 April 1919 Schöneberger Lichtspieltheater, Berlin

CAST: Conrad Veidt *the Stranger/Button Maker*; Heinz Salfner *Peer Gynt*; Lina Lossen *Solveig*; Georg John *Prof. Dr. Begriffenfeldt*; Irmgard von Hansen *Ingrid*; Hanna Lierke *Anitra*; Richard Senius *the Fence Builder*; with Gertrud von Hoschek

CREDITS: *Producer* Richard Oswald; *Directors* Richard Oswald, Victor Barnowsky; *Based on* Peer Gynt *by* Henrik Ibsen; *Photographed by* Max Fassbender

SYNOPSIS: The prologue shows how Peer's parents run a hospitable home, but Captain Gynt (Hans Sternberg) is a gambler. He loses everything, leaving his wife, Aase (Ilka Grüning), in abject poverty after his death.

The first part (*Peer Gynts Jugend*) shows how Peer (Heinz Salfner) lives the life of an idler. After he carries off the wife of his neighbor, Matz Moen (Georg John), into the mountains, he comes upon the Woman in Green (Maria Forescu), who is, in reality, the daughter of the Troll King (John Gottowt). On top of this, his mother, Aase, dies alone.

In the second part (*Peer Gynts Wanderjahre und Tod*), Peer sets his eye on adventure, which means a constant flow of beautiful women. During his often-fantastic travels (he wanders across the globe from North America to Africa and back again to Norway) he meets four lovelies (Irmgard von Hansen, Hanna Lierke, Anita Berber, Gertrud von Hoschek), all of whom seduce and abandon him. In the course of these relationships—during which he is a gold prospector, a slave trader, a prophet, and "king of the desert"

(in a lunatic asylum in Cairo)—he enjoys riches and comfort, only to be left ultimately penniless and discouraged.

After years of such experiences, he returns as an old man to his hometown of Gubrandsdale. The bizarre Button Maker (Conrad Veidt) is all for putting him into his melting pot, so that he can be reshaped and reinvigorated. Before this can occur, however, Solveig (Lina Lassen), Gynt's childhood sweetheart who has remained true to him all these years, effects his salvation through her pure love and devotion.

REVIEW: "There is no other play that has been presented onstage than *Peer Gynt*—the Nordic *Faust*—a chief work of the late dramatic grandmaster, Henrik Ibsen. Little wonder, then, that *Peer Gynt* has now been adapted for the screen. Viktor Barnowsky, on whose stage (the Lessing Theatre, Berlin) the play has often been performed, has naturally allied himself more closely to Ibsen's original script than to the version usually seen performed, which is often mistaken for complete.

"The cast is the same as in the original cast of the Lessing Theater. Heinz Salfner, perhaps the best stage Peer Gynt, provides an excellent performance (apart from some trifling misfires). Ilka Grüning as the lonely mother Aase, Lina Lossen as Solveig—although she is still noticeably a bit uncomfortable within the film medium, she adapted well in the ensemble—Irmgard von Hansen in the role of Ingrid... In smaller parts, but good and just right for their roles—Maria Forescu (the troll king's daughter), Conrad Veidt (the button maker), Georg John (Matz Moen), Hans Sternberg (the father), and John Gottowt (the troll king).

"There's nothing that need be said against this adaptation of the Peer Gynt theme to the screen, but one wishes that this difficult task would have been attempted by the best dramaturge and the most experienced director. Viktor Barnow-

The Button-Maker (Connie, right) exchanges words with old Peer (Heinz Salfner). (*Peer Gynt*)

sky — excellent on stage — is too inexperienced in film direction to conquer the medium; the fact that he adapted the script himself must also be regarded as a mistake. Had he lived, Henrik Ibsen would certainly have concocted the film much differently.

"In terms of effect, acting and technical form (photography: Max Fassbender), *Peer Gynt* surpasses the so-called average production by far, and it will find a grateful audience. Not to mention that it will become a box-office hit anyway because of its world-famous title. But one has to mention every detail that is not perfect when a work that is so dominant in literature and the art of acting is concerned. And that was done with the above…"

> *Der Film* (Berlin), No. 15;
> 12 April, 1919 — B. von Joachim

NOTES AND QUOTES: Henrik Ibsen's eponymous play — which had premiered on stage in Christiana, Norway, in 1876 — provided fodder for a number of cinematic adaptations. The fledgling Paramount Pictures Corporation distributed the first filmed effort in 1915. Charles Ruggles, who would go on to international fame as a comic actor, essayed the role of the Button Maker under Oscar Apfel's direction, while Cyril Maude enacted the title role.

Some 16 years after Conrad Veidt had tried to stuff Heinz Salfner into the pot, Hans Albers was avoiding the same fate for director Fritz Wendhausen and Bavaria Films. (Also headlining the 1934 German production was actress Olga Tschechowa, who had appeared with Veidt in *Die grosse Sehnsucht* [1930] and *Die Nacht der Entscheidung* [1931]. In what can only be termed an odd coincidence, Miss Tschechowa was the niece of playwright Anton Chekov, who was no slouch himself when it came to penning immortal tales for the stage, which were later usurped by filmmakers for the screen.)

In 1941 — back in the USA — Peer Gynt (now impersonated by 17-year-old Charlton Heston, heading a group of virtual unknowns) trotted off per the established formula for independent filmmaker David Bradley. The only legitimate "name" in the cast list was that of Francis X. Bushman. Ironically, the silent star went unseen; his disembodied *voice* took on the narrative chores. An obscure 1976 motion picture and a couple of made-for-TV specials followed, but it took until 1993 — and a big budget TV miniseries based on Ibsen's fantasy — for *Peer Gynt* to be produced in Norway.

As per the Oswald film version, a bit of mystery remains on the plate, and this is due mainly to the extant critique from *Der Film* (cited above). In the movie ad, Georg John is listed as Professor Doctor Begriffenfeldt; in the extant cast listing, he is cited as playing Matz Moen. It has been suggested that John doubled, playing the former role in the first part of the production, and the latter role in the second. A similar problem arises when one source (a trade ad in the 4 September 1919 *Der Kinematograph*) has Hanna Lierke playing Anitra, while another (the aforementioned *Der Film* review) lists Anita Berber in the part. Without additional information or the film itself, both puzzles are open to conjecture.

Opium (Die Sensation der Nerven)

Monumental-Filmwerke GmbH, Berlin — 1918/1919; Photographed at Bioscop-Atelier, Neubabelsberg; World Premiere (& prospective exhibitors' showing): 29 January 1919 Residenz-Theater, Düsseldorf; Berlin premiere: February 1919 Marmorhaus; *Nachzensur*: 10 June 1921 — 6 Acts, 2286 meters; Forbidden to adolescents

CAST: Conrad Veidt *Richard Armstrong*; Werner Krauss *Nung-Tschang*; Eduard von Winterstein *Professor Gesellius*; Hanna Ralph

Maria, his Wife; Sybill Morel *Sin, later Magdelena*; Friedrich Kühne *Dr. Armstrong*; Sigrid Hohenfels *the Opium Woman*; Alexander Delbosq *Ali*

CREDITS: *Producer/Director* Robert Reinert (Dinesen); *Scenario* Robert Reinert; *Photographed by* Hjalmar Lersky; *Music at theatrical premiere* I. Poltschuk

SYNOPSIS: Professor Gesellius (Eduard von Winterstein) has been studying the effects of opium in China, for over a year. When told that a certain Nung-Tschang (Werner Krauss) has a purer, more potent (and, therefore, more dangerous) opium than anyone else, Gesellius pays the man a visit. While at the den, a Chinese girl calls out for help, and Gesellius is seized by Nung-Tschang and his men and cast into a locked room. The Chinese man hates all Europeans—a white physician had once seduced Tschang's wife—and Sin, the girl pleading for release, is the dearest person in the world ... his daughter.

Tschang leaves Gesellius with a quantity of the pure opium and the professor, despondent, tries it. As he is in the throes of an opium dream, Sin (Sybill Morel) frees herself and him, and the two make their escape. Hot on their heels is Tschang, who swears that he will steal the dearest love of the professor, just as Gesellius has stolen his daughter.

Back home, Sin adopts the name Magdalena and begins to work at Gesellius' sanitarium. The professor, busy with his projects, fails to notice that his wife, Maria (Hanna Ralph), has fallen in love with Dr. Richard Armstrong (Conrad Veidt), Gesellius' favorite student and son of the colleague who had disappeared some 17 years earlier in China. Coincidentally, the elder Dr. Armstrong (Friedrich Kühne) returns and, in a very bad state, becomes a new patient at the sanitarium. Gesellius promises both to help him and to keep his identity a secret from his son.

Son Richard is likewise in a bad way,

feeling extremely guilty for having fallen in love with the wife of his mentor and protector. He tries to do himself in, but Maria comes upon him (he is badly injured) and brings him back to the sanitarium. The couple speaks of their love for each other just as Gesellius enters and, of course, overhears. Leaving in a fog, the professor comes upon Nung-Tschang, who smiles wickedly at him. The Chinese opium seller leaves some of the deadly powder on the desk. Disconsolate, Gesellius takes some of the drug to bury his sorrow. In his drug-induced state, he imagines that he has killed Richard. Tragically, as this is happening, Richard does commit suicide. Out of his lethargy, Gesellius is informed of the younger man's death and feels responsible for it.

Maria also feels that her husband has killed her lover, so Gesellius and Magdalena make for India, where they intend to further their research on the drug. They are followed by Nung-Tschang, who keeps the professor so well supplied that he becomes addicted. Finally, the researcher arrives home again, only to discover that Dr. Armstrong—fully recovered—is now head of the sanitarium. Gesellius expects cooperation and understanding from his old friend. He gets none, as Dr. Armstrong believes the professor has killed his son, Richard. Secretly in love with Gesellius, Magdalena claims that *she* killed Richard. She is arrested, convicted and sent off to prison.

Armstrong now seeks to care for the professor, who is failing rapidly. Nung-Tschang appears, and Dr. Armstrong recognizes him as the husband of the woman he loved in China. Tschang gloats that his revenge is complete: Armstrong's son, Richard, is dead, and the doctor has sent his own daughter—Magdalena—to prison. Armstrong is devastated.

Tschang tries to rescue Magdalena, but she refuses to accompany him. Guards

For today, at least, Richard Armstrong (Connie) is on the mend. (*Opium*)

rush in, a struggle ensues, and Tschang is shot. Meanwhile, Gesellius finds Richard's suicide note and takes this to Maria, who goes to the police at once. Magdalena is freed.

Gesellius dies while again having an opium vision, but a pleasant one, in which all his loved ones are present.

REVIEWS: "Robert Reinert has finally completed a work he can call his own. His *Opium* is a full-length, 6-Acter, quite different from other films. First of all, it has no 'star role,' which might hinder the integrity of the work. Second, he doesn't concentrate only on the fate of the two main characters, but shows how they connect with the fates of a half-dozen other persons. Third, this epic film has not only one or two 'highlights,' but revels in sensationalism in wholesale quantity... The greatest praise belongs to director Reinert, who succeeded in making the beauty and

exotic charm of China and India real in Neubabelsberg."

> *Der Kinematograph* (Düsseldorf)
> No. 631; 5 February 1919
> Egon Jakobsohn

"A precise, well-thought-out plot... effective, detailed sets, built without thought of the cost ... perfect technique ... never boring ... the characters are true-to-life ... a picture one won't easily forget..."

> *Lichtbildbühne*

NOTES AND QUOTES: Reinert wrote and directed *Nerven* for Decla-Bioscop, which produced the film some moths after *Opium*. More of a sequel than a continuation of the original story, *Nerven* was nonetheless regarded by some reviewers as Part II of the earlier picture. Available information indicates that only Eduard von Winterstein appeared in both pictures.

Opium is considered by some to be part of the first wave of the "sex education" films (see *Es Werde Licht!*, above), which included items which targeted other vices besides sex.

The picture is really built on a familiar story, albeit draped with a great deal of colorful theatrics and melodrama. *Opium* anticipates by several years the popularity of "Yellow Peril" themes, so the novelty of some of the situation is a redeeming factor. Nonetheless, none of the principals clearly stands above the grand achievements of the nameless art director, whose splendidly crafted settings tend to distract the viewer from attempting to make sense of the hoary betrayal/infidelity/guilt/revenge/murder slumgullion that's underneath it all. Connie does what he can to look alternately lovesick, remorseful and suicidal, and he's not bad. It's just that virtually everyone else is also emoting to the hills nonstop — Werner Krauss makes some faces that are reminiscent of Emil Jannings' glowerings in *Die Augen der Mumie Ma*— and the thought that a bit of opium might be just the ticket to slow things down to a more natural pace is not out of place here.

Die Reise um die Erde in 80 Tagen

[LOST] *Around the World in 80 Days*; Richard Oswald-Film GmbH, Berlin — 1918/19; Distributed by Westfalica-Monopol-Film-Vertrieb; Original Release: 8 Acts, 2705 meters; World Premiere: 20 March 1919 Marmorhaus, Berlin; Zensur: 8 July 1921 — 8 Acts, 2578 meters; Then re-cut to 2563.50 meters; Admissible to adolescents; 1921 re-release title: Die Reise um die Welt; Approved for adolescents

CAST: Conrad Veidt *Phileas Fogg*; Anita Berber *Aouda*; Reinhold Schünzel *Archibald Corsican*; Eugen Rex *Passepartout*; Max Gülstorff *Detective Fix*; Käte Oswald *Nemea*; Paul Morgan *John Forster*

CREDITS: *Producer/Director* Richard Os-

wald; *Scenario* Richard Oswald; *Based on the eponymous novel by* Jules Verne; *Photographed by* Max Fassbender; *Musical score (for the theatrical premiere)* S. Radzitzki

SYNOPSIS: Phileas Fogg (Conrad Veidt) wagers the members of his London-based gentlemen's club that, due to radical improvements in modes of international travel (like railway trains), a man might very well be able to travel around the world in 80 days. When his wager is accepted, Fogg and his new valet, Passepartout (Eugen Rex), proceed on a series of adventures that offer excitement while bringing the pair ever closer to circumnavigating the globe. From the outset, the men are relentlessly pursued by Detective Fix (Max Gülstorff), who is certain that Fogg's hasty departure from the city has something to do with a daring robbery of the Bank of England. Accompanied by rich eccentric Archibald Corsican (Reinhold Schünzel), Fogg and the ever-resourceful Passepartout endure capture, shipwreck and murderous attack, and come within inches of losing their lives so that the princess Aouda (Anita Berber) — an Indian widow about to be cremated alongside her husband's cadaver — may regain hers.

Back in England, there is some doubt as to whether Fogg had actually accomplished the journey in the prescribed time. There remains nothing left to do, therefore, but pack and start out again.

REVIEWS: "Jules Verne's exciting novel *Around the World in 80 Days* has finally been filmed. We say 'finally,' because this wonderful adventure tale was truly made for the cinema, and one has to wonder why no director has battled for this wonderfully cinematic book. Richard Oswald, whose elaborate efforts are always eclipsing the 'average' picture ... has taken up the gauntlet, and ... has enjoyed tremendous success. This film is much more than a series of illustrations from the novel, as the story actually comes alive on the screen and the

Connie (left foreground) seems preoccupied, while Reinhold Schünzel (center) and Eugen Rex appear to be having words. Everyone else is seven shades of indifferent. (*Die Reise um die Erde in 80 Tagen*)

viewer experiences what he formerly could only read.

"This is due not only to the genius of the director, but also to the exquisite artistry of the cast. Names like Anita Berber, Käthe Oswald, Conrad Veidt, Reinhold Schünzel and Max Gülstorff need no explanation..."

Neue Berliner 12 Uhr, undated

"...Director Richard Oswald has cannily constructed [the film] around every comic incident in the novel and, scene by scene, has produced a delightful, action-filled picture. It got a very favorable reception, due to the casting of the ladies, Anita Berber and Käthe Oswald, and Messrs. Conrad Veidt, Reinhold Schünzel, Eugen Rex, and Max Gülstorff."

Berliner Tageblatt, undated

"Richard Oswald, the most courageous and adventurous in the realm of filmmakers, takes Jules Verne, takes the novel best suited for filming—*The Journey around the World in 80 Days*—and makes a film. This is in contrast to the older French 'Éclair' film, where the subject was treated as one thrilling sensation. Oswald moves the story along the novel's most grotesque lines, and the ploy is successful. The world tour becomes a ramble through the Green Forest... Widow burnings, Indian downfalls, sunken ships, arrests, attempted suicides—everything is here, and so unbelievably funny, that one's eyes are never bored throughout the 8 acts."

Der Kinematograph (Düsseldorf),
No. 639; 2 April 1919

"Jules Verne's *The Journey around the World in 80 Days* now fills the program at the Marmorhaus in Richard Oswald's adaptation. The book was filmed before the War by the French "Éclair" company, when the French directors made the bet at the Eccentric Club a gripping and exciting event. Oswald, though, has concentrated on the comical element of the story. He picked out the funniest scenes and thus created a mirthful comedy…"

B.Z. am Mittag, undated

Nocturno der Liebe

[LOST] *Nocturne of Love*; aka **Chopin**; Nivelli-Film-Fabrikation, Berlin—1918/1919; Censorship information: unknown; Released in 4 Acts

CAST: Conrad Veidt *Frederic Chopin*; Gertrude Welcker *Sonja Radkowska*; Rita Clermont *Mariolka*; Erna Denera *George Sand*; with Clementine Plessner

CREDITS: *Director* Carl Boese; *Scenario* Hans Brennert, Friedel Köhne; Based on episodes from the composer's diary

SYNOPSIS: This is the story of Frederic Chopin's life and loves, told in episodic form.

Chopin (Conrad Veidt) passionately loves the renowned singer Radowska (Gertrude Welcker), but the woman tries to involve him in intrigue and he is pursued by the Polish police.

Fleeing to Paris with his childhood friend Mariolka (Rita Clermont), Chopin meets and becomes infatuated with George Sand (Erna Denera). The couple begins a torrid affair.

An old gypsy once warned Chopin: "Beware of women. They will bring you the greatest happiness and the most profound misfortune." This pronouncement, sadly, proves to be true. George Sand ultimately makes Chopin miserable, and the composer dies in the arms of Mariolka, the only woman whose love for him has been selfless and true to the end.

REVIEWS: "Conrad Veidt plays the leading role and, by his powerful performance, gives riveting humanity to this strange, vivacious and, at the same time, magnetic character."

Der Kinematograph, No. 627;
8 January 1919

"Conrad Veidt in the main role of Chopin offers a finely polished performance, which shows the cerebral and inner suffering of the [Chopin] personality even in moments depicting sheer happiness."

Der Film, No. 2; 11 January 1919

Die Japanerin

[LOST] *The Japanese Woman*; Stern-Film GmbH, Berlin—1918; Censorship date: unknown—5 Acts; World premiere: 24 January 1919 Tauentzien-Palast, Berlin

CAST: Conrad Veidt *Thomas Harvell*; Max Landa *the Detective*; Helene Voss *Lieschen, his Housekeeper*; Leopold von Ledebour *Robert Raymond*; Ria Jende *Mary, his Niece*; Manja Tzatschewa *Man-to, his Niece*; Bernhard Goetzke *the Arab Servant*; Marie Grimm-Einödshofer *the Cook*; Rose Lichtenstein *the Parlor Maid*; Camillo Sacchetto *Henry Clavering, a young Englishman*; Georg Baselt [Basilk] *Spitzkopf, a Private Detective*; with Loni Pyrmont

CREDITS: *Director* Ewald André Dupont; *Scenario* E.A. Dupont; *Photographed by* Charles Paulus; *Set Decorations* Eugen Stolzer

SYNOPSIS: The detective (Max Landa) has fallen in love for the first time. The apple of his eye is Man-to (Manja Tzatschewa), a delicate Japanese girl living with her uncle Robert Raymond (Leopold von Ledebour) and her cousin Mary (Ria Jende).

One day, terrible news reaches the detective; Robert Raymond has been found murdered in his apartment. With the help of Raymond's secretary, Thomas Harvell (Conrad Veidt), the detective begins his investigation. Raymond had worked with Harvell the previous evening; when the

(Standing and emoting, left to right): Connie, Bernhard Goetzke, Manja Tzatschewa, Ria Jende. (Seated, defunct) Leopold von Ledebour. (*Die Japanerin*)

secretary left, nothing more was heard from Raymond. Come morning, Harvell found the study door locked. Suspecting the worst, he summoned Raymond's nieces; when they broke through the door, they found Raymond, shot in the head.

The detective locates the murder weapon: one of Raymond's own Smith and Wesson revolvers, which was cleaned and reloaded after the murder. The handkerchief used to clean the pistol, however, is one of Man-to's! Harvell reveals to the detective that the Japanese girl had only recently been questioning him as to how the weapon worked. Nonetheless, when in the presence of the beautiful Japanese maiden, the detective is unable to confront her with his suspicions. Taking her into his arms, he notices a key hanging about her neck. He removes the key without the girl's

knowledge and discovers that it fits the study door!

Soon, there is evidence that another crime has been committed: a huge diamond was stolen following Raymond's death.

Despite this, the detective cannot bring himself to believe that Man-to is guilty of these crimes, and allows her to move in with her aunt. It is there that he discovers a letter from a Mr. Clavering (Camillo Sacchetto) to Raymond, in which it is revealed that Clavering married one of Raymond's nieces. Man-to confirms the detective's hunch that Clavering's bride was Mary.

Nearly sure of the circumstances, the detective separately invites Harvell, Mary and Man-to to visit him; he makes sure that none of the three realizes that the others have been invited, too. First, he tells Man-to that he suspects Mary. When Mary arrives, he places her under arrest. Immediately, Harvell — who had been eavesdropping — storms into the room and confesses to both crimes. The detective has anticipated this. He already knew that Harvell was madly in love with Mary and would not stand by and see her harmed in any way. Harvell killed Raymond because the man was about to disinherit Mary for her clandestine marriage to Clavering.

Harvell confesses to the theft of the diamond as well, but refuses to disclose the whereabouts of the gem. In a moment of confusion, Harvell flees, but the detective is hot on his heels. After a dramatic chase, both men end up in the barn where Harvell has secreted the diamond. A fight ensues and a fire breaks out. The detective succeeds in finding the diamond and escaping, as Harvell perishes in the blaze.

REVIEWS: "The detective film *Die Japanerin*, which had its premiere at the Tauentzien-Palast, shows an undoubted improvement over its predecessors. It is calmer, less hectic, sharper and clearer in its plot, and has more vivid photography. Again the task of revealing a murderer's secrets falls to Max Landa... Performance and direction are very carefully wrought. In addition to Landa, Manja Tzatschewa, Georg Basilk and the interesting Reinhardt actor, Conrad Veidt, were very strong..."

Lichtbildbühne, No. 4;
25 January 1919

"This film offers few novelties, but it is technically sound, it develops skillfully and the acting is mostly decent. The central focus of the ensemble is, of course, Max Landa, who seized the opportunity to display his aloof, cool detective once again. His partner is Manja Tzatschewa, a young

Bulgarian, who we've already seen in several films. Special contributions were made by Conrad Veidt (as the secretary) and Ria Jende (as Mary). The rest were average to good."

Der Film, No. 5; 1 February 1919

NOTES AND QUOTES: The fifth entry in the Max Landa-Detektivserie of 1918/1919.

Die Japanerin was E.A. Dupont's first turn at directing Conrad Veidt; the second would be 1930's *Menschen im Käfig*. Neither film is currently available.

Die Mexicanerin

[LOST] *The Mexican Woman*; Kowo-Gesellschaft für Filmfabrikation GmbH, Berlin; 1918/1919; Censorship information: unknown — 5 Acts

CAST: Conrad Veidt *Dr. von Dossen*; Ferdinand Bonn *Don Herta*; Magda Elgen *Juanita, his Daughter*; Kurt Katsch *Bueblo, a Young Mexican*; with Curt Brenkendorf

CREDITS: *Director* Carl Heinz Wolff; *Scenario* Dr. O. Schubert-Stevens

SYNOPSIS: see trade ad copy below

NOTES AND QUOTES:

*From a trade advertisement
(for the Zentral-Kinema):*
"Only three more days— The excellent hit of the Wild West —*Die Mexicanerin*
An extremely thrilling drama of the Wild West in 5 Parts, with daring riding scenes and speedy pursuit scenes.
The action takes place partly in a city [*sic*], partly in Mexico."

*From a trade advertisement
announcing Magda Elgen
Dramen-Serie 19/20 (The Magda Elgen
Dramatic Series for 1919/1920):*
"The great *Ausstattungsfilm** in 5 Acts by Dr. O. Schubert-Stevens

---

*Film historian Werner Mohr translates this term as "fully outfitted in terms of design, sets, and accoutrements."

Magda Elgen and Connie in the first (or maybe the second) production of *Die Mexicanerin*.

Shortly, through the Wolff & Company Film Distributing Company, Berlin, it will be premiered in July."
From a newspaper advertisement (for the U.T. Lichtspiele):
"Only until April 8, the first class feature film, *Die Mexicanerin*. Sensational detective and Wild-West adventure-drama from Mexico, in which elegance, fashion, love, craftiness, slyness and poison have the leading part."

"*Die Mexicanerin*: A new production of the recently destroyed [burned] film is in progress." [Conrad Veidt's name is listed prominently.]
Der Film, No. 16; 1919

Per Veidt biographer Pat Wilks Battle, "The negative burned and the film was reshot. Veidt was most likely in the first version."
Per *CineGraph*, Connie appeared in both versions.
The second version was released in 1919, and Ferdinand Bonn may have assisted Carl Heinz Wolff in directing the second version.

Opfer der Gesellschaft

[LOST] *Society's Victim*; Messter-Film GmbH, Berlin—1918; Distributed by Hansa-Film-Verleih; Filmed at: Messter-Film-Atelier, Blücherstrasse, 32; *Nachzensur*: 6 April 1921— 5 Acts, 1597 meters; Forbidden to adolescents
CAST: Conrad Veidt *Prosecutor Chrysander*; Annaliese Halbe, Vilma Born-Junge, Kurt Brenkendorf, Carl Wallauer, Willy Grunwald
CREDITS: *Director* Willy Grunwald; *Scenario* Robert Wiene, Robert Heymann

SYNOPSIS: Prosecutor Chrysander (Conrad Veidt) successfully convicts Martha Bellina (Vilma Born-Junge) of murder, bypassing all consideration of extenuating circumstances. The prosecutor is a hard, idealistic man, who is driven to rid society of undesirables like Martha. As a result of the case, Chrysander is celebrated and promoted, and becomes engaged to the daughter (Annaliese Halbe) of the chief judge. Before the wedding, however, he comes across Martha's diary, in which he discovers the hard

Having shouldered the weight of injustice for quite some time, Prosecutor Chrysander (Connie, left) finally gets a hand. (*Opfer der Gesellschaft*)

circumstances of the woman's life. Seduced and abandoned when she was with child, then cheated and extorted, Martha finally shot her husband in a pathetic effort to make him stop blackmailing her.

Taken aback by what he has read, Chrysander puts his life on hold to devote himself to writing a book, *Society's Victim*. Into the midst of all this walks the prosecutor's former fiancée, who has married in the interim. Unaware of this, Chrysander reacts romantically, only to be rebuffed when the woman's husband arrives. A fight breaks out, and the husband is accidentally killed. During the ensuing trial, Chrysander is accused of perjury (for his statements regarding his ignorance of his former fiancée's marriage) and sentenced to death for murder.

Martha Bellina tries to intercede on the prosecutor's behalf, appealing to the minister of justice himself. The minister, in turn, is revealed as the man who seduced and abandoned Martha — and their child, Chrysander — when they both were young. Due to a technicality, the death sentence cannot be commuted, and Chrysander is led away to his execution, another of society's victims.

NOTES AND QUOTES: Scenarist Robert Wiene would return to this same theme some ten years later, for *Die Andere* (1930).

Die Prostitution

[LOST] *Die Prostitution 1. Teil: Das gelbe Haus*; *The Yellow House*; aka *Im Sumpfe der Grosssstadt—In the Big City Gutter*; Richard Oswald-Film GmbH, Berlin —1919; Ein "Sozial-hygienisches Filmwerk"; Original release: 7 Acts, 2566 meters; World premiere (and press preview): 19 March 1919 Schadow-Lichtspiele, Düsseldorf; Berlin press preview: 27 April 1919 Marmorhaus; Berlin premiere: 1 May 1919 Marmorhaus; *Nachzensur*: 14 April 1921—7 Acts, 2544 meters, then recut to 2526.5 meters; Forbidden to adolescents; Retitled *Das gelbe*

Haus for rerelease; *Nachzensur*: 30 January 1922 — 6 Acts, 2544 meters; Censored locally at Württemberg

CAST: Conrad Veidt *Alfred Werner*; Fritz Beckmann *Klassen*; Anita Berber *Lola, his Daughter*; Gussy Holl *Hedwig, his Daughter*; Reinhold Schünzel *Karl Döring*; Rudolf Klein-Rhoden *Hiller, the Landlord*; Rita Clermont *Vera, his Daughter*; Ferdinand Bonn *Michalsky*; Marga Köhler *Madame Riedel*; Kissa von Sievers *Prostitute*; Preben J. Rist *Servant of Righteousness*; Werner Krauss *Man*; with Ernst Gronau, Wilhelm Diegelmann, Emil Lind

CREDITS: *Producer/Director* Richard Oswald; *Scenario* Richard Oswald, Magnus Hirschfeld; *Photographed by* Max Fassbender, Karl Freund (?); *Set Design* Emil Linke

SYNOPSIS: The film consists of several episodes about the fate of girls forced into prostitution, either by accident or by design.

Hiller's daughter, Vera (Rita Clermont), is seduced and, given her sensual nature, it's a short trip into the world's oldest profession. Instead of running off to her music lessons, she heads to a brothel. One day, unwilling to surrender her (empty) handbag, she is strangled by a man. Accused of her murder is the man who had first seduced her, her friend and pimp.

Another episode shows how Alfred Werner (Conrad Veidt) storms into the brothel to free a girl who is working as a prostitute against her will. He is successful, but the police decide to send her back to her father, the very man who had forced her to prostitute herself in the first place. In the end, Werner saves her.

REVIEWS: "…according to recent standards, the photography is flawless. Oswald has created a 'portrait of Germany.' In reality, for all its picturesque beauty, Old Berlin is a foul place, both within and without… Conrad Veidt, the rescuer, shows his unsentimental side and a flexibility that is new for him."

Lichtbildbühne, 3 May 1919

DIE PROSTITUTION
SOCIALHYGIENISCHES FILMWERK

RICHARD
OSWALD
UNTER MITARBEIT
VON SAN. RAT DR.
MAGNUS
HIRSCHFELD

MARMORHAUS
KURFÜRSTENDAMM 236 DIR.: SIEGBERT GOLDSCHMIDT

"So many emotions are evoked upon seeing this film that they are hard to contain. The picture is not a wildly sensational piece, but a substantial work that depicts the struggle between a 'square' and a prostitute. The prostitute ... is a prisoner of society, brought before society's court. To her rescue comes a young, educated man, and the two are the foundation of the piece."

"County Court Decision" in *Film-Kurier*, 3 January 1923

"To illustrate the life of suffering for the unhappy victims of 'buyable' love, the scenarist used the technique of the 'folk play' for the screen. He has a good nose for contrasts... Conrad Veidt and Reinhold Schünzel are very good in the male leading roles..."

Deutsche Lichtspielzeitung, 12 April 1919

NOTES AND QUOTES: Per Gerhard Lamprecht, the original title, *Die Prostitution*, was forbidden when censorship was reintroduced, so the film was renamed *Das gelbe Haus* prior to its rerelease in 1921.

[LOST] *Die Prostitution 2. Teil: Die sich verkaufen*; *Those Who Sell Themselves*; Richard Oswald-Film GmbH, Berlin—1919; Ein "Sozialhygienisches Filmwerk"; World premiere: end of June 1919 Sondervorführung, Berlin; General release: 30 August 1919 Richard-Oswald-Lichtspiele, Berlin; *Zensur*: 7 August 1920—7 Acts, 2436 meters; Forbidden; Retitled *Die sich verkaufen* for rerelease; *Nachzensur*: 20 September 1922—7 Acts, 2400 meters; Forbidden to adolescents

CAST: Conrad Veidt *Günter Hofer, editor of the "Tagesboten"*; Reinhold Schünzel *Otto Sasse*; Gertrude Hoffmann *Klara, Hofer's Girlfriend*; Ilka Grüning *Frau Bürger, Klara's Mother*; Eduard Von Winterstein *Albert Hartwig, the Judge*; Kissa von Sievers *Else, his Wife*; Paul Morgan *Paul, Hartwig's Son by his first Marriage*; Preben Rist *Erich Schulte, editor of the "Blitzschlag"*; Gussy Holl

CREDITS: *Producer/Director* Richard Oswald; *Scenario* Richard Oswald, Robert Liebmann; *Photographed by* Max Fassbender

SYNOPSIS: Prologue: A prostitute (Kissa von Sievers) is arrested. At her trial, she says, "I'm selling only my body, but the others..." The "others" are seemingly respectable persons, who sell their entirety for riches and power.

Frau Bürger (Ilka Grüning), a high society lady, and Otto Sasse (Reinhold Schünzel), acting as her manager, have been swindling the public by selling shares in nonexistent or tapped-out silver mines. In this fashion, they have bilked hundreds of hopeful "shareholders." To lure more of the wealthy citizens into her scam, Frau Bürger holds open houses, wherein business is conducted against a background of gambling and drinking. One night, Sasse catches Paul Hartwig (Paul Morgan), son of the examining magistrate Albert Hartwig (Eduard von Winterstein), cheating at cards; he had hoped to pay off his debts with his winnings. He forces the young man to write out a confession on a playing card. When his father refuses to help him, Paul turns to his young stepmother, but she, too, has debts she cannot bring to reveal to her husband. She approaches Sasse for a loan, but the unscrupulous man merely tries to force himself upon her.

With excellent publicity from the dishonest newspaper *Der Blitzschlag*, Frau Bürger's enterprise is doing very well. Editor Günter Hofer (Conrad Veidt) of the respectable *Tagesbote*, however, decides to fight the swindlers with all his resources; he remains so busy doing so, he has no time to see his fiancée, Klara (Gertrud Hoffmann), and her mother, an elderly woman who has retired to private life. Hofer's crusade causes Magistrate Hartwig to issue warrants for Frau Bürger and Herr Sasse. The woman flees, but Sasse is

Opposite: Berlin's first-run movie palaces usually printed their own posters. (*Die Prostitution*)

Conrad Veidt   Gussy Holl   Preben Rist

Gertrud Hoffmann   Conrad Veidt   Ilka Grüning

brought in; during the interview, he produces the playing card with young Hartwig's confession. Appalled, Magistrate Hartwig abandons the investigation.

Exonerated, Sasse demands that Hofer print a retraction, and the editor has no choice but to do so. Magistrate Hartwig has approached his son in the meanwhile, suggesting that the young man either go to prison or have himself declared insane. Not keen on prison, Paul allows his father to take him off to a private asylum. En route to his fiancée's villa, Hofer hears a cry for help. It is Klara, who is struggling to free herself from Sasse's embrace. Hofer is horrified to learn that Klara's mother has given permission for Sasse to wed her daughter. On closer examination, however, Hofer discovers that Klara's mother is the erstwhile fugitive Frau Bürger! Klara tries to persuade her lover to keep silent about her mother's predicament, but the editor is resolved to expose the scam in all its seamy detail.

The next day, Hofer publishes a complete account of the fraud. The shareholders storm the company offices, but Frau Bürger has fled yet again. Sasse is seized and, when another attempt at blackmailing Magistrate Hartwig goes nowhere, poisons himself. Frau Bürger is subsequently caught and Editor Hofer finds himself alone; Klara, unable to forget that he caused her mother's downfall, leaves him to his newspaper.

REVIEW: "Richard Oswald searched for real human beings, and created an interaction, a truly dramatic conflict, such as is rarely seen on the screen.

Conrad Veidt is the honest, upright man. His posture, his gestures, his whole being ... demonstrate such pure character that he doesn't need to playact much at all."

Lichtbildbühne, No. 29;
19 July 1919 — L.K.

NOTES AND QUOTES: Very few of the *Aufklärungsfilme* made at the end of the teens have weathered the years, and one might ask if this was the ultimate result of public outrage or shame, the wartime destruction (by happenstance) of film vaults throughout Germany, the instability of nitrate film stock, or merely the luck of the draw. They were wildly successful moneymakers upon their initial release, and therein lies the reason for the head scratching: cash cows are normally treated with sufficient reverence to assure their being able to be milked time and again. How could the body of an entire subgenre — churned out in abundant quantity within the short span of its "life" — virtually disappear *in toto*?

The kernel of the problem may lie in the fact that the pictures were a) produced for domestic distribution only, and b) niche-marketed to lower class audiences, chiefly blue-collar workers and soldiers. Without an eye to exporting the product, there was no need for additional prints to drive up production and distribution costs. A limited number of positives would make the rounds of the more notorious sections of the major cities (Berlin's Kurfürstendamm district comes to mind) as well as the "neighborhood houses" in smaller towns. Being thus targeted at the hoi polloi, the films could be shot and shipped cheaply, which usually guaranteed healthy revenues. (As far as producers of *Aufklärungsfilme* were concerned, critical comment on technical competence or artistic vision ran a distant second to black ink in the company ledgers.) The downside to such economy is that fewer prints meant reduced chances that the picture itself would survive being edited (or run) to pieces. Following the spate of *Nachzensur*

Opposite, top: **The fast life hits a speed bump. (Left to right) Connie, Gussy Holl, Preben Rist.** (*Das gelbe Haus*) *Bottom:* **Ilka Grüning (right) keeps an eye on lustbirds Gertrud Hoffmann and Connie** (*Die sich verkaufen*)

in the early 1920s, the existing individual positive prints—not the negatives—were cut and pasted individually; any remaining money that could be skimmed from the product would be retrieved without spending a pfennig extra.

Certainly no effort was made by Josef Goebbels to preserve them as precursors to the cinematic output of the Third Reich. While they might have "received praise from Reichstag delegates" upon their initial release just after the end of World War I, these cheaply made, naïve accounts of illicit behavior and debauchery as practiced within the boundaries of the Fatherland by its citizenry had no place in a catalogue of motion pictures designed to project the desired image of the Übermensch on the world's screens.

If only a lengthy list of titles exists after some eight decades, their profusion is witness to their popularity. Targeted to the hoi polloi by canny filmmakers, they were wildly successful moneymakers upon initial release and most were reissued profitably, even when cut and recut at the whim of almost anyone in authority. Then, as now, the tag "Verboten" did little other than increase the appeal of a film or a series of films. Everybody knew that.

Anders als die Andern (Sozialhygienisches Filmwerk II)

Different from the Others; "Sozialhygienisches Filmwerk II"; Ein Aufklärungsfilm; Richard Oswald-Film GmbH, Berlin—1919; *Zensur*: 6 Acts, 2280 meters; Special performance: 28 May 1919 Apollo-Theater, Berlin; World premiere: 30 May 1919 Prinzess-Theater, Berlin; (per the Deutsches Kinemathek, the world premiere took place at the Apollo-Theater in April, 1919) ; *Nachzensur*: 18 August 1920—6 Acts, 2115 meters; Forbidden, as contrary to the law, unless the specific approved showing will be for physicians and medical personnel, in schools, or in institutions of higher learning.

CAST: Conrad Veidt *Paul Körner*; Reinhold Schünzel *Franz Bolleck*; Leo Connard *Paul's Father*; Ilse von Tasso-Lind *Paul's Mother*; Alexandra Willegh *Paul's Sister*; Ernst Pittschau *Her Husband*; Fritz Schulz *Kurt Sivers*; Wilhelm Diegelmann *Kurt's Father*; Clementine Plessner *Kurt's Mother*; Anita Berber *Else Sivers*; Helga Molander *Mrs. Hellborn*; Magnus Hirschfeld *Doctor*; Karl Giese *Paul as a Schoolboy*

CREDITS: *Director/Co-Producer* Richard Oswald; *Co-Producer* Magnus Hirschfeld; *Scenario* Magnus Hirschfeld, Richard Oswald; *Photographed by* Max Fassbender; *Set Designer* Emil Linke

SYNOPSIS: Paul Körner (Conrad Veidt) is a homosexual concert pianist who finds himself blackmailed by Franz Bolleck (Reinhold Schünzel), who led Körner on in order to gain a hold over him with regard to Statute 175, which makes the practice of homosexuality illegal. Körner pays Bolleck regularly, but when the blackmailer ups his demands—because Körner has fallen in love with one of his male music students—Körner goes to the authorities, charging Bolleck with blackmail. Bolleck goes to prison, but both he *and* Körner get three months' prison time on Statute 175 violations. Returning from prison, the pianist finds that all of his concert dates have been canceled due to adverse publicity about his homosexuality; he poisons himself. The fragment ends with Magnus Hirschfeld speaking out against intolerance for the "third sex."

REVIEWS: "Yesterday the Oswald Film Company showed their new work at a press screening in front of invited guests at the Apollo Theater. After the performance, experts and non-experts criticized the film, before finally tearing it to pieces.

"I simply cannot agree with this general opinion. Oswald has treated a very delicate topic in a decent and noble way. Maybe this was his chief mistake: he intended that his film appear as an academic treatise and strongly underestimated the effect it would have. [Many people] were secretly pleased by its failure. But Oswald has treated so many serious problems successfully that I can't bypass this film statement without a serious critique. The topic is doubtless a delicate one. Men who might be said to be plumbing the depths of the human soul have tried to create a picture worthy of its predecessors... In this, Richard Oswald and Dr. Magnus Hirschfeld have failed. It is surely not the fault of these men, who crafted this film with love and dedication, mindful that they were confronted with a difficult task. The topic is thankless, and I believe it is completely impossible to create a picture about it.

"The audience, hoping to understand by sharing all of the yearnings of the human soul, is thwarted by the theme; it is here that Oswald will find the cause of his failure. But the film will have its say, like all the others Oswald has produced. Direction and photography are beyond praise, and the acting was very good as well.

"Conrad Veidt approached his certainly difficult role with assurance and precision. Fritz Schulz, his partner, has to master the same problems, but does so less well. Reinhold Schünzel is a good actor, no doubt about it, and that's why he should not draw his characters—here, he is a blackmailer—along comical lines."

Deutsche Lichtspielzeitung,
No. 24; 16 June 1919

"*Anders als die Andern* is the title of the social-hygienic film being shown at the D.K. Lichtspiele. It depicts the life of a homosexual violinist in thrilling scenes, arousing compassion. This man's fate opens one's eyes as to how § 175 caused and still causes disaster.

"Although homosexuality has been proven by expert doctors to be an unfortunate predisposition, little has been done to abolish § 175. Now this *Aufklärungsfilm*

appears on the scene and calls for the abolition of the statute in the pure name of human love and justice..."

Lichtbildbühne, No. 3;
26 July 1919

"At the premiere of the picture *Anders als die Andern* at the Lessing Theater in Hamburg, pamphlets were handed out to the audience, decrying the film with the wildest and meanest prose. There were heated scenes, after which the agitator and his few fellow-rebels were thrown out, and the performance went on with no further interruption.

"Because of this incident, Hamburg's newspapers became interested in the picture twice (and watched it twice), and, the next day, the following reviews appeared:

General-Anzeiger fuer Hamburg-Altona

We live in the age of the so-called "enlightening films." Among those, few can be called irreproachable. The enlightening film *Anders als die Andern*, now shown at the Lessing Theater, has nothing to do with the usual trash, but nonetheless has been rejected via wild protests by a part of this audience. Per a letter we received from a local association, this is because the film would seduce our youth in a most unpleasant manner.

After watching the film, we found it to be tendentious, looking to influence the opinion of the masses regarding § 175 and hoping to reach a plebiscite to abolish this law against human beings with an unhappy predisposition. The film is constructed and directed with remarkable tact; it cannot offend anyone watching it...

Hamburger Volkszeitung

Anders als die Andern: an enlightening film at the Lessing Theater by the well-known sexologist, Dr. Magnus Hirschfeld. § 175, which punishes intimate homosexual contact between two men, seems to encapsulate a perfect example of filth from a homespun view of morality, although in reality it really has nothing to do with moral principles at all. It punishes only sexually active homosexual men, which proves that

Fritz Schultz is weeping on Connie's chest; that's Leo Connard with the silk topper; Anita Berber is looking you in the eye. (*Anders als die Andern*)

the government intended to forbid only this 'infertile' sexual intercourse for fear that otherwise we would lose too many new soldiers and tax payers... This is why we greatly appreciate that our comrade, Dr. Magnus Hirschfeld, has undertaken to enlighten the masses in an academic way.

And while he is for abolishing the disastrous § 175, it has nothing to do with morality or culture, but rather is the demand of a scientist who has, through his studies, arrived at the conclusion that homosexuality is no crime, but rather a sickness or just a different path nature has chosen in her wondrous way...

Neue Hamburger Zeitung

A delicate film. At the Lessing Theater ... a film is now being shown which is titled *Anders als die Andern*; it reproaches the problem of homosexuality. At the premiere last Friday, there were strong protests — even rebellion — among audience members, and we had to take a look at this picture ourselves, assuming the attitude of a prudish spectator with a slightly hesitant mental attitude... Thus, we were being totally objective. We therefore had a most prissy attitude, filled with concerns for the public welfare; and so, we sat down.

We say in advance: homosexuality is a predisposition, a very unhappy one in Germany ... and we demand that this injustice, which is couched in the insistence that this unhappy predisposition be dishonorably punished, be made to vanish from the codex... And this is the honest and — we convinced ourselves by the strictest standards — the academic purpose of this film. And yes, we acknowledge the decency, discretion and dignity with which the problem was not so much flogged out but discussed in a serious way. It is offered to the audience in a solid way, which is also relevant artistically...

Der Film, No. 37;
14 September 1919

NOTES AND QUOTES: The film initially may have run for some 100+ minutes. In 1974, the Gosfilmofond in Moscow presented a copy of *Inace, cem drugie* (*Different from the Others*) to the State Film Archive of the former German Democratic Republic that was a 45-minute fragment (871 meters) with Ukrainian subtitles. (Subsequently, the Gosfilmofond presented copies to the sundry film repositories of Munich, the Netherlands, and Brussels.) Copies circulating currently are either cutdowns from this fragment, or the fragment itself.

The working title of film was *§ 175*, then *Anders wie die Andern* (*§ 175*); the subtitle frequently appeared in later publicity materials, perhaps to compensate for the ambiguity of the main title. A Swedish film, *Vingarne* (*The Wings*, 1916), based on the Danish novel *Mikaël* (1908) by Hermann Bang and filmed by Maurice Stiller, is the only picture that might challenge the status of *Anders als die Andern* for earliest gay film. Luna-Film's *Aus eines Mannes Mädchenjahren* (*A Man's Girlhood*) was released in October 1919.

The wording of the censor ruling (cf. the *Nachzensur* text, above), shows, the "Forbidden" notwithstanding, that the authorities accepted the scientific importance of this work of Richard Oswald's.

Although the film opened to decent reviews and some popular acclaim, it was soon banned in many cities throughout Germany. In 1930, Hirschfeld (director of the Scientific Humane Committee, which he founded in 1897) fled from the Nazis and settled in France; in 1933, his library was burned by the Nazis, and (apparently) the only complete prints of *Anders als die Anderen* went up with it.

"Prior to the premiere, Oswald had prepared thirty to forty prints of the film and had arranged for distribution points in Hanover, Cologne, Frankfurt am Main and Vienna, as well as Berlin. That summer, the film opened in numerous other cinemas in Berlin and throughout Germany; within a year, it was also exported to Austria and the Netherlands. A major box-office hit, it frequently played to sold-out houses and was still running in Berlin in March of 1920...

"These two films [*Anders* and *Die Prostitution*] were produced and distributed during a unique window of opportunity that opened just days after Germany's defeat in World War I. On 12 November, 1918, the acting government—the 'Council of People's Commissars'—promulgated its first decree, the third point of which read: 'Censorship will not take place; theatre censorship is abolished.'"

"Cinema and Censorship in the
Weimar Republic" by
James D. Steakley.
Film History (magazine),
Volume 11, 1999; pp. 188–189

English novelist and screenwriter Christopher Isherwood recalled that the Nazis breaking up screenings of the film. In addition, Isherwood recounted segments from the original film that have not survived the years:

"Three scenes remain in my memory. One is at a ball at which the dancers, all male, are standing fully clothed in what seems about to become a daisy chain. It is here that the character played by Conrad Veidt meets the blackmailer who seduces him and then ruins him. The next scene is a vision which Veidt has of a long procession of kings, poets, scientists, philosophers and other famous victims of homophobia, moving slowly and sadly with heads bowed. Dr. Hirschfeld himself appears. I think the corpse of Veidt, who has committed suicide, is lying in the background. Hirschfeld delivers a speech (that is to say a series of titles) pleading tolerance for the Third Sex."

Homosexuality in the Movies by
Vito Russo. New York: Harper
and Row, 1987; pp. 20–21

"'You see,' chatted Veidt once, while we were discussing the never-ending subject of roles, 'even if I wanted to, I couldn't do things like *Anders als die Andern* anymore. I admit that those jobs were necessary and useful to me, because those films were a product of there times and had to be made — [those issues] had to be overcome... But even if I admit that they were useful and necessary, I could not return to them again'."

Conrad Veidt: Ein Buch vom Wessen und Werden eines Künstlers by Paul Ickes. Berlin: Filmschriftenverlag GmbH, 1927; p. 101

Die Okarina

[LOST] *The Ocarina*; Bayerische Film-GmbH, Fett und Wiesel, Munich — 1919; World premiere: 8 August 1919 Kant-Lichtspiele, Berlin; *Nachzensur*: 29 April 1921— 6 Acts, 1829 meters; Forbidden to adolescents

CAST: Conrad Veidt *Jaap Eden, the Cook*; Charlotte Böcklin *Regine*; Rudolf Lettinger *Captain Svarrer*

CREDITS: *Director* Uwe Jens Krafft; *Scenario* B.E. Lüthge (1st film scenario); *Based on a novel by* Karin Michaelis

SYNOPSIS: "The film shows us the moral conflicts of sailors who, separated from their wives and children for months, are exposed to danger and the temptations of the flesh in far off harbors."

REVIEW: "After the many disappointments the multitude of film adaptations of famous novels has brought us lately, one can happily note that, in this case, Karin Michaelis' exciting novel was successfully transformed into an exceedingly affecting, thrilling and engrossing cinematic drama. This is especially praiseworthy because the scenarist didn't render the source novel unrecognizable by neglecting its subtle psychology ... but, on the contrary, encourages the audience to go further and

read the novel, with which it might have been unfamiliar. This is perhaps the highest praise possible for an adaptation.

"Any film drama that, like *Die Okarina*, shows the story clearly and logically without any distractions from over-direction or knickknacks, is both pure literature and a literary achievement, because it introduces intellectual works to a vast part of our society that is completely unfamiliar with literature. Therefore, the educated reader of novels enjoys the picture as much as the uneducated 'cinema visitor.' Both would enjoy the splendidly artistic pictures of this drama and the marvelous acting of the beautiful, vivacious Charlotte Böcklin, the lively Rudolf Lettinger, and the demonic Conrad Veidt.

"All in all, a great success..."

Film-Kurier; 10 August 1919

NOTES AND QUOTES: Additional bits and pieces on the plotline of the film may be found in the following unknown review:

"*Die Okarina*, adapted for the screen by B.E. Lüthge after Karen Michaelis' novel, shows us the lives of sailors, who spend most of their lives at sea, having left their relatives at home. The sailor's tragic destiny fully engages us, all the more so as the woman left behind by Captain Svarrer is beautiful and anguishes over her longing for him. She knows of his sensual needs and the temptations that follow a sailor, who goes ashore "to stretch his limbs" after a long sea journey. Hence, her life is agonizing, frightened and jealous as she is.

"Svarrer returns, but the woman continues to experience nagging doubt. Regine, their oldest daughter, is to accompany her father on his next trip and watch out so that he remain faithful to her mother.

"The part of Regine was charmingly enacted by Charlotte Böcklin in a lifelike manner."

DIE OKARINA

Karin Michaelis Roman »Treu wie Gold« gab den Stoff zu diesem Film, der in einer Reihe schöner Bilder Szenen aus dem Seemannsleben wiederspiegelt. Der Film zeigt uns die Gewissenskonflikte der Seeleute, die monatelang von Weib und Kind entfernt, in weiten Häfen den Gefahren und Lockungen des Fleisches ausgesetzt sind. Charlotte Böcklin und Conrad Veidt sind in den Hauptrollen beschäftigt. Der Film wurde von Uwe Jens Kraft für die Bayerische Film Co. aufgenommen.

A montage from the original program. (*Die Okarina*)

Prinz Kuckuck

[LOST] *Prince Cuckoo*; aka **Leben und Höllenfahrt eines Wollüstlings;** The Life and Descent into Hell of Some Libertines; Gloria-Film GmbH, Berlin—1919; Filmed at: Bioscop-Atelier, Neubabelsberg; World premiere: 9 February 1919 Marmorhaus, Berlin; *Nachzensur:* 26 May 1921—6 Acts, 2575 meters; Forbidden to adolescents

CAST: Conrad Veidt *Karl Kraker*; Olga Limberg *Sara Asher*; Niels Prien *Henry Felix, her Son* [*Prince Cuckoo*]; Annaliese Halbes *Berta Kraker*; with Hanna Ralph, Eric Charell, Fritz Kortner, Wilhelm Diegelmann, Magnus Stifter, Margarete Schlegel, Marga Kierska, Max Gülstorff, Margarete Kupfer, Paul Biensfeldt, Gertrud Wollan, Toni Zimmerer, the Ballet Erik Charell

CREDITS: *Director* Paul Leni; *Scenario* Paul Leni and Georg Kaiser*; *Based on the eponymous novel by* Otto Julius Bierbaum; *Photographed by* Carl Hoffmann; *Set Design* Paul Leni; *Set Construction* Otto Moldenhauer (debut); *Musical score (for theatrical premiere)* Friedrich Holländer

SYNOPSIS: Henry Felix (Niels Prien) is the illegitimate son of Sara Asher (Olga Limberg), a free spirit who comes to Germany from parts unknown. Henry might be the son of a Russian nobleman or a street musician; who can tell?

She abandons her son, who is brought up by farmers. Later, he is adopted by Herr Kraker, an eccentric millionaire, who tries to make a good man of him. Alas, he is only partly successful. Henry grows up to be a hedonist, caring only for himself and his pleasure. After his adoptive father dies and the will has been read, he first meets Herr Kraker's niece and nephew, Karl (Conrad Veidt) and Berta (Annaliese Halbes). Kraker's kin are outraged that their uncle's millions have been left to "Prince Cuckoo," the foundling who was left in their nest, so they conspire to get the money back from Henry.

Karl becomes Henry's constant companion, and tries to overwhelm "Prince Cuckoo" in the swamp of sexual excess, but in vain. Finally, Karl attempts to stab his "cousin," but Henry fends off the attack and Karl falls to his death from a high cliff. Henry is finally free to enjoy the sweet pleasures of life. Or so he thinks...

REVIEWS: "Unlike most others, this is way beyond what we would call 'film.' One forgets he is sitting in front of a technical invention; one drowns in pictures and plot...

"Every little scene shows the wonderful devotion of the director... As I've said before, it is not necessary to go abroad to film atmospheric locations... Paul Leni, creator of this film, built Venice—with palaces, towers, and channels—in Neubabelsberg. He has built a Sicilian grotto and has animated these landscapes so wonderfully, so believably, that you can only sit and wonder...

"As Karl Kraker, Conrad Veidt makes the greatest impression; he makes the decadent, soft side of his character as believable as his occasional fits of rage. If not his best, it is one of his best performances."

Der Film, No. 30;
1919—Carl Boese

"Quietly—very quietly—a picture has been completed which dwarfs everything that cinema has brought forth to this point. Not just German cinema, but cinema, period.

"Within a few days, Gloria-Film ... will release its version of the first part of Otto Julius Bierbaum's renowned novel, *Prinz Kuckuck*. What a great achievement! [It is] a literary motion picture, the dream which has so far gone unrealized for all those who see cinema as more than mere entertainment... New perspectives! Doggedly reproducing the content of a literary

---

*Not the famous dramatist

Another splendid *Marmorhaus* poster. (*Prinz Kuckuck*)

work on the screen does not allow for psychological subtlety. But [new perspectives], together with the great importance of the visual element ... these two elements help one enjoy the psychological slant of the film, while the dramatic tension remains to great effect.

"How can this be? At first glance, one looks at this picture as a puzzle; only slowly does one see beyond the surface to the artistic truth. What we do *not* have is a screenwriter's manuscript, which is rearranged for motion pictures by a director before being recorded on film by a photographer... Here, everything gives way to the vision of one prodigious personality, in whom the creator and the adaptor meld seamlessly.

"This man is Paul Leni, the Artist/Director. He is the force that controls all the technical ends, just as it is his zest that draws the viewer further into the picture. This is a new stratagem, one that has emerged from the move to creative independence: one does not always run to the library [for inspiration], but rather follows the muses inherent in one's individual humanity.

"The acting herein also moves in new directions... Conrad Veidt, who plays Karl, has eclipsed the roles from his past..."

Der Kinematograph (Düsseldorf),
No. 665; 1 January 1919

NOTES AND QUOTES: *Prinz Kuckuck* is the first of four pictures in which Paul Leni directed Conrad Veidt. Contemporary documents indicated (vaguely) that there would be a second part or continuation to this feature, but there is no hard evidence that such a sequel was ever produced.

Prinz Kuckuck is usually classified as a *Sittenfilm*, a sex-education hybrid with sexual themes incorporated into a thriller.

Wahnsinn

[LOST] *Madness, Insanity*; Veidt-Film, Berlin — 1919; Zensur: 1919 — 5 Acts, 1662 meters; Forbidden to adolescents; World premiere: 15 October 1919 Marmorhaus and Theater am Moritzplatz, Berlin; *Nachzensur*: 20 September 1921 — 5 Acts, 1482 meters; Forbidden to adolescents

CAST: Conrad Veidt *Friedrich Lorenzen*; Reinhold Schünzel *Jörges* (some sources say *Jörsen*), *a Street Merchant*; Gussy Holl *the Girl*; Grit Hegesa *Marion Cavello, a Dancer*; with Heinrich Peer, Esther Hagan

CREDITS: *Producer/Director* Conrad Veidt; *Scenario* Margarete Lindau-Schulz, Hermann Fellner; *Based on a novella by* Kurt Münzer; *Photographed by* Carl Hoffmann (Karl Freund?); *Sets* Willi A. Herrmann

SYNOPSIS: Banker Friedrich Lorenzen (Conrad Veidt), an eccentric misanthrope, travels around the world. One day, he meets up with a band of gypsies, and they tell his fortune: "A chest will bring you a great fortune and luck, but death as well. Find the chest!"

The command to "Find the chest" becomes an *idée fixe*. He begins to obsess about the chest. He sees it in visions, and beside it, a beautiful girl (Grit Hegesa). He hunts about constantly, incessantly. Madness.

After a long and fruitless search, he decides to return home. En route, he comes upon a street merchant (Reinhold Schünzel), who offers him a strangely designed key. To Lorentzen, the merchant's face turns into that of the beautiful girl; he buys the key.

Back home, he receives a parcel from the merchant. "In addition to the things you bought, I'm sending along a chest. Un-fortunately, the key has been lost." It is the chest! Stunned, Lorentzen tries the strange key; it fits!

He is torn between his desire for a great fortune and good luck, and his fear of death, but eventually opens the chest. Like a ghost, the girl of his vision rises from the chest. He takes her into his arms, and moves to kiss her; the girl turns into the grinning old gypsy woman.

Terrified, Lorentzen flees. For three days, he feverishly recalls his happy childhood, his youth, and his first love. He then expires.

(Note: Some sources indicate that, for the denouement, Lorentzen manages to lock himself in the trunk and suffocates.)

Reviews: "The first Conrad Veidt film, *Wahnsinn*, is ready for exhibiting. The script is from Margarete Lindau-Schulz, after a novel by Kurt Münzer, and offers the artist a rare opportunity to show exactly what lies closest to his soul: the presentation of a decadent, hysterical, overwrought man who is driven to madness by malevolent fate. The submission under strong[er] influences, the fanatical clinging to fixed ideas, the apathy of relaxation: all these are tasks that this very artist, with his rich means of expression (just recall the nervous business with his hands), can perform perfectly.

"As great as Veidt's achievement may have been, one wishes to see the actor not always doing the same or similar roles in future productions, a fear that seems to be justified in view of the presumed success of this work, and even more so as there is always the danger that the artist may become rigid in his style. Veidt's direction is the equal of his art of acting, although one may detect a certain influence from Leni (*Prinz Kuckuck*). Where he copied, at least he copied with good taste and ... style.

"Reinhold Schünzel as Jörges, Miss Grit Hegesa as Marion Cavallo (who let her facial mimicry speak as well as her bodily rhythm) and Gussy Holl, as the girl from the trader's shop, complemented Veidt's performance as an excellent ensemble."

Der Film (Berlin), Vol. 4, No. 42; 19 October 1919 — P — I (Podehl)

"In the Marmorhaus, one can meet Conrad Veidt in his starring film, *Wahnsinn*, which shows off his powerful dramatic abilities. Reinhold Schünzel and vivacious dancer, Grit Hegesa, also demonstrate some potent acting. In a smaller role is the charming Gussy Holl..."

Berliner Tageblatt ("Die Films der Woche"), Vol. 48, No. 494; 19 October 1919 (early edition)

"The film *Wahnsinn* with Conrad Veidt was just inevitable; it was 'in the air,' so to speak. This narrow, angular, almost transparent face; those gloomy, expressive eyes, that blaze unsteadily with a dark glow in scenes of psychological depression, called for full dramatic utilization in a film concerning a pathological lost soul.

"Margarete Lindau-Schulz wrote the script; Veidt was his own director: a collaboration of rare, outstanding homogeneity. There is something of E.T.A. Hoffman's spirit in this fantastic mix of reality and horror; something of his characteristic half-bizarre, half-horrific [mix], which comes effectively to life both scenically and pictorially.

"The film concentrates entirely on Veidt. He gives his leading character sense and form with piercing intensity, with a wonderfully restrained, yet eager command of gesture, with the fascinating expressiveness of his eyes, indeed, with his every movement. That Schünzel is able to remain in the forefront is certainly proof of his strong personality. A quick movement of his head, a twitch of the corners of his mouth, a twinkle in his eyes is enough to change the atmosphere from one of happy laughter to sheer horror and, in the next moment, to relieve the tension again.

"Grit Hegesa as the careless-lascivious pure female is very good, but Gussy Holl should give up film [acting]. It is pitiful to watch this artist — who is peerless in her own sphere — at a task which she cannot master despite her best efforts."

Film-Kurier (Berlin), Vol. 1, No. 116; 19 October 1919 — Dr. J.B. (J. Brandt)

NOTES AND QUOTES: *Wahnsinn* marked Conrad Veidt's debut as a director.

One source hypothesizes that Richard Oswald was involved with this production.

Gussy Holl (to Lotte Eisner): "This film was not only called *Madness*, it *was* madness as well, and I can't remember anything about the story." (*Murnau*. London: Secker and Warburg, 1973; p. 130, note.) Rumor had it that Murnau had helmed the picture, just prior to filming *Sehnsucht*, but author Margarete Lindau-Schultz told Eisner that it was directed entirely by Veidt. "An advertisement in the *Lichtbildbühne* confirms this."

Preproduction notice: "The great sensation-film, *Wahnsinn*, script by Margarete Lindau-Schulz, was just sold to Otto Glücksmann & Company. In the main roles: Conrad Veidt, Reinhold Schünzel, Grit Hegesa, Gussy Holl."

Film-Kurier (Berlin), Vol. 1, No. 65; 21 August 1919

Pre-release publicity: "It seems to me that even the stagehands work calmly and with restraint as they break down the grand staircase. As if even the strokes of their hammers were blunted ... as they peeped into the little room, constructed in a corner of the Zoo studio, that lacks only the fourth wall to completely resemble [a home]. It has carpets, old pictures, a ceil-

WAHNSINN
IN DER HAUPTROLLE
CONRAD VEIDT

Original artwork from *Wahnsinn*, the first picture Connie directed.

ing and a real, functional fireplace. In the armchairs sit two women who, at first glance, look surprisingly similar, almost like two sisters. They sit with their legs crossed and seem to be bored. Now I rec-ognize Gussy Holl, the witty, charming actress, and Esther Hagan.

"Someone is sitting at a table, leafing through a manuscript: a lean figure with an angular face, high forehead, thin mouth and flickering eyes. A few others, like Heinrich Peer and Huch, sit at a different table. They talk to each other quietly, slowly, hesitantly. Break! Nitandando [*sic*].

"What is going on here? Is this a film shoot or a private party? But there is Freund at the camera, adjusting it. Now Veidt stands slowly and stretches himself like a sleepy marabout. He walks past the camera and sinks into a low armchair. Gussy Holl gets up as well and ends up standing beside him. Veidt seems to have forgotten his surroundings. Holl takes a note out of her pocket, reads it, opens her eyes wide, crumples up the note, walks off, sits down again, and plays with her child. Esther Hagan hums. Veidt awakens. Freund has long since finished [filming] the scene. He changes film canisters. And so it goes…"

Film-Kurier (Berlin),
Vol. 1, No. 103;
4 October 1919

Unheimliche Geschichten

Eerie Tales aka *Weird Tales, Five Sinister Stories, Tales of the Uncanny, Tales of Horror*, etc.; Richard Oswald-Film GmbH, Berlin—1919; Press preview: October 1919 Richard-Oswald-Lichtspiele, Berlin; World premiere: 6 November 1919 Richard-Oswald-Lichtspiele, Berlin; *Nachzensur*: 16 July 1920 — 6 Acts, 2318 meters; Forbidden to adolescents

CAST: Conrad Veidt *Death, the Stranger, the Bon Vivant, the Traveler, the Club President, the Count*; Reinhold Schünzel *The Devil, the Husband, the Bon Vivant, the Drunkard, Inspector Silas, the Baron*; Anita Berber *The Courtesan, the Plague Victim, the Dancer, the Wife, the Countess*; with Georg John, Paul Morgan, Hugo Döblin

CREDITS: *Producer/Director* Richard Oswald; *Scenario* Robert Liebmann, Richard Oswald; *Based on*: Anselm Heine (**Die Erscheinung**—1st episode), Robert Liebmann (**Die Hand**—2nd episode), Edgar Allen Poe (**The Black Cat**—3rd episode), Robert Louis Stevenson (**The Suicide Club**—4th episode), Richard

Oswald (**Der Spuk**—5th episode); *Photographed by* Carl Hoffmann

SYNOPSIS: Prologue: Midnight in an old bookstore. Three pictures hang from the wall: Death, the Devil, and a courtesan. At the last stroke of the clock, the pictures come to life and browse through the books lying around. The spectator watches as the stories unfold.

Die Erscheinung (*The Apparition*): A woman (Anita Berber) is constantly being bothered by the husband (Reinhold Schünzel) she has divorced. When this occurs in a park, a stranger (Conrad Veidt) steps in to rescue her. Having fallen in love with her on the spot, he takes her to his hotel, where he arranges for her to have a room. He bids her a good night, then heads out on the town for a previously arranged date with some friends. When he returns, it is late and he is drunk. Getting no answer to his knock on the woman's door, he opens it and finds the room empty, devoid of furniture, with the wallpaper stripped from the walls. Presuming that he's not thinking clearly due to the alcohol, he returns to his own room and passes out.

The next morning he finds the room freshly papered, with new furniture. Completely shaken, he asks the manager what has happened to the woman he brought the night before. The manager replies that the man arrived alone; there was no woman. The hotel staff and the police support the manager's statement: there *was* no woman.

In the street, the man witnesses a funeral procession. Filled with dark thoughts, he bribes one of the men to tell him what has happened. He learns that the woman he brought to the hotel died from plague, and that every effort was being made to hush things up, lest the city fall into a panic. Aghast, the stranger staggers away and collapses in the park.

Die Hand (*The Hand*): Two bon vivants visit a nightclub, where they both fall for the charms of the same woman

Die Hand— The bizarrely coiffured Connie (second from left) and Reinhold Schünzel (second from right) will discover that lust can lead to death and to horror that transcends death (and then to more death…). (*Umheimliche Geschichten*)

(Berber). She doesn't want to decide which man will receive her favors, so the men cast dice for her. The loser (Schünzel) strangles his friend (Veidt) and flees.

Years later, the bon vivant again meets up with the woman, who invites him to attend her debut as a dancer that evening. While the man watches the performance, a clawlike hand appears at the curtain on the side of the stage. When it appears again, followed by the complete figure of the murdered friend, the murderer faints in his box. Brought to after the performance, he is invited to a séance, where the spirit of the dead man appears repeatedly. As the woman watches helplessly, a ghostly figure materializes behind

the terrified man, who is strangled from behind, much as he had murdered his friend years earlier.

Die schwarze Katze (*The Black Cat*): A drunkard (Schünzel) neglects his young wife (Berber), although he remains very jealous of her. One day, he meets a traveler (Veidt) while in a bar and offers him the hospitality of his home. The wife and the traveler are quickly attracted to each other and are just as quickly caught nuzzling by the drunken husband. When the traveler leaves the house, the husband kills his wife with a beer stein and walls her up in the cellar. Upon his return, the traveler is told that the wife has left on a journey. Not believing this for an instant, the traveler makes for the police, who agree to search the house. In the cellar, they are greeted by a peculiar sight: the wall appears to be moving. The cat — which was walled up alive with its mistress — has dug through the still-soft material. The murder is discovered, the murderer apprehended.

Der Selbstmörderklub (*The Suicide Club*): Police Inspector Silas (Schünzel) keeps his eye on a strange house, where people enter, but never leave. Climbing up assorted vines and trellises, he notes activity within the supposedly deserted mansion. Once inside, he finds himself in a very unusual men's club.

The president of the club (Veidt) explains to him that he is now in a suicide club, whence none of the members leave voluntarily. Over the portal to the main room hangs a sign in Italian — fresh from Dante: "Abandon hope, all ye who enter here!" The members gather to draw cards: the man drawing the ace of spades is to commit suicide. Silas draws the ace of spades.

As the others withdraw from the room, the president seats Silas in his chair and shows him a row of buttons, each assisting with suicide. The first button binds the occupant to the chair; the second causes instant death. On his way out of the room, the president tells Silas he must do away with himself by midnight, which is to strike in ten minutes. Despairing, Silas spends the time thinking of a way to escape. An idea hits him; he climbs onto the table and lies there, feigning death. Returning at midnight, the president thinks Silas has died of fright. When he sits in his chair, Silas leaps up and pushes the first button. The president is held firm and Silas leaves the suicide club unharmed.

Der Spuk (*The Ghost*): A lighthearted story with a happy ending.

The baroness (Berber) feels neglected and unloved by her husband (Veidt). One day, a gentleman (Schünzel) has an accident near the castle, and asks for medical assistance and lodging. The baroness is happy for the diversion and spends lots of time with him. He, in turn, enjoys the lady's company and loves telling stories about his prowess and heroic deeds. The baroness is impressed by so much manliness, but the baron becomes suspicious, so he devises a plan to put his presumptuous guest in his place.

The baron leaves suddenly, having announced that business demands his presence elsewhere for a few days. That evening, while the baroness and her guest are having supper, the pictures and the lamps in the room start moving by themselves. Both diners are terrified, and when hooded figures appear out of nowhere, the gentleman ups and flees the castle. The baron reveals himself and lets his wife in on his plan. Each falls into the other's arms and laughs about the "disappeared" hero.

REVIEWS: "These five one-act photoplays show how cinematic success may be found with outstanding clarity. As far as I know, nothing of this type has been produced so impressively since *Der Student von Prag*... Alongside the fantastic, flamboyant makeup of these thrilling stories, the tedious ballroom and literary films ... pale terribly. The theater and the cinema will always remain separate worlds, and the film studios, which are now slowly recording the body of world literature onto the silver screen, should point to this picture as a fine example of adapting the source material... Richard Oswald has succeeded admirably.

"Conrad Veidt is a splendid actor, especially so as the dread figures in the five acts; he is tremendously effective in each role. As with Reinhold Schünzel, one has to admire his extremely fine pantomime; only rarely are titles required.

"The production is bright and stylish throughout. From start to finish, one is spellbound by each story and this is at least due

Grausige Nächte
mit
Conrad Veidt
Reinhold Schünzel
Anita Berber

in part to the lovely and amazing special effects. Ending these eerie tales with a witty ghost story was a very good idea, too."

Der Kinematograph, 1919

"A one-act play evening in the cinema ... both as a whole and in the individual stories, a definite success. Unnecessary to say anything about the acting ... except that Schünzel's enormous versatility is surprising... Anita Berber demonstrates, as usual, charm and mature ability... Conrad Veidt does not only vary the demonic element of his parts, but shows smiling humor as well in the last story."

Der Film, No. 45;
9 November 1919

"The crowd has been pressing around the Richard-Oswald-Lichtspiele for three weeks now. The police have had to come regulate traffic... The leading critics and commentators are demanding a sequel to these one-act pictures..."

Illustrierter Filmkurier,
No. 9; 1919

NOTES AND QUOTES: As if in (rather protracted) response to this critical cry for more cinematic weirdness, Oswald produced a second, "talkie edition" of *Unheimliche Geschichten*, in 1932. Anchoring these proceedings—which featured one erstwhile (Paul Wegener) and one future Golem (Ferdinand Hart)—were sound renditions of Poe's *The Black Cat* and Stevenson's *The Suicide Club*.

Veidt, Schünzel and Berber are quite enjoyable throughout the quintet of "uncanny tales," but they haven't the monopoly on weirdness. The apelike antiquarian bookseller who opens the narrative scampers through the crowd and over tables to (apparently) drive every potential customer out the door so that he can turn off the lights and go to bed!

Satanas

[LOST*] Viktoria-Film-Co. GmbH, Berlin — 1919; Filmed at Bioscop-Atelier, Neubabelsberg; World premiere: 30 January 1920 Richard-Oswald-Lichtspiele, Berlin; *Zensur*: 13 December 1920 — 6 Acts, 2561 meters; Forbidden to adolescents; Ein "Episodenfilm"

CREDITS: *Producer* Ernst Hofmann; *Director* F.W. Murnau; *Scenario & Supervision* Robert Wiene; *Photographed by* Karl Freund; *Sets & Costumes* Ernst Stern

SYNOPSIS: The frame shows how Satan, the fallen angel, suffers from the loss of the Light. He pleads and wrangles with God, but God's voice repeats the condemnation, concluding, "You are cursed until one person, a single person, brings good out of evil." Satan traverses time and space, seeing only evil and despair, but his eyes betray a yearning for the Light, a yearning for Good...

1st episode (*Der Tyrann; Eine Tragödie aus der Pharaonenze/The Tyrant*)

CAST: Conrad Veidt *the Hermit of Elu/ Satan*; Fritz Kortner *Pharaoh Amenhotep*; Margit Barnay *Phahi, Pharaoh's wife*; Sadjah Gezza *Nouri, a harp player*; Ernst Hofmann *Jorab*

Pharaoh Amenhotep (Fritz Kortner) is in love with Nouri (Sadjah Gezza), a young slave harpist. He appoints the young man Jorab (Ernst Hofmann) as inspector of his gardens; Nouri pretends Jorab is her brother, but she is really in love with him. Jorab, however, cannot stop thinking of a

*35mm positive elements of *Satanas* have been identified at the Filmoteca española in Madrid. The 40-meter tinted fragment of the seduction scene with Margit Barnay and Fritz Kortner (from episode 1, *Der Tyrann*) is believed to be a fragment of the Spanish export version of the picture.

Opposite: The picture was released (and rereleased) under various names. One-sheet from an early '20s turn. (*Unheimliche Geschichten*)

girl he once met by a well when he was still a shepherd. The hermit of Elu (Conrad Veidt), the only man able to interpret a dream of Pharaoh's, refuses all rewards and asks to attend one of the courts of justice. He is unimpressed when Amenhotep pardons an adulteress, and warns the Pharaoh that he will have the chance to show he is a wise judge before dawn.

While still a child, Nouri witnessed a woman save her (Nouri's) mother from being unjustly stoned to death; she now asks the hermit for help in finding this woman. Nouri had promised her mother to devote herself to this benefactress, whom she will recognize by means of a brooch bearing the likeness of the goddess Phta. The hermit tells Nouri to ask Pharaoh for the key he wears around his neck; this will open seven doors, and behind the seventh, she will find the woman she seeks. Then the hermit takes Jorab through the seven doors to the room of Phahi(Margit Barnay), the Pharaoh's neglected young wife; she turns out to be the woman Jorab loves.

Nouri cries out when she finds Phahi and Jorab in each other's arms, and this brings Pharaoh onto the scene. The adulterers are sentenced to die before dawn. Left alone with them, Nouri recognizes Phahi from her brooch as the woman who saved her mother. She covers Phahi with the royal cloak the Pharaoh has given her, not to save Phahi, but so that she herself might die with Jorab. The executioners take her and the young man away, and at dawn, Pharaoh finds Phahi, half-mad with grief. She begs him to tell her her lover's name, so that she might die with it on her lips.

The hermit changes into a huge angel of death — Satan — who goes through the palace crushing the sundry mortals scornfully. There is no hope for his salvation here.

2nd episode (*Der Fürst; Lucrezia Borgias Tod/The Prince*)

Based on Victor Hugo's romantic melodrama *Lucrezia Borgia*

CAST: Conrad Veidt *Gubetta/Satan*; Kurt Erhle *Gennaro*; Elsa Berna *Lucrezia Borgia*; Ernst Stahl-Nachbauer *Alfonso d'Este*; Jaro Fürth *Rustinghella*

The name "Lucrezia Borgia" is hated and feared throughout Italy. She loves only one, her son — born secretly, out of wedlock, ignorant of the identity of his mother. Lucrezia (Elsa Berna) confides in Gubetta (Conrad Veidt), an elegant and mysterious Spaniard with yearning in his eyes, who takes her from Ferrara to Venice so that she can see her son at least once in her lifetime.

She sees her son, Gennaro (Kurt Erhle), a most handsome young man — at a masked ball. Gennaro likewise sees her, momentarily unmasked, and falls in love with her. The rumor that Lucrezia Borgia is present fills the hall. Five of Gennaro's friends search for him, and find him in the arms of a masked woman. They tear off the mask, recognize Lucrezia, and scream "Murderess!" "Adulteress!" "Incestuous Woman!" Lucrezia is appalled that her son should have heard these words and swears revenge.

Gubetta lures the five friends to a meal at the palazzo and secretly invites Gennaro, as well. Lucrezia prepares the infamous Borgia poisoned wine, but before it is served to the young men, Gubetta asks her whether she really intends to take five innocent lives. Blinded by rage, Lucrezia nods. Gennaro, who does not realize what is happening until it is too late, stabs his mother to death, and Satan, once again, succumbs to the heavenly curse.

3rd episode (*Der Diktator; Der Sturz eines Volkstreben/The Dictator*)

CAST: Conrad Veidt *Waldemar Grodski/ Lucifer*; Martin Wolfgang *Hans Conrad, a young student; later, "Führer" of the Revolution;* Marija Leiko *Irene, his Sweetheart;* Max Kronert *Father Conrad;* Elsa Wagner *Mother Conrad*

The young poet Hans Conrad (Martin Wolfgang) lives in Zurich, the city of refugees and the damned. He lives for his work, quietly writing and dreaming. One day he meets Waldemar Grodski (Conrad Veidt), a Russian revolutionary whose eyes burn with fanaticism. Grodski persuades the poet to follow the ideals of brotherly love, revolution and Communism, and Hans become an ardent follower of the cause. When the Russian Revolution breaks out, Hans, hoping to become champion of the oppressed, sets off with Grodski for the small town in Germany where he was born. There, the revolutionary crowd chooses him as its leader and seizes the castle.

Hans finds it is difficult to hold the power he has received without resorting to violence and bloodshed. He is horrified by how staggeringly different his dreams and reality are. Acting on Grodski's counsel, he takes hostages, has them killed, and — finally — declares what amounts to war. Two of the first victims in the outbreak of fighting are Hans' parents. The young man is shattered, but Grodski spurs him on and on.

Hans' only secret from Grodski is that the poet has secretly wed Irene (Marija Leiko), a good young woman who has no idea who Hans really is or what he has been doing.

When the counterrevolution starts, it is decided that the bloodthirsty dictator must die. A girl volunteers to do the deed, as she knows of a secret passage that leads to the dictator's bedroom in the castle.

The plan is uncovered, though, and Hans awaits the assassin when she enters. It is Irene! When they understand what is happening, neither can move, but Grodski warns Hans that unless Irene be executed

Satan (Connie, left) has Martin Wolfgang on his way up the primrose path in *Der Diktator,* episode III of *Satanas.*

as an example to all those who dare rebel, he will fall from power. Hans opts for power over love, and hands Irene over to the firing squad.

Hans goes mad when Grodski transforms into the gigantic fallen angel. Satan, once again denied salvation because of the weakness of mankind, soars into the darkness, undelivered for all eternity...

REVIEWS: "The screenplay of this very powerful film, rich in artistic quality, comes from Robert Wiene. A grand idea, Satan's yearning for salvation, forms the backbone of this work... The treatment, exciting from beginning to end, is by F.W. Murnau, who undertook the direction, and by Ernst Stern, who created the décor and costumes. Nowhere is anything obtrusive or importunate; everything fits into the setting to the advantage of the overall artistic effect. The film is mightily dependent upon mood and creates a potent atmosphere, which is quite substantially supported by the precise and graphic photography of Karl Freund.

"The cast is first rate throughout the film. Sadjah Gezza, whose work becomes more balanced and mature in film after film; Margit Barnay, who plays the Egyptian queen; Elsa Berna, who embodies the character of Lucrezia Borgia in a saucy manner; and Marija Leiko, who creates quite an intensive figure of her heroine. Male leads are in good hands with Fritz Hortner [*sic*], Ernst Hofmann, Kurt Ehrle, and Martin Wolfgang.

"The most extraordinary achievement of Conrad Veidt as Satan merits a somewhat detailed inspection. Here, he seems to attain the perfect model of the film actor. No exaggeration; no moment "unsuitable" for films; but rather a profundity, a personal mimetic experience that causes the audience's nerves to quiver along with him, almost forcing it to lipread the actor's words before they appear in the titles. His expressive, animated face creates an unforgettable impression. An interior experience is graphically, consummately conveyed.

"If the public, usually completely focused upon eroticism and sensationalism, brings a modicum of taste to this artistic film, the Victoria-Film production might enjoy great success with this effort."

Der Film (Berlin), Vol. 4, No. 46;
16 November 1919 — H.L.

"Regarding the world premiere of the film *Satanas*...

"Conrad Veidt plays Satan. He has already often displayed his prowess for enacting the demonic spirit, and his acting here is at the same high level of his earlier performances. The final shot [of the picture] is not so happily chosen, however. The beaten Satan has to disappear into a cave in front of the gates of Hell. One sees Veidt turning his back to the audience, clad only in a *very* short shirt. The amusing reaction to this scene can certainly not have been the intention of the producer.

"The rest of the actors do not stand out above average; some are even below that. The plot, which leads us through different epochs, gives [the filmmakers] the opportunity of striving with all their considerable skill. It must be said that the director did not allow this opportunity to slip away."

Berliner Börsen-Courier, No. 53;
1 February 1920

NOTES AND QUOTES: The surviving screenplay indicates that Satan opened and closed a curtain before and after each episode. Murnau used a similar device in *Faust*, when the Devil gloats over the seduction of the Duchess of Parma.

Satanas' structure (3 episodes, each of which takes place in different eras) was clearly influenced by D.W. Griffith's *Intolerance*. It, in turn, undoubtedly influenced such other episodic features as *Blade af Satans Bog* (*Leaves from Satan's Book*; Carl Dreyer, 1920), *Der Müde Tod* (*Destiny*; Fritz Lang, 1921) and *Das Wachsfigurenkabinett* (*Waxworks*; Paul Leni, 1924). In addition, the Egyptian episode may have had an effect on Ernst Lubitsch's *Das Weib des Pharao* (1921); both *Pharao* and *Satanas* were designed by Ernst Stern.

Friedrich Wilhelm Murnau (né Plumpe) was born in Bielefeld, Germany, in December 1888. Most recently reintroduced into current popular film consciousness via *Shadow of the Vampire* (2000), a fictional examination of the production of his seminal vampire saga, *Nosferatu* (1922), Murnau is probably most renowned for his mainstream classics *Die Letzte Mann* (*The Last Laugh*, 1924), *Tartuffe* (1926), and *Sunrise* (1927), which he shot for the Fox Film Corporation in Hollywood. Like so many of his cinematic contemporaries, he was a pupil of Max Reinhardt before moving on to motion pictures.

Sadly, apart from *Der Gang in die Nacht* (1920), every one of the films Murnau made with Conrad Veidt remains lost.

Actor-director-scenarist Fritz Kortner (born Fritz Nathan Kohn in May 1892 in Vienna) first joined Connie on-screen in *Satanas*. While the Austrian actor's most notable credit in a Veidt-Film is that of Nera, the knife-hurling murderer of *Orlacs Hände* (1924), his most fascinating work lay within his provenance as screenwriter. Having made for the United States during the outset of the Nazi era, Kortner (and fellow émigré Joe May) wrote the screenplay for *The Strange Death of Adolf Hitler*, an exploitative melodrama released by Universal in 1943. Active in the industry until a few months prior to his death (of leukemia, in 1970), Kortner's last role was that of Shylock in an Austrian television production of *The Merchant of Venice*.

Nachtgestalten

[LOST] *Figures of the Night*; aka *Eleagabal Kuperus*; Richard Oswald-Film GmbH, Berlin — 1919/1920; Filmed at Bioscop-Atelier, Neubabelsberg; Distributed by Deutsche-Bioscop AG, Berlin; World premiere: 9 January 1920 Richard-Oswald-Lichtspiel, Berlin; *Zensur*: 16 July 1920 — 6 Acts, 2192 meters; Forbidden to adolescents

CAST: Conrad Veidt *Adalbert Semilasso, the Comedian*; Paul Wegener *Thomas Bezug, Multibillionaire*; Reinhold Schünzel *Hainx, his Secretary*; Erik Charell *Arnold, Bezug's Son*; Erna Morena *Elisabeth, Bezug's Daughter*; Anita Berber *Nella, a Dancer*; Paul Bildt *Hecht, an Inventor*; with Theodor Loos, Willi Allen

CREDITS: *Producer/Director* Richard Oswald; *Scenario* Richard Oswald; *Based on the story* **Eleagabal Kuperus** *by* Karl Hans Strobl; *Photographed by* Karl Hoffmann; *Set Design* Hans Dreier

SYNOPSIS: Thomas Bezug (Paul Wegener) — the richest man in the world — is also the poorest, in terms of friends. Crippled, he is protected by a cadre of musclebound bodyguards and amused by a group of misshapen dwarfs. He sees everyone surrounding him as being envious and greedy, or full of hatred because they are so dependent upon him.

Using his enormous wealth, he buys and sells people, usually destroying them in the process. Despite these freakish games he plays with human beings, he is lonely, desperately lonely. The dancer (Anita Berber) he has fallen in love with decides to leave him, although he has showered her with gifts and offers of money, and has even engaged a comedian, Adalbert Semilasso (Conrad Veidt), to keep her amused.

Moved by frustration and anger, he resolves to become master of the world. When a crazed inventor (Paul Bildt) tells him of a machine of his own design — one that can draw the oxygen from the air — Bezug forces a group of billionaires to come up with the money needed to make the idea a reality. The insane plan: to blackmail the world into submission by threatening total destruction. The whole idea is nonsense, of course. It fails miserably when the inventor calls Bezug, reveals that he has taken poison, and confesses that he really hasn't invented anything.

Bezug's secretary, Hainx (Reinhold Schünzel), smugly watches his master's plans fail, one after another. The canny Hainx maneuvers to make himself heir to the billionaire's fortune. Standing in his way are Bezug's children: Arnold (Erik Charell), his apelike son, upon whom is lavished ceaseless paternal love and devotion; and Elisabeth (Erna Morena), his daughter, for whom the opulence of her surroundings are as meaningless as her life is empty.

Through it all, Bezug remains alone, suspicious and aloof — a true creature of the night.

REVIEWS: "The fact that this incredibly convoluted material [has produced] a cinematic work of art that has a powerful effect on the viewer is due to the extraordinary talent of producer/scenarist Richard Oswald. In his portrayal [of Bezug], Paul Wegener has underscored the director's vision. The make-up he uses is un-

NACHTGESTALTEN

From the original program: Connie and Erna Morena (at rear) watch as Reinhold Schünzel gets physical. That's Paul Wegener with the crutches and fright wig. (*Nachtgestalten*)

usually effective; its dourness provides quite a contrast with [the actor's] normal appearance. Reinhold Schünzel is impressive in his aloof arrogance. His brazen displays of cool detachment has one thinking from the start that there lurks a criminal genius behind that immobile face, one who is moving ever closer to his goal of taking over his employer's fortune.

"Eric Charell characterizes the apish son with excellent acting and appropriate dexterity. Erna Morena as the daughter, Paul Bildt as the inventor, and Conrad Veidt and Anita Berber as the entertainers of the piece … contribute to the success of the picture."

Der Kinematograph, 1920

Sehnsucht (Alternative titles: Die Leidensgeschichte eines Künstlers [The Story of the Suffering of an Artist] and Tragödie eines Tänzers [A Dancer's Tragedy])

[LOST] *Desire* aka *Bajazzo* (*Sehnsucht*'s working title); Richard Mosch-Film GmbH (per film ad), but according to Margarete Lindau-

Schultz, Lipow-Film, Berlin, 1920; World premiere: February 1921(?); *Zensur*: 18 October 1920 — 5 Acts, 1765 meters; Forbidden to adolescents

CAST: Conrad Veidt *the Student, Danker*; Gussy Holl *Russian Grand Duchess*; with Albert Bennefield, Ellen Bolan *Dancer*, Paul Graetz, Helene Gray, Danny Gürtler, Eugen Klöpfer, Margarete Schlegel, Marcella Gremo

CREDITS: *Director* F.W. Murnau; *Scenario* Carl Heinz Jarosy; *Sets* Robert Neppach; *Photographed by* Carl Hoffmann; *Costumes* Charles Drecoll (*haute couture* company)

SYNOPSIS: Danker (Conrad Veidt), a young Russian student in Geneva (the publicity calls him an artist, and some-

Original trade ad. Gussy Holl is again at Connie's feet. (*Sehnsucht*)

times even a dancer; perhaps this is what he was studying), gets himself sent on a mission by the Nihilists so that he can return to his native country at someone else's expense. In Russia he meets and falls in love with a girl (Gussy Holl). He is arrested, but manages to escape. But he cannot find his beloved, and he searches for her everywhere until at last he learns that she died while he was in prison.

REVIEW: "Actually, there is hardly any action in this 'Story of a Love'; this is compensated for by all sorts of tasteful and cleverly used décor. The fact that the hero is a dancer allows for the pantomime of a dance performance — the fact that Conrad Veidt plays the dancer gives artistic weight to the drama. By very, very subtle means, Veidt makes the most insignificant occurrence seem fateful. Although the milieu and the story (nihilists and their opponents) are not especially interesting, his acting, gentle as always, affects [the viewer]. Eugen Klöpfer and Margaret Schlegel are worthy of mention, as is the lighting, which brings quality to the film."

Unknown review,
November 1920

NOTES AND QUOTES: "Gussy Holl remembers that it was about the unhappy love of a Russian dancer, Conrad Veidt, for a grand duchess played by herself." Lotte Eisner asks: It is just possible that the student might have become a famous dancer, but whatever had the grand duchess to do with all this saga of love and renunciation? (Eisner, *Murnau*; p. 130.)

Das Cabinet des Dr. Caligari

Decla-Film-Gesellschaft, Holz & Co., Berlin, 1919; Original running time: 71 minutes; Filmed at Lixie-Atelier, Berlin-Weissensee; Distributed by Decla-Bioscop; World premiere 26 February 1920 — Marmorhaus, Berlin; *Nachzensur*: 11 March 1921 — 6 Acts, 1703 meters; Forbidden to adolescents; USA premiere: 3 April 1921; *aka **Das Kabinett des Dr. Caligari; Das Kabinett des Dr. Kaligari***; BxW (originally tinted in green, brown, steel blue)

CAST: Conrad Veidt *Cesare, the Somnambulist*; Werner Krauss *Dr. Caligari*; Friedrich Faher *Francis*; Lil Dagover *Jane*; Hans Heinz von Twardowski *Alan*; Rudolf Lettinger *Dr. Olson*; Rudolf Klein-Rogge *A Criminal*; Ludwig Rex *A Rogue*; Elsa Wagner *Landlady*; with Henri Peters-Arnolds and Hans Lanser-Ludloff

CREDITS: *Producer* Erich Pommer, Rudolph Meinert; *Director* Robert Wiene; *Orig. Story & Scenario* Carl Mayer, Hans Janowitz; *Set Designers* Hermann Warm, Walter Reimann, Walter Rohrig; *Photographed by* Willy Hameister; *Original Musical Score (Theater)* Giuseppe Becce

SYNOPSIS: In the course of an extended conversation with an older man in a garden, Francis (Friedrich Faher) tells of Dr. Caligari (Werner Krauss), who came to the town of Holstenwall in order to exhibit Cesare, a somnambulist, in the local fair. Cesare foretold the untimely death of Francis's friend Alan (Hans Heinz von Twardowski): "How long will I live?" "Until dawn." When Alan is found murdered, Francis asks the police to interrogate Caligari about his comatose protégé. As they do so, another man is arrested for attempted murder, and the police leave, hoping to pin Alan's slaying on him, too. Jane (Lil Dagover), a young girl whom Francis loves, arrives at the fair and is presented to Cesare by Dr. Caligari.

Later, while the suspicious Francis watches Caligari and the sleeping Cesare through a window of their wagon, the real Cesare kidnaps Jane from her bed and carries her off across the village rooftops; the figure Francis has seen in the wagon was a mannequin. In fleeing from the pursuing townspeople, Cesare drops Jane and falls down a hillside. After periods of confusion and bewilderment, Francis returns to the wagon with the police, who discover the figure in the casket to be a dummy. Caligari flees to a local insane asylum, where he is caught. It is revealed that he is the head of the asylum, and that he became fixated on a medieval mountebank, Caligari, who was known to control an entranced individual who murdered on command. When a somnambulist was brought under the asylum head's care, he in essence became Caligari and used the sleepwalker for his own experiments. Upon being presented with the body of the dead Cesare, Caligari becomes violent and is put into a straitjacket.

Connie's portrayal of Cesare the Somnambulist in *Das Cabinet des Dr. Caligari* led to an international awareness of the German actor.

Back in the present, Francis leaves the garden and walks into a courtyard, which is the asylum he told about in his narrative. Persons recognizable as Jane, Cesare, and others are seen, and the man Francis identified as Caligari is, in fact, the wise director of the real mental asylum. Francis, who is a patient of the asylum, goes berserk and is himself restrained with a straitjacket; he is then put into the same cell that "Caligari" had occupied in the narrative.

REVIEW: "*The Cabinet of Dr. Caligari* strikes a pitch akin to that heard in the stories of Hoffmann, Poe, FitzJames O'Brien and Ambrose Bierce. It should be said that while the interpretation has added immeasurably to the photoplay, yet the profounder reason for the thrill which it awakens lies in the actual story of Dr. Caligari."

Arthur Ziehm, as quoted in "A Cubistic Shocker," *New York Times*, 20 March 1921

"Opinions about *The Cabinet of Dr. Caligari*, at the Capitol this week, will probably be sharply divided — and that's the first thing that recommends this picture, for, although individuality so pronounced that it breeds active disagreement does not necessarily denote peculiar excellence, it is bound to have a strong appeal for habitual motion-picture spectators depressed by stock stuff.

"The most conspicuous individual characteristic of the photoplay is that it is cubistic, or expressionistic. Its settings bear a somewhat closer resemblance to reality than, say, the famous *Nude Descending a Staircase*, but they are sufficiently unlike anything ever done on the screen before to belong to a separate scenic species. A house, for instance, is recognized as a house, but, with its leaning, trapezoidal walls, its triangular doors and its bizarre floor patterns, it does not look like any house anybody ever lived in — likewise the irregular alleyways between inclined buildings, the crazy corridors and the erratic roofs.

"Doubtless, these expressionistic

scenes are full of meaning for the specialist in the form of the art they represent, but the uninitiated, though they will now and then get a definite suggestion from some touch here or there, and enjoy it, are not asked to understand cubism, for the settings are the background, or rather an inseparable part, of a fantasy story of murder and madness such as Edgar Allan Poe might have written. This story is coherent, logical, a genuine and legitimate thriller, and after one has followed it through several scenes the weird settings seem to be of its substance and no longer call disturbing attention to themselves.

"The two principal characters in this horrific story are Dr. Caligari, an uncanny old wizard, and Cesare, an unearthly somnambulist completely in his power, who is his agent in the commission of crime for crime's sake. Werner Krauss as the doctor gives one of the most vivid performances recorded on the screen, and Conrad Veidt is no less the embodiment of the ghostly, ghastly sleep-walker. The others in the cast are also effective, and if they all act with exaggerated gestures and facial contortions, this, too, is in keeping with the story and its settings. Everything is unreal in *The Cabinet of Dr. Caligari*. There is nothing of normalcy about it."

New York Times, 4 April 1921

"Berlin has yet another new slogan: 'You must be Caligari!' For weeks now, this enigmatic categorical imperative has screamed out from every kiosk, has leapt forth from every newspaper centerfold. Those in the know ask: 'Are you Caligari, too?' much in the same fashion one asked in past years, 'Are you Manoli?' and one whispered furtively about 'expressionism,' 'film' and 'madness.'

"Well, this first expressionistic film is out and about, and even though it takes place in a lunatic asylum, there is nothing mad about it. No matter what one's opinion is of modern art, here, the term has a completely different meaning...

"Werner Krauss, accoutered as the fantastic Dr. Caligari, equals a masterpiece that no one can readily match. Alongside him, Conrad Veidt's demonic reading of the somnambulist affects one in a most uncanny fashion. People with nervous conditions might well get nightmares from this... Robert Wiene provides the direction per his usual splendid form, and the brilliant photography melds well with the work of artists Warm, Reimann and Röhrig.

"With its latest picture, the Decla Film Company has demonstrated that the art of film has not as yet gone as far as it could and that undreamt of possibilities still lie in the future."

Kinematograph, 1920

"The most important and the most original photoplay that has come to this city of Chicago the last year.... That is the way some people say it.

"The craziest, wildest, shivery movie that has come wriggling across the silversheet of a cinema house. That is the way other people look at it.

"It looks like a collaboration of Rube Goldberg, Ben Hecht, Charlie Chaplin and Edgar Allan Poe — a melting pot of styles and technique of all four....

"Cubist, futurist, post-impressionist, characterize it by any name denoting a certain style. It has its elements of power, technique, passion, that make it sure to have an influence toward more easy-flowing, joyous, original American movies."

Chicago Daily News,
12 May 1921—
Carl Sandburg

NOTES AND QUOTES: *The Cabinet of Caligari*— scripted by the late Robert Bloch and starring Glynis Johns and Dan O'Herlihy — was produced by 20th Century–Fox

The death of his somnambulist has put a serious kink in the career plans of Dr. Caligari (Werner Krauss, center). (*Das Cabinet des Dr. Caligari*)

in 1962. With nary a trace to be found of sideshow quackery or black-clad somnambulists, the film bore only the most tenuous of ties to the Decla German-language original and disappeared from sight rather quickly. It remains both difficult to see and difficult to watch.

"I am a firm spiritualist, a quite good medium, and I've known since my youth the power of suggestion. This has affected nearly every aspect of my artistic and human lives. That's why I always present 'my last will and testament' in this way, for I know that a great deal of my success lies therein. And that's also the reason why such a good role as Cesare in *Caligari* (for example) has always excited me."

Conrad Veidt in
Kino-Album (undated)

Lil Dagover was born Marie Antonia Sieglinde Martha Seubert in Madiven, on Java, on September 30, 1887. The prolific actress (she was a member of Berlin's prestigious Deutsches Theater, in addition to having appeared in well over 100 motion pictures) partnered Veidt in five features, apart from their mutual breakthrough film, *Caligari*. Among the more notable German silent pictures in the Dagover catalogue are both parts of Fritz Lang's *Die Spinnen*, *Dr. Mabuse der Spieler* and *Der müde Tode*, and F.W. Murnau's *Phantom* and *Tartüff*; come the sound era, Lil worked steadily for five decades to come. Remaining in the Fatherland during hostilities, she was awarded the War Merit Cross in 1942. Her last film role was that of Helene in Maximilian Schell's 1979 production of *Geschichten aus dem Wiener-*

Rerelease ad art; note the prominence of Connie's name. (*Das Cabinet des Dr. Caligari*)

wald (*Tales from the Vienna Woods*). Lil Dagover — ever the "frail-seeming heroine with the haunted look"— died, at age 92, on January 24, 1980.

Erich Pommer, chief executive of Decla-Bioscop, had originally approached Fritz Lang to direct *Caligari*, but as *Die Spinnen* (also a Decla picture) was enjoying tremendous box-office success, it was felt that moving Lang to another would be financially foolhardy. Lang was assigned to assemble the second part of the Kay Hoog serial, and Robert Wiene was thus engaged. Lang, however, had already given some thought to *Caligari*. According to Siegfried Kracauer:

> Weine suggested, in complete harmony with what Lang [see pp. 30–31 of David Robinson's *BFI Film Classics* volume on *Das Cabinet des Dr. Caligari* for an additional wrinkle on Lang's "rebuttal" to this statement] had planned, an essential change of the original story — a change against which the two authors violently protested. But no one heeded them. The original story was an account of real horrors; Weine's version transforms that account into a chimera concocted and narrated by the mentally deranged Francis. To effect this transformation, the body of the original story is set into a framing device which introduces Francis as a madman, and which perverted — if not out and out reversed — Janowitz and Mayer's intrinsic intentions. While the original story exposed the madness inherent in authority, Weine's *Caligari* glorified authority and convicted its antagonist of madness... In its changed form, *Caligari* was no longer a product expressing, at best, sentiments characteristic of the intelligentsia, but a film supposed equally to be in harmony with what the less educated felt and liked.
>
> *From Caligari to Hitler.* Princeton (NJ): Princeton University Press, 1947; pp. 65–67

Much has been written about *Caligari*'s widespread influence on the cinema, as if there was a rush to emulate the bizarre sets concocted by art design team Her-

mann Warm, Walter Röhrig and Walter Reimann. Not so. Lotte Eisner ("Carl Mayer's Debut," by Erich Pommer. *The Film Till Now*, by Paul Rotha. London: Vision Press, 1930) writes that producer Erich Pommer's overriding concern was monitoring costs, and this led to using materials (obvious canvas backdrops) and techniques that were then popular in theater. Pommer penned his own version (Eisner, The *Haunted Screen*; pp. 18–19) of the situation, in which he says the *Caligari* "look" was due to Warm, Röhrig and *Robert Herlth*. No matter. While the German critics did wax rhapsodic after the Marmorhaus premiere, apart from Wiene's enthusiastic leap back on the bandwagon the following year with his (and Carl Mayer's) *Genuine*, this "Expressionism *in extremis*" movement went nowhere. (Wiene, in fact, appears to be the only filmmaker who was determined to milk the *Caligari*/Expressionistic cow. Despite the fact that *Genuine* [1920] lost money, the Breslau-born director proceeded with *Raskolnikov* [1923], the last of his Expressionist features. It, too, failed at the box office.)

Although *Caligari* was widely hailed as an important film, a perceptive film and a monumental film, no one saw it as being the prototype of a subgenre. German cinema picked up on the picture's underlying theme — man as puppet, torn between madness and subjugation — and dealt with it in a variety of ways time and again for the next several years; granted. Still, much of its allure lay in the fact that it was *sui generis*; most of its impact lay in the novelty of its approach. Herr Kracauer reports that the picture was neither terribly popular with the average German filmgoer ("too high brow"), nor terribly influential on French or American cinema. [Apologies to Carl Sandburg, above.] It may well have been "the most widely discussed film of the time"; nonetheless, "It stood out lonely, like a monolith" (Kracauer p. 72).

Unlike the majority of Veidt's earlier films, many of which were lucky to see comprehensive distribution throughout Germany, *Das Cabinet des Dr. Caligari* led to international awareness of Connie (and Lil Dagover and Werner Krauss).

Patience

[LOST]; aka *Patience: Die Karten des Todes* (*Death's Calling Cards*); Gloria-Film GmbH, Berlin, 1920; Distributed by Progress-Film GmbH, Berlin; World premiere: 6 April 1920 U.T. Kurfürstendamm, Berlin; *Nachzensur*: 24 June 1920 — 5 Acts, 1869 meters; Forbidden to adolescents

CAST: Conrad Veidt *Sir Percy Parker*; Adele Sandrock *the Matriarch*; Aenderly Lebius *William, Her Son*; Maria Santen *Lady Parker*; Wilhelm Diegelmann *Tom, the Fisherman*; Irmgard Bern *Jane*; Karl Platen *Edward*; with Felix Basch, Marga von Kierska, Loni Nest, Carl Krieger, Paul Wald, Marta Santen, Rudolf Meinhard-Jünger, Max Winter

CREDITS: *Directors* Paul Leni, Felix Basch; *Based on a Scotch ballad*; *Photographed by* Carl Hoffmann; *Set Design* Paul Leni

SYNOPSIS: In the old castle of the proud Scottish Parker family, the matriarch (Adele Sandrock) is hated for her suspicions and prejudices. The only thing she believes in is her fortune-telling cards; thus, she passes her time in her room playing patience. The cards tell her time and again that her son William (Aenderly Lebius), who long ago ventured abroad, will return. Should he not return, the matriarch's grandson, Percy (Conrad Veidt), will become the new laird. The old lady despises Percy — who is physically deformed — and she maneuvers Edward (Karl Platen), a close relative, into line as master of the estate. Edward, now laird of the castle, is a wicked man, and life at the estate becomes more torturous and unbearable.

Suffering from the hate and rejection of his relatives, Percy flees. He finds shelter and good friends among the fishermen living on the coast. One night, during a terrible storm, Percy displays his courage to his new friends. He runs into the stormy night to rescue people on a ship sinking off the coast. He is able to save only one person, however, a small girl. He decides to rear the child as if she were his own.

Years go by. The young girl has become a beautiful young lady and the paternal love Percy felt for her has become the love of a man for a woman. In addition, Sir William Parker has returned home. Revealing nothing that befell him during his years away from home, Sir William is quick to see into Edward's evil heart.

Sir William searches for Percy, even though Edward tells him the deformed man is long dead. With the help of Tom, the fisherman (Wilhelm Diegelmann), both Percy and Jane are found in their happy home. It transpires that Jane is Sir William's long-lost daughter, also thought dead because of the shipwreck. Sir William returns with Percy and Jane to the castle, which finally becomes a bright and happy place.

REVIEWS: "One is content with this well thought-out work, content with the photography, and, most of all, content with the work of Paul Leni, who created a picture which is not only art, but thrilling, as well."

Erste Internationale Filmzeitung, No. 5; 1920 — R.P.

"This well-conceived, well-executed production will hold the audience's interest. In Paul Leni, we have a splendidly perceptive director, capable of melding artistry with technical know-how; he well knows how to introduce scenes of great natural beauty into his story.

"The excellent photography is courtesy of Carl Hoffmann. The cast members — all of whom are masters of their parts — are Conrad Veidt, Wilhelm Diegelmann,

Connie as Sir Percy Parker. (*Patience*)

[Marga] von Kierska, Irmgard Bern, Adele Sandrock, Felix Basch and Karl Platen."
Der Kinematograph, 1920

"Paul Leni directed. He did a good, commendable job, trying to charm the eye when the brain wanted to go on strike; still, he showed delightful pictures... Conrad Veidt as the deformed, but noble-thinking nephew ... thrills with his peerless mimicry and his knack for precise characterization."
Der Film, No. 17; 24 April 1920

Die Nacht auf Goldenhall

[LOST] *The Night at Goldenhall*; Veidt-Film, Berlin, 1919; Distributed by W.E.P.-Film GmbH, Berlin; Original Release: 5 Acts, 1808 meters; *Zensur*: 21 March 1921—5 Acts—1770 meters; Forbidden to adolescents; World premiere: 16 April 1920 Richard Oswald-Lichtspiele, Berlin

CAST: Conrad Veidt *Lord Reginald Golden and his nephew, Harald Golden* (dual role); Esther Hagan *Ellen von Lehden*, Gussy Holl *Rajah*, Heinrich Peer *Baron von Lehden*

CREDITS: *Producers* Conrad Veidt, Richard Oswald (?); *Director* Conrad Veidt; *Screenplay* Hermann Fellner, Margarete Lindau-Schultz; *Art Direction* Willi A. Hermann; *Sets* Robert Neppach; *Musical Score for Theatre* Paul Kursch; *Photographed by* Karl Freund

SYNOPSIS: Following the death of Lord Reginald Golden (Conrad Veidt), his nephew Harald (Conrad Veidt)—who had once been disowned for his dissolute lifestyle—takes over both title and property.

Some weeks later, Baron von Lehden (Heinrich Peer)—a friend of Lord Reginald's—arrives at Goldenhall with his

Without the film itself, it's impossible to determine whether this is Connie as Lord Reginald Golden, or as the nephew, Harald. (*Die Nacht auf Goldenhall*)

daughter, Ellen (Esther Hagan). The baron is very surprised at hearing that his old friend died by his own hand, but he is astounded to find that Harald — whom he knows to be dishonest — is at the castle, instead of in America.

While the baron cannot puzzle this out, the young Lord Golden reveals all to Ellen himself. Tortured by pangs of conscience, he tells the young woman how he returned from America, hat in hand, but found that he was unwelcome at Golden-

hall. That night, he forced his way into his uncle's bedroom and pleaded for forgiveness, threatening to shoot himself on the spot if his pleas went unheeded. Lord Reginald struggled with him for possession of the pistol; it went off, and the elder man was killed instantly.

Harald then arranged things to look like suicide, and forged his uncle's will, substituting his own name for that of Ellen, Lord Reginald's intended heiress.

After confessing to all these misdeeds,

Harald returns to Ellen everything that rightfully belongs to her, and begs her forgiveness, for he loves her. Ellen accepts both the inheritance and Harald's proposal of marriage.

REVIEW: "This picture is a wonderful piece of work with regards to the photography and the direction. It is a step up from Veidt's first film, *Wahnsinn*. Veidt himself plays the leading part, demonstrating excellent mime and avoiding any indication of nervousness."

Der Film, No. 44; 1919 — P

NOTES AND QUOTES: This film was the second to be shot by Veidt's production company and the last film Connie would direct himself.

Kurfürstendamm (Ein Höllenspuk in 6 Akten)

[LOST] Richard Oswald-Film GmbH, Berlin — 1920; *Zensur*: 12 July 1920 — 6 Acts — 2424 meters; Forbidden to adolescents; World premiere: 30 July 1920 Richard-Oswald-Lichtspiele, Berlin (Ein *Sondervorführung*— A "Special Performance" with piano accompaniment by Hans May)

CAST: Conrad Veidt *the Devil*; Erna Morena *Frau von Alady*; Asta Nielsen *Lilly* and *Maria the Cook [and later Film Star]*; Rudolf Forster *Ernst Duffer*; Theodor Loos *Raoul Haselzwing*; Paul Morgan *Fritz*; Henry Sze *Dr. Li*; Rosa Valetti *Frau Lesser*

CREDITS: *Producer/Director* Richard Oswald; *Scenario* Richard Oswald; *Set Design* Hans Dreier; *Photographed by* Karl Hoffmann, Axel Graatkjaer; *Music (for theater)* Eduard May

SYNOPSIS: The Devil (Conrad Veidt) has become bored with Hell. He notices that many of the ever-growing legions of lost souls come from the Kurfürstendamm district and decides that he would like to see this Kurfürstendamm for himself. After his grandmother provides him with

a money printer, the long-tailed demon enters the human world from the Kaiser Wilhelm Memorial Church! His first view of the world, in fact, is from the church tower. Printing up a few bills, he makes for a tailor shop, where — under the pretext that his clothes were stolen at a masquerade — he outfits himself so as to blend in with the humans.

Posing as a gentleman, he walks through the streets, rents a room in a boarding house, and begins the sort of adventures one can have in the Kurfürstendamm. Led about by a Chinese "guide" (Henry Sze), he revels in the beautiful girls (like Lilly — Asta Nielsen), and even in some of the married women. He starts a film company with disastrous results. He is awash in the moral corruption of the area; at one point, he is swindled and robbed! Finally, he realizes that not even the Devil is a match for the Kurfürstendamm. He heads back to his grandmother's side, in the security of Hell, where he begins to feel like himself again.

REVIEWS: "With this latest picture, Richard Oswald has ventured into some pretty weird territory. It has some of the attributes of a grotesque film, for which — lately — there has been tremendous demand...

"An outstanding cast wrestles with the plot, jumping about through the six grotesque acts. Conrad Veidt — the Devil, complete with hooves — is unbelievably agile. Truly bizarre, he hops over tables and chairs like a kangaroo, and — with the total lack of self-consciousness that only a film actor can have — rushes headlong down the street in broad daylight costumed as the Devil. [The scene where] he founds a film company gives [everyone] the chance to do a parody on dreadful films.

"Title cards are used very sparingly, as they are for the most part unnecessary. The photography is good."

Der Kinematograph, 1920

A montage from the original program: two studies of Connie as the devil; Erna Morena wields the parasol (center); Asta Nielsen is both of the remaining women; at the bottom are Henry Sze and Rudolf Forster. (*Kurfürstendamm*)

"*Kurfürstendamm — ein Höllenspuk in 6 Akten* is the name of Richard Oswald's latest film, which demonstrates, once again, that the director has ideas that no one has ever thought of before (but will, now). The broad street itself, the little girls in their silk stockings, the cavaliers, the honky-tonk bars, the elegant pensions, the courtesans and the frenzy of film — all this rollicks in a hellish tempo, in a hell spook... Apart from a few sequences, the grotesque and burlesque [*sic*] power of the scenes is mostly strong. The quality of the tableaux is good; sometimes they remind one of Breughal [*sic*], sometimes they recall an E.T.A. Hoffmann–like atmosphere. Sometimes the playing becomes rather primitive, like an old Hans Sachs folk play, but it's always amusing.

"Casting sets a new record. The devil is Conrad Veidt: lanky, mobile, comical, satanic, drunk, acrobatic; he carries the role (sometimes he even lugs it) throughout the six acts. There is Asta Nielsen: as the Kurfürstendamm girl, a cook, the movie star, the mulatto at the masked ball; she is always good, often exemplary. Erna Morena, who has the most beautiful camera face (and knows it), is a cold courtesan. Rosa Valetti is excellent as the pension keeper; the mimicry she does with her mouth is great. Henry Sze, the well-known Chinese film actor, is not quite vivid enough... Theodor Loos is a funny, if somewhat overdone, ham actor... Paul Morgan and Rudolf Forster are too cold and immobile in the hurly-burly of the others...

"The main plot line is interrupted by funny, grotesque and striking jokes and bits; Veidt and Nielsen's ideas are inexhaustible. Oswlad has created a funny (but never silly) parody of life by combining the saga of the devil with a much more devilish reality. We sat in the overcrowded cinema and saw this *Midsummer Night's Dream* of a hell-spook rush by, and, some-

how touched to the core by this satire, stepped out afterwards onto the Kurfürstendamm."

Film-Kurier, 31 July 1920 —
Martin Proskauer

"Richard Oswald subtitled his latest work, *Ein Höllenspuk in 6 Akten*. That sounds like an excuse, like a justification for the loosely and inconsistently composed plot. One expects originality; especially after the first act, one expects a mixture of satire, comedy, grotesquerie. There is that, and there would be more, if a few passages didn't inflict upon one the impression that the whole thing should be taken more seriously, that one should search for a deeper meaning. The highlight is the fifth act, the funniest... This tale allows Conrad Veidt to shine as an enactor of grotesquerie. His play is nuanced and he deviates from his usual manner of expression."

Der Film, No. 32; 7 August 1920

Der Reigen

The Merry-Go-Round; aka **Ein Werdegang** (*An Evolution*); Richard Oswald-Film der Deutschen Bioscop AG, Berlin, 1920; Distributed by Bioscop-Verleih; Filmed at Bioscop Studios, Neubabelsberg; World premiere: 28 February 1920 Richard-Oswald-Lichtspiele, Berlin; *Zensur*: 17 July 1920 — 6 Acts, 2025 meters; Forbidden to adolescents

CAST: Conrad Veidt *Peter Karvan*; Asta Nielsen *Elena*; Theodor Loos *Fritz Peters*; Eduard von Winterstein *Albert Peters*; Irmgard Bern *His Wife*; with Willy Schaeffers, Hugo Döblin, Ilse von Tasso-Lind, Loni Nest, Willy Karin

CREDITS: *Producer/Director* Richard Oswald; *Original Story & Scenario* Richard Oswald; *Set Design* Hans Dreier; *Cinematography* Carl Hoffmann, Axel Graatkjaer

SYNOPSIS: Some time after the death of her mother, Elena (Asta Nielsen) falls in love with her (Elena's) piano teacher, only to be thrown out of her house by her

The cat that ate the canary: Asta Nielsen and Connie. (*Der Reigen*)

stepmother, who regards the man as being too poor to offer her his hand in marriage.

Elena goes on to meet a number of men; among them is Peter Karvan (Conrad Veidt), a friend of her piano teacher. Peter introduces her into the world of cabaret. Elena tries to become a singer, but hasn't the talent to succeed at it.

Finally, she obtains a job working as a governess in the home of a rich couple. The man of the house pursues her romantically and, after the death of his wife, marries her. Elena doesn't really love him, but she does love his brother, who loves her, as well.

Karvan, her former lover, finds her and proceeds to blackmail her. When her husband discovers Elena's past, he throws her out of the house. She ends up with Karvan in a honky-tonk. Disgusted with life, she shoots Karvan and takes poison to do herself in.

REVIEW: "An average picture, nothing more. One has seen better work from Richard Oswald, and Asta Nielsen, returning after quite a number of years, disappoints... The script, as well, really offers nothing that's particularly interesting... Conrad Veidt, splendid as usual, gives the down-at-the-heels musician real life. Eduard von Winterstein and Theodor Loos do their best in less rewarding parts."

Der Kinematograph
(Düsseldorf),
3 March 1920

NOTES AND QUOTES: There is some controversy as to whether the scenario of *Der Reigen* was based on a renowned work by playwright Arthur Schnitzler, or taken from an original composition by producer-director Richard Oswald. A monograph on Richard Oswald's career published by Berlin's Deutsche Kinemathek in 1970 advises pointblank that Schnitzler's "dialogue" had nothing to do with the picture at hand. Nonetheless, the Deutsches Film-institut holds that Oswald had plundered Schnitzler for *Der Riegen*. (Schnitzler's name is nowhere to be seen in existing prints of the film.) A preproduction trade announcement, citing no source material for the screenplay, remarked only that the picture would be a succession of five one-act vignettes. When or if additional documentation is unearthed, the debate may well be resumed.

Max Ophüls' *La Ronde* (1950; released as *Der Reigen* in West Germany) allots Schnitzler on-screen credit, although the playwright shares responsibility for the scenario with director Ophüls and Jacques Natanson. A German television production from 1995 —*Der Reizende Reigen nach dem Reigen des reizenden Herrn Arthur Schnitzler*— needed go no further than its title to proffer who wrote what to the casual viewer.

Der Reigen marked Veidt's first of two films with Asta Nielsen, one of the true silent superstars. Born in Copenhagen in 1881, "Die Asta" made a handful of Danish features before settling in Germany with her husband, Urban Gad. Gad, who had not set the world afire as a set designer, managed to gain some notice as director of a number of early German pictures starring his wife and actor Max Landa. (Veidt would appear with Landa in two of the "Max Landa-Detectivfilme"—*Die Japanerin* [1919] and *Moriturus* [1920].) The unconventional Nielsen (who had shocked Danish society by giving birth as an unmarried teenager) joined the ranks of such maverick actresses as Eleanora Duse and Sarah Bernhardt in daring to play Hamlet, but Nielsen's silent film version (in 1921) indulged in a little kinky one-upmanship: Die Asta's Danish prince was a woman *disguised* as a man! Although she retired from the screen in 1932 (feeling that her true milieu had been the silent narrative), Nielsen whiled away the next 40 years as an artist,

writer, and stage actress; she died, at age 90, in 1972.

Die Augen der Welt

[LOST] *The Eyes of the World*; Carl Wilhelm-Film GmbH, Berlin, 1920; Distributed by Terra-Film AG, Berlin; *Zensur*: 21 July 1920 — 6 Acts, 2083 meters; Forbidden to adolescents; World premiere: 23 July 1920 Berlin

Cast: Conrad Veidt *Juliane's lover*; Ressel Orla *Juliane von Derp*; Wilhelm Prager *the Silhouette Cutter*; with Anton Edthofer, Henny Steinmann, Lotte Coopmann, Emil Heyse, Julius Sachs, Carl Platen, Berthold Rosé, Fritz Witte-Wild, Max Zilzer, Fritz Rimpler, Wladimir Enders-Saniwitsch

Credits: *Director* Carl Wilhelm; *Scenario* Ruth Götz, Carl Wilhelm

Synopsis: The only available information concerning the plot of this picture is that it concerns "the fight of a father and son for the love of a woman."

Reviews: "The first film of the Terra Film group is very promising. It is a solid, careful work and demonstrates, without a doubt, a strong artistic approach. The director is not limited to guiding the actors, but works hand in hand with the photographer so as to find a unique background for the story. This is a great achievement for director Carl Wilhelm.

"A major role is played by Conrad Veidt. It was memorable, watching this artist together with his colleagues, who were not really bad on their own, but who seemed almost dead, as if without soul, when compared with him. Only he seems to have a beating heart. His inner life can be seen to an incredible degree in his every movement... Ressel Orla deserves mention; we were happy to see her again, following the long hiatus she took, and also W. Prager, who made the most of his difficult role..."

Der Film, No. 31;
31 July 1920

The largest "demonic Veidt" in history seems a bit at odds with the extant reviews of the film. (*Die Augen der Welt*)

own frame, a stylized base must be prepared and used overall. Conrad Veidt's performance dominates the others as if from a mountaintop. [He shows] a richness of soul and enormous tension in his every gesture."

Erste internationale Filmzeitung,
No. 29-30; 31 July 1920

"At the top of the new program is a drama entitled *Die Augen der Welt*, and it stimulates deep thoughts. Conceived as a chamberplay [Kammerspiel] and divided into six acts and three intermezzi, its dazzling lighting evokes pictures of light and shadow from life's heights and depths. In a part fantastic, part realistic manner, the notion that a man is, in a sense, dictated by the severe role of fate ('The eyes of the world inexorably destroy every happiness on earth!') is handled quite well. Hand in hand with splendid performances goes tasteful décor, which provides a rather peculiar feast for the eyes. Cast in principal roles are Ressel Orla, favorably renowned in cinema circles as a tragedienne, and the character player Konrad Veidt, who heads the list of actors who are an acquired taste."

"The Screen-Stages,"
unknown source,
date unknown

"The film, *Die Augen der Welt*, written by Ruth Götz and Carl Wilhelm, is extraordinarily thrilling. The tension isn't produced through logically sequenced events, but because at the beginning of the film, the spectator is placed at a far advanced point in the action and is only informed in later intermezzi as to what has been going on. What's not obvious is why the picture is considered a *Kammerspiel* (chamberplay). The whole story is domi-

"This picture, written by Ruth Goetz and Carl Wilhelm ... is very original. It starts with the climax, as it were, and the story is then slowly explained by the tales of the three different persons involved. The finale wraps in a sort of fantastic grandness, but nowhere near the limits of good taste. The subject itself is very delicate, but it may be said that it has been adapted perfectly to the screen.

"From the outset, one thing is quite pleasing: the director thinks in pictures. This provides the essential basis for the milieu, for, when each tale is embedded in its

nated by a horror that marks the thrilling performances of leading actors Conrad Veidt, Wilhelm Prager and Ressel Orla. The film, now showing at Munich's Regina-Theater, is technically one of the best."

Unknown review — M.

Der Januskopf

[LOST] *The Janus Head*; aka *The Head of Janus*, *Love's Mockery*, **Schrecken**; "Decla Bioscop Sensations Klasse"; Originally subtitled **Eine Tragödie am Rande der Wirklichkeit**; (*A Tragedy Bordering on Reality*); Lipow-Film, Berlin 1920; Distributed by Decla-Bioscop AG, Berlin; Filmed at Film-Ateliers am Zoo and Cserépy-Atelier; World premiere (prospective exhibitors' showing) 28 April 1920, Berlin; *Zensur*: 21 August 1920 — 6 Acts, 2222 meters; Forbidden to adolescents; General Release: 26 August 1920 Marmorhaus, Berlin

CAST: Conrad Veidt *Dr. Warren/Mr. O'Connor* (*Dr. Jeskyll* [*sic*] *& Mr. Hyde* in Janowitz's script); Margarete Schlegel *Grace*; Magnus Stifter *Utterson, Warren's friend and lawyer*; Bela Lugosi *Dr. Warren's Butler*; with Willy Kaiser-Heyl, Margarete Kupfer, Gustav Bötz, Jaro Fürth, Marga Reuter, Lanja Rudolph, Danny Gürtler, Hans Lanser-Ludolff

CREDITS: *Director* Friedrich Wilhelm Murnau; *Scenario* Hans Janowitz; *Based on the novel* Dr. Jekyll & Mr. Hyde *by* R.L. Stevenson; *Photographed by* Karl Freund, Karl Hoffmann; *Sets* Heinrich Richter

SYNOPSIS: Coming upon a bust of Janus, the two-faced Roman deity, in a curio shop, Dr. Warren (Conrad Veidt) buys it on impulse. Although he presents it to his fiancée, Grace (Margarete Schlegel), she returns it to him, repulsed by its appearance. The doctor, who has been working feverishly on the enigma of the two sides of human nature, begins to fall under its influence. He concocts an elixir to separate the good and evil natures of man, as well as an antidote, with which to restore matters afterwards. Quaffing the liquid himself, he transforms into Mr.

O'Connor (Conrad Veidt), a hideous, hunchbacked brute.

O'Connor lets a flat in Whitechapel, London's criminal district, and commits all types of horrendous crimes, including beating an old man to death and raping Grace. (By some accounts, O'Connor also forces Grace into prostitution.) Warren finds that he turns to the transforming liquid more and more, and discovers — to his horror — that stronger and stronger doses of the antidote seem to be producing shorter and shorter periods of normalcy.

The day comes when, on the run from the police, he cannot return to his residence. (In a hallucinatory sequence, O'Connor bludgeons a young girl and — as a horrified Dr. Warren watches nearby — the image of the brute multiplies and intensifies. It is unclear from existing synopses where this segment occurred.) The chemist is out of the necessary chemicals, so — via a note — Warren's old friend Utterson (Magnus Stifter; in some accounts of the screenplay, the character is named "Laue") is sent to retrieve the chemicals from Warren's laboratory; there are enough for one final transformation. In the presence of Utterson and Grace, O'Connor reverts to Warren. The shock is too much: Utterson dies from fright and Grace goes mad.

Distraught, O'Connor rushes back to his home to do away with himself. Taking poison, he sits down to write a full confession, but, as he writes, he changes yet again into the brute. A friend, who has hurried over to the house, finds the letter and the corpse of O'Connor, which is clutching the bust of Janus.

(This synopsis formulated from Janowitz's script and contemporary critiques of the film.)

REVIEWS: "The theme of this fantastic film has remained popular throughout time, and because of this, this style of film has progressed. We saw *Nachtgestalten*,

Grace (Margarete Schlegel) watches her fiancé, Dr. Warren (Connie), give a finger wave to a recent purchase. At right, making himself at home, is liberated butler Bela Lugosi. (*Der Januskopf*)

Unheimliche Geschichten, Das Kabinett des Dr. Caligari, the film *Die Andere* (from the novel by Lindau) and with this latest, *Schrecken*, we come back to the precursor of such films. This film is modeled after the world-famous novel by Stevenson, *Dr. Jekyll & Mr. Hyde*.

"It is generally known that Jekyll and Hyde are the same person — a gentleman from London — who is driven by the secret force of a double identity, during which time he degenerates into a wild animal and commits gruesome acts while in a dazed state. This role, that of both a proper man of high standing *and* of a possessed criminal, might make some actors wince. Here, Conrad Veidt is the enactor of this double role. He plays— he *lives*— this role as no other German actor could. One distinguishes two distinct main roles in this fantastic film: the hysterical man who acts as if he were subject to hypnotic trances, and

the epileptic, he who is organically ill. Veidt totally personifies this first role, as his very appearance reeks of foreshadowing (one thinks of the Somnambulist in *Caligari*); the other character is in from Werner Krauss territory (*Dr. Caligari*, Smerdjakoff in *The Brothers Karamazov*.)

"Here in *Schrecken*, only Veidt truly acts. One is excited and captivated, even if he knows how the story will develop, because one wants to see how he portrays the growing hardships of this difficult double-role. When Veidt acts, he speaks with his body and with his hands (others have learned this 'hand-language' by watching him), not with his mouth. Veidt's talent is so great that even his lurking crouch, or his over-the-shoulder glance, is phenomenal... When Veidt does something, he lifts it out of the conventional, and gives it expression and individuality.

"Worth mentioning is the moment in

which the audience's powers of reason are put to the test—the scene in the laboratory, half-shrouded in darkness. Veidt's transformation from gentleman to criminal is so good, the metamorphosis so peculiar, that his barber had to be specifically instructed how to take his shaggy hair and turn it into something fashionable."

"An Interesting Production
from Lipow-Film" *Schrecken*
in *Film-Kurier*, 29 April 1920;
p. 1— Martin Proskauer

"Conrad Veidt brings an admirable virtuosity to the character of Dr. Jekyll. On the one side, an admirable gentleman; on the other, a criminal compelled to carry out abominable deeds. Only a true artist like Veidt could handle such a role."

Lichtbildbühne, No. 18;
1 May 1920; p. 18

"The handling of this role bears witness to Conrad Veidt's excellence. With him as the character, Dr. Warren, the whole thing would either fall apart, or move right along. It moves right along. That was the main thing; that and the writer and director's securing rights to the subject matter.

"[As Warren], Conrad Veidt possesses a world-class elegant, gentleman-like calm, a noble passion, and the intellect, spirit and composure of a man of the world. He also has the sharp-edged characteristics of his other character [O'Connor], such as expressive gestures, compelling movements, and grotesque/disgraceful overtones."

Film-Kurier, 27 August 1920;
p. 2— L.K. Fredrik

"We are devoting this notice to Veidt, whose gratuitously titled film *Schrecken* opened Thursday at the Marmorhaus. Let it be said that the film—right from its opening title—is not only inspired, but—as we predicted—has enjoyed great success because of its breathtaking excitement. Conrad Veidt should be praised for his unsurpassed performance, as should the Bioscop Distribution Company for acquiring this masterwork."

Lichtbildbühne, No. 35;
28 August 1920; p. 39 — R.G.

"This thoroughly amazing story is spine-tingling from start to finish. The metamorphosis—which takes place in plain sight—is a masterpiece of technical accomplishment. What is basically impossible onstage is no problem at all on the screen. The lean, intelligent face of Conrad Veidt—who portrays Dr. Warren with undeniable authority—transforms almost imperceptibly into a hateful, unkempt visage; with his body doubled over, [Veidt] becomes an entirely different man. It is very unsettling to get an extremely good look at the man.

"Conrad Veidt brings his usual virtuosity to play in enacting such a weird character, and his range of expression is astonishing. Along with him, Willy Kaiser-Heyl, Magnus Stifter, Margarete Schlegel, and all the other actors are simply marvelous.

"The photography is excellent throughout, with both scenes and individual images rich [*sic*]; the blue-tinted street scenes (shot in the studio with special lighting) are especially memorable."

Kinematograph, 1920

"This latest film work, which Decla-Bioscop is releasing, recalls to mind a certain quality shared by its predecessors, *Caligari* and *Kurfürstendamm*. This certain quality, however, is the only thing that these pictures do have in common. It can be said that this new film measures up to *Caligari*, even surpassing it in some instances... This might well be due to the acting of Conrad Veidt, whom we have never before seen in a role of such degree of difficulty and contrast, placing on him [as it does] enormous physical and emotional demands...

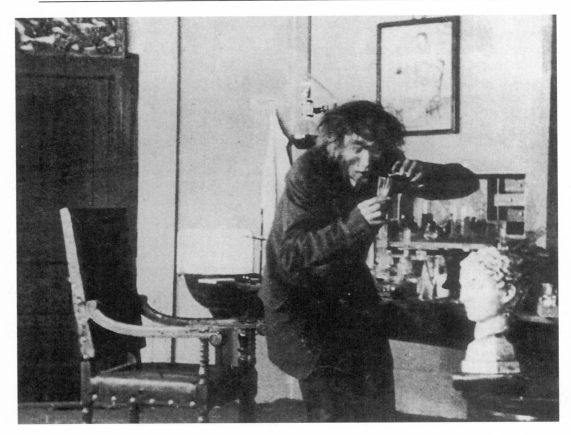

This time 'round, it's Mr. O'Connor at the Janus-head! (*Der Januskopf*)

"Imbued with many melodramatic highlights, the picture is entertainingly suspenseful, and succeeds in bringing the quasi-scientific problem — the duplicity within people — closer to the viewer. And that is one argument in favor of [Hans Janowitz's] script. As far as casting goes, here, too, we have nothing but the best. Director F.W. Murnau — with his broad vision, photographic good sense and taste, and his sure, steady director's hand — permits his actors to give all they are capable of giving.

"Above all, Conrad Veidt. This great artist has totally outdone himself, has topped all his past work with this role. As Dr. Warren, he replicates his well-known study of a sensitive man. What he produces as O'Connor, however, is the most admirable work we've yet had from him. He exudes reality and authenticity, right down to the smallest gesture. In this, he has been helped immensely by Karl Freund and Carl Hoffmann's technical genius in photography..."

H.-U. Dörp. 1920

NOTES AND QUOTES: *Der Januskopf* marks the only time Conrad Veidt appeared with Hungarian actor Bela Lugosi. Lugosi would go on to fame as the screen's foremost impersonator of Bram Stoker's Dracula, in the eponymous Universal production of 1931. Coincidentally, Connie was Carl Laemmle's first choice for the role of the vampire (with Lon Chaney the undisputed frontrunner in the eyes of Carl Laemmle, Jr.). Following Veidt's return to

Germany and Chaney's death, Universal initiated a well-publicized search for the actor who would don the cloak. Lugosi, who had introduced the role to the Broadway theatergoers, got the part only after a carload of other thesps had been scrutinized and found wanting.

F.W. Murnau was no stranger to *Dracula*, either. As he had with *Der Januskopf*, in 1922, the maverick director would once again "borrow and adapt" a literary work without paying royalties. What had proven successful with Robert Louis Stevenson, though, didn't work with Bram Stoker. Stevenson had died in the South Seas in 1894, and his kith and kin were literally in no position to care much about plagiarism. Stoker shuffled off this mortal coil scarcely a decade before Prana Films unveiled *Nosferatu*, however, and the widow Stoker was determined that no one was to make a brass farthing from *Dracula*—which she rightly perceived as her husband's most lasting legacy to her and the world — without obtaining full rights from the estate. Murnau clearly learned his lesson. His next (and last) full-blooded excursion into the world of Expressionistic fantasy and horror would be his splendid *Faust* (1926), based on the masterwork by Johann Wolfgang von Goethe, who had thoughtfully passed on nearly a hundred years prior to the film's initial release.

Der Januskopf was one of three major adaptations of the Stevenson work to hit the screen in 1920; it was the only one to disappear subsequently into the abyss. The other versions included a major Paramount/Artcraft production, top-lining John Barrymore, and a five-reel "modernized" rendition by Louis Mayer, starring the silent era's perennial Grinch, Sheldon Lewis. (If we consider a low-comic treatment by Arrow Pictures—featuring ex–Keystone Cop, Hank Mann — the number of Jekyll and Hyde turns hit *four* that year.) The good versus evil dichotomy would become one of the most oft-filmed themes in the course of cinematic history.

Abend ... Nacht ... Morgen

[LOST] *Evening ... Night ... Morning*; Attributed variously to Helios-Film, Berlin; Schneider-Film, Berlin; and Decla-Bioscop A.G., Berlin; Distributed by Decla-Film; Filmed at Lixie-Atelier, Berlin-Weissensee; Original length: 5 Acts—1700 meters; *Zensur*: 6 September 1920 — 5 Acts, 1713 meters; Forbidden to adolescents; World premiere: 24 September 1920 Decla-Lichtspiele-Unter den Linden, Berlin; Ein Decla Detectiv Film der Decla-Bioscop

CAST: Conrad Veidt *Brilburn, Maud's Brother*; Otto Gebühr *Ward, a detective*; Gertrude Welcker *Maud, a demi-mondaine*; Bruno Ziener *Chester, a Rich Gentleman and Maud's Lover*; Carl von Balla *Prince, a Gambler*
CREDITS: Producer *Erwin Rosner*; Director *F.W. Murnau*; Sets *Robert Neppach*; Scenario *Rudolf Schneider*; Photography *Eugen Hamm*

SYNOPSIS: Maud (Gertrude Welcker), a young woman of the world, is being kept by millionaire Chester (Bruno Ziener), who overwhelms her with gifts. Brilburn (Conrad Veidt) is a ne'er-do-well who gets money from Maud, who is his sister. He has Maud ask her lover for a beautiful pearl necklace in a jeweler's window, thinking that he (Brilburn) will get hold of it, sooner or later. After promising to give the matter some consideration, Chester buys it for Maud. While doing so, he meets up with his friend Prince (Carl von Balla), a heavy gambler. They drive to their club, where Chester shows the necklace to all his friends.

That night, Prince — heavily in debt — breaks into Chester's house to steal the necklace. In order to find out where it is, he deliberately breaks a vase. Chester, hearing the noise, comes in and opens the safe to make sure the pearls are still there. Prince knocks him out and hangs him

large lump of coal so as to make room for the jewel case. Police-men find Brilburn unconscious near the yard—he has been knocked out by that flying lump of coal—and they take him to the police station as a drunk.

Ward, the great detective (Otto Gebühr), investigates. Chester has been revived, so there is no question of suicide. It's also clear that two people had been at the crime scene, in-dependently of each other. A cigarette butt of an expensive type leads Ward to Prince, who gets his explanations balled up; the dagger and the button make Brilburn suspect number two. Thanks to the piece of coal that hit Brilburn, Ward finds the place where the necklace is hid-den. All he has to do is wait for Prince — who has run away — to come to look for the necklace in the coal yard.

REVIEWS: "This is a Conrad Veidt film in which he does not play the leading role. Nor does Gertrude Welcker, whom we like to see for more than her beautiful legs. The film some-times seems to be a satire on de-tective pictures, but it's not sup-posed to be. After all, it supplies the thrills that are expected from a good detective story. It builds skillfully, although the detective, masterfully played by Otto Gebühr, reveals who the murderer is much too easily... Still, there is suspense and a certain structural logic to this Con-rad Veidt film."

Film-Kurier,
25 September 1920

From the original program (*Abend ... Nacht ... Morgan*)

from the chandelier. Smoking a cigarette, Prince types a suicide note (supposedly from Chester), and then goes off with the necklace.

Soon afterwards, Brilburn breaks in, hoping to steal the necklace. He sees the man hanging and—horrified—cuts him down and runs away, having first unwit-tingly dropped his dagger and torn a but-ton off his coat. Prince hides the necklace in a heap of coal, having thrown away a

"The new detective film from Decla is quite good. The plot is a little transparent, but it nevertheless has its thrilling moments and is pulled off by an excellent cast...

"Without a doubt, Otto Gebühr as the detective is the picture's most sympathetic character. His detective has an element of the American [detective], with his unruffled demeanor and his dramatic gestures. Gertrud Welcker imbues her demimondaine with a bit too much bland dignity, but Conrad Veidt is quite a convincing criminal."

Der Kinematograph, No. 716; October 1920

"For a detective drama, Munich's [*sic*] Rudolf Schneider-Film's five acts merit raves. This is certainly due to the casting of the main parts. By the way, here's something new: a film with Conrad Veidt, in which he by no means has the leading role. Nevertheless, again he is fabulous, authentic in his acting — part pimp, part burglar — in spite of exhibiting a certain crudeness at some moments and a certain good natured attitude at others. His pantomime when he's examined at the police department is unsurpassed.

"Otto Gebühr can't be blamed for portraying detective Ward; he plays him well, and very sharply outlined. Gertrude Welcker also gives an excellent performance as the coquette. She looks beautiful, is dressed with refinement, and has blossomed, actingwise. Bruno Zeiner as a well-off elderly gentleman and Carl von Balla, as the gambler/murder, are worthy of mention.

"The whole thing was quite satisfying, as far as the direction goes... Robert Neppach's sets were in good taste, and [Eugen] Hamm's photography was flawless."

Der Film, Number 40; 2 October 1920

NOTES AND QUOTES: *Detektivfilme*— most of which were patterned after American models — were quite popular at this time, and Decla-Bioscop produced a series of its own in 1920-1921. Connie had appeared in a couple of Max Landa's series' entries (*Die Japanerin* and *Moriturus*) prior to the release of *Abend ... Nacht ... Morgen*. Lack of mention of the director in the contemporary critiques of the film suggests that he may have had his name removed from the credits prior to release. If, as Lotte Eisner opines, "the plot was ... horribly banal," Murnau may have opted to participate in this production solely out of boredom or for the money.

Moriturus

[LOST] Hilde Wörner-Film-Fabrikation, Berlin, 1920; *Zensur*: 6 September 1920 — Prologue and 5 Acts, 2026 meters; Forbidden to adolescents; World premiere: 23 September 1920 Marmorhaus, Berlin

CAST: Conrad Veidt *Wilmos*; Max Landa *the Detective*; Reinhold Schünzel *Baron von Mohrungen*; Hans Tillo *von Liebenau, his Cousin*; Hilde Wörner *Siegnis, a Maid*; Marga von Kierska *Frau von Riberac*

CREDITS: *Producer* Hilde Wörner; *Director* Carl (Müller-)Hagen; *Based on the novel* Liebeshörigkeit *by* Ferdinand Runkel; *Photographed by* Kurt Lande

SYNOPSIS: The impoverished von Liebenau (Hans Trillo) is hopelessly in love with Frau von Riberac (Marga von Kierska). Her brother Wilmos (Conrad Veidt) will not consent to a marriage between the two unless he (Wilmos) is somehow made heir to von Liebenau's cousin, Baron von Mohrungen (Reinhold Schünzel).

Desperately in love — and unable to stop himself — von Liebenau mixes a powder into von Mohrungen's drinks and meals, believing it to be a powder which would make his cousin sterile and thus unable to produce an heir. The maid Siegnis (Hilde Wörner) becomes an accomplice,

Wilmos (Connie, left) tries to get on the good side of the Baron von Mohrungen (Reinhold Schünzel). (*Moriturus*)

as she is secretly in love with the baron, and von Liebenau has convinced her that the powder is a potion that would cause the baron to return her affection.

Neither conspirator realizes that the potion contains morphine. Wilmos, who has supplied the powder, hopes that von Mohrungen will die and that his future brother-in-law will stand to inherit his fortune.

However, Mohrungen's good friend is a police detective, who notices what's happening and, after many misadventures—including the death of one of von Mohrungen's friends—exposes the villainy and saves the baron from a certain death.

REVIEW: "This detective story is accurate and logical; the subject matter is novel and interesting... Max Landa portrays his detective tastefully, and without resorting to any of the usual devices. Reinhold Schünzel is never completely convincing as the baron being destroyed by morphine, while Conrad Veidt is a little too demonic as Wilmos..."

Der Kinematograph, No. 716;
October 1920

NOTES AND QUOTES: Another Max Landa Detektiv film. See also: *Die Japanerin*.

Max Landa had appeared opposite Asta Nielsen in 7 German feature films between 1913 and 1914; all were directed by Nielsen's husband, Urban Gad.

Manolescus Memoiren

[LOST] *The Memories* [Memoirs] *of Manolescu* aka *Fürst Lahovary, der König der Diebe*;

Count Lahovary, the King of Thieves; Richard Oswald-Film GmbH, Berlin — 1920; *Zensur:* 25 September 1920 — 7 Acts, 2346 meters, then recut to a Prologue & 6 Acts, 2341.5 meters; Forbidden to adolescents; World premiere: 1 October 1920 Richard-Oswald-Lichtspiele, Berlin

CAST: Conrad Veidt *George Manolescu*; Erna Morena *Diane/Irene von Montignan*; Rudolf Forster *Alfons, the Fiancé*; Clementine Plessner *Mother Manolescu*; Alfred Kühne *Old Manolescu*; Adele Sandrock *Countess Anastasia Worutzky*; Hedda Vernon *Cecilie*; Käthe Waldeck *Inge*; Lilli Lohrer *Leonie, the Porter's Daughter*; Robert Scholz *Secret Policeman Schröder*; Preben J. Rist *Man in Pyjamas*; Hermann Wlach *Rudolf Berg*

CREDITS: *Producer/Director* Richard Oswald; *Scenario* Richard Oswald; *Based on the memoirs of* Georges Manolescu; *Photographed by* Max Lutze; *Art Director* Hans Dreyer

SYNOPSIS: (Note): Contemporary accounts of the picture reveal two somewhat disparate plot summaries; both follow.

Plot I *(according to the* Illustrierter Film-Kurier *program):*

George Manolescu's start in life is a difficult one. His father (Alfred Kühne) is a drunkard, and young George (Conrad Veidt) is left on his own. He is an emotional weakling — always looking for love — who grows adept at theft and betrayal. George loves women and women, who sometimes call him the "King of Thieves," love him, but he is unhappy for all this. He spends half his life in prison; at times, he is grateful that the police have arrested him again. He searches for a personal salvation, but as soon as he is released from prison, he goes back to his old ways and is incarcerated again.

He feels that the right woman might be able to save him, and when he meets Diane von Montignan (Erna Morena), he thinks he has found her. It soon devolves, however, that Diane wants the "King of Thieves," and not the good Manolescu. She helps him with his misdeeds and assists him in assuming the character of "Lord Lahovary." Together, they enjoy a short period of glamour and luxury, given to them by people who cannot — or chose not to — see beyond the elegant, dreamlike façade of "Lahovary."

Of course, this cannot last. Manolescu discovers that Diane has betrayed him — with the headwaiter of a restaurant! For a while, he is a broken man ... but then he meets Cecilie (Hedda Vernon), a good, gentle girl. George allows himself to be arrested again; in prison, he writes his memoirs. Once again, the highlights (and lowlights) of his life parade by: the bad home, the many women, the imprisonments, the luxurious life as Lord Lahovary, and the gentle Cecilie. When his sentence ends, he leaves the prison and goes straight into the arms of his gentle Cecilie, who has been waiting for him, all this time.

Plot II *(according to a review in* Der Kinematograph *[Düsseldorf] and other reviews):*

George Manolescu grows up in bourgeois surroundings: his father is a drunkard who regularly beats his wife (Clementine Plessner), and George himself is an idler. When he steals for the love of a porter's daughter (Lili Lohrer), his father repudiates him. He becomes a waiter — and then a room-service waiter — in an elegant hotel. There he meets a beautiful confidence woman, Irene von Montignan (Erna Morena), who likes him and hires him to be her secretary. Soon, she is teaching him her scams and the two enter a life of full-time swindles. As the demands of their lifestyles increase, they decide to abandon small-time operations, and go for the big coup. Manolescu now impersonates Lord Lahovary, and Irene is his secretary.

When a Russian countess (Adele Sandrock) commits an indiscretion, George and Irene quickly seize the opportunity to blackmail her. Disaster strikes, however, when the hotel headwaiter (Herman

Program art. (*Manolescus Memoiren*)

Wlach) recognizes George as the erstwhile room-service waiter; to silence him, the pair makes the headwaiter a partner. Things get worse.

With the police hot on his heels, George seeks to hide in an occupied hotel room. There, he meets Cecilie, a kind and gentle young woman. Without really knowing why, he confesses all his past crimes to her. She utters a single word: "Atone." He sees in her his angel of deliverance and allows himself to be captured by the police. After he has finished his sentence in prison, he finds Cecilie awaiting him at the gate. A life of freedom and righteousness awaits him.

REVIEWS: "Finally! An excellent, captivating and witty adventure picture, taken straight from the life of the notorious hotel thief and swindler who was the center of official investigations some time ago. Fact and fiction may get blurred, but, even so, fascinating images are created by the cast in a manner that could not have been improved upon.

"A large part [of the picture's] success is due to the brilliant acting. Konrad [*sic*] Veidt as Manolescu is a tour de force of the art of mime. His Manolescu isn't his usual haunted figure — which has been seen repeatedly from Veidt recently — but [is] totally a man, fully developed, and yet capable of change at any moment. [Veidt has] a great capacity for observation and a profound understanding of human behavior. His acting here is completely devoid of hyperbole and pretense. Watching him is a genuine pleasure... Erna Morena plays the villainess per the formula and is a great deal more interesting in the role of the male secretary, which appears to suit her very well."

Der Kinematograph
(Düsseldorf), No. 717;
10 October 1920

"Among the natural-born criminals who have some sort of innate glory, George Manolescu might be number one. [The historic] George Manolescu was a rough person, who didn't know himself how he came to enjoy such success as 'King of Thieves.' Actually, such a story wouldn't make an interesting film. But, if one tried to show his motivations, or the odd qualities a man like Manolescu must have had, an attractive film could be had. In fact, something wonderful has been achieved: the Manolescu case has been shown, but from a moral, and not a tragic, viewpoint.

"Conrad Veidt is not that [first] Manolescu; not that low, suspicious, limited sort, not that smarmy half-gipsy... Something very tender, almost boyish, unconsciously beams around him."

Film-Kurier, 1920

"'The art of film!' was my first thought, when I left the Richard Oswald Theater. What Oswald has created here is splendid, a sign of real artistic genius. Motifs in the life of an adventurer, he calls it... Conrad Veidt is a spiritualized [*sic*] Manolescu, as only Conrad Veidt can be. A wonderful performance..."

Der Film, No. 41;
9 October 1920

"Richard Oswald, who has always gone his own way, now tries to convince us that his way is the right way with his film about a thief, *Manolescus Memoiren*. It seems to us, however, that Oswald has emphasized the literary angle too much. He stresses the spiritualized [*sic*] aspect of the theme, which he obviously considered worth making a film about, but doesn't work the logistics out well enough in terms of film. His treatment remains on the surface...

"Would Mr. Oswald admit that without the dazzling performance of Conrad Veidt and the coquetry of Erna Morena — the best in this field — his new film would really be a poor film, because of its implausibility, its incoherent development and that sentimental ending? Thanks to the excellent acting, *Manolescu* becomes a highly imaginative thief comedy in the last seconds, quite amusing to an audience and thus worthy of being seen. He who looks to amuse himself doesn't ask about probabilities or possibilities. The new Oswald film fulfills its task to entertain to a high degree. And watching Conrad Veidt eager to learn how to serve as a waiter is itself worth the price of admission."

Erste internationale Filmzeitung,
No. 35–39; 28 September 1920

Künstlerlaunen

[LOST] *Temperamental Artists*; aka ***Der Maler, die Liebe und das Fräulein***; *The Artist, the Lover and the Young Woman*; Vera-Filmwerke GmbH, Hamburg, 1920; *Zensur*: 7 October 1920 — 6 Acts, 2079 meters; Forbidden to adolescents

CAST: Conrad Veidt *Arpad Czaslo*; Aud Egede Nissen *Dagmar*; Albert Bozenhard *the Russian Lord*; with Philine Leudesdorff-Tormin, Gertrude Arnold, Frida Richard, Ludwig Max, Alkfred Haase

Director Paul Otto; *Screenplay* Robert Liebmann, Georg Jacoby; *Based on the novel* Romantik *by* Olga Wohlbrück

SYNOPSIS: The Russian lord (Albert Bozenhard) discovers the talented painter Arpad Czaslo (Conrad Veidt) and becomes his patron. Soon after, however, the painter falls in love with Dagmar (Aud Egede Nissen), the Russian's fiancée, and she returns his affection. The nobleman withdraws his support from Czaslo, and the artist and Dagmar run off together. They try to start a new life together, and — at first — all is happiness and love.

Czaslo, however, is an artist, and soon he begins to withdraw from Dagmar — and the rest of the world — so that he can paint without distraction. Dagmar cannot understand this and leaves Czaslo. Surprisingly, the Russian nobleman has recovered from his disappointments and brings the two together once again. He, himself, goes on to marry the artist's sister.

REVIEWS: "Robert Liebmann and Georg Jacoby have adapted the novel ... very well and to the fullest... They have drawn the characters up perfectly... But there are truly excellent artists who really LIVE in this film ... among them... Conrad Veidt, who feels and plays with extreme sensitivity..."

Erste internationale Filmzeitung,
No. 42-43; 6 November 1920

"Robert Liebmann and Georg Jacoby have produced [*sic*] a nice feature film

The plot: Connie, as a painter, falls in love with his benefactor's honey. (*Künstlerlaunen*)

after Olga Wohlbrück's novel, *Romantik*. Romantic novels have a great chance of success, especially in this materialistic age of ours, because one always enjoys seeing what one is missing out on. The thrilling plot of the film, which is currently showing at the Imperial Theatre, fortunately exhibits a good portion of comfortable humor. The performances are excellent, with Conrad Veidt (who seems to exaggerate things a bit), Aud Egede Nissen and Frida Richard in the leading parts. Paul Otto is in control, with tight, skillful direction."

Unknown review

"The subtitle is *A Romantic Affair in Six Parts*, after themes from Olga Wohlbrück's novel, *Romantik*. And, I don't think the tricky transformation of novel into film has ever been handled with more luck than in this case. It has simultaneously

found great success in mastering the book's plot and becoming an acceptable film in its own right. Paul Otto directed with great skill; he didn't give the horse the bridle, but showed reserve and moderation.

"The acting was quite excellent, both the solo performances and the ensemble work. Once again, Conrad Veidt, as the rather eccentric, gifted painter, gave a wholly perfect performance. His partner was Aud Egede Nissen, who was equally good beside him."

Der Film, Number 45; 1920

Liebestaumel

[LOST] *Love and Passion*; Vera-Filmwerke GmbH, Hamburg, 1920; *Zensur*: 11 October 1920 — 5 Acts, 1623 meters; Forbidden to adolescents; World premiere (and press preview): 2 January 1921; Kammer-Lichtspiele, Hamburg

CAST: Conrad Veidt *the gypsy, Jalenko*; Maria Zelenka *Mira* [some reviews call the character *Cira*]; Erich Ziegel *the Judge*; with Max Zawislack, Heinrich Schroth, Margarete Lanner, Gustav Adolf Semmler, Otto Marlé, Marie Gindra

CREDITS: *Director* Martin Hartwig; *Producer* Viggo Larsen (?); *Scenario* Dr. Artur Landsberger; *Photography* Hans Kämpfe; *Art Design* Georg Meyer

SYNOPSIS: No coherent synopsis could be found. See below.

REVIEWS: "'I want to live with the actors, feel what they feel, just understand...' said he [*sic*], expressing the basic ways in which an audience judges a movie. This part is not fulfilled in the new 'Vera' film *Liebestaumel* by A. Landsberger.

"The spectator will not understand the strange behavior of a young bride, who runs away on her wedding day from splendor and glamour, into the uncertainty of a gypsy wagon; nor will he understand the fiery romantic air of two jealous women, fighting. He'll neither understand the judge, who marries a blond tramp only to be removed later, nor his successor, who thinks up the most dazzling tortures for the woman who has betrayed him, instead of simply throwing her out of the house. The audience will ask: 'How did this fragile little girl survive in that miserable gypsy cart?' and 'How can a prison be so poorly guarded that it's possible to have a romantic rendezvous in it?' and 'Why the acquittal?' And because the answers to these questions are missing from the picture, the

Mira (Maria Zelenka) is falling under the spell of Jalenko's (Connie's) gypsy violin. Her husband will regret not hiring an accordion player. (*Liebestaumel*)

audience will take everything humorously, will count out by number the lovers of the blond tramp, and will amuse themselves by their foolishness.

"The average person will never be able to recognize the effects of an eerie primal power in all those colorful events. They will forget that the film is called *Liebestaumel* [Ecstasy of Love] and that such an ecstasy might well throw overboard everything that is rational and logical...

"Conrad Veidt reaches into the soul of a wandering man, fills it with the marvelous power of his personality, and ultimately fails, because of missed opportunity..."

Film-Kurier, 2 February 1921—
Margot Meyer

"Quite fancifully constructed and strongly mixed with purely cinematic effects—which shouldn't be tolerated in modern film any longer—is *Liebestaumel*, a film drama in four acts with an introduction, made by Artur Landsberger and shown for the first time at the Sportpalast [theater]. Things that have no bearing on reality happen in this picture. The heroine of the movie, the beautiful Mira, staggers from one love affair to another, from one man to another, until there are four whom she has married, one after the other, before leaving them all in the lurch. When she betrays the fourth, the deceived man strikes out at her violently, in revenge. He sets fire to the pavilion where his unfaithful wife and her lover are sitting, and both perish in the flames.

"Nevertheless, the picture is rich in events and occasions, and it's fascinating because of the agile performance of Maria Zelenka as Mira and Conrad Veidt as the Gypsy fiddler, Jalenko. Décor and photography are pleasant enough."

"News on Film"—
Unknown review

"It takes a certain point of view to correctly appreciate this film by Dr. Artur Landsberger (which ran as a press performance in Hamburg's Kammerlichtspiele), because the author's intent clearly exceeded the mundane process of filming...

"Martin Hartwig bravely struggled with the difficulties the scenario placed in the director's way. While on the whole he found the right tone for the film, he gave the plot absurdity a pleasant, acceptable flavor only by changing some [of the original] circumstances. Hans Kämpfe stood at Hartwig's side, by virtue of his most satisfactory photography. Georg Meyer's architectural skills had little free play, however.

"The acting, which posits a level not all partners can reach, requires a chapter of its own. Maria Zelenka plays Cira; she acts well, even excellently. But she only acts. There are several moments when you feel what she has lived through, but these are isolated. Beside her stands Conrad Veidt, trying unsuccessfully to give real life to his [unfortunate part as a] gypsy. Erich Ziegel is excellent as the destitute, but warmhearted judge..."

Der Film, Number 6;
1921—M.M.

Der Gang in die Nacht

The Walk in the Night aka *Journey into the Night*; Goron-Films, Berlin—1920—2000 meters; Filmed at Cserépy-Atelier and Filmateliers am Zoo; *Zensur*: 20 October 1920—5 Acts, 1927 meters; Forbidden to adolescents; Trade showing: 13 December 1920; World premiere: 21 January 1921 Richard-Oswald-Lichtspiele *and* Schauberg Theatre, Berlin

CAST: Conrad Veidt *the Blind Painter*; Olaf Fönss *Dr. Eigil Boerne*; Erna Morena *Hélène*; Gudrun Braun-Steffensen *Lily*; Clementine Plessner

CREDITS: *Director* F.W. Murnau; *Sets* Heinrich Richter; *Photographed by* Max Lutze; *Scenario* Carl Meyer; *Based on the Danish screenplay* The Conqueror *by* Harriet Bloch

The plot: Connie, as a painter, falls in love with his benefactor's wife. (*Der Gang in die Nacht*)

SYNOPSIS: Dr. Eigil Boerne (Olaf Fönss) has been engaged to Hélène (Erna Morena) for some time. He takes her to a cabaret to celebrate her birthday. Lily (Gudrun Braun-Steffensen), a young dancer, is fascinated by him and pretends to sprain her ankle in order to meet him. She succeeds in seducing him and it isn't long before he has broken off with Hélène. The professor marries Lily and the two move to a picturesque fishing village on the coast, where they meet a young painter who has become blind (Conrad Veidt). He restores the man's sight via a very difficult operation and brings him into his home. Boerne leaves to try and comfort Hélène — having heard that her broken engagement has resulted in poor health — but he returns without seeing her. He does, however, learn that his wife has taken up with the painter. He storms away furiously.

Several years later, Lily shows up at his office and begs him to operate a second time on the painter, whose sight has failed again. Boerne rails that she is incapable of true love and that he would consider helping the painter only if she were out of the picture entirely. Lily runs from the house while Boerne, overcome with emotion, faints. When he comes to, he heads for Lily's house, only to find that she has committed suicide so that Boerne will cure the painter. She has poisoned herself, proving she was able to love truly. The painter forgives the doctor, thanking him for having made it possible for him to see Lily in the first place.

The next morning, a servant finds Dr. Boerne dead in his study. In his hand is a letter from the painter; now that Lily is dead, he prefers to remain in darkness.

REVIEWS: "Where does the writer's

skill leave off? Where does the director's skill begin? Or that of the actors? One has no idea. Everything has slipped, everything has merged seamlessly, one into the other. There can be no feeling other than total completion. In his scenario, Carl Mayer has composed a work of poetry."

Film-Kurier,
14 December 1920

"This film marks a new epoch in the art of cinematography. It is the first attempt to integrate a chamberplay [*Kammerspiel*]—a strong, thrilling plot, with few characters and fully nuanced psychological composition—into a screenplay... What we have, then, is not merely a picture of interest to regular audiences... but a polished gem, that will also please the most demanding and particular of film connoisseurs.

"The cast is perfect, filled with excellent actors, of whom Olaf Fönss is the best. Murnau's direction is masterful."

Der Kinematograph,
No. 728; 30 January 1921

NOTES AND QUOTES: In her appraisal of the picture, however, Lotte Eisner found

> Olaf Fönss ... is stiff and foppish and grimaces horribly to indicate anger or passion... Conrad Veidt ... is dark and inflexible, and acts like Cesare in *Caligari*, apart from wringing his hands like Orlac. This Expressionistic style clashes with Gudrun Braun's naturalistic and unconvincingly sprightly interpretation of Lily. Only Erna Morena as Helene is really at home in this *Kammerspiel*, the tragic mask of her face that of Asta Nielsen.

Murnau; pp. 94–95

Der Gang in die Nacht is the earliest surviving Murnau film, thanks mainly to the involvement of the Cinémathèque Française. The only extant print was discovered—sans titles—by Henri Langlois among boxes of negatives in East Berlin's Staatliches Filmarchiv. As Murnau nor-

mally used a plethora of titles to complement his visuals, this print, then, returned only a part of the director's work to the public. (A video of the film currently circulating has but a handful of titles, reconstructed and inserted out of a dire need to explain the action; as such, they can do little to underline the psychological nuances that Murnau was striving to record. Without inserts of Hélène's diary, sundry missives of import, and a fortuitous newspaper announcement, the film's extant narrative path would be even more winding and difficult.) Contemporary commentary (by director Willi Haas, in the 14 December 1920 *Film Kurier*) examined Carl Mayer's scenario in detail; thus, we know that the surviving elements are also missing at least one scene. Within this less than integral framework, Murnau's recurrent inserts of the sea and its many faces—meant to parallel the calm-to-roiling emotions surging within our protagonists—lose both a great deal of impact and not a little coherence.

Viewing the picture *as it stands today* leads one to agree for the most part with Lotte Eisner's assessment of the acting. Husky, avuncular Fönss (only in a scenario such as this one could he possibly bedevil two younger women) goes totally overboard when called upon to register passion of any kind. Returning home from his unsuccessful jaunt to cheer up Helene, his Boerne catches Lily doing little more than strolling down the hillside aside the nameless painter, whereupon he reacts as though he had stumbled onto the pair *in flagrante delicto*. As he was being directed by Murnau while the camera was rolling, his has to be a case of shared negligence. Gudrun Braun-Steffensen's Lily (surely the most graceless dancer ever to hit the international silent screen) was likewise guided through her excesses, and her "mad scene"—wherein she dons her old theatrical costume and prances about defiantly to assuage her fears of an early morning thunderstorm — is as awkward as it is embarrassing. In contrast to these histrionics, Erna Morena's Hélène provides a textbook example of understatement: when informed by the professor that's he's vacating the premises, she merely hangs her head, neck and a good part of her chest in despair. Later, she is invigorated in her sickbed when she reads that Boerne has apparently returned to his pre–Lily habits and dispositions; a satisfied smile and a bit of newspaper stroking is all it takes for Miss Morena to bring it home.

Connie's artist does stalk about — clad entirely in black, Cesarelike — for most of the footage where he's not required to be bedridden or intertwined with Lily. While he handles his infrequent closeups with flare (the brief sequence in which his sight fails him a second time is enacted well enough), his hands become almost talon-like in appearance (presaging Max Shreck's Nosferatu) in scenes in which he stumbles about blindly. And the whole business about the artist and Lily using their free afternoon to fall for each other is no more dramatically convincing (especially after Lily's initial revulsion to the man, his condition, and the idea of his staying on with the Boernes) than Herr Fönss' supposed irresistible charms.

Filmmaker-historian Gerhardt Lamprecht opined that this picture, which he regarded as stylistically old-fashioned (even for the beginning of the 1920s), was reminiscent of Danish motion pictures from the previous decade. As if in response to this observation, Miss Eisner explained how Murnau "was obliged for *Der Gang in die Nacht* to make use of one of the many scenarios that the declining Nordisk Film Company had thrown on the German market" (Eisner p. 120). Nonetheless, the film — rife with what was perceived as psychological detail — was heralded as a cinematic milestone when it was first released, and the combination of Murnau's vision and

Max Lutze's camerawork imbued this *Kammerspiel* with true *Stimmung*, the much sought-after palette of light and shadow.

With *Der Gang in die Nacht*, Veidt and Murnau parted ways professionally, although both artists would turn up in Hollywood in 1927.

Christian Wahnschaffe

1.Teil: Weltbrand; *Conflagration*; Terra-Film GmbH, Berlin, 1920; Distributed by Terra-Filmverleih GmbH; *Zensur*: 26 October 1920 — 6 Acts, 2083 meters; Forbidden to adolescents; World premiere: 6 November 1920 Schauberg, Berlin; Prior to the premiere, there was a press and trade showing at Berlin's Hotel Esplanade; an orchestra (under the direction of Karl Muck) played behind the screen. General release: 12 November 1920

CAST: Conrad Veidt *Christian Wahnschaffe*; Leopold von Ledebour *Grand Prince*; Fritz Kortner *Ivan Becker*; Franz Sutton *Kroll*; Lillebil Christensen *Eva Sorel*; Theodor Loos *Amadeus Voss*; with Ernst Matray, Margarete Schlegel, Reinhold Schünzel, Rosa Valetti, Hugo Flink, Hermann Vallentin, Aruth Wartan, Esther Hagan, Paula Barra, Maria Reisenhofer, Paul Graetz, Fritz Feld, Josef Peterhans, Helga Molander, Sylvia Torf, Leopoldine Konstantin, Frida Richard, Ilka Grüning

CREDITS: *Director* Urban Gad; *Scenario* Paul Georg, Robert Michel; *Based on the novel* Christian Wahnschaffe *by* Jakob Wassermann; *Photographed by* Max Lutze; *Set Design* Robert Dietrich

SYNOPSIS: Europe, 1905. Christian Wahnschaffe (Conrad Veidt) is son and heir to a rich industrialist. In spite of the luxuries of his youth, he has always been warmhearted and compassionate. In addition, he is an idealist, always searching for goodness in man.

One day, he meets Ivan Becker (Fritz Kortner), a Russian anarchist possessed of a good heart. Becker wishes to change society for the sake of making life better, not for his own selfish ends. Christian is en-

(Left to right) Connie, Fritz Kortner, Theodor Loos: *Weltbrand.*

thusiastic about Becker's dreams and follows him to St. Petersburg. Among the Russian's other followers is Eva Sorel (Lillebel Christensen), a dancer who falls in love with Christian. The mistress of the grand prince (Leopold von Ledebour), Eva is also Becker's confidante; she has in her possession some of Becker's papers, in which he has outlined preparations for a revolution.

All is well until these papers are stolen by the prince's underlings. Both revolution and revolutionaries are revealed to the Czar. Soldiers rush through the streets, firing indiscriminately on the people. The revolutionaries try to seize the grand prince's palace, in order to burn it down, but soon realize that they are fighting a losing battle. Looking for someone upon whom to pin the blame for the dreadful uprisings, the people blame Eva, who (in their view) *gave away* the plans for the revolution.

The prince says nothing to warn his former mistress of her peril, and the revolutionaries kill her. She dies in Christian's arms.

REVIEW: "This Terra film proves that... the style and intellectual kernel of a novel can be adapted very well to the screen... Such results are achieved only with an exceedingly good staff and cast..."
Der Kinematograph (Düsseldorf),
14 November 1920

2. Teil: Die Flucht aus dem goldenen Kerker; *The Flight from the Gilded Prison*; Terra-Film AG, Berlin —1921; Distributed by Terra-Filmverleih GmbH; *Zensur*: 17 March 1921— 6 Acts, 2050 meters; Forbidden to adolescents; Recensored & abridged: 19 March 1921— 6 Acts, 2032 meters; Forbidden to adolescents; World premiere: 30 March 1921— Scala Lutherstrasse, Berlin (with the participation of the Philharmonic Orchestra, under the direction of Alexander Schirmann); Moved to the Terra-Theater Hardenbergstrasse (Motivhaus) on 1 April, after the premiere.

CAST: Conrad Veidt *Christian Wahnschaffe*; Esther Hagan *the Prostitute*; Werner Krauss *her Brother, Niels Heinrich*; Margarete Kupfer *her Mother*; Fritz Feld *the Lunatic*; Rose Müller *the Pure Young Woman*; with Ernst Pröckl, Emil Heyse, Jenny Marba, Magda Madeleine

CREDITS: *Director* Urban Gad; *Scenario* B.E. Lüthge, Hans Behrendt; *Based on the novel* Christian Wahnschaffe *by* Jakob Wassermann; *Photographed by* Willy Hameister; *Set Design* Robert A. Dietrich

SYNOPSIS: Tired of being one of the idle rich, Christian Wahnschaffe (Conrad Veidt) begins to frequent a dive that is also a criminals' den. He befriends a prostitute (Esther Hagan)—riddled with venereal disease—and he protects her from some brutal treatment by her very own brother, Niels Heinrich (Werner Krauss). When he takes the poor woman back to her mother's house, however, the mother (Margarete Kupfer) sees this as an opportunity to extort money from Christian. In the midst of all this, he meets a pure young woman (Rose Müller) who is devoting her life to helping the aged, the poor and the sick.

Completely in love with her, Christian renounces his wealth, adopts her simple lifestyle, and consigns to the fire all the goods his concerns manufactured, as he realizes that they have not reduced poverty, but rather have sparked greed and jealousy. The young girl is murdered by Heinrich; he lusted after her and also coveted a pearl necklace she received from Christian. With the death of his true love, Christian's dream of using his talents and his wealth to make a better world is shattered. When the murder is made public, he—like Christ—offers himself to the maddened crowd, who thinks him the underlying cause of the death of the girl whom all loved.

REVIEWS: "This second episode of *Christian Wahnschaffe* is less mired in the literary aspect [than the first] and is more readily understandable without any dilution of the artistic element. This time, all the rough edges have been smoothed and this new episode unreels as a complete story all to itself. Urban Gad's technical artistry, along with a string of the cinema's top actors, has produced a captivating picture taken right from real life... With this production, Terra Films has aligned itself with the handful of production companies striving to elevate the cinema's artistic standards.

Ud af det gyldne Bur

Filmatiseret i 6 Akter efter 2. Del af Jacob Wassermanns berømte Roman: „CHRISTIAN WAHNSCHAFFE"

I Hovedrollerne:

Conrad Veidt, Werner Krauss
og Rosel Müller

The original Danish program cover. (*Die Flucht aus dem goldenen Kerker*)

"...Conrad Veidt raises the standards of acting to the pinnacle of greatness in his final scenes... Werner Kraus is right along [by] his side, as the whore's brother: hefty, brutal, driven by passion..."

Der Kinematograph (Düsseldorf),
No. 738; 10 April 1921

"Urban Gad, the director, planned out the scenes very carefully, and he made the extras show real empathy. He created a coherent scenic atmosphere and has that so-important 'eye for pictures' that alone will allow picturesque effects in a film. Conrad Veidt is so soul-related to the figure of Wahnschaffe that he can play this 'pure fool' with warmest empathy..."

Der Film, No 14; 1921

NOTES AND QUOTES: "Christian Wahnschaffe" is more than the title character's name. *Wahnschaffen*— an adjective in dialectic German — means deformed or misshapen; hence, Jakob Wassermann's protagonist personifies a Christianity (or, in a wider sense, any set of religious or ethical beliefs) that has been manipulated or has gone awry. Both *Weltbrand* and *Die Flucht Aus Dem Goldenen Kerkor* are in the collection of the F.W. Murnau Stiftung.

Der Graf von Cagliostro

[LOST] *Count Cagliostro*— Coproduction of Vereinigte; Filmindustrie Micheluzzi & Co. (Micco Film), Vienna & Berlin, and Lichtbild-Fabrikation Schünzel-Film, Berlin —1920; *Zensur*: 7 January 1921— 6 Acts, 2158 meters; Subsequently recut to 2156 meters; (Censored as a German film)— Forbidden to adolescents; World premiere: 21 December 1920 Busch-Kino, Vienna; German premiere: 17 February 1921 Marmorhaus, Berlin

CAST: Conrad Veidt *the Minister*; Reinhold Schünzel *Giuseppe Balsamo [Count Cagliostro]*; Anita Berber *his Love*; Hugo Werner *his Servant*; Carl Goetz *the Senile Prince*; Hilde Wörner *the Prince's Mistress*; Hanni Weisse *her Maid*; with Heinrich Jensen, Walter Huber, Armin Seidelmann, Ferry Sichra, Hugo Werner-Kahle

CREDITS: *Director* Reinhold Schünzel; *Scenario* Reinhold Schünzel, Robert Liebmann; *Photographed by* Kurt Lande, Karl Hoffmann; *Artistic Advisor* O.F. Werndorff

SYNOPSIS: Count Cagliostro (Reinhold Schünzel) is really Giuseppe Balsamo, a Sicilian conman born in Palermo in 1743. Together with his servant (Hugo Werner), the "count" separates gullible men — nobles and commoners alike—from their money, while robbing women of their honor. He prefers to deal with the wealthy, however, as their social position usually precludes their admitting to having been swindled, thus allowing Cagliostro to escape without punishment.

He comes close to being made a noble himself—due to more of his lies and pretenses—only to have to flee the country.

Hiding out in a small principality in Austria, he poses as the Grand Master of an Egyptian Freemason society (which he has just concocted himself). Taken for an august personage, he is approached by the minister (Conrad Veidt) and asked to help rid the area of the old prince's mistress (Hilde Wörner); the woman is breaking the principality with her profligacy. The count endeavors to do so, with the result that one intrigue follows another (at one point, he falls in love with the mistress himself) and the whole affair becomes outrageously scandalous. The prince (Carl Götz) is poisoned, and Cagliostro flees to Paris.

REVIEWS: "The biography of the most notorious adventurer and the most brazen scoundrel, who—at the end of the 18th century—imperiled all of Europe, is marvelously effective cinema; one could make 10 or 20 films from his life without running out of material. The fact that there is just barely enough here for even one film is not his fault, but that of the script, which is the weakest element in the entire production. The picture must credit the incredible success of its Viennese premiere to the location shooting."

"Against the splendor [of Vienna] the cast pales slightly, but the acting is excellent in spots. Reinhold Schünzel enacts Cagliostro as more than a mere cunning knave. Hugo Werner... is a bit too blatantly sly as his servant and partner in crime. If the pair acted in real life as they are played here, one would have to marvel at the degree of stupidity needed to fall for such obvious tricks...

"Apart from the actors named above, Carl Götz ... gives the best performance of all. Conrad Veidt as the minister is also very effective in his opulent costumes, and he plays without a false note... Hilde Wörner demonstrates that she's capable of playing something other than a waif from Berlin."

Der Kinematograph, 1921

"This film could have been a masterpiece... Scenarist Robert Liebmann didn't expend any extra energy and what he did manage doesn't come close to the demands of this subject. The adaptation is less than adequate... Carl Götz and Conrad Veidt are the only actors whose every gesture is perfect."

Film-Kurier, 9 February 1921

Surprisingly, Veidt did not play Cagliostro, but rather the Austrian minister. (*Der Graf von Cagliostro*)

Original poster art. (*Der Graf von Cagliostro*)

Das Geheimnis von Bombay

[LOST] *The Secret of Bombay* aka ***Das Abenteuer einer Nacht***; *One Night's Adventure*; Decla-Bioscop AG, Berlin — 1920/21; *Zensur*: 21 December 1920 — 5 Acts, 1670 meters; Forbidden to adolescents; World premiere: 6 January 1921 Marmorhaus, Berlin

CAST: Conrad Veidt *Tossi*; Lil Dagover *Gabriela Farnese/Concha*; Bernhard Goetzke *Hobbins*; Anton Edthofer *Dr. Vittorio*; K.A. Roemer *Tschou*; with Hermann Böttcher, Nien-Sön-Ling, Lewis W. Brody

CREDITS: *Director* Artur Holz; *Scenario* Rolf E. Vanloo, Paul Beyer; *Set Designs* Robert Herlth, Walter Röhrig; *Photographed by* A.O. Weitzenberg

SYNOPSIS: Famous singer Gabriela Farnese (Lil Dagover) is aboard a cruise ship, which stops for the night at Bombay. Having learned from Dr. Vittorio (Anton Edthofer), the ship's physician, that a dancer at a local tearoom bears a striking resemblance to her, she decides to venture out to see her "double" that night. At the last moment, Dr. Vittorio must remain aboard ship, so he entrusts Gabriela to the care of his friend the poet Tossi (Conrad Veidt); the two make for Tschou's Tearoom, where they are invited in to view a waxworks by Tschou himself. Tossi, who knows how dangerous the bazaar can be, asks the singer to wait in the rickshaw, while he checks the place out first. Inside, the poet sees a group of wax figures and, among them, one of Gabriela! Tossi runs out and brings Gabriela back in to see the figure; it is gone! Gabriela heads back to the safety of the rickshaw while a mysterious Indian (Bernhard Goetzke) — who has followed

NOTES AND QUOTES: In 1928 Richard Oswald, with whom Veidt had worked in 21 full-length motion pictures, directed (but did not produce) *Cagliostro: Leben und Liebe eines grossen Abenteurers* for Albatros-Wengeroff productions. Not surprisingly, Oswald's first choice for the title character was Veidt, who was in Hollywood, working for Universal at the time.

Nien-Sön-Ling (left) has some pointed advice for Connie. (*Das Geheimnis von Bombay*)

the couple, unseen, for some time — offers to sell Tossi the figure resembling his lady friend. During the negotiations, the rickshaw driver runs in and tells Tossi that Gabriela has vanished.

Tossi hurries outside, where he finds Gabriela sitting peacefully in the rickshaw. Unbeknownst to the poet, the Indian, Hobbins— the lover of the dancer, Concha (Lil Dagover)— has had the idea of substituting Gabriela for Concha, who is currently hiding from the Indian police in connection with the robbery and murder of a rajah. Gabriela was snatched from the rickshaw and taken to an underground chamber, which can only be entered through a secret trapdoor. Hence, when Tossi finally makes his way out of the tearoom, he is met by Concha, who is now wearing Gabriela's clothing. The poet is completely taken in by the masquerade, and it is only later that he becomes aware of what has happened. While he and Dr. Vittorio rush to rescue her, Gabriela is forced to dance in Concha's place at Tschou's tearoom.

Hobbins has sent an anonymous tip to the police, who arrive at the tearoom and arrest the woman they believe to be Concha. A rich American, who also believes her to be the dancer with whom he is in love, rescues her from the police. When he learns the truth, he takes her back to her ship, which is on the verge of sailing. Back at the tearoom, Tossi gets between the police and Concha (whom he believes to be Gabriela) and is shot for his trouble. When Concha tries to flee in the confusion, she is shot down as well.

REVIEWS: "[This is] an adventure picture with exotic trappings [which should] appeal to the public. Both in terms of plot and exposition, it's straight out of the *Herrin der Welt* (*Mistress of the World*) school. The story is captivating, and, gratefully, the acts are brief, without any unnecessary padding... The underlying framework of this... production is extraordinarily lovely and stylish, even if [it is] really more Chinese than it is Indian. The only fault is the inadequacy of a painted backdrop [representing] the harbor.

"In the double role of chanteuse and dancer, Lil Dagover demonstrates not only that she is indeed very beautiful, but also that she is a mistress of mime, capable of any number of surprises and possibilities. Despite their uncanny resemblance, her characters were both completely different from each other and thoroughly developed.... Conrad Veidt as the poet Tossi [is] very effective, and Bernhard Goetzke is first rate in his get up as the Indian adventurer."

Der Kinematograph, 1921

"The 'Decla' discovered the Orient. This time around, India is the scene. We let those who are more capable judge the authenticity of the foreign customs, and are content, like children, to simply adore the beautiful pictures. And there are a lot of them. Artur Holz had enough material and made full use of it. Conrad Veidt plays the poet as a devoted youth, avoiding all sarcastic sharpness…"

Der Film, No. 2; 8 January 1921

"The acting is excellent. Conrad Veidt [is] restrained and dreamy, playing simply but impressively, the performance of a total film expert…"

Film-Kurier, 7 January 1921

Menschen im Rausch

[LOST] *People in Ecstasy*— subtitled: **Film-tragödie**—1920/21; Internationale Filmindustrie GmbH (Intern-Film), Heidelberg; Filmed at Interfilm Studios, Heidelberg-Schlierbach; World premiere: 6 January 1921 Motivhaus, Berlin; *Zensur*: 12 January 1921— 5 Acts, 1905 meters; Forbidden to adolescents
CAST: Conrad Veidt *the Composer, Professor Munk*; Aenne [Ullstein] Gebharda *Asta*; Grete Berger *Frau Munk*; Julius Geisendörfer *Anton*; Klara von Mühlen *Gina, Fraulein Munk*; Fritz Alberti *Feld*; Robert Garrison *Theater-Agent*; Heinz Ullmann *Dr. Ritter*; with Atti Ottendörfer
CREDITS: *Assoc. Producer* Conny Carstennsen-Wirth; *Director* Julius Geisendörfer; *Scenario* Dr. Artur Landesberger; *Photographed by* Ernst Vachenauer; *Set Design* Walter Reutlinger

SYNOPSIS: Professor Munk (Conrad Veidt) is a most successful composer. One day, he attends a premiere, leaving his wife (Grete Berger) and daughter (Klara von Mühlen) at home. After the performance, he meets Asta (Aenne Gebharda), a young woman in the street; she pleads with him to save her from a lover, who follows her every night into the club where she performs. Blinded by her beauty, he takes her with him; his wife and daughter await his return home in vain.

Asta is likewise blinded — by Munk's wealth. She persuades him to divorce his wife and marry her, hoping to become a

celebrated artist through his famous name. During a performance, however, the two are hissed at, even though Munk is at the keyboard.

The professor's relations try to prevent his decline, but they cannot. Making matters worse, Professor Munk's nephew also falls victim to Asta's great charms.

Grown old before his time, Munk crumbles completely following the death of his first wife, Asta having already left him. Reduced to playing the violin in the same honky-tonk that Asta came from, he meets up with her again and strangles her in a fit of madness.

REVIEWS: "This thrilling picture follows the themes from Dr. Artur Landsberger's novel. Conrad Veidt's performance as Professor Munk is true to life, believable, and thought out to the limit. Veidt is a great artist… The photography is sharp and some splendid scenes result."

Der Kinematograph (Düsseldorf)— Frank Goetz

"The script finds the essential role, the keynote part… and there is only one — Conrad Veidt. His figure, his whitened temples and the juvenile face conspire to form a great contrast. He gives style to the whole film, even to the theme, itself; but he is all alone, without any coactors of equal balance…"

Film-Kurier, 7 January 1921

"The Heidelberger-Film-Industry is distributing a five-act [film] written by Artur Landesberger. It deals with the tragedy that befalls a successful composer, who, his temples already gray, is torn from a long, happy and harmonic marriage by a devil of a woman. He does *not* garner new artistic inspiration from this experience, however. On the contrary, through the woman's cunning and total disregard for him, he is pulled down from the artistic heights, loses his reputation, is thrown

Aenne Gebharda and Connie: original program cover. (*Menschen im Rausch*)

over by her, and becomes a lowly musician. When, one day, he finds her again, this woman he rescued from the gutter and who now rolls in luxury, he strangles her in a mad, hateful frenzy.

REVIEW: "Conrad Veidt portrays the musician. Not for the first time does he portray a weary, aging artist, so [the viewer] won't find his palette enriched. But when one adds what is already familiar to that which is newly experienced, once again there is a portrait of sharpness and intensity. The wife is played by Greta Berger-Ly [*sic*], who ought to become better known as a wonderful character actress... Aenne Gebharda is the cat, partly Orska [actress Maria Orska], partly [Asta] Nielsen to a lesser extent, herself; but equipped in equal parts with emotion and style, and completely qualified to make the part her own. Typically, Julius Geisendörfer withheld a little too much from the pimp to make him seem fully human. The unbilled composer's son-in-law offered a semicaricature of [Reinhold] Schünzel and should start a row over not being credited.

"The director was Geisendörfer. The settings were well chosen throughout, properly framed, not overloaded, and rich in variety."

Unknown review

Der Leidensweg der Inge Krafft

[LOST] *The Suffering of Inge Krafft*; May-Film GmbH, Berlin, 1920-1921; Filmed at May-Film-Atelier, Berlin-Weissensee; *Zensur*: 8 March 1921— 5 Acts, 2095 meters; Forbidden to adolescents; World premiere: 11 March 1921 Tauentzien-Palast, Berlin

CAST: Conrad Veidt *Hendryk Overland*; Mia May *Inge Krafft*; Albert Steinrück *the Prince*; Heinz Stieda *Harry Rhaden*; Margarete Schön *Dagmar*; with Paul Rehkopf, Harry Frank, Adolf Klein, Paul Passarge, Hermann Leffler, Waldemar Pottier, Lia Eibenschütz, Sylvia Torf, Harry Hardt

CREDITS: *Producer* Joe May; *Director* Robert Dinesen (Reinert); *Scenario* Joe May; *Based on an idea by* Thea von Harbou; *Photographed by* Sophus Wangoe; *Set Designs* Otto Hunte

SYNOPSIS: Young, pretty Inge Krafft (Mia May) is in love with Hendryk Overland (Conrad Veidt), but she still piques the interest of a Russian prince. Seeing a chance to save her father from financial ruin, she breaks her engagement to Overland and marries the prince (Albert Steinrück), going off with him to his estates in the Caucasus. The prince is brutal and domineering; Inge feels inadequate and isolated. She begins to take long rides on horseback, and — on one of these — she comes upon the hovel of a young shepherd, whom she finds attractive.

After a while, noticing her absences, the prince follows Inge, and he surprises her with her shepherd. The shepherd is shot and Inge is tossed to the estate workers, who rape her before chasing her off the grounds. Inge seeks to find peace by taking the veil, but — before she can take her vows— Overland turns up and asks that he be allowed to speak to her. He is preparing for a years-long expedition to new Zealand, and convinces Inge to come live with his sister for the duration. Inge agrees and is taken to Overland's sister, Dagmar (Margarete Schön), and her husband, the composer Harry Rhaden (Heinz Stieda). With the happily married couple, it's expected that she will recover her spirit without so drastic a move as taking religious vows.

After some months, terrible news arrives: the expedition has been attacked by savages and has been decimated. Shortly thereafter Dagmar's son accidentally drowns, and, unable to cope with this, Overland's delicate sister is taken to an asylum, where she is pronounced incurably insane. Harry and Inge grow closer due to their grief, and some time later they prepare to be married. On the very day of the wedding, however, Overland appears. A bit taken aback by the proceedings, he makes for the asylum where — upon seeing him — Dagmar miraculously regains her sanity.

Overland phones Harry with the good news that he is bringing Dagmar back home with him, but warns Harry to say nothing of his second marriage to her. Inge is willing to sacrifice herself, but Harry —

Hendryk Overland (Connie) at a low point while on expedition. (*Der Leidensweg der Inge Krafft*)

his passions aroused — vehemently objects. Despairing of finding a solution to the situation, Inge throws herself out the window. Overland rushes to her side. Dying, she swears her love for him and asks that she be buried in the cloister.

REVIEWS: "The May-Film Company has found a truly sensitive and perceptive collaborator in Thea von Harbou. Her scenarios are exquisitely simple and clear in both plot development and character outline. These are absolutely essential quali-ties for the feature film. Here, we have splendid sets, exceptional photography and magnificent performances by the cast, all of which help to classify this May film as a masterpiece...

"Mia May has the lead, and, as always, she is not only one of the most beautiful of actresses, but also one of the most technically perfect actresses for this kind of film. Her acting is natural and true to life; her vivid eyes and eloquent gestures express her every emotion... Conrad Veidt, as outstanding a portrayer of characters as ever, [plays] Hendryk.

"There can be nothing but praise for the direction and the cinematography."

Der Kinematograph, No. 735;
20 March 1921

"After *Die Frauen von Greifenstein*, May-Film tries yet again to adapt a psychological condition for the screen… Compared with the first film, [this picture] is a step forward, no doubt, but the psychology is treated only in passing, as it were… Not actual kitsch, but not art, either.

"Robert Dinesen's direction is very detailed; he works meticulously and makes excellent use of the actors' qualities. The brutality of Steinrück needs no special emphasis, but Margarete Schön's reserve is remedied by him. Apart from his talent, Conrad Veidt is just what is needed in the role; he has many strong moments."

Der Film, No. 11; 1921

"If a young lady is determined to make her life a life of suffering, there is absolutely no reason to force the German cinema patrons to do the same. The only mitigating circumstance in this case is the really excellent direction of Robert Dinesen…"

Deutsche Lichtspielzeitung,
No. 12; 19 March 1921

"Audiences in Bomst, Meseritz and the surrounding areas will again completely enjoy the lovely blonde, Mia May. *The Suffering of Inge Krafft*, which stretches from the cloister through life and into Africa and Europe, hurls us back to 1914 and the times of glorious cinematic twaddle.

"Without a doubt, this film will become a box-office hit, and there is also no doubt that the script — on the [premiere] invitation, Thea von Harbou's name appears, although it is coyly concealed in the credits — is aimed at reaching the masses. [This is] regrettable, actually, because Robert Dinesen's excellent direction provides shots of outstanding rural beauty in both location scenes and decorative interiors. As far as the leading roles go, the acting is stirring throughout. This time, Conrad Veidt avoids decadent impact, which has become almost a given with him. He shows control, moderation, and he doesn't serve the cliché (with which we have become accustomed), but the human being, just as the author of the film had envisioned. Beside him stands Albert Steinrück, who was entrusted with [the role of] the Caucasian pasha, which he portrayed with astounding virtuosity.

"Mia May, for whom the film was written, adjusts to her cast in a fashion that is exemplary for star-cinema. Nonetheless, she's given the chance to show off some excellent dramatics. She gives the strongest support to the whole enterprise, without allowing her contributions to come forth obtrusively.

"A prominent personality in the film industry recently coined a splendid dictum: 'When it's not applauded, it's literature.' Yesterday evening, there was enormous applause."

Unknown review —
"Aros" (Alfred Rosenthal)

Die Liebschaften des Hektor Dalmore

[LOST] *The Love Affairs of Hector Dalmore*; Richard Oswald-Film GmbH, Berlin, 1920/21; World premiere (Special showing for theater owners/exhibitors): 22 February 1921 Richard-Oswald-Lichtspiele, Berlin; *Zensur*: 25 February 1921 — 6 Acts, 2045 meters; Forbidden to adolescents

CAST: Conrad Veidt *Hektor Dalmore*; Lia [Lya de] Putti *Zofe*; Erna Morena *Theresa*; Kitty Moran *Errie*; Helene Ford *Lela*; Maja Servos *Lona*; Sascha Gura *Rosanna*; Aenne Ullstein

Erna Morena is just one of the six women Connie manages to juggle as Hektor Dalmore. (*Die Liebschaften des Hektor Dalmore*)

Magde; Otto Bennefeld *Hektor's Double*; Henry Sze *Servant*; Hans Junkermann *Theresa's Husband*; Anton Pointner *Young Man*; Preben Rist, Georg Langer *Two Scoundrels*

CREDITS: *Producer/Director* Richard Oswald; *Scenario* Richard Oswald; *Photographed by* Otto Kanturek; *Set Design* Hans Dreier

SYNOPSIS: Hektor Dalmore (Conrad Veidt) enjoys the company of *six* women, who fight each other like cats and dogs over the lucky man. He can take it or leave it; half cynic, half Lothario, he finds his adventures amusing. Nonetheless, he knows enough to avoid serious consequences— there are concerned fathers who insist on engagement as they fear for their daughters' honor, and jealous husbands who insist on duels fearing for their own honor; he employs a double to take his place at times such as these.

At one point, his double (Otto Bennefeld) goes off for an assignation with a young woman whose father is eager to marry her off. While this is unfolding, Hektor is pursuing another woman — Rosanna (Erna Morena) — who is prim, quite respectable, and married. At first, his attempts to woo and win her are in vain. Slowly, however, the lady begins to come around.

All goes awry when the husband (Hans Junkermann) discovers what has been going on and demands satisfaction. Things get worse when Hektor's double hands in his resignation, as he has fallen in love with one of the women he was hired to deceive. Tragically, Hektor is then made to fight a duel with the husband of the woman he has been chasing, and is killed.

REVIEWS: "Once again, Richard Oswald has made the right choice for his films... He knows what the public wants and he knows how to give it to them. His latest picture, *Die Liebschaften des Hektor Dalmore*, is quite witty and unusual; one enjoys it as it unreels, not knowing what will transpire next. It's a little risqué,

and — unfortunately — more than a little bit sentimental.

"The picture begins with an explosion of humor — lighting up like a *Don Juan* film — but it ends on a false note, like a joke without a punch line. You wait ... for the crowning moment in this tale of ardor and adventure, smiling at [Hektor's] situations and even chuckling at the acts of knavery which could very well lead to catastrophe. But that crowning moment — although totally unexpected — fails to satisfy; it's an easy way out, even a little dull.

"Conrad Veidt plays Hektor Dalmore with disarming cheek and studied insouciance. Erna Morena stands out (of the array of beautiful women) as the respectable wife... and Sascha Gura also as the voluptuous woman at the bar. Lia Putti gives legs to a pretty little maid (and those are quite shapely legs, too). Henry Sze offers a puckish Chinese manservant...

"Oswald's direction deftly manipulates this convoluted love story. The sets and photography are in veterans' hands and nothing more could be desired [from them]."

Der Kinematograph
(Düsseldorf), No. 733;
6 March 1921

"A modern Boccaccio plays with the superficialities of his theme, only to invoke tragic justice suddenly at the end. Another genuine Oswald, with an original idea, roughly sketched, just what the audience likes... Conrad Veidt in the title role [is] absorbingly human, as always..."

Der Film, No. 9; 26 February 1921

Landstrasse und Grossstadt

[LOST] *Country Roads and the Big City*; subtitled: **Musikanten des Lebens** (*Musicians of Life*); Carl Wilhelm-Film GmbH, Berlin, 1921;

Distributed by Terra-Film AG, Berlin; *Zensur*: 21 April 1921— 6 Acts, 2218 meters; Forbidden to adolescents; World premiere: 22 April 1921 Terra-Theater, Berlin

CAST: Conrad Veidt *Raphael Strate*; Fritz Kortner *Mendel Hammerstein*; Carola Toelle *Maria*; with Franz Schönemann, Richard Georg, Edmund Heinek

CREDITS: *Director* Carl Wilhelm; *Scenario* Dimitri Buchowetzki; *Sets* Karl L. Kirmse; *Photographed by* Carl Hoffmann

SYNOPSIS: The country road sometimes makes strange partners of people: violinist Raphael Strate (Conrad Veidt), for example, has thrown his lot in with organ grinder Mendel Hannerstein (Fritz Kortner) and the timid Maria (Carola Toelle), who has taken to the road after being beaten by her aunt. The trio is headed to the big city, where jobs may be easier to find and life ought to be more worth living.

Fortune smiles on them.

A wealthy man becomes Raphael's patron, and the violinist soon gains renown. Mendel, always a practical and realistic man, becomes Raphael's business manager, and — before long — the men open a large musical concert agency. Then... disaster! Raphael's hand is slashed during a robbery attempt at night. Unable to play his violin, he watches his livelihood wither; he soon becomes horribly depressed. Maria stands by him during his time of trial, while Mendel — who has always desired Maria and has been jealous of Raphael — turns his back on his comrade. Although she despises him, Maria secretly becomes Mendel's mistress, so that with the money and gifts she receives, she can care financially for Raphael, whom she has always loved.

Raphael does recover slowly, however, and, after a few years, he finds that he can once again play with his former artistry. At a soiree thrown by Mendel, Raphael and Maria find themselves together, and the seeds of their love for each other blossom immediately. Mendel, outraged and appalled at what he sees, is felled by a heart attack.

REVIEWS: "This unusually touching film is the result of both cinematic instinct and a touch of *La Bohème*. The heady progress made by the three is a bit unlikely, especially their quick jump from rustic roots to ultramodern sophistication. Still, meticulous attention to the smallest details — along with the exquisite direction and brilliant cast — makes one forget such quibbles...

"Conrad Veidt and Fritz Kortner play the musicians. Veidt is the dreamy idealist. Kortner's Jewish organ grinder is a pragmatist, and, in his becoming a social 'upstart,' [the actor] shows his great range of characterization. Along with them is the quiet yet elegant Carola Toelle, who [is] a natural for roles such as these.

"Designer Kirmse has created some wonderful settings for the office sequences as well as appropriate vistas for the scenes on the country road. A good part of the success of the film is due to the extraordinarily sharp photography."

Der Kinematograph, No. 741; 1 May 1921

"Carl Wilhelm presented his new six-act film, with a scenario by Dimitri Buchowetzki... a top quality film, based on the excellence of the acting, coming from a unique trio of players: Conrad Veidt, Fritz Kortner and Carola Toelle... The simple theme is imbued with Kortner's natural humor. Conrad Veidt's versatile sensitivity and Carola Toelle's charm and warmth add harmony of their own. Carl Wilhelm has succeeded not only in toning down the play, but also in increasing the thrills by deviating from the subject's straightforward approach several times."

Der Film, No. 17; 1921

"*Landstrasse und Grossstadt*, a film I consider tolerable in terms of plot and direction, without spotting any particular style, which probably was far from what was intended. Kortner was excellent, as almost always, and Carola Toelle was somewhat too spherical [?]. Conrad Veidt got on my nerves with his—Christ!—interminable air of megalomania. During the first acts, the photography was beneath contempt!"

Unknown review

"The Terra-Cinema is showing a Carl-Wilhelm-Film with the title *Landstrasse und Grossstadt*. The subject: Two poor musicians come to the big city; through happenstance, the violist's talent is revealed. He becomes a celebrated virtuoso while his colleague rises as his impresario. Coming between them is Maria, who loves the violinist, who is being robbed by the impresario; she finally finds her way back into his arms… Closeup; the end. Well, the plot would have been tolerable had it stemmed from the hands of a capable director who would have crafted three tight acts. Instead, three long acts were added which undermined our patience with their tiresome unimportance and boundless repetition.

"Fritz Kortner alone was somewhat able to reconcile things… Conrad Veidt as the violinist had lots of opportunities to cast demonic looks while wearing peculiar, archaic dress clothes. Carola Toelle is Maria. She has an enormous assortment of dresses and a rather small array of expressions. This, however, may be due to the fact that this 'tragic play' had her playing a Madonna in décolletage. She should be more careful in choosing her film roles from now on."

Unknown review—"Pol"

"A splendid film: an interesting fable, with excellent direction and outstanding performances. Carl Wilhelm deserves the top prize—about 10 years ago he started a suburban studio at Bolten-Baeckers. Leo

Peukert, the amiable Mizzi Parla—who remembers this famous singer of gay parts from Vienna?—and Rudolf Christians, who died in America, all acted in that small studio at the same time, while I struggled with the beginnings of aesthetic cinema. Today Carl Wilhelm is at the summit and has a company bearing his name that is affiliated with the excellent Terra-Konzern. He found and still has the opportunity to release his artful projects. When Wilhelm acquired (with an eye to filming it) Dimitri Buchowetzki's manuscript, which bore the subtitle *Musicians of Life*, he immediately realized that only first-rate acting would be proper for the delicate psychological plot. Hence, he called Fritz Kortner, Conrad Veidt, and Carola Toelle…

"Conrad Veidt brings profound warmth to the violinist, something Christlike, a nervous spirituality that is the direct opposite of the rough, brutal, cunning huskiness of Fritz Kortner's hurdy-gurdy man. Besides these two strong, impressive performances stands the Maria of Carola Toelle. She has never been as good as she is in this picture, showing tender loveliness and feminine charm while brimming with melancholy… Like Karl Hoffmann's photography, Karl L. Kirmse's exterior settings are very good.

"The film was the kind of joy one only rarely experiences."

Unknown review—L.F.K.

Lady Hamilton

[LOST] Richard Oswald-Film AG, Berlin—1921; Distributed by National-Film; *Zensur*: 15 October 1921—7 Acts, 3673 meters; Subsequently recut to 3667.4 meters; Forbidden to adolescents; World premiere: 20 October 1921 Richard-Oswald-Lichtspiele AND Marmorhaus, Berlin

CAST: Conrad Veidt *Lord Nelson*; Liane Haid *Emma Lyon, later Lady Hamilton*; Werner

Krauss *Lord William Hamilton*; Reinhold Schünzel *Ferdinand IV, King of Naples*; Else Heims *Marie Caroline, Queen of Naples*; Anton Pointer *Greville*; Julie Serda *Adele Nelson*; Georg Alexander *George, Prince of Wales*; Paul Bildt *Caraciollo, King's Minister*; Theodor Loos *George Romney, a Famous Artist*; Hans Heinrich von Twardowski *Joshua Nesbit, Nelson's Stepson*; Gertrud Welcker *Miss Arabella Kelly*; Adele Sandrock *Headmistress*; Käte Waldeck-Oswald *Jane Middleton*; Hugo Döblin *Dr. Graham*; Celly de Rheydt *Phryne*; Heinrich George *Captain Sir John Willet Payne*; Friedrich Kühne *Tug*; Louis Ralph *Tom Kid*; Ilka Grüning *Landlady*; Claire Krona *Emma Lyons' Mother*; Max Adalbert, Hanns Sturm, Max Gülstorff *Three Beggars*; Rudolf Meinhard-Jünger, Karl Geppert *Barbers*; Adolf Klein *Minister of the Navy*; Karl Platen *King's Valet*; with Georg John, Karl Römer, Clementine Plessner

CREDITS: *Producer/Director* Richard Oswald; *Scenario* Richard Oswald; *Based on the novels* Liebe und Leben der Lady Hamilton *and* Lord Nelsons letzte Liebe *by* Heinrich Vollrath Schumacher; *Photographed by* Carl Hoffmann; *Asst. Photographer* Karl Voss; *Set Designs* Paul Leni; *Set Construction* Hans Dreier; *Costumes* Paul Leni, Hans Dreier

SYNOPSIS: The life of Emma Lyon (Liane Haid) does not start off very promisingly. She is poor, but is more than beautiful and charming enough to compensate for her poverty. These qualities—and a couple of coincidences—make it possible for her to meet Lord Hamilton (Werner Krauss), who falls in love with and then marries her. On Emma's part, this is a loveless union; her husband is a conceited, mildly inept diplomat. Still, she follows him to the court of Ferdinand IV, King of Naples (Reinhold Schünzel), where, thanks to her beauty and charm, she soon becomes a court favorite.

It is an open secret that Emma is passionately in love with Horatio Nelson (Conrad Veidt), British hero and head of the admiralty. Nelson—himself married—is Emma's true love, and he believes her to be the real reason for his many successes. Lord Hamilton turns a blind eye to the affair, as he is both afraid of losing his position should he offend the British hero and proud of the influence he wields by being the husband of such a celebrated woman.

The strange ménage à trois ends when revolution breaks out in France. Afraid for his life, Ferdinand turns to Britain for help, but receives no assurances. Now terrified, the King of Naples dismisses the British ambassador. Hamilton is devastated; he seeks revenge on Emma and Lord Nelson, whom he somehow regards as the cause of all his trouble.

As he cannot harm Nelson himself, he influences the admiralty to send him out to sea. With the naval hero out of the way, Hamilton confronts Emma: apart from Lord Nelson, what does she love most? Power? Riches? Knowing that he hasn't much time left, Hamilton strips his wife of her title and position, screaming that he has always known that she betrayed him, cuckolded him. Emma stays calm, regretting none of the loss; all she wants and needs is Nelson's love. She leaves the dying Hamilton as she was when she first met him, poor, and returns to England to meet the love of her life again.

Penniless and bearing in her arms her and Nelson's child, she awaits his return from the Battle of Trafalgar. Bad news travels fast, however. Although Napoleon has been defeated, Nelson has been shot in battle, and has died—a picture of Emma in his hand. The former Lady Hamilton collapses in the London streets, unnoticed by the jubilant crowds, celebrating the victory at sea.

REVIEWS: "The first Richard Oswald million-mark production—and, at the same time—the film that spurred the most heated discussions, pro and con, even before its release, had its premiere at both the Marmorhaus and the Richard-Oswald-Lichtspiele at the same time. It was, one must mention at the outset, a remarkable success in both locations, with much spon-

Blind in one eye and missing an arm, Connie's Lord Nelson gets comfortable on Emma Lyon's shoulder. Emma (Liane Haid) seems none the worse for wear. (*Lady Hamilton*)

taneous applause during the showings. Because of its strengths and weaknesses, [it is] a film that cannot easily be compared with others. There are scenes that look like Hogarth engravings or Teniers paintings come to life... Another strength, the brilliant palette of vivid ideas, big and small, almost becomes a 'packed topic'—a disadvantage.

"On the whole, however, Oswald's 'leap' into the historical costume film succeeds remarkably well... Regarding the acting, what Oswald has achieved with Liane Haid, who plays the role of Emma, is amazing. If she cannot compete with Conrad Veidt's monumental Nelson and fails to show [her side] as an ambitious politician, it is her own fault..."

Der Film, No. 43;
23 October 1921

"...This is an interesting story of ... a ... greengrocer's daughter [who], through love affairs, finally achieved the station of Lady Hamilton and her affair with Lord Nelson, by whom she had a child just prior to her husband's death. And, oh boy, the manner in which it is done! Even in the American censored version there is enough to slip the thrills over the plate when it comes to the undraped...."

Variety, 6 December 1923 — Fred.

"Like most historical films, this one [attempts to] confine itself to the objective recording of events, but mixes anecdotes in with historical records and burdens itself with too many petty details, thus giving too much and too little at the same time... Apart from this, as a plain and simple historical costume picture it is a remarkable affair. Where an actual 'on the spot' item was lacking, Paul Leni (design) and Hans Dreier (execution) created an effective substitute…

"The program lists so many famous actors that one can only note that even the smallest part is played by an excellent actor. The best performance was Conrad Veidt as Admiral Nelson…"

Der Kinematograph, No. 767;
30 October 1921—
Ludwig Brauner

"… The dramatic tension in evidence [in *Lady Hamilton*] enjoys great success due to the excellent teamwork of the three principals. …Top marks in terms of performance go to Conrad Veidt. His face, battered with pain from war injuries, with passion and ambition, remains unforgettable…."

Unknown review

"Richard Oswald's direction is masterly, his seven acts varied and colorful… It has been proven that Conrad Veidt belongs to the strongest forces in motion pictures today. He is, perhaps, the actor with the deepest understanding of film. His every motion becomes a pictorial effect. His mime and the glint of his eye express everything to such a degree that text titles seem unnecessary…"

8 Uhr *Abendblatt*,
24 October 1921

"The biggest success in this film is Conrad Veidt. The conclusion we can draw, after all the premieres [we've had] so far this year, is that—from the perspective of acting—Conny is the top. Maybe we imagined Nelson, the admiral, differently, but Nelson, the man, cannot be thought of differently…"

Berliner Lokal-Anzeiger,
24 October 1921

NOTES AND QUOTES: *Lady Hamilton* enjoyed extensive location shooting, as producer Richard Oswald was determined that director Richard Oswald should have every opportunity to display the essence of the scenario (of writer Richard Oswald) against authentic backdrops. Thus, not only did cinematographers Hoffmann and Voss shoot extensive background plates in a variety of locales (including Hamburg and Lübeck, Germany; Naples, Rome and Florence, Italy; and sundry vistas in England), but the principals went along for the ride(s). Made at the outset of Germany's fling with *Kostümfilme*, *Lady Hamilton* would prove that Oswald hadn't lost the knack of latching onto popular, new genres that he had demonstrated several years before, with his *Aufklärungsfilme*.

Per *Films in Review* (October 1958): *Lady Hamilton* "…was sold to the US for $175,000 before the final editing, on the strength of the first rough cut" (p. 446). As the *Variety* review quoted above was printed some *two years* after the film's German premiere, one can only guess at the arduousness of the process of converting the German original to a format that would be understood and enjoyed by American audiences. For all that, *Lady Hamilton*—like virtually all foreign-language releases at the time—played exclusively in American "art houses," where it attracted only a fraction of the viewers it had at home.

Austrian actress Liane Haid (1895–2000) started her professional life as a dancer. Graduating to the legitimate stage in her native Vienna—as well as in Budapest and Berlin—she was discovered in 1917 by the *Erste Wiener Kunstfilmgesellshaft*, for which concern she made some 18 films. Haid moved to Germany in late 1919, where her film career began in earnest. In *Lady Hamilton*, the actress essayed the title role, appearing on-screen with some of the country's most renowned film personalities. Haid retired from the film industry in the early 1950s, when she moved to Fribourg, Switzerland. She died in Bern several months past her 105th birthday.

Das indische Grabmal

The Indian Tomb (aka *Mysteries of India; Above All Law*); May-Film GmbH, Berlin—1921; Photographed at the Jofa Studios (Berlin-Johannisthal), May-Film Studios (Berlin-Weissensee), and at "May-Film-City" (Wolterdorf); Distributed by Ufa
    CAST: Conrad Veidt *Ayan, the Maharajah of Bengal*; Olaf Fönss *Herbert Rowland*; Mia May *Irene, his Fiancée*; Erna Morena *Savitri, the Maharani*; Bernhard Goetzke *The Yogi, Ramigani*; Lya de Putti *Mirrjha*; Paul Richter *Mac Allan, an English Officer*; Karl Platen *Rowland's Servant*; Hermann Picha *Professor Leyden*; Wilhelm Diegelmann *Captain*; Georg John *Penitent*; Lewis Brody *Black Servant*; with Wolfgang von Schwind, Max Adalbert
    CREDITS: *Producers* Joe May, Robert Wüllner (and Erich Pommer, Pt. 1 only); *Directors* Gunnar Tollnes, Joe May; *Photographed by* Werner Brandes, Karl Puth; *Screenplay* Fritz Lang; *Based on the eponymous novel by* Thea von Harbou; *Art Direction* Erich Kettelhut, Karl Vollbrecht; *Sets* Otto Hunte, Martin Jacoby-Boy; *Costumes* Martin Jacoby-Boy; *Musical Score for theaters* Wilhelm Löwitt

2 parts: Part I—*Die Sendung des Yoghi* (120 mins.); *Zensur*: 20 October 1921—6 Acts, 2957 meters; Forbidden to adolescents; World premiere: 22 October 1921 Ufa-Palast am Zoo, Berlin

    SYNOPSIS: Ayan (Conrad Veidt), Maharajah of Bengal, has lost his wife, Savitri (Erna Morena)—who was everything in the world to him — not to death, but to an English officer, Mac Allen (Paul Richter). Torn between grief and a thirst for revenge, he decides to build a monument to the love he has lost.

    He awakens Ramigani (Bernhard Goetzke), a yogi who has buried himself alive in his quest for perfection. Now Ramigani, according to the holy rules, must fulfill the wish of the one who has awakened him. Ayan commands the yogi to travel to England, where he is to fetch the well-known architect Herbert Rowland (Olaf Fönss), without having anyone near and dear to Rowland — especially his fiancée, Irene (Mia May) — know of his mission. Ramigani, who can see into the future, warns the maharajah against carrying out his plan, but Ayan will not be moved.

    It is not long after arriving in India that Rowland learns that the monument he is building is meant to be a tomb for a woman still alive, and that the maharajah plans to kill his wife and enshrine her within. The architect asks to be relieved of his duties and to be allowed to return to England, but Ayan refuses.

    At this moment, Irene disembarks in India. She overheard part of the conversation the yogi held with her fiancé, and followed him across the world. The maharajah receives her in his palace, and asks that she not yet inform Rowland of her arrival, so that he might concentrate fully on his work. Ayan cannot help notice that Irene is quite beautiful, and his attentions terrify her. Repulsed by the maharajah's approach, she flees through the labyrinth of walls and corridors. Rowland spots her as she runs past and follows her. In the dark, he accidentally runs into a fakir, who curses him: "Your white skin shall be eaten by leprosy!"

    Both Irene and Rowland are brought back to their rooms. Through a servant, Rowland learns of the danger facing Mac Allen and Savitri, so he tries to bargain: he will build the tomb, if and when Mac Allen and Savitri are released, unharmed. But Ramigani reveals the power of India's mys-

Opposite: **Ayan interrupts his wife at prayer. The maharajah is clearly upset with Savitri (Erna Morena). (*Das indische Grabmal*)**

Connie as Ayan, the maharajah who builds a monument to lost love. (*Das indische Grabmal*)

ticism: "You won't be building any tomb. You have leprosy, sahib."

Part II—*Der Tiger von Eschnapur* (100 mins.); *Zensur*: 17 November 1921—7 Acts, 2534 meters; Forbidden to adolescents; World premiere: 19 November 1921 Ufa-Palast am Zoo, Berlin

SYNOPSIS: Irene, who has not heard of Rowland's condition, asks Ayan that she be allowed to see her fiancé. He agrees and shows her Rowland, suffering in the 'Hall of Lepers.' Ayan leads Irene to believe that it was her fault that her love will have to suffer and die, as a consequence of her running away from the maharajah. When she asks whether there is anything she can do to save the leprous man, Ayan replies that she must sacrifice herself to the god of penitence. In the temple she watches as Ramigani mystically cures Rowland, and then she draws a knife to sacrifice herself, per the bargain. Ayan stops her, still want-

ing her alive so that he may love her. He allows her to see Rowland.

Having done all that has been demanded of him, Ramigani departs, but not before warning Ayan once again that he will have his revenge, but at the cost of everything he holds dear.

Meanwhile, Mac Allen, who has been captured in the jungles by Ayan's hunters, has been returned to the palace. The Englishman escapes from the dungeon and wanders throughout the palace corridors. Savriti's faithful servant finds him and brings him to Rowland and Irene. The palace guards storm the room, however, and Ayan orders Mac Allen to follow him. Irene pleads for mercy, and the maharajah seemingly relents: "No human being will harm him." Ayan is true to his word. The officer is hurled into a tigers' den, and Savitri is forced to watch as her lover is savaged by Bengal tigers.

Rowland and Irene conspire to escape from the palace, and resolve to take Savitri with them. Making their way through the jungle, they come to a canyon, but Ayan and his trackers are not far behind. Rowland and Savitri make it to the other side of the canyon, but Irene, who has been running behind them, is seized by Ayan. The maharajah then demands that Rowland come back with him. Before the architect can stop her, Savitri throws herself into the canyon in order to save Irene.

Rowland builds the monument to Savitri and leaves India with Irene. Ayan, however, has fulfilled Ramigani's prophecy. Completely broken in spirit, he spends his days—garbed in penitential robes—sitting on the steps of the tomb.

REVIEWS: "What makes this film so charming is the sharp photographic composition of the shots, the balance (even in terms of detail) of scenic and optical effects, the contrast of light and shadows, and the logical formulation of pictures. Apart from the director's vision, the designer Jacoby-Boy — who built this picturesque India from a meld of fantasy and reality — contributed a great deal to the artistic worth…"

B.Z. am Mittag,
6 November 1921

"… The audience, with its thunderous applause, was completely correct. The production is impressive, a spectacle of high style."

Berliner Boersen-Zeitung,
November 1921

"Perhaps Herr May will be pleased when we say that his new work is a worthy successor to "*Herrin der Welt*," that it is a jewel."

Berliner Lokal-Anzeiger,
November 1921

NOTES AND QUOTES: In Germany, following their separate premieres, the two parts were shown on consecutive evenings; for foreign distribution, these were edited into a single 8-reel feature and called *Mysteries of India* (later, *Above All Law*). This, presumably, was the version that was (briefly) released in the United States in 1922. David Shepard, president of Film Preservation Associates and the man who spearheaded the recent restoration of the entire *Das indische Grabmal* saga, told Veidt historian Paula Vitaris how "special negatives" were prepared for editing prior to distribution within the United States by Russian and European filmmakers:

Apparently the practice was to send over second negatives that had not been edited, along with a print of the European version as a guide, which the American distributor could follow or ignore. The distributor would then prepare these American versions with English titles, which would often be quite different from the original versions, but which were sometimes successful.

Thus was Fritz Lang's haunting fantasy *Der müde Tod* (1921) reworked when it was released (some two years later) as *Between Two Worlds* for an extremely limited run in the USA.

When questioned by Vitaris as to his opinion of Connie's performance in the saga, Shepard offered:

Conrad Veidt waltzes away with the whole movie. It's very interesting in terms of the structure of the film. A whole hour goes by before Conrad Veidt gets his entrance. In order to solve that problem, they had a scene at the very beginning which is a kind of background explication as to where the yogi Ramagani (Bernhard Goetzke) comes from. Conrad Veidt has a small part in that opening scene. So we see him at the beginning and people don't have to wait an hour to see the star. But then he really does disappear because his surrogate, the yogi, carries the action at least an hour into the film. Veidt is then reintroduced. From then on, really nobody else has to be in the movie at all.

To me the most extraordinary scene with him is the one where Irene, who is being held more or less captive in his palace, demands to see her fiancé, who is being held separately. This man [Veidt's Majarajah] is not used to hearing demands, and he is shocked at facing the demand, but he's also too inscrutable to allow us to see how shocked he is. And so Veidt does the whole thing by straightening up. His eyes get a little wider. But his performance is completely free of histrionics. He plays scenes with his eyebrows. He plays scenes with his cheekbones. It is the most astonishingly subtle performance and you absolutely can't take your eyes off him…

Joe May's *Das indische Grabmal* cost 20 million marks, and although it "confined" itself to India and normal footage, it

outdid the serials in thrilling episodes. This super-production, which imparted the same sinister moral as the Lubitsch pageants, not only adapted the miraculous practices of yoga to the screen, but showed rats gnawing on the fetters of its captive hero, elephants forming a gigantic lane and an all-out fight against tigers. Circuses at

Denna sida förkunnar nyheter av stort intresse för den svenska biografpubliken ~ ~

RIALTO-TEATERN

en av Stockholms ledande filmteatrar

visar dem.

Den **första** av dessa filmens storverk blir

Joe Mays världsberyktade film

Drömmarnas tempel.

(Das indische Grabmal)
Officin: E. F. A.
vilken får sin premiär mån-
dagen den 27 febr.

I denna film föres åskådaren in i den indiska mystikens hemlighetsfulla värld, i romantikens solskimrande rike, där kärlek, hat och ädelmod kämpa mot den råa, realistiska verkligheten.

Den **andra** av dessa blir

Kung Dam Joker

Lustspel i fem akter med **Sidney Chaplin** i huvudrollen.
Där föres åskådaren in i glädjens tempel.

Dessa filmer levereras av **Continentalfilm**, Stockholm.

Connie's German features always enjoyed tremendous popularity in Sweden. Original trade ad. (*Das indische Grabmal*)

that time made nice profits out of animal rentals [Kracauer p. 56].

As it was made prior to the invention of the Schüfftan process (a trick photography technique involving a photograph of a scale model reflected into the camera lens off an inclined mirror), Bengal — in all of its romantically envisioned enormity — was duplicated at, or greater than, life-size. From *Das grosse Biderbuch des Films* (1922/23): "Construction of the massive sets began in 'Maytown,' Joe May's Weissensee studios in Wolterdorf (outside of Berlin) in May 1920. The renowned Stosch-Sarrasani Circus provided the horses, elephants and zebras used in the production, and the Hagenbeck Zoo lent their tigers."

Fritz Lang and Thea von Harbou had written the screenplay — based on von Harbou's 1917 novel — in 1920, with the tacit understanding that Lang would direct the film. At the last moment, Joe May decided to direct it himself, citing the fact that his American investors — the Famous Players-Lasky/Paramount organization — didn't want a novice director at the helm of such a monumental production. Lang, furious at having been displaced (it's been reported that he felt May had stepped in as director because it was perceived that *Das indische Grabmal* couldn't fail) never worked with May again. Lang finally directed his and von Harbou's material himself in 1958. In the interim, the scenario had been filmed a second time (under Hitler's government) as *The Indian Tomb* (1938) by Richard Eichberg.

"These German films excel in pictorial effect because artistic Europe has eyes. Europe is all color, scenery, variety, a clash of cultures. She is theatrical — she is always looking for 'effects' ... and it is just here that pictures like *Doctor Caligari, The Mistress of the World, The Golem, The Loves of Pharaoh, The Triumph of Truth,* and *The Indian Tomb* are having their effect on American producers and directors. We need better and greater stories and more imagination in their treatment. We need more of the bizarre and the grotesque, the exotic in our productions — but always retaining those things that we have achieved and that every motion picture producer in Europe admits that we excel in — storytelling, mechanical technique and picture tempo."

"Our Domestic Movies and the Germans" by Benjamin De Casseres.
New York Times, 26 March 1922

Lucrezia Borgia

(aka *Cesare Borgia*; *Lukrezia Borgia*); Richard Oswald-Film AG, Berlin —1922; Filmed at Ufa-Messter-Atelier, Berlin-Tempelhof; Distributed by Hugo Engel/Universum-Film-Verleih GmbH; *Zensur*: 6 October 1922 — 7 Acts, 3286 meters, then recut to 3284.4 meters (Other sources indicate 2191 meters after censorship); Forbidden to adolescents; World premiere: 20 October 1922 Marmorhaus, Berlin, *and* Richard-Oswald-Lichtspiele, Berlin (Other sources aver the premiere was held on 23 October 1922 at the Ufa-Palast am Zoo, Berlin); US Distributor (1928) — Unusual Photoplays

CAST: Conrad Veidt *Cesare Borgia*; Albert Bassermann *Pope Alexander VI*; Anita Berber *Countess Julia Orsini*; Wilhelm Dieterle *Giovanni Sforza*; Alfons Fryland *Alfonso, Prince of Aragon*; Heinrich George *Sebastiano*; Liane Haid *Lucrezia Borgia*; Alexander Granach *a Prisoner*; Lothar Müthel *Juan Borgia*; Lyda Salmonova *Diabola*; Adele Sandrock *Abbess*; Wilhelm Diegelmann *Wirt*; Adolf Edgar *Licho*; Max Pohl *Fratelli, an Armorer*; Hugo Döblin *Cesare's Servant*; Käthe Waldeck-Oswald *Naomi*; Clementine Plessner *Mrs. Fratelli*; Mary Douce *Florentina*; Victoria Strauss *Rosaura*; Tibor Lubinsky *Gennaro*; Paul Wegener *Micheletto*; with Philipp Manning, Ernst Pittschau

CREDITS: *Producer/Director* Richard Oswald; *Asst. Director* Karl Freund; *Scenario* Richard Oswald; *Based on the novel by* Harry Scheff, *and the diaries of* Bishops Burcardus *and* Gregorovius; *Photographed by* Carl Drews, Karl Voss, Karl Freund, Frederik Fuglsang; *Asst. Cameraman* Robert Baberske; *Photographic*

Cesare Borgia (Connie) cowers before the crucifix held by Pope Alexander VI (Albert Bassermann), his father. (*Lucrezia Borgia*)

Supervision Alfred Kern; *Costumes* Robert Neppach; *Set Designs* Robert Neppach, Botho Höfer

SYNOPSIS: Italy, 16th Century: Rodrigo Borgia (Albert Bassermann), head of the notorious Borgia family, has become Pope Alexander VI.

His son Cesare (Conrad Veidt) is feared as an unscrupulous murderer. His other son, Juan (Lothar Müthel), informs the pope that Cesare is insanely and incestuously in love with their sister, the beautiful Lucrezia (Liane Haid), and that he has sworn to kill any man he perceives to be a rival. The pope neither believes nor cares, but the very accusation proves fatal to Juan. Cesare sends three violent men to "execute" Juan and his fiancée, Naomi (Käthe Waldeck-Oswald).

Appalled, Lucrezia accuses Cesare of the double murder, and he confesses, at the same time warning her that he would kill anyone who dared to love her. Lucrezia fears for her fiancé, Alfonso of Aragon (Alfons Fryland), whom she plans on marrying. Shortly after the wedding, one of Lucrezia's spies finds a letter that reveals Cesare's plan to rid himself of his sister's new husband.

With this as proof, she goes to the pope, who writes to Cesare, expressly forbidding him from doing Alfonso any harm. Lucrezia brings the papal letter to her brother — who pretends that he will obey — but on her way home she is abducted by Cesare's three henchmen and taken off to a convent. At midnight, she makes good her escape, but returns home to find Alfonso has been murdered. Lucrezia returns to the papal palace and informs Alexander of the murder. Cesare is summoned into his father's presence. When Lucrezia reveals that Cesare has also murdered Juan, the pope has heard enough. He curses his degenerate son and banishes him.

Uncertain of what the future will bring, Lucrezia heads to the castle of Giovanni Sforza (Wilhelm Dieterle), her first husband (whom she never really loved) to beg shelter and safety. Sforza, still in love with the beautiful Lucrezia, agrees and proposes marriage once again. She accepts, *if* he will kill Cesare.

Learning where his sister has gone, Cesare plans to attack Sforza's castle and kill him. The battle is fierce. Sforza's men succeed in turning back the attack a number of times. To prevent further bloodshed, Sforza challenges Cesare to single, mortal combat. The fight proves fatal to both men.

REVIEWS: "...The director of this film, Richard Oswald, is said to be a German. He made this picture in Italy. The leading players are Conrad Veidt, Lina Haid [*sic*], Paul Wegener and John Winship [*sic*]...."

"Mr. Veidt gives a studious performance as Cesare Borgia. The others are only fair."

New York Times,
25 December 1928 —
Mordaunt Hall

"Robert Neppach has constructed a castle that is one of the most powerful buildings in film yet. The whole battle scene is an enormous triumph for Richard Oswald."

Film-Kurier, 1923

"In the seven acts, one sensational event is followed by another. The highlight is the battle scene, where more than 5000 people performed."

Verdens Gang (Kristiania)

"*Lucrezia Borgia* is here! Much has already been said about this film, almost mythlike narratives have been told, and much will be said in the future. One quickly notices that Oswald crafted this film for international tastes— or, at least, he wanted to— and that's why not much attention has been paid to the rules and parameters of German taste in film. Although taste is subjective, and film taste abroad and in Germany is very different, there are similarities... and within these *Lucrezia Borgia* was made...

"The acting is mostly strong. Bassermann as pope has the strongest effect on the audience. Conrad Veidt, who plays a Cesare desperately in love also has powerful moments, but a consistency is missing from his performance. As Juan Borgia, Lothar Müthal is deliberately noble while being deliberately melancholic. And Dieterle as Sforza is every bit his equal. There's little to say about the females... Liane Haid here and there... Anita Berber has some good shots... but they are overshadowed by the men."

Der Film (Berlin),
No. 44; 1922

"Richard Oswald has used poetic license very freely — almost to the point of falsifying history, in fact — but cleverly, as well."

Der Kinematograph
(Düsseldorf),
No. 819; 1922

"The historic film requires an element of fantasy, one that provides guiding motifs instead of spontaneous ideas; a fantasy that — unlike a ballad, consisting of words— is composed in stanzas of 'picture,' in 'refrains' of movement. The Lucrezia Borgia theme could have made such a wondrous ballad, with the motifs (or movements) being interwoven, like a musical theme. But Oswald confuses the plots ... at will, and demotes Pope Alexander VI's motif from being the underlying force to being makeshift. ... If the events had been concentrated, as in a ballad, no one would have questioned the historicity. But a film that merely pretends to show historic events falls apart when one finds improbabilities in the plot.... The events depicted are often directed clumsily, reminding one of *Graf Essex*..."

Bnoersen-Courier, No. 24:
October 1922 —
Herbert Ihering

"*Lucrezia Borgia* is without a doubt one of the most outstanding films we have ever seen.... The film is never tiring, in spite of its length. In fact, interest increases throughout the film. The leading parts are played by Conrad Veidt and Liane Haid. Conrad Veidt as Cesare Borgia is simply masterful, as he is in all his roles..."

El Día Gráfico (Spain),
2 February 1923

NOTES AND QUOTES: *Lucrezia Borgia* was an epic historical pageant, another type of picture that was in vogue after the war. The bean counters at Ufa, mindful of the tremendous popularity (and box-office revenues) of such spectacular Italian imports as *Cabiria* and *Quo Vadis*, pushed Germany into the market. Such a move not only did wonders in terms of bolstering domestic attendance (which was normally near capacity, anyway), but also served to put foreign ticket buyers and investors on notice that the German economy had rebounded to the extent that its feature films could now be readily produced on as grand a scale as any in the world.

Joseph May's *Veritas Vincit* (1918) was one of the stepping-off points for this grandest of subgenres, but it fell to Ernst Lubitsch (with his *Madame du Barry*, 1919, and *Anna Boleyn*, 1920) and Dimitri Buchowetski (*Danton*, 1921) to keep the opulent war-horses up and running for as long as possible. As is always the case, interest in the historical pageant soon gave way to interest in more contemporary, intimate drama, but — by virtue of their initial expense and subsequent market value — most of the "superspectacles" managed to avoid falling into the black holes of apathy and neglect during the switch from silence to sound.

Both *Lucrezia Borgia* and *Lady Hamilton* were seen as somehow derivative of the Lubitsch superepics, which were notable for expensive (and — thought some — excessive) fidelity to architecture, costume, and accouterment. They were also noteworthy for their determination to avoid having "given facts" about the historicity of the story get in the way of the narrating of its moral.

Connie's Cesare Borgia is another of his demons, with this one firmly rooted in reality. As a result of Oswald's interesting twist on the Borgia family saga, though, Lucrezia, history's favorite poisoner, is the sacrificial lamb led hither and yon by circumstances essentially beyond her control. Cesare has become a practitioner of villainy on an operatic level. His incestuous leanings so pervade the narrative that the picture won arguably higher box-office returns when released in certain markets under its alternative title: *Cesare Borgia*. Connie plays Cesare as an elemental force — neither possessed of any redeeming traits, nor mindful of any need for redemption — so the characterization, while powerful, is not the multifaceted portrayal a different scenario (or a different director) might have evoked.

Paganini

[LOST] Conrad Veidt-Film GmbH, Berlin — 1923; Distributed by Richard Oswald-Film AG,

Opposite: Connie's turn as Niccolò Paganini — in the last of the Veidt-films — was regarded as one of his very finest performances. (*Paganini*)

Berlin; *Zensur:* 20 January 1923 — 5 Acts, 2064 meters; World premiere: 31 March 1923 Tauentzien-Palast, Berlin; Principal Photography: September-December, 1922

CAST: Conrad Veidt *Niccolò Paganini*; Harry Hardt *Duke Marsini*; Greta Schrödter *Antonia Paganini*; Alexander Granach *Ferruccio, the Flower Seller*; Eva May *Giulietta, his Daughter*; Gustav Fröhlich *Franz von Liszt*; Hermine Sterler *The Duchess*; Jean Nadolovitch *Hector Berlioz*; Martin Herzberg *Achille, Paganini's Son*; with Hans Wassmann, H. Jontscher

CREDITS: *Producers* Conrad Veidt, Richard Oswald; *Director* Heinz Goldberg; *Artistic Supervision/Assistant Director* Conrad Veidt; *Scenario* Heinz Goldberg; *Based on an idea by* Paul Beyer; *Photographic Direction* Karl Vass; *Camera Operators* Karl Vass, Stefan Lorant; *Sets* Robert Neppach; *Costumes* Maxim Frey; *Musical Score for Theaters* Mischa Spolianski; *Production Supervisor* Alfred Kern

SYNOPSIS: Niccolò Paganini (Conrad Veidt) has apparently died in Paris, but after the interment, rises from the grave and returns to his home in Italy. Was he buried alive? Back home, his wife (Greta Schrödter), who could never understand him, becomes even more of a stranger to him, and only his son, Achille (Martin Herzberg), brings joy to his life.

His bizarre experience in Paris has driven him to visit the cemetery regularly. He plays his violin there, and it is there that he meets Giulietta (Eva May), daughter of the flower seller Ferruccio (Alexander Granach). The young, innocent girl also restores his zest for life. Unbeknownst to anyone, Ferruccio has been hired by Duke Marsini (Harry Hardt) to slay Paganini, as the duchess (Hermine Sterler) has fallen passionately in love with him. Giulietta learns of the arrangement, and when Marsini encounters the violinist, it is Paganini who kills the nobleman. Fleeing for his life, Paganini takes Giulietta with him. Before long, though, the duke's soldiers have captured the fugitive, who is sentenced to die for his crime.

In his cell, Paganini begins to play his violin. As if by magic, the cell doors open, the guards — deeply moved — retreat, and the mobs outside rejoice. As the people carry Paganini off on their shoulders, the duchess Marsini appears. Knowing that, because of Giulietta, she can never possess the handsome violinist, she orders her retinue to shoot him. Astonishingly, the bullets miss Paganini and strike the young woman.

Paganini buries Giulietta in the cemetery where they first met. Shattered emotionally, he leaves on a world tour with his son, Achille, and it is during one of these concerts that he collapses and dies.

REVIEWS: "On the whole, a little shortening of the film is in order..."

Film-Kurier, 1 April 1923

"The photography leaves a great deal to be desired... Veidt plays this tailor-made role with his usual virtuosity."

Lichtbildbühne, 31 March 1923

"One might want to hold his breath in view of Conrad Veidt's magnificent climb to the pinnacle of classic film artist, to hold his breath that he doesn't stumble over the many inherent obstacles... For Conrad Veidt has shown us that the full spectrum of pantomimic expression surpasses the spoken word, and because of this, he is not only the greatest, but also the most dedicated of film actors...."

Der Tag (Vienna),
6 November 1923 —
B. Balázs

NOTES AND QUOTES: "The indoor photography was completely done in the rooms of the 'Kaiserliches Schloss Schönbrunn' at Vienna. All the furniture items were originals and were the private property of the Austrian imperial family. The coaches were drawn by horses sired by the former imperial stud, Lippizza."

Paganini film program

Wilhelm Tell

Althoff-Ambos-Film AG (Aafa), Berlin; Distributed by Althoff-Ambos-Film AG, Berlin; *Zensur*: 22 June 1923 — 7 Acts, 2885 meters; Admissible to adolescents; World Premiere: 23 August 1923 Marmorhaus, Berlin

CAST: Conrad Veidt *Gessler*; Hans Marr *Wilhelm Tell*; Erna Morena *Bertha von Bruneck, a Wealthy Heiress*; Käte Haack *Agi, her Companion*; Erich Kaiser-Titz *Emperor Albrecht*; Fritz Kampers *Rudolf*; Emil Rameau *the Chancellor*; Otto Gebühr *Heinrich von Melchthal*; Karl Ebert *Arnold, his Son*; Max Gülstorff *Attinghausen*; Johannes Riemann *Ulrich von Kudenz, his Nephew*; Eduard von Winterstein *Werner Stauffacher*; Agnes Straub *his Wife, Gertrud*; Hermann Vallentin *Wolffenschiessen*; Josef Peterhans *Landenberger*; Xenia Desni *Hedwig Tell*; Willi Müller *Walter Tell*; H.P. Peterhans *Wilhelm Tell*; Theodor Becker *Konrad Baumgartner*; Grete Reinwald *his Wife, Armgard*; Robert Löffler *Pastor Rösselmann*; Wilhelm Diegelmann *"The Bull" of Uri*

CREDITS: *Producer* Fritz Feld; *Directors* Rudolf Dworsky, Rudolf Walther-Fein; *Photographed by* Guido Seeber, Toni Mülleneisen, Georg Lemkie; *Director of Photography* Guido Seeber; *Still Photographs* Georg Lemkie; *Scenario* Willy Rath; *Based on the eponymous drama by* Friedrich Schiller; *Set Design* Ernst Stern, Rudi Feld; *Costumes* Ernst Stern, Rudi Feld; *Make-up* Jacques Buck

SYNOPSIS: Under the Holy Roman Emperor Albrecht (Erich Kaiser-Titz), the central Swiss cantons are placed under the authority of the Austrian prefects Wolfenschiessen (Hermann Vallentin), Landenberg (Josef Peterhans) and Gessler (Conrad Veidt). Each man is autonomous ruler of his own district, and all three rule with an iron hand. They are determined to tax the Swiss into the ground while exploiting the beautiful countryside for all it's worth.

The Swiss are becoming concerned about this oppression. Attinghausen (Max Gülstorff), an elderly man of property, sends his nephew Ulrich (Johannes Riemann) to talk with the Chancellor. Heinrich von Melchthal (Otto Gebühr) angers the tax collectors when he refuses to be bullied into paying more than he should. Later in the day, Heinrich's son, Arnold (Karl Ebert), is almost seized by tax officials while he is plowing the fields; Arnold escapes, but his oxen and plow are confiscated.

Untroubled for the moment is Wilhelm Tell (Hans Marr) — a bit of a local hero for his prowess with the crossbow — his wife, Hedwig (Xenia Desni), and their two small sons.

Real trouble begins when Prefect Wolffenschiessen (Herman Vallentin) stops at Frau Baumgartner's (Grete Reinwald) home and demands something to drink. Attracted by the woman's beauty, he attacks her. Frau Baumgartner's cries bring her husband, ax in hand, down from the hillside. Soon, Wolffenschiessen is lying in a puddle of his own blood, and Baumgartner (Theodor Becker) is fleeing for his life. Word reaches Gessler of his fellow prefect's "murder" just as Wilhelm Tell helps Baumgartner escape his pursuers by ferrying him across the lake in a small boat during a storm.

Through all of this, Gessler has found himself attracted to Bertha von Bruneck (Erna Morena), a beauteous young woman with monetary assets. His rival for the heiress's hand is none other than Ulrich, who is a bit cowed by Gessler's office and authoritative demeanor. Meanwhile, Landenberger, angered at Heinrich's attitude and unable to locate Arnold, has the elder von Melchthal blinded for his arrogance and orders the von Melchthal farmstead burned down. Heinrich is taken in by Getrud Stauffacher, his neighbor and a good Christian woman, but it isn't long before the Austrian troops invade the Stauffacher home to berate Gertrud. In a fracas, Gertrud is killed by a soldier; her husband, Werner, returns moments after the soldiers flee, only to discover his wife.

As the Swiss reach their collective boiling point (men from all over the countryside secretly meet and pledge allegiance to each other and to Swiss freedom), Gessler orders that every man must make obeisance to the prefect's helmet, which has been mounted in the courtyard atop a pole. When Tell refuses to perform such a ridiculous action, Gessler has his son led to the pole, where he is to stand with an apple on his head. If Tell can shoot the apple with his crossbow, he shall have life and freedom. He does, but is arrested anyway when he reveals that he kept back a second arrow — for Gessler — had he accidentally shot his son. Tell is led off to jail, his son is spirited away and taken back home, and the Swiss men grow more earnest in their plans to fight for liberty.

Gessler orders Ulrich put into the dungeon, where he will languish until death overcomes him unless Bertha agrees to marry the prefect. After struggling with her conscience, Bertha gives in, Ulrich is released (he flees for his Uncle Attinghausen's property) and Tell is sentenced to be brought to the emperor. The Swiss, united at last, plan to attack their Austrian captors when a signal fire is lit atop a nearby Alpen crag. As the boat bearing Tell crosses the lake, another storm arises and the Swiss captive is released in order to keep the craft from foundering. Tell brings the boat up to the shore and, snatching his crossbow, leaps onto land and makes his escape.

The storm having passed, Gessler leads his band ashore to find Tell, but finds death instead; from a place of concealment, Tell fires an arrow into the villainous prefect's throat. As this is happening, the Swiss arise, defeat their captors and liberate their country from Austrian rule.

REVIEWS: "...AAFA offers a *Wilhelm*

Gessler, dressed for the Swiss winter. Who knew apples were in season? (*Wilhelm Tell*)

Tell for the people, somewhat in the style of a cheap novel. ... Apart from the [lack of] artistic value, [though,] it has to be welcomed.

"The protector Gessler is played by Conrad Veidt with a touch of decadence. He depicts Gessler as a hysteric. This contradicts history as much as does the love story surrounding Bertha von Brunneck..."

Unknown review

"...[*William Tell* is] a most interesting picture, well made, finely directed, extremely well cut....

"...the Tell character is commanding in stature, besides an actor of the first grade. There are other good actors in this picture play, men and women.... The picture cost some money to make and it has everything in its favor, excepting for America."

Variety, 20 May 1925 — Sime.

"We may mention that the press screening of the film *Wilhelm Tell* on September 9th was an exceedingly great success at the Artistic Cinéma. The film was praised."

Der Kinematograph, No. 969; 13 September 1925

NOTES AND QUOTES: Marked by impressive sets, costumes and lighting schemes—as well as by Conrad Veidt's splendid Gessler—the 1923 *Wilhelm Tell* is a clever, if somewhat clumsy, account of the familiar folktale. Codirector Rudolf Walther-Fein, chief cinematographer Guido Seeber and a handful of the principals spent a couple of weeks in Switzerland for requisite shots of Alpen majesty and Lake Geneva. These background sequences were then interwoven (not always seamlessly) with backlot exteriors and more than a few decent and pointedly solid sets. When the meld worked, it worked well; when it didn't — as when inserts of various

Swiss patriots trundling uphill from the lake were mixed with shots of the ever-growing group standing on what appears to be wrinkled outdoor carpet set against a featureless, black background — the discrepancy between the ill-matched sequences is appallingly obvious.

Nonetheless, some of the technicians' artifices are fascinating for their cleverness. Shots of Tell and Baumgartner, their little boat being heaved hither and yon on the storm-tossed lake, were achieved by having the craft mounted on a pivot which was placed in the midst of a series of wire-supported canvas "waves." As the boat was rocked, the "waves" were manipulated with rods, and the resultant image — aided by quantities of water sprayed this way and that — is, if not completely credible, entrancing and thus acceptable within the framework of the tale.

Neither the renowned piercing of the apple nor the requisite piercing of Gessler is handled well, however. In both instances, the jump cuts from a view of Tell steadying his weapon to the sight of arrows sticking out of fruit and villain are jarring and not at all satisfying.

Hans Marr does a decent enough job as Tell, even if the portly actor offers quite a contrast to the more traditional image of a heroic physique. Marr's portrait of the Swiss icon is straightforward and unnuanced: when that crossbow is nestled in the crook of his arm, his Tell strikes poses worthy of oil paintings or matte-finished movie stills. Nonetheless, one unfortunate instance apart, the Polish born actor consistently avoids the sort of overwrought display that has become associated with the worst of "silent movie acting"; would that Karl Ebert (Arnold von Melchthal) had followed Marr's lead.

Veidt's Gessler, whose makeup treatment is reminiscent of that of the actor's character "Death" in *Unheimliche Geschichten*, is a classic bully. He is self-assured to the extent that he doesn't bat an eyelash when the lovesick (and obviously inept) Ulrich threatens to draw a knife in his presence, yet almost crawls under a rock during a happenstance encounter with Tell on a mountain road. Gessler's bravado—never so blatant as when he's surrounded by oddly accoutered soldiers—reaches its apex in the unfortunate "Marry me or your lover dies" type of tripe injected into the larger proceedings as a sop to the romantic leanings of the distaff ticket buyer. This subplot device, mercifully missing from the 1934 sound reworking, only serves to reduce the Machiavellian prefect to the stock, mustache-twirling heavy of dime novels and low-rent stage melodramas.

In an effort to reach the widest audience possible, AAFA registered *Wilhelm Tell* as an *educational* film on 11 November 1924; the film was subsequently reissued without being recensored.

Glanz gegen Glück

[LOST] aka Gold and Luck; **G.G.G.**; (*Eine Filmtragödie in fünf Akten*); Mercator Filmausstellungs und Vertriebs-AG, Berlin—1923; *Zensur*: 6 September 1923—5 Acts, 2179 meters; Forbidden to adolescents

CAST: Conrad Veidt *the Count*; Erna Morena *the Beauty*; Eduard von Winterstein *the Peasant*; Georg John *the Profiteer*; Margot Nemo *the Nurse*; Walter Neumann *the Physician*; Karl-Heinz Klubertanz *the Worker*; Erich Völker *the Clergyman*; Margarete Kupfer *the Comedian*

CREDITS: *Director* Adolf Trotz; *Scenario* Adolf Trotz, Erich Pabst; *Photographed by* Max Lutze, Paul Holzki; *Set Designs* Robert Neppach

SYNOPSIS: The count (Conrad Veidt) is desperately ill. His physician (Walter Neumann) tries an experimental medicine that can produce a dangerous side effect: vivid hallucinations. The count falls victim to this.

In his deluded state, the count "buys" the health of a peasant (Eduard von Win-

terstein). Now suffering the pains of the count's former illness, the peasant hounds the count via some terrifying visions. In the end, however, the count is cured; he is also relieved to discover that his perilous adventures have only been feverish dreams.

Das Wachsfigurenkabinett

Waxworks aka *The Wax Works*; *Three Wax Men*; *The Three Wax Works*; Neptun-Film AG, Berlin—1924; Distributed by Hansa-Leih der Ufa *and* Wiking-Film AG; Filmed at May Studios, Berlin-Weissensee; *Zensur*: 14 February 1924—4 Acts, 2142 meters; *Zensur*: 12 November 1924—7 Acts, 2147 meters; Forbidden to adolescents; World Premiere: 13 November 1924 U.T. Kurfürstendamm, Berlin

CAST: Conrad Veidt *Czar Ivan the Terrible*; Emil Jannings *Haroun-al-Rashid*; Werner Krauss *Jack the Ripper*; Wilhelm Dieterle *the Poet, the Baker, the Fiancé, the Lover*; Olga von Belajeff *the Daughter, the Baker's Wife, the Nobleman's Daughter, the Lover*; John Gottowt *the Director of the Waxworks*; Paul Biensfeld *Vizier*; Ernst Legal *the Preparer of Poisons*; with Georg John

CREDITS: *Producer* Leo Birinski; *Director* Paul Leni; *Asst. Director* Wilhelm Dieterle; *Scenario* Henrik Galeen; *Photographed by* Helmar Lerski; *Still Photographer* Hans Lechner; *Set Designs* Paul Leni, Alfred Jünge; *Set Construction* Fritz Maurischat; *Costumes* Ernst Stern; *Production Supervisor* Alexander Kwartiroff

SYNOPSIS: "Poet wanted, paid by the hour."

If it weren't for the beautiful daughter (Olga von Belajeff) of the waxworks owner (John Gottowt), the poet (Wilhelm Dieterle) would never have agreed to write tales about the figures in the exhibit: wax models of Haroun-al-Rashid (Emil Jannings), Ivan the Terrible (Conrad Veidt), and Jack the Ripper (Werner Krauss).

As soon as he starts to write, however, the poet's stories take on a life of their own and he becomes Assad the baker, and the beautiful girl his wife. Haroun-al-Rashid is

Connie and frequent co-star Erna Morena. (*Glanz gegen Glück*)

irritated by the smoke rising from the baker's ovens and orders that Assad be executed. The guards are stunned by the beauty of Maimune (von Belajeff), Assad's wife, and report about this to their master.

As usual, Haroun sneaks out of the palace that night, in order to see for himself the baker's wife.

The couple is having a terrific argument, and, to calm his wife, Assad promises that he will steal Haroun's fabled ring—the one that can grant wishes—for her. The baker leaves, and the caliph enters the house and speaks with Maimune.

Slipping into the palace, Assad spies the sleeping form of Haroun; to steal the ring, he hacks off the caliph's arm and, after a wild chase, returns to his home with it. Maimune, terrified of Assad's jealousy, hides the caliph in the oven. As the guards reach the house, Maimune—aware that Assad has *not* killed Haroun—learns from the caliph (still in the oven) that when he sneaks out of the palace, he leaves a wax image of himself in his bed. Quickly, Maimune turns the ring on the finger of the wax arm and wishes the caliph to be alive and well again. Haroun climbs out of the oven and reveals himself to an astounded Assad and the palace guards. Delighted by Maimune's cleverness, he makes Assad his court baker.

Finishing his first story, the poet turns to the next figure: Ivan the Terrible.

Czar Ivan (Conrad Veidt) is a suspicious and superstitious despot. He has a poison preparer who has invented a toxin that causes death at an interval that can be timed to the second. Using an hourglass, Ivan can watch the last seconds of a victim's life run out along with the grains of sand. The court astrologer warns Ivan to beware the poisoner, who is then led away to be executed. Before dying, the man plots revenge upon the Czar by secretly painting Ivan's name and three crosses on the hourglass.

Invited to a wedding, the ever-suspicious Czar has the bride's father change clothing with him. An arrow is loosed and the man dressed as the Czar is killed. The wedding party is stunned by this turn of events, but Ivan forces them to continue drinking and dancing. He makes to carry off the bride—threatening to have her new husband murdered if she refuses—but, at that moment, the hourglass bearing his name and the crosses is found. Terrified, the Czar lets the bride and groom go, and falls into a trance, watching the sands flow through to the bottom and then turning the glass over to postpone the moment of death. This he does again, and again, and again…

Tired out by all his writing, the poet falls asleep. Haroun-al-Rashid and Ivan appear in the ensuing wild nightmare, giving way to the figure of Jack the Ripper (Werner Krauss). Spring-heeled Jack chases the beautiful waxworks' owner's daughter with a knife, as the poet tries to shield the girl. Jack follows the couple through an eerie panorama and finally stabs the poet in the chest.

The poet awakens from the nightmare—he has accidentally pushed his sharpened pencil into his side during his dream. The beautiful young woman comforts him and her kiss eases the pain of both the pencil and the nightmare.

REVIEWS: "Paul Leni has created a highly stylized picture à la *Caligari* after the script by Henrik Galeen; the film will receive the highest praise from people greatly interested in the arts, but will not reach the mass audiences…"

Die Filmwoche, No. 48;
26 November 1924

"… [The part of *Das Wachsfigurenkabinett* featuring] Ivan the Terrible may be called a masterpiece, as it shows the rich expressive possibilities of the film. It has an impressive unity and ever-increasing dramatic force…. The portrait of Ivan the Terrible is a coup by Conrad Veidt; the actor and the scenery meld into one."

Die Bildwart, Vol 12;
December 1925

"Three stories in one are hitched together… Ivan the Terrible is largely a costume affair with a gripping scene of the Czar torturing victims in the Kremlin… Much triple exposure work which made

German photography the Hollywood rage for a time. All sets are freakish."

Variety, 6 February 1929

"This fantastic film consisted of three weird tales, the last of which was by all means the most interesting. In it Emil Jannings gives a startlingly fine performance as a grotesque Caliph.... Conrad Veidt renders an excellent portrayal in the role of Ivan the Terrible, and Werner Krauss is quite impressive as Jack the Ripper."

New York Times, 19 March 1926

"Conrad Veidt is arresting as Ivan; his portrayal of the bloodlust and final insanity of the Czar are noteworthy in every respect. Werner Krauss has little to do as Jack the Ripper, but has a wonderfully malig-

nant expression. Emil Jannings is a sheer delight as the fat, lecherous, but nevertheless good-hearted Haroun al Raschid.... William Dieterle plays very well as the lover in each episode...."

Der Kinematograph Weekly, 12 July 1928

NOTES AND QUOTES: The American premiere (as *The Three Wax-Works*) was at the Cameo Theatre on March 18, 1926. From the program:

This extraordinary film when shown in London a few months ago before an audience of the leading intellectuals of England made such notables as George Bernard Shaw, H.G. Wells and Sir James Barrie, who were present, express their complete amazement at the artistry of the direction, photography, story and acting of this film.

A splendid portrait of Connie as Ivan the Terrible. (*Das Wachsfigurenkabinett*)

"The cycle of imaginary tyrant films came to a close with *Das Wachsfigurenkabinett*. Released as late as November 1924 — at a time when life was just beginning to look normal again — *Waxworks* marked the end of that period in which the harassed German mind retreated into a shell. The script was written by Henrik Galeen, who, in *Nosferatu*, had identified the tyrant with pestilence. He peopled the new film with no less than three tyrants, but reduced them all to wax figures...

"The imagery in *Waxworks* culminates in scenes which, exceeding their task of illustrating the plot, penetrate the nature of tyrannical power... One shot of the Ivan episode reveals the magic spell power radiates: Ivan appears in a folding door, the portrait of a saint in life-size on each leaf, and as he stands there, vested with all the insignia of his dignity, he seems a living icon between the two painted ones. Another picture unit of the same episode shows the bride whom Ivan wants to make his mistress looking through the iron bars of a window into the torture-chamber where her husband is undergoing terrible sufferings; and the shot of her face, distorted with horror, is followed by a close-up of Ivan's well-groomed, ring-adorned hand clasping those iron bars... Here the Germans intuitively visualize an aspect of tyranny which the Russians, doubtless on the strength of experience, were to emphasize as the basic one."

Kracauer, pp. 84, 86.

"For my film *Waxworks* I have tried to create sets so stylized that they evince no idea of reality. My fairground is sketched with an utter renunciation of detail. All it seeks to engender is an indescribable fluidity of light, moving shapes, shadows, lines and curves. It is not extreme reality that the camera perceives, but the reality of the inner event, which is more profound, effective and moving than what we see through everyday eyes, and I equally believe that the cinema can reproduce this truth, heightened effectively."

Paul Leni, as quoted in
CinemaTexas Program Notes,
Vol. 22, No. 1; 9 February 1982

Waxworks was influenced by *Caligari*, and not only in terms of Expressionism. Both films unfold on a fairground, but Leni's traveling show is in constant motion: electric signs and lights are superimposed over the shadowy, circular movements of the ferris wheel and carousel. Leni's picture also owes a structural debt to Fritz Lang's *Destiny* (1921), in that each film is comprised of three episodes, and no two episodes occupy the same time period or locale.

The picture's first two episodes feature views of the reigns of a brace of infamous tyrants. True to the Expressionistic philosophy, each ruler is at once the cause and the effect of his environment. Jannings' obese Haroun-al-Raschid embodies the rotund and seemingly soft contours of the caliph's surroundings, while CV's angular Tsar Ivan is constantly seen measured between iconostases or against towering spires. (In the Ivan the Terrible sequence, Leni's use of low-ceilinged sets makes the tsar seem all the taller, and renders everyone's movements awkward and unsettling.) Both rulers deal with their lust according to their respective standard operating procedures that, also, are in keeping with physical appearances. The caliph's pursuit is initially frenzied, yet quickly subsides; is this due to physical impotence, laziness, or a willingness to accept a ménage à trois? The tsar's favorite method is to eliminate the competition, and so he has the woman's father executed and her husband tortured; no hint of lethargy or compromise here.

The third episode unfolds back at the fairgrounds in the present day, and it is, really, the chase that closes many action pictures (and comedies) of the period. The episode — at least in the edited version that has survived the years — is the briefest of the three; perhaps the mundane, present-day settings were perceived as being less enthralling than the more exotic times and locales the earlier chapters evoked. Still, per Freddy Buache ("Leni," *Anthologie de Cinema* No. 33, March 1968), this part

is full of scintillating, feverish beauty interlaced by an expanding lyricism. The filmmaker blended his art as a visionary designer with a dazzling technique of ghostly movement, elaborate framework, odd angles, and ... superimposition.

The episodic character of the picture works against a sustainable tension; likewise, the differing degrees and kinds of menace enacted by the three wax men guarantee an uneven playing field.

A fourth segment was scrapped.

"Of the three starring actors Conrad Veidt comes off best as Ivan the Terrible, who enjoys forcing his poisoned victims to watch the sand drain from an hourglass, pin-pointing the exact moment of their death."

Horror in Silent Films
by Roy Kinnard.
Jefferson (NC): McFarland &
Company, 1995; p. 167.

"The second story, concerning Ivan the Terrible, is brooding and intense in tone, and both its mood and its visual style clearly influenced [Sergei] Eisenstein's treatment of the same subject some twenty years later. Conrad Veidt's Ivan, lean and angular, with pointed beard and wild, staring eyes, anticipates Cherkassov's performance; and Leni, like Eisenstein, exploits the low-ceilinged architecture of the Czar's palace and the vaulted chambers that force him to stoop as he enters them, to reflect the character's inner torment in the physical poses that he is forced to strike."

Hollywood Destinies:
European Directors in America
1922–1931 by Graham Petrie.
London: Routledge &
Kegan Paul, 1985; p. 169.

Carlos und Elisabeth (Eine Herrschertragödie)

aka ***Don Carlos und Elisabeth***; Richard Oswald-Film AG, Berlin 1923/24; Distributed by Rudolf Berg-Filmvertrieb; *Zensur*: 20 February 1924 — Prologue and 5 Acts, 3153 meters; Forbidden to adolescents; World premiere: 26 February 1924 Richard-Oswald-Lichtspiele, Berlin

CAST: Conrad Veidt *Charles V and Don Carlos*; Martin Herzberg *Carlos, as a Boy*; Eugen Klöpfer *Phillip II*; Robert Taube *Duke of Alba*; Adolf Klein *Grand Inquisitor Espinosa*; Aud Egede Nissen *Princess Eboli*; Rudolf Biebrach *Duke of Valois*; Dagny Servaes *Elisabeth, his Daughter*; Wilhelm Dieterle *Marquis of*

Posa; Friedrich Kühne *Don Perez, King's Minister*

CREDITS: *Director and Producer* Richard Oswald; *Scenario* Richard Oswald; *Photographed by* Karl Hasselmann, Kurt Vass, Karl Puth, Theodor Sparkuhl; *Art Direction* Oskar Fritz Werndorff; *Sets* O.F. Werndorff, Josef Junkersdorf; *Costumes* O.F. Werndorff, J. Kaufmann; *Based on the play* Don Carlos *by* Friedrich Schiller; *Theatrical Music at Premiere* Willy Schmidt-Gentner

SYNOPSIS: Prologue: The deeply religious Charles V (Conrad Veidt) has instituted the Holy Inquisition in Spain. His son Philip (Eugen Klöpfer) has worldlier goals: he wants the Spanish crown. The Church urges Charles to oppose his son's ambition, but the emperor is old and weary and Philip has no problem usurping the throne. Before leaving the court for the sanctuary of the Convent of St. Just, Charles asks Espinosa (Adolf Klein), the Grand Inquisitor, to bless his son's reign. Philip agrees to support the Inquisition and to defend the Church, and he is crowned with Espinosa's blessing.

The Inquisition sweeps over Spain, persecuting heretics and innocent souls with equal fervor. At first Philip is appalled by the brutality of the Church's arm, but Espinosa and the Duke of Alba (Robert Taube) — who helped Philip assume the throne — convince him that to show pity is to show weakness...

The Play: Over the years, Philip's reign has become one of cruelty and bitterness, with the Inquisition growing ever more ruthless. In Flanders, where the new religion of Protestantism has taken root, the people are suffering greatly. The people look to Philip's son, Carlos (Conrad Veidt), for support, but Carlos has other problems: he is violently in love with the Princess Elisabeth of Valois (Dagny Servaes). Before he can confess his love to her, however, Philip proposes to her for reasons of state, and Elisabeth accepts. When Carlos confesses his love for the princess to his father, Philip angrily banishes him from court. Seven months after their marriage, a son is born to Philip and Elisabeth. A miraculous birth?

A year later, as Carlos is still in exile, his friend, the Marquis de Posa (Wilhelm Dieterle), informs him that the people of Flanders desperately needs Carlos' help. Returning to court, Carlos is refused permission to go to Flanders; the Duke of Alba is sent instead, and the fate of Flanders is thus sealed. Carlos sees Elisabeth again, and the princess confesses that she loves him, as well. Their meeting is cut short by the king's arrival.

Later Carlos receives an anonymous letter and, convinced it's from Elisabeth, rushes off to the clandestine meeting. After pouring his heart out to the woman he encounters there, he finds it is not Elisabeth, but Eboli (Aud Egede Nissen), a noblewoman and confidante to Elisabeth, who is also in love with Carlos. The prince spurns her advances. Furious, Eboli runs to the king and the Duke of Alba and informs them of Elisabeth's and Carlos' relationship. Philip demands proof, so Eboli and the duke search for evidence of the illicit affair, going so far as to inform the king of the gossip about the "seven-month pregnancy."

Alba convinces the king that Carlos doesn't just want the queen, but the throne, too. The prince is arrested for treason, a move that angers the people, who love the infante. The Marquis de Posa, fearing that the political situation will soon become intolerable, forges a letter in which he stands accused of treason, thus moving the finger of guilt from Carlos to himself. The ruse works. Philip kills Posa himself and Carlos is freed, but he has lost all feelings of love and respect for his father.

Philip suspects that Elisabeth and Carlos still care for each other, and the queen admits as much to her husband. Philip pleads for her love on his knees, but she leaves him to his agony. This pain turns to fury, and the king sends Carlos to the Inquisition for adultery. Carlos openly declares his love for Elisabeth, the queen and his stepmother, and he is sentenced to die. Philip visits Carlos as the young man is in prison, awaiting execution. The king is sorry for what he has done and wishes to save his son, but Carlos refuses to renounce his love.

Philip watches as Carlos is decapitated. Elisabeth, who arrives too late to plead for a stay of execution, collapses at the sight and soon afterwards dies of a broken heart.

Alone, despairing, Philip leaves the court and goes to the Convent of St. Just, where his father sought sanctuary years earlier.

REVIEWS: "Dramatic pictures which stun the normal human being with deep theatric color, like the escape of Carlos down dark corridors with the queen; a door is opened, and there on the golden stairs is the complete royal household... The overall impression of this solid, sometimes brutal, always folksy work is splendid. Sometimes is seems like an untamed predator, sometimes like a child's dream..."

Film-Kurier, 27 February 1924

"The greatest success of Richard Oswald. A film that shows the strong, secure hand of its director."

Film Echo, 3 March 1924

"Rarely has Conrad Veidt had such splendid moments, such painful renunciation and impulsive opposition to the inevitable..."

Montag Morgen, 3 March 1924

Opposite: Posa (Wilhelm Dieterle, left) demands Carlos' (Connie's) sword, as the Infante has been foolhardy enough to draw it in the presence of the king. Original Ross-Verlag postcard, bearing Dieterle's autograph. (*Carlos und Elisabeth*)

674/6
Wilhelm Dieterle   Conrad Veidt
phot. Krabbe

Carlos und Elisabeth

Verlag „Ross" Berlin SW 68

Connie as the emperor Charles V. *Carlos und Elisabeth* was one of his first non–Episodenfilme pictures in which he played a dual role.

"…Of the whole cast, only one figure was really successful, that of Aud Egede Nissen as Eboli. Eugen Klöpfer lacked entirely the distinction needed for Philip, and Conrad Veidt as Carlos was bad.

"A hurrah must be given to the photography of Sparkuhl and Hasselmann, and most of all for the scenery and costumes of O.F. Werndorff.…

Variety, 16 April 1924 — Trask.

NOTES AND QUOTES: "What Richard Oswald has already tried to achieve in *Lucrezia Borgia*— to create a real 'moving picture' from a romantic, warm basic sensation—he manages here, but stronger, richer, and at the same time, denser."

Dr. Oskar Kalbus,
*Vom Werden deutscher
Filmkunst — Der Stummfilm*

Carlos und Elisabeth is representative of the spate of historical films that were ubiquitous in Germany c. 1920–1924. Commonly entitled *Kostümfilme*, these pictures sought to convey the "historicity" of old, familiar tales (more often than not set during the Renaissance) via meticulous attention to period detail. Many reviewers felt that the most successful of these owed a tremendous debt to Max Reinhardt, and Lotte Eisner has suggested that director Richard Oswald modeled his film's lighting schedule on the Deutsches Theater's production of *Don Karlos*. While that may well have been the case, viewers keen on seeing an Oswald photoplay faithful to the Schiller original came away disappointed. The addition of Elisabeth of Valois' name to the title assured that politics and heretics would be thrust into the Reinhardt-inspired shadows, thus making the motion picture inches from being a mute clone of Méry and Du Locle's libretto for Verdi's grand opera.

Another dual role for Connie, with the actor impersonating grandfather/grandson this time around, rather than twin brothers. (*The Man Who Laughs* would see him doing sire/offspring.) Veidt's Charles V is of a proper vintage, with fatigue, displeasure, and the smallest joy of befuddlement playing across his face. His infante is closer to Hamlet than to Romeo, however, as the prince's outrage at the throne's political and religious persecution of the "heretics" gives him as much pause for thought as does his frus-trated love for his "stepmother," Elisabeth. A superb job, all around.

In addition to *Carlos*, Oswald engaged Veidt for *Lady Hamilton* (1921) and *Lucrezia Borgia* (1922). Most critics regarded Rudolf Dworsky's and Heinz Paul's respective versions of *Wilhelm Tell* as *Kostümfilme*, despite the fact that they were drawn from a theatrical piece — another of Friedrich Schiller's popular plays—which was itself based on folk mythology and not on independent historical records.

Originally Emil Jannings had been signed to play Philip II, but the chance to play Nero in D'Annunzio's production of *Quo Vadis?* (to say nothing of a nice, long stay in sunny Italy, with all those *belle signorine*) saw him beg to be released from his contract; Eugen Klöpfer assumed the role.

Nju

aka *Husbands or Lovers?*; aka ***Nju: Eine Unverstandene Frau*** (*Nju: A Misunderstood Woman*); Rimax-Film AG, Berlin—1924; Filmed at Efa-Atelier am Zoo *and* Staaken; Distributed by DEWEST-Filmverleih GmbH; *Zensur*: 20 August 1924 — 6 Acts, 2227 meters; Forbidden to adolescents; World premiere: 21 November 1924 Alhambra, Kurfürstendamm *and* Richard Oswald-Lichtspiele

CAST: Conrad Veidt *the Poet*; Elisabeth Bergner *Nju*; Emil Jannings *Her Husband*; Migo Bard *the Nanny*; Nils Edwall *the Child*; with Margarete Kupfer, Aenne Röttgen, Karl Platen, Max Kronert, Walter Werner, Grete Lund, Maria Forescu, Fritz Ley

CREDITS: *Director* Paul Czinner; *Scenario* Paul Czinner; *Based on the eponymous play by* Ossip Dymow; *Set Design* Paul Rieth; *Set Construction* Gottlieb Hesch; *Photographed by* Reimar Kuntze, Axel Graatkjaer; *Music* Bruno Schulz (*at the Alhambra premiere*)

SYNOPSIS: Nju's marriage with her husband seems a happy one: he adores her as much as his prosaic nature will permit, his wealth allows him to grant her every

Connie watches as Emil Jannings and Elisabeth Bergner square off. Original American release lobby card. (*Nju*)

wish, and they have a wonderful young son. Nonetheless, Nju (Elisabeth Bergner) comes to feel that her husband (Emil Jannings) regards her as just another luxury; she is just a precious toy for him to play with between the stock exchange and business meetings.

She meets a stranger (Conrad Veidt) at a ball. Being a poet, he is quite the opposite of her robust husband, and the lady and her stranger spend much of the evening coyly flirting with each other. It's not long afterwards that the unsuspecting husband realizes his wife has changed and, when the poet comes to visit their home, the husband also realizes where her affections have flown.

The husband begins to fight for his wife. He visits the poet, who just laughs at

him, and when he returns home from work the next day, the husband enters Nju's room to find the poet there. Blinded with rage, he draws a revolver and shoots, but the shot misses.

Now completely repulsed by her husband, Nju leaves; she is willing even to abandon their child in order to go off with the man she feels she loves. She takes a room in a shabby pension, living for the poet. Soon, however, she comes to understand that the poet is not so terribly different from her husband. He is also self-absorbed and very soon, Nju — the loving, clinging woman — becomes a burden to him.

When her husband visits to offer his help and friendship, she sends him away. That same evening, the poet breaks up with her, using harsh words to get his point across. She runs after him through the stormy winter night, but the poet refuses to let her step into his house. While she walks back through the streets, she sees her husband strolling into a hotel with another woman.

There is nothing left of her world, and she throws herself off the city wall.

REVIEWS: "One of the most shattering events that was ever shown in film or onstage... Full of the deepest tragedy of human life.... [This is] an achievement that puts [Paul Czinner] in the front row of German directors... Conrad Veidt is "He," the poet who breaks up the marriage. This is a role tailor-made for him, and he is stronger and more impressive here than in any previous film."

Vossische Zeitung,
23 November 1924

"Director Paul Czinner had the marvelous task of molding the three concepts, Bergner, Jannings, Veidt, into one idea, and he did this with caring hands. The sketch of the simple plot was always illuminated with good ideas."

Berliner Tagblatt,
22 November 1924

"...one of the strongest (and surely highest grossing) film successes of the season... Conrad Veidt lent the poet his young/old furrowed face... He is the only German film actor who is casually elegant; the pelt of the seducer fits him naturally..."

Montag Morgen,
23 November 1924

"It is not often that one has the pleasure of witnessing in the same film two such intelligent actors as Emil Jannings and Conrad Veidt....

"Mr. Veidt is ... excellent as the intruder. In most Hollywood productions, Mr. Veidt would have looked as if he had just stepped out of a bandbox. Here Mr.

Veidt dresses his part without wondering whether his trousers are well pressed and if he has enough cuff showing..."

New York Times, 22 November
1927 — Mordaunt Hall

"A winner for art film houses and good enough for regular program theaters in spots....

"Elizabeth Bergner and Conrad Veidt are implausible. Veidt does not make the grade either as the lover or the heavy....

"Veidt does not register for the kind of man who would be supposed to win the affections of a happily married woman from her husband and child...."

Variety, 23 November 1927

NOTES AND QUOTES: "But [Dr. Czinner] said he could suggest another picture for me... *Nju*, after Ossip Dymoff's drama. The script was ready and the finances had been secured. Czinner came to speak about the cast and said, 'You can choose whomever you want for the two main male characters.' Fantastic! I chose Emil Jannings and Conrad Veidt at once."

Elisabeth Bergner, as quoted
in *Bewundert viel und viel
Gescholten.* Munich: Wilhelm
Goldmann Verlag; 1978.

Nju is considered to be an excellent example of *Kammerspiel*, a German cinematic subgenre in which rather mundane themes are presented in a very natural narrative style with a minimum of dramatis personae and locations. Film historian Felix Bucher further delineates films of this type as having "a strict unity of action, theme and place," if only to distinguish them further from their more brooding (and sprawling) Expressionistic counterparts.

Emil Jannings (born Theodor Emil Janenz in 1884, in Rohrschach, Switzerland; died 1950) and Conrad Veidt crossed paths professionally thrice during the silent era: *Das Wachsfigurowk* (1924), before *Nju* and *LMB* (1925) afterwards. Jannings, who started in films in 1914, came to America in the mid to late '20s along with a good number of German compatriots and Swedish colleagues, including F.W. Murnau, Ernst Lubitsch, Paul Leni, Victor Sjöström, and Greta Garbo. The burly actor quickly won over American critics and audiences (a 1929 issue of *Picturegoer* magazine held that "Nine people out of ten, if asked to say who is the greatest actor of the screen, would unhesitatingly reply Emil Jannings"); he also won the first Academy Award for best actor for his performance in Josef von Sternberg's *The Last Command* (1928). Only the coming of sound — which revealed in Jannings and others accents a bit too pronounced to be overlooked — saw his return to Germany. When Veidt then fled the Fatherland with the rise to power of Hitler's regime, Jannings stayed on to enjoy the fruits of being one of the Nazis' greatest actors-cum-publicity triumphs. Nonetheless, following the war (and an investigation of his activities by the Allied authorities), it was determined that he did so in order to continue in his craft (while making good money), rather than because he bought the Nazi line. The actor made more than 70 features in his four-decade career.

Although Jannings and Veidt differed regarding political expediency and ethical niceties, they did find common ground in the affections of actress Gussy Holl, whom each man married. Veidt started the trend in 1918 (he and Gussy divorced a year later); Jannings claimed the woman as his own in the early 1920s.

Like Emil Jannings, character actress Margaret Kupfer appeared in three films with Veidt: *Der Januskopf* (1920) and *Der Kongress tanzt* (1931) bracketed *Nju*. Kupfer, who was born in Freystadt, Germany, in 1881, made her film debut in *Der schwarze Moritz* (1916) and was still acting in fea-

tured roles in 1951. The actress, who had some 50 films to her credit, died in 1953.

Orlacs Hände

The Hands of Orlac; Pan-Film, Vienna (Austria), 1924/25; Distributed by Berolina-Film, Berlin; Conflicting information on release dates; *Zensur*: 24 September 1924 — 7 Acts, 2507 meters; Forbidden to adolescents; World premiere: 25 September 1924 Haydn-Kino, Berlin (per DFI); World premiere: 31 January 1925 U.T. Nollendorfplatz, Berlin (per Cine-Graph); Austrian premiere: 6 March 1925 Vienna; Original running time: 90/92 minutes; Running time of surviving print: c. 63 minutes

CAST: Conrad Veidt *Paul Orlac*; Paul Askonas *Servant*; Carmen Cartellieri *Regine, the Maid*; Fritz Kortner *Eusabio Nera*; Alexandra Sorina *Yvonne Orlac*; Fritz Strassny *Orlac's Father*; Hans Homma *Dr. Serral*

CREDITS: *Director* Robert Wiene; *Producer* Karl Ehrlich; *Scenario* Ludwig Nerz; *Based on the eponymous novel by* Maurice Renard; *Photographed by* Günther Krampf; *Assistant Cameraman* Hans Androschin; *Art Direction* Stefan Wessely, Hans Rouc, Karl Exner; *Music* Pierre Oser, Jan Kunkel

SYNOPSIS: Famous pianist Paul Orlac (Conrad Veidt) is seriously injured in a train accident, and his hands are later amputated. The body of Vasseur, a man just executed for committing murder, is brought into the same hospital and the doctor grafts Vasseur's hands onto Paul's wrists. After the operation, Paul is haunted by visions of a strange man. When he learns of the transplant, the pianist despairs and refuses to touch his loving wife, Yvonne (Alexandra Sorina), and his piano. His sleep is filled with nightmares, as he sees Vasseur's hands push a dagger marked with a cross into a man's chest. One morning, he finds just that dagger in his own house. Paul nearly goes insane, feeling that the murderer's soul is taking possession of him; even his handwriting isn't his own anymore.

With Paul unable to play, the Orlacs soon run into money problems. Looking for some financial help, Yvonne visits Paul's father (Fritz Strassny), but the old man refuses to assist her. Regine (Carmen Cartellieri), the maid, persuades Yvonne to have Paul go himself to see his father. Yvonne doesn't know that Regine is acting on instructions from the man in Paul's visions, who is very real, indeed.

Paul reluctantly goes off to see his father, but he finds the old man dead, stabbed with a dagger marked with a cross. He summons the police, who discover not only that the dagger had belonged to Vasseur, but also that the fingerprints on the dagger were Vasseur's as well. While the police are investigating, Paul sneaks out and is confronted by the very man who has haunted his dreams. This unknown man leads Paul to a tavern, where he demands a million marks from the pianist's freshly acquired inheritance. When Paul asks why he ought to pay, the unknown man reveals that he was Vasseur, and that Orlac owes him for his hands.

Paul goes to the police, telling them about the blackmail. He is told to meet with Vasseur again at the tavern; the police will be waiting. The plan works well and the man is arrested. He is not Vasseur, but Eusebio Nera, a conman well known to the police. Nera admits to the attempted blackmail, but accuses Orlac of killing his own father. At that moment, Regine arrives. She confesses to the police that Nera, a former friend of Vasseur, made rubber gloves bearing Vasseur's fingerprints and that Nera murdered the elder Orlac. Not only this, Regine insists; Nera also committed the crime for which Vasseur was executed.

As Nera is taken away, Paul slowly realizes that he and his new hands are innocent of any and all crimes.

REVIEWS: "...It is hardly fair to say that Conrad Veidt goes a bit far in his efforts to strike terror into the hearts of his spectators. Nevertheless, one can assert with safety that Mr. Veidt and the others would have added to the reality of their Grand Guignol tale if they had been a bit more restrained...."

New York Times, 5 June 1928 — Mordaunt Hall

"Orlac is one of the best of Conrad Veidt's achievements. [He is] always interesting and thrilling, with all of his personality engaged... the applause of the audience at the premiere — who called him again and again in front of the curtain — was well deserved."

B.Z. am Mittag, 3 March 1925

"Veidt succeeded in creating with his sensitive artistry the figure of a lamentable man, filled with dread. Showing superior character development, Veidt's grand art uncovered every facet of the subject."

8 Uhr *Abendblatt*, 3 February 1925

"An exceptionally thrilling and fantastic film, carried by the remarkable creative power of Conrad Veidt."

Der Kinematograph, 8 February 1925

"Full of endless genius is the byplay with his [Conrad Veidt's] hands. Their eloquence alone reveals the drama of the soul. Veidt is one of the few select portrayers of man in German cinema."

Film-Kurier, 2 February 1925 — H. Michaelis

"Were it not for Veidt's masterly characterization, *The Hands of Orlac* would be an absurd fantasy in the old-time mystery-thriller class. As the musician who learns that the hands he lost in a train wreck have been supplanted by those from a man guillotined for a murder, Veidt keeps his audience highly tensed in spots...."

Variety, 27 June 1928

Top: Original trade ad. (*Orlacs Hände*); *bottom:* Paul Orlac (Connie) (left) is horrified. The recently executed murderer Vasseur (Fritz Kortner) has seemingly returned from the grave to demand the return of his hands. (*Orlacs Hände*)

NOTES AND QUOTES: Robert Wiene's *Orlacs Hände* marked the first time that Maurice Renard's novel was brought to the screen. In 1935, MGM bought the property, reworked it from psychological thriller to full-blown horror film, and cast hypertense actor Colin Clive as Orlac. Peter Lorre headlined the cast in the role of the lunatic surgeon — a thankless part in the German original — which was expanded and made kinkier; lovely Frances Drake, as Yvonne Orlac, likewise saw her role enlarged. Released as *Mad Love*, the picture has acquired a cult status in the years since. In 1961, the film was remade — under its original title — by Riviera International Film. This time around, Mel Ferrer was Orlac, and British horror-film star Christopher Lee was featured prominently in the cast.

Recently, newly discovered footage — as well as a meticulous re-editing of the existing film — has resulted in a "restored" version of *Orlacs Hände*. Per film historian Henry Nicolella, the "new" footage includes a sequence in which Orlac envisions a murder committed with the X-marked knife, and the entire last scene, as originally filmed.

Schicksal

[LOST] *Fate*; aka *Schichsal*; Lucy Doraine-Film GmbH; für Messtrofilm; Distributed by Landlicht-Verleih GmbH and Messter-Ostermayr-Film GmbH, Munich; Filmed at Efa-Atelier am Zoo; Exteriors shot in Stockholm, Copenhagen; *Zensur*: 22 September 1924 — 6 Acts, 2307 meters; Forbidden to adolescents; World premiere: 12 February 1925 Tauentzien-Palast, Berlin

CAST: Conrad Veidt *Count L.M. Wranna*; Eduard von Winterstein *Minister von Glayn*; Lucy Doraine *Yvonne, his Daughter*; Friedrich Kayssler *President H. Milner*; Paul Bildt *Martin, a Servant*; Lia Eibenschütz *Heddy*; Hilde Radnay *Rita Varene, a Dancer*; Rolf Loer *Frederick Holm*; Hadrian M. Netto *Jockey B. Craddock*; with Willi Kaiser-Heyl

CREDITS: *Producer* Fritz Klotzsch; *Director* Felix Basch; *Scenario* Walter Wassermann, Felix Basch; *Based on the novel* Das verlorene Paradies *by* Guido Kreutzer; *Director of Photography* Franz Planer; *Photographed by* Franz Planer, Josef Blasi; *Music* Giuseppe Becce; *Set Design* Carl L. Kirmse

SYNOPSIS: Minister von Glayn (Eduard von Winterstein), a respected and honorable man, has lost his heart to Rita Varene (Hilde Radnay), a dancer. He showers her with gifts, running through not only his own savings, but his daughter Yvonne's fortune, as well. Yvonne (Lucy Doraine), a happy girl who loves to help others, is unaware that she is now penniless. She wiles away the days in the orphans' home she has founded.

Today is a big day at the home. A generous donor — Mr. Milner (Friedrich Kayssler) — is on hand and he presents Yvonne with a check for 50,000 krone. Yvonne is too happy to notice the passionate glances she's receiving from Count Wranna (Conrad Veidt), chairman of the orphans' home and husband to Yvonne's best friend, Heddy (Lia Eibenschütz). Yvonne has eyes only for Frederick Holm (Rolf Loer), a secretary, and he returns her love.

Von Glayn has another rendezvous with Rita, who demands 50,000 krone for herself. The minister refuses at first but, unable to withstand her charms, relents and promises to bring the woman the money the next day. He does not suspect that Rita is planning to use the money to run off with her lover, Craddock (Hadrian M. Netto), one of Count Wranna's jockeys. Back home, von Glayn confesses all to his daughter, while bemoaning that he needs another 50,000 krone quickly; suicide is his only alternative. Struggling against her better judgment, Yvonne gives her father Mr. Milner's check; she now realizes she has lost both her honor and any chance of happiness with Frederick.

Connie, about to show his etchings to Lucy Doraine. (*Schicksal*)

The embezzlement is found out by Count Wranna, who smoothes things over by returning the money from his own personal fortune. He asks Yvonne to come to his house, where he confronts her with his discovery and forces the woman to sign an IOU. Looking to capitalize on the moment, Wranna takes Yvonne into his arms. She faints, however, and is ministered to by Heddy.

The next day's mail brings a note from Wranna, along with a copy of the IOU that now bears the admission "the money I stole from the orphans' home." Aghast at reading the phrase she did not write, Yvonne heads for the address on the note, which turns out to be the flat that was occupied by Rita; Wranna has now rented it. Wranna tries to force his attentions upon Yvonne, but is stopped when both hear that someone has entered the flat. It is von Glayn, hoping to see Rita once again. Yvonne hides in the bedroom, where she finds her father's love letters to Rita, including the one about the 50,000 krone. Appalled, she realizes that she has sacrificed everything for her father's mistress, a dancer. Just then, Heddy and Fredrick walk in. They found out about the count's intended rendezvous with Yvonne and rushed to help Yvonne. Yvonne, however, cannot bring herself to look her fiancé in the face and runs out.

She takes the next train, whereon she finds herself with the good, gracious Mr. Milner. This is too much for her. She runs through the train, fully intending to throw herself to her death; she is stopped from doing so by Mr. Milner. He takes her to Paris, where she works in the orphans' home he runs there. As time passes, she becomes more like her old self again. Then, at a celebration honoring her for her selfless work, she meets up with Wranna, who tells her he has divorced Heddy and wants to marry her. When she refuses, Wranna threatens to reveal everything. Mr. Milner appears just then, and Yvonne confesses everything to him. Mr. Milner understands and gives her another check with which to buy her freedom.

Wranna refuses to accept the check. Tearing up the IOU, he draws a pistol and shoots at Yvonne, crying that if he cannot have her, no one else will. Thankfully, he misses her; he then shoots himself.

Yvonne is free, her honor has been restored and — before long — Frederick Holm arrives in Paris.

REVIEWS: "The thrilling plot unfolds with great skill around the sundry cliffs, which play a large part in the story, as has been shown in so many films and novels before. The capable hand of Felix Basch was lavish with the society scenes..."

Die Filmwoche, No. 8;
18 February 1925

"The way Felix Basch succeeds in telling this common story tastefully, how he fills it with both thrills and flesh and blood realism, is not art, but significant ability at film direction. Conrad Veidt as Lucy Doraine's counterpart? Very interesting..."

Die Filmwoche, No. 9;
25 February 1925

Le Comte Kostia

[LOST] *Count Kostia*; aka **Graf Kostja**; Art et Cinégraphie, Paris/Westi-Film GmbH, Berlin; Distributed by Cinématographes Phocéa; Zensur: 7 February 1925 — 6 Acts, 1747 meters;

Forbidden to adolescents; World premiere: 29 May 1925 Paris

CAST: Conrad Veidt *Count Kostia*; Génica Athanasiou *Stéphane*; Claire Darcas *Countess Kostia*; André Nox *Vladimir Paulitch*; Florence Talma *Madame Lerins*; Pierre Dalfour *Gilbert de Saville*; Paul Pauley *Pope Alexis*; Henri Desmarets *Ivan*; Farney *Fritz*; with Daniel Mendaille, Louise Barthe, Yvette Langlais, Roby Guichard

CREDITS: *Producer/Director* Jacques Robert; *Based on the novel by* Victor Cherbuliez; *Photographed by* Georges Lucas, Lucien Bellavoine

SYNOPSIS: Count Kostia (Conrad Veidt) is a feudal lord in Czarist Russia, and he is strict with his serfs. When Valdimir Paulitch (André Nox), the son of a serf, attempts to woo Kostia's sister, the count expels him in disgrace. Paulitch swears revenge and begins to pursue the Countess Kostia (Claire Darcas). The countess, shamed yet insisting that she is innocent, commits suicide after bearing a daughter. Kostia, convinced of his wife's guilt, does not regard the newborn Stephanie as his child. Embittered, he moves into an old castle on the Rhine where, in memory of his son who died, he forces Stephanie to wear boy's clothing, and she is educated as a boy. Torn by hatred and distrust, he causes his supposed "child of sin" to go through life without a smile.

The count's suffering plays itself out again and again in the form of tormented dreams. His newly engaged secretary, Gilbert de Saville (Paul Dalfour), thus overhears all the details of the Kostia tragedy.

Gilbert tries to comfort Stephanie, who has grown to become a young woman (Génica Athanasiou), and slowly she comes to trust and to love him. When Kostia falls ill, Dr. Paulitch is called to his bedside. Feeling that his vengeful plan has not yet reached completion, Paulitch begins to pursue Stephanie. Stephanie flees the lecherous man and, in the act of freeing herself from his embrace, she causes the doctor to fall onto the rocks by the Rhine. Dying,

Le Comte Kostia marked Connie's second venture into Czarist Russia.

Paulitch is brought to Kostia's castle, where he confesses all the evil he has done and reveals that Stephanie is, indeed, Kostia's daughter.

Freed of his eternal nightmare, Kostia allows Stephanie to marry Gilbert.

REVIEWS: "... [In *Le Comte Kostia*, they] found ... a theme that could be placed on the noble, thoroughbred shoulders of Conrad Veidt. ... Veidt blends the successful elements of his Ivan the Terrible and ... Orlac with a sure hand. The way in which his face turns from being grief-torn to being the pure picture of peace after the comforting words of the doctor proves how much this master of mimicry can do without the makeshift bridge of words...."

Reichsfilmblatt, No. 18;
2 May 1925

"The performance of *Comte Kostia* has been a great triumph for Conrad Veidt.... The audience followed the great [actor's] performance enchanted. Highly praised also was the up-to-now unknown Romanian actress, Génica Athanasiou, who has worked only on the stage; this is her first film. ... On the whole, it is a film closer to the German style than to the French."

Der Film, No. 10;
8 March 1925

NOTES AND QUOTES: Again, if I may defer to Pat Wilks Battle:

"Director Jacques Robert lured Veidt to France for his production of *Le Comte Kostia*, based on a 19th-century Gothic romance. According to the novel's introduction, 'There are some great lords, such as Count Kostia, whom marital unhappiness has so embittered that they have become three-quarters monsters.' The count also suffered bouts of somnambulism, and of this part of the film a French critic commented, 'The sleepwalking scene is the most impressive of all. In a setting of curtains and tapestries, old pieces of furniture and bric-a-brac, Kostia Leminoff, a single person, holds the screen for ten minutes, and harasses the nerves of the spectators by his intensely dramatic performance. Conrad Veidt, the great German actor, proves here his talent for tragic mime.'"

Le Comte Kostia was censored as if it were a German production.

Liebe macht blind

[LOST] *Love Makes One Blind; Love Is Blind*; Universum-Film AG (Ufa), Berlin — 1925; Filmed at Ufa-Atelier, Neubabelsberg; *Zensur*: 29 August 1925 — 5 Acts, 1856 meters; Forbidden to adolescents; World premiere: 2 October 1925 Mozartsaal, Berlin (inaugural presentation) and U.T. Turmstrasse and Ufa-Palast, both Königstadt

CAST: Conrad Veidt *Dr. Lamare*; Lil Dagover *Liane*; George Alexander *Viktor, her Husband*; Emil Jannings *Himself*; Lilian Hall-Davis *Evelyn*; Jack Trevor *the Director*; with Jenny Jugo, Alexander Murski

CREDITS: *Director* Lothar Mendes; *Photographed by* Werner Brandes; *Scenario* Robert Liebmann; *Based on the farce* Die Doppelgängerin *by* Viktor Leon; *Set Designs* Hans Jacoby

SYNOPSIS: Liane (Lil Dagover), Viktor's beautiful wife, knows what really goes on at the "meetings" her husband (George Alexander) frequently attends in the evenings. He returns with confetti in his hair, his wedding ring in his pocket, and scribbled notes, which he hides in both obvious and unlikely places.

She struggles to retain her husband's affection. When a film is produced locally for charity, she tries to prevent her un-

Dr. Lamare — himself half blind behind those Coke-bottle glasses — was Connie's first purely comic role in a motion picture. (*Liebe macht blind*)

faithful Viktor from meeting Evelyn (Lilian Hall-Davis), the beautiful star, by slipping him a drug, Veronal. Her plans go awry, however, when Dr. Lamare (Conrad Veidt), thinking that Liane is planning to commit suicide, provides her with bicarbonate of soda instead.

Desperate, Liane disguises herself and flirts outrageously with her husband. She succeeds in pushing Evelyn out and manages to steal her husband's wedding ring. Back home, she confronts Viktor with this proof of his infidelity and reveals her intrigue. Half-ashamed, half-enthralled that his wife went to such ends to regain his love, Viktor pleads for Liane's forgiveness, and they fall into each other's arms.

REVIEWS: "Conrad Veidt can be seen

here in his first comic role. For him alone, this picture is worth watching..."

Berliner Morgenpost,
4 October 1925

"Another surprise is Conrad Veidt, who satirizes his vocation and himself in a most priceless fashion..."

Germania, 4 October 1925

"Ufa... has a new film comedy that is worth seeing; indeed, that one must see. A flowing plot, highly imaginative, tasteful direction, excellent acting... Conrad Veidt, here as a comedian for the first time, is a charming surprise."

Berlin Boersen Courier,
4 October 1925

"...The players who do most of the work are Lil Dagover and Conrad Veidt. There is no complaint about their performances....

"Emil Jannings appears in a few scenes [and] is seen in his dressing room and is exploding with mirth at the actions of Veidt, who has to pretend in this particular sequence that he can't act.

New York Times,
23 August 1927 —
Mordaunt Hall

Ingmarsarvet

Ingmar's Inheritance aka **In Dalarna and Jerusalem**; aka **Die Erde ruft** (*The Earth Cries Out*); Nordi-Westi Film AB, Stockholm; Original Running Time: 92/90 minutes; World premiere: 26 December 1925 Röda Kvarn, Stockholm; German premiere: 19 November 1926 Mozartstaal, Berlin

CAST: Conrad Veidt *John Helgum*; Lars Hanson *Ingmar Ingmarsson*; Mona Martenson *Gertrud Storm*; Jenny Hasselqvist *Barbro*; Ivan Hedqvist *Stark Anders*; Nils Ahrén *Schoolmaster Storm, Gertrud's Father*; Gabriel Alw *Christ*; Knut Lindroth *Berger Sven Person*; Hugo Björne *Captain of "L'Univers"*; Carl Browallius *Ingmar's Father*; Mathias Taube *Tims Halvor*; Märta Halldén *Karin Ingmarsdotter*; Bengt

Djurberg and Sten Lindgren *Gunhild's Brothers*; John Ekman *Eljas*; Lili Lani *Gunhild*; Sven Bergvall *Passenger*; Wilhelm Tunelli *Pastor Dagson*; Gösta Richter *Bertil*; with Emmy Albiin, Joshua Bengtsson, Anna Lindahl, Gösta Gustafson, Liskulla Jobs, Nils Jacobson, Arne Lundh, Joshua Bengtsson, Gunnar Maegerstolpe, Sven Quick, Nils Ohlin

CREDITS: *Producer* Oscar Hemberg; *Director* Gustav Molander; *Screenplay* Ragner Hyltén-Cavallius, Gustav Molander; *Based on the novel* Jerusalem I: I Dalarne *by* Selma Lagerlöf; *Photographed by* Julius Jaenzon, Ake Dahlqvist; *Makeup* Manne Lundh; *Music* Eric Westberg, Oskar Lindberg, Helmer Alexandersson; *Art Direction* Vilhelm Bryde; Filmed on location in Jaffa, Jerusalem, and in Torsang and Jämtlands Län, Sweden

SYNOPSIS: The unreliable Eljas (John Ekman) becomes master of the Ingmarsson farm and guardian of the young Ingmar through marriage to Karin Ingmarsdotter (Märta Halldén). Eljas is a drunkard, and he squanders the inheritance. He dies while driving his horse and carriage, without anyone knowing he has hidden away a large sum of money in a cushion.

Ingmar Ingmarsson grows up and becomes the assistant to Storm, a schoolteacher. Karin is now paralyzed in both legs, and her second husband, Tims Halvor (Mathias Taube), has taken over the Ingmarsson farm. Ingmar (Lars Hanson) longs for the farm, but despairs of ever owning it. A faithful old servant, Stark Anders (Ivan Hedqvist), persuades Ingmar to build a saw and thus to set out on making money with which to buy the farm.

One stormy night, Ingmar and Gertrud (Mona Martenson), Storm's daughter, realize that they are in love with each other. At the same time, the preacher John Helgum (Conrad Veidt) speaks fervently about founding a new congregation in Jerusalem. Many of the villagers are converted by Helgum's eloquence, among them Tims Halvor and — later — Karin, when she is healed. They and many others wish to join Helgum and leave for Jerusalem.

The Ingmarsson farm is put up for sale and Ingmar, who is also planning his wedding to Gertrud, is struggling to find the money with which to reclaim what he feels is rightfully his. He is offered the money by wealthy Berger Sven Persson (Knut Lindroth), the district judge, on condition that Ingmar marry Persson's daughter, Barbro (Jenny Hasselqvist).

On the day of the auction, Ingmar chooses to buy the farm by marrying Barbro; he deserts Gertrud and renounces their love. In the meantime, Gertrud finds the money hidden by Eljas in the cushion. She gives the money to the shamefaced Ingmar and tells him that she also has been converted by Helgum. Together with the other "Helgumians," she starts off toward Jerusalem.

REVIEWS: "Perhaps Conrad Veidt's Helgum makes the strongest impression. He is the religious fanatic, the man who blindly feels his calling and who, in the midst of a flood of misfortune, seizes on the straw which carries him through the rest of his life…"

Arbetaren, 28 December 1925

"From the standpoint of the direction, the highlights include the description of the steamship wreck and the horrendous, stormy night when Helgum wins his greatest triumph. This character is strikingly played by the German Conrad Veidt, a well known name from many German films…"

Folkets Dagblad,
28 December 1925

"Perhaps it is Conrad Veidt's Helgum who is the most memorable of all. The soft-spoken madness which proves so fascinating to the people makes quite a strong impression on the audience, too."

Socialdemokraten,
27 December 1925

"Helgum's part has been entrusted to the German actor, Conrad Veidt. His per-

formance is sterling and any facet of the character that appears less than totally genuine is, of course, due to the fault of the director."

Aftonbladet,
28 December 1925

"It is difficult to really say anything about the actors' work after seeing only this first part [of the saga]. Here, however, the hypnotic performance of Conrad Veidt as Helgum dominates completely."

Stockholms Dagblad,
27 December 1925

"Helgum is played by Conrad Veidt, who touches you by giving the impression of fervent and implicit faith while, at the same time, revealing a frightening, pathological character. It is an interesting study, artistically performed."

Stockholmstidningen,
27 December 1925

"And then we come to the best performance of the film: Conrad Veidt! … He made the religious dreamer likable and reasonable, even for those who would normally adopt a negative attitude toward figures such as this. In his calm, unexaggerated fanaticism, there was something attractive, something trustworthy which raises his performance to real art…"

Svenska Dagbladet,
27 December 1925

"As the fervent, fanatical Helgum, Conrad Veidt stands out in sharp relief to this rustic existence, and it is readily understandable how his mystical, Christlike figure gets a strong hold on the minds of the Delecarlian peasantry."

Dagens Nyheter,
27 December 1925

"The underlying motif of this picture is the effect of intense religious feeling upon a simple folk.…

"The picture is an excellent study of Swedish folk life and the Jerusalem

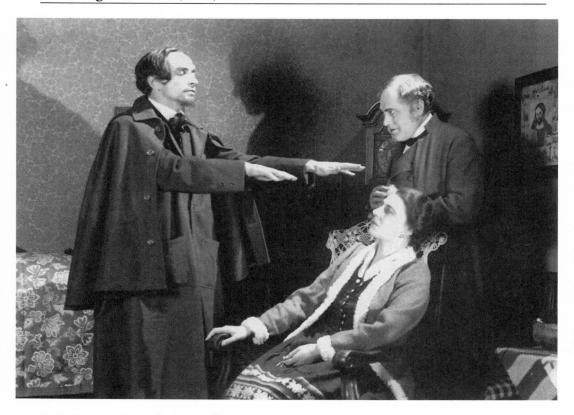

Karin Ingmarsdotter (Märta Halldén) won't be paralyzed much longer, now that the Rev. Helgum (Connie, left) has got his arms working. Karin's other half—Tims Halvor (Mathias Taube)—is admiring Helgum's technique. (*Ingmarsarvet*)

episodes were actually photographed in the Holy Land. There is noteworthy acting by a large cast and while the picture is unusually long the interest is well sustained throughout."

National Board of Review
Magazine, Vol. IV, No. 2;
February 1929

NOTES AND QUOTES: Following his sojourn in Paris (for *Le Comte Kostia*), Connie was lured to Sweden with the promise of working on a film based on the *Jerusalem* saga of author Selma Lagerlöf, one of that country's national treasures. Gustav Molander, an insightful director whose vision and palette were held as reminiscent of fellow countrymen Mauritz Stiller and Victor Sjöström, guided Veidt

through what was to be the first part of a two-part work. (The actor did not appear in the second part, *Till Österland*—based on Lagerlöf's *Jerusalem II: I det heliga landet*—which enjoyed some location shooting in the Holy Land.)

Molander, who—like Veidt—emigrated from his native country late in his career, won a fair shame of acclaim in the United States due to his professional affiliation with Ingrid Bergman. Molander had directed the beautiful actress in the original Swedish production of *Intermezzo* (1936), the scenario of which he had co-written. Two years later, David O. Selznick bought not only Molander's screenplay, but also the rights to the Swedish movie itself. The underlying rationale was that Selznick International Picture's version of

Intermezzo— which was to mark Ingrid Bergman's debut in English-language cinema — would benefit both in terms of economy (predetermined camera angles and edits would save time and money) and security (there would be no "rival" production to siphon off revenues or encourage comparisons).

Der Geiger von Florenz

The Violinist of Florence; aka *Impetuous Youth* (USA); Universum-Film AG (Ufa), Berlin 1925-26; Filmed at Efa Studios, Berlin; Exteriors filmed in Florence; Distributed by Decla-Bioscop-Verleih; *Zensur*: 9 March 1926 — 5 Acts, 2260 meters; Admissible to adolescents; World premiere: 10 March 1926 Gloria-Palast, Berlin

CAST: Conrad Veidt *Renée's Father*; Elisabeth Bergner *Renée, a Young Girl*; Walter Rilla *the Painter*; Greta Mosheim *his Sister*; Nora Gregor *the Stepmother*; with Ellen Plessow

CREDITS: *Director* Paul Czinner; *Scenario* Paul Czinner; *Photographed by* Adolf Schlasy, Arpad Viragh; *Music* Dr. Giuseppe Becce; *Set Designs* Erich Czerwonski, O.F. Werndorff

SYNOPSIS: After the death of her mother, Renée (Elisabeth Bergner) transfers all her love to her father (Conrad Veidt). When he remarries, she becomes extremely jealous of his new wife (Nora Gregor). Soon the situation at home becomes intolerable, so her father sends Renée to a boarding school in Switzerland.

Renée becomes a problem student at the school, as she wants to be sent home to rejoin her father. As things turn out, however, she is punished for her misbehavior by being forced to remain at the school when all of the other students go home for the holidays. She decides to run away, and she makes it as far as the Italian border. As she has no passport, she disguises herself as a shepherd boy to get into Italy.

In Italy she is free and — still in disguise — she earns something of a living as a street musician. One day a painter catches sight of her while she is playing the violin in her own, dreamy fashion. Fascinated, he takes her with him to Florence, where he paints her as "The Violinist of Florence." The painter has no idea that his new companion is a girl, nor is he aware that she is falling in love with him.

The painting is a huge success and is heralded all throughout Europe. News of it reaches Renée's home, where her father recognizes "The Violinist." He makes his way to Florence, confronts the painter, and demands that his "comrade" be turned over. The painter refuses, saying that he "likes the boy." When the painter discovers that his protégé is a girl, he asks her father for her hand in marriage. After some tribulation, the father agrees and the painter and his "Violinist" — and the father and his new wife — look forward to a happy future.

REVIEWS: "...The central idea of the story [of *Impetuous Youth*, now at the Fifth Avenue Playhouse] is almost absurd, for some of the characters are so easily deceived by a girl masquerading as a boy. ... Mr. Veidt is capital as the father and husband, but unfortunately his role is not nearly as important as [Elizabeth] Bergner's. Others in the cast give competent performances."

New York Times, 13 June 1927 — Mordaunt Hall

"A subtle picture... not so much a display of filmed art as— like *Goldrausch* (*The Gold Rush*) — a work of art itself."

Reichsfilmblatt, No. 11; 13 March 1926 — Felix Henseleit

(as *Impetuous Youth*)

"Very pleasant slight comedy, well acted and directed. Elizabeth Bergner is deliciously vivacious and clever as Renée. Conrad Veidt is good, but has little to do as the father. Walter Rilla makes a good artistic lover.

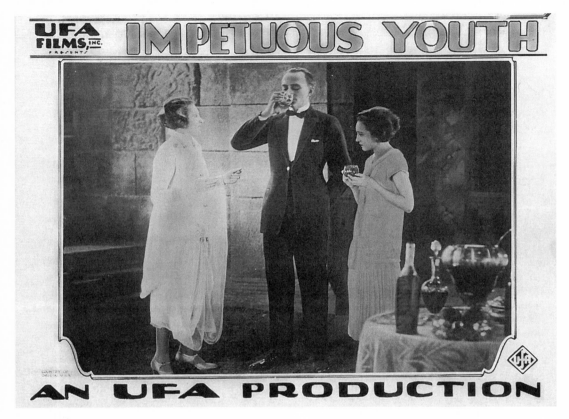

Flanked by his second wife (Nora Gregor) and his daughter (Elisabeth Bergner), Connie needs that drink. (*Der Geiger von Florenz*)

"The somewhat unusual theme has been pleasingly handled by Paul Czinner…. Continuity is jerky, probably owing to cutting.

"Very good photography…."

Kinematograph Weekly,
7 October 1926

"The film *Der Geiger von Florenz* passed all the exams of its enemies…"

Die Filmwoche,
24 March 1926

NOTES AND QUOTES: Director Paul Czinner (born in Budapest in 1890; died 1972) held doctoral degrees in literature and philosophy. Czinner married actress Elisabeth Bergner (born Elisabeth Ettel in either 1897, 1898, or 1900 in Drogobycz, Galizia) in 1933, and, in all, directed a dozen of her

early films. The couple emigrated to England at the start of the Nazi era, where they again collaborated to produce such popular English-language features as *Catherine the Great* (1934) and *Escape Me Never* (1935). Their last film together was *A Stolen Life* (1939); they separated not long thereafter. Bergner returned to film (and later, television) work in Germany following the war, and was active in the industry until 1984; she died in 1986. From 1955 (with *Don Giovanni*, starring basso Cesare Siepi), Czinner — who remained in England — chose to concentrate on recording on film the world of ballet and opera.

Composer Dr. Giuseppe Becce (born in Padua in 1887; died 1973) started his career as a composer for the cinema in 1913, working with Oskar Messter. That same year, he made his acting debut as the eponymous *Richard Wagner* (also for Messter); this screen appearance was also his swan song. During the silent era, Dr. Becce composed and orchestrated accompaniments designed for world premiere performances. As was the custom in Germany, first-run theaters (with resident orchestras available for major motion pictures) retained performance rights to these scores. Smaller movie houses and rerelease theaters were left to their own devices. When sound took root, he scored over 50 features, and also provided incidental music (uncredited) for films such as *Frankenstein* (1931; director James Whale ultimately opted to release the picture with music under the titles only) and *The Crosby Case* (1934). In addition to *Der Geiger von Florenz*, Dr. Becce also composed premiere music for *Das Cabinet des Dr. Caligari*.

Die Brüder Schellenberg

The Brothers Schellenberg aka *Two Brothers*; Universum-Film AG (Ufa), Berlin—1925/26; Filmed at Ufa Studios (Jofa) and Ufa-Tempelhof; Distributed by Decla-Bioscop-Verleih; *Zensur*: 11 March 1926—7 Acts, 2834 meters; World premiere: 22 March 1926—Ufa-Palast am Zoo, Berlin

CAST: Conrad Veidt *Wenzel* and *Michael Schellenberg*; Lil Dagover *Esther Raucheisen*; Henry de Vries *Herr Raucheisen*; Werner Fütterer *Georg Weidenbach*; Bruno Kastner *Kaczinsky*; Liane Haid *Jenny Florian*; Frieda Richard *her Mother*; Julius Falkenstein *Esther's First Suitor*; Wilhelm Bendow *Esther's Second Suitor*; Erich Kaiser-Titz *Esther's Third Suitor*; Paul Morgan *A Gangster*; with Jaro Fürth

CREDITS: *Director* Karl Grune; *Scenario* Karl Grune, Willy Haas; *Based on the eponymous novel by* Bernhard Kellermann; *Photographed by* Karl Hasselmann; *Set Designs* Karl Görge, Kurt Kahle; *Music for the Theater* Werner Richard Heymann; *Conductor (Theater/Premiere)* Erno Rapee

SYNOPSIS: A terrible accident occurs at the Raucheisen gas works—a huge explosion kills and injures more than a hundred workers. Herr Raucheisen (Henri de Vries) is more concerned about the 5 million marks of insurance money covering the property damage than he is about the loss of life. He does react—angrily—when he discovers that his secretary, Wenzel Schellenberg (Conrad Veidt), is again late for work; Wenzel is discharged.

Wenzel's brother, Michael (Conrad Veidt)—the plant foreman—is appalled by the accident and has worked the night through helping the injured. When Raucheisen hints that Michael may have somehow been responsible for the tragedy, the foreman hands in his notice. Now at liberty, Michael decides to devote his life to helping the poor and the unemployed. Wenzel doesn't share his concern (his dream has always been one of wealth) and the brothers go their separate ways.

Using what he has learned from Raucheisen's business practices, Wenzel starts a successful career. At an antiques auction, he first meets Jenny and her mother. Jenny, an unemployed actress, is a warm and beautiful girl. Wenzel soon falls in love with her and arranges for her to be employed in a famous theater. He courts her and, slowly, Jenny begins to reciprocate, going so far as to break off with her fiancé, Georg Weidenbach (Werner Fütterer), who is recovering from the injuries he sustained at the Raucheisen explosion.

Meanwhile, Michael's project—a colony for the unemployed—has grown prodigiously; some 3000 men are already living there. To the colony comes Georg. Abandoned by his fiancée and still physically weak, he looks for a new start.

During an economic downturn, Raucheisen loses a lot of money when Wenzel engineers a buyout of Raucheisen stock at the exchange. The magnate's beautiful daughter, Esther (Lil Dagover), cannot deal with this turn of events and continues to spend money as if there were no tomorrow. At a posh restaurant, she crosses paths with Wenzel and Jenny, who have come to celebrate their impending marriage. Wenzel's secret admiration for his ex-boss's daughter is reawakened by Esther's exotic beauty. Without thinking twice, he follows Esther to Paris, leaving behind his unsuspecting fiancée. He discovers that Esther is in Paris for a tryst with her secret lover, Kraczinsky (Bruno Kastner), who is badly in need of money. Wenzel agrees to help Kraczinsky, *if* Esther will marry him.

Jenny, suspicious of her fiancé's long journey abroad, follows him to Paris. Depressed, she runs into Michael, who is also en route to ask his brother for a monetary contribution for his colony. Michael comforts Jenny. When they arrive at Wenzel's hotel, they learn that Jenny's fears have

been realized; Esther and Wenzel are to be married. Overwhelmed, Jenny tries to commit suicide by diving off the hotel balcony. Michael takes the injured woman back to the safety of his colony.

Wenzel is less than satisfied with Esther as his wife. She is frigid, sarcastic and uncaring: Wenzel realizes that she has married him only for his money. Slowly his unrequited love drives him mad. When he learns that Esther and Kraczinsky are planning to elope, he strangles his faithless wife in a fit of blind rage.

Completely shattered, Wenzel makes his way to Michael's colony, where Jenny and Georg have become reconciled. The colony and the reunited young couple look forward to a bright future while Wenzel, lost in madness, is removed to an asylum.

Esther (Lil Dagover) has frustrated poor Wenzel (Connie) for the last time. (*Die Brüder Schellenberg*)

REVIEWS: "…Out of all the actors, we first have to name Conrad Veidt, who plays the double role of the two brothers. The two characters are studies [done] with the utmost refinement, both continuously revealing new nuances. As the elegant adventurer, he is all charm and appealing kindness, the type that strongly appeals to women, and as the idealistic founder of the city, Veidt has the deep introversion of the all-wise man who suffers."

Lichtbildbühne,
23 March 1926

"…Grune … has created a film that is, with all its spiritual delicacy, a thriller. Grune brings thrills, diversion, even effects, that are thrown hard into the audience; in the next moment, he is the incomparable messenger of the soul, whom we admired in *Die Strasse*…"

Der Kinematograph, No. 997;
28 March 1926

"…In this film, Conrad Veidt portrays both the good and the bad brother. He is himself for the money-mad mundane creature, and wears spectacles, a fair wig and beard for the spiritual brother, Michael. [Any] fault, however, lies with the director or the scenarist and not with Mr. Veidt, who in both instances does exceedingly well…."

New York Times,
21 August 1928 —
Mordaunt Hall

"…Conrad Veidt plays a dual role of two brothers, one an avaricious businessman and the other a sappy philanthropist.
"You have to sit through [the movie] to appreciate how badly capable actors can do under certain circumstances."
Variety, 22 August 1928 — Rush.

NOTES AND QUOTES: Due to the parameters of Willy Haas and Karl Grune's scenario, Veidt's dual role, while handled competently, is rather flat and unimpressive. Goody-goody Michael Schellenberg appears only intermittently throughout the photoplay — at times, just as one is on the verge of forgetting that there are *two* Schellenberg brothers — and that's just as well: vapid and one-dimensional, Michael's face consistently reflects his bearing the weight of the world on his shoulders. Karl Hasselmann's extreme closeups of Veidt as the benevolent brother verge on those ghastly studies in self-martyrdom with which Hollywood burdened Christ in any of its overlong renditions of the gospel accounts.

It's only with ne'er-do-well Wenzel Schellenberg that Connie has a shot at indulging in a little character development. Wenzel drips distasteful realism from every pore, at least up until the point when he begins to realize that Lil Dagover's Esther — replete with bee-stung lips and eyeshadowed à la Cesare in *Das Cabinet des Dr. Caligari* — will sashay seductively for everyone *but* him. Triggered by Lil's reaction to an over-the-shoulder ECU of the "demonic Veidt," Connie abruptly abdicates realism in favor of the broadest imaginable strokes of lust and frustration. It's anybody's guess as to whether he and Fraulein Dagover are burlesquing their material, or have wandered into some sort of *Aufklärungsfilme* throwback. Dagover's spoiled Aryan princess is reduced in either case to a second-generation knock-off of Theda Bara at *her* most outrageous. Whether the fault ultimately lay with the script, the direction, or the actors' interpretation, none of this is a pretty sight, and the film — which does not come close to meriting the superlatives tossed about in the contemporary German critiques — suffers because of it.

Dürfen wir schweigen?

[LOST*] *Should We Be Silent?*; Nero-Film GmbH, Berlin—1926; Filmed at Jofa Studios, February—March 1926; Distributed by Bayerische Film GmbH; *Zensur*: 17 March 1926—7 Acts, 2686 meters; Forbidden to adolescents; World premiere: 6 April 1926 Alhambra Kurfürstendamm, Berlin

CAST: Conrad Veidt *Paul Hartwig*; Walter Rilla *Dr. Georg Mauthner*; Henri de Vries *Henry Pierson*; Mary Parker *Leonie, his Daughter*; Betty Astor *Inge*; Elga Brink *the Assistant*; Fritz Kortner *the Doctor*; John Gottowt *his Assistant*; Ernst Laskowski *the Young Man*; Maria West *the Young Woman*; Maria Forescu *First Patient*; Else Plessner *Second Patient*; Frieda Richard *the Old Woman*; Ernst Verebes *Gerd*; Albert Paulig *the Waiter*; Ernst Stammer *the Proprietor*; Bella Pollini *the Dancer*

CREDITS: *Director* Richard Oswald; *Scenario* Richard Oswald; *Photographed by* Gustav Ucicky, Eduard von Borsody; *Set Design* Heinrich Richter; *Theatrical Music at Premiere* Hans May

SYNOPSIS: Dr. Mauthner (Walter Rilla) is a specialist in venereal diseases. He is engaged to Leonie (Mary Parker), but the young woman — due to her fiancé's dedication to his work — feels neglected. Thus, she falls in love with Paul Hartwig (Conrad Veidt), a painter whose passionate character is quite different from the subdued nature of the physician. It's not long before Leonie breaks up with Mauthner and becomes engaged to Hartwig.

Hartwig does not want to lose Mauthner's friendship, however, and when the doctor advises him to have a blood test done, the painter agrees. The test turns out positive, showing the signs of venereal disease; Hartwig reacts angrily, feeling that Mauthner intended to get his revenge on him in this fashion. He marries Leonie despite the blood test results, and soon has a sick wife and a sickly daughter.

Meanwhile, Mauthner has married his assistant (Elga Brink), and they are the parents of a healthy boy.

Leonie dies. Convinced that he has caused his wife's death and his daughter's tragic condition, Hartwig leaves town and takes up the vagabond life. Many years later, as a sick, down-at-his-heels sort, Hartwig returns to inquire after his daughter. To his great relief, the dying man discovers that she was healed by Dr. Mauthner and that she is engaged to Mauthner's son.

REVIEWS: "...The tricky subject matter is handled with discretion, and the actors— above all, Conrad Veidt — labor mightily to stay within artistic boundaries. The film is very well capable of opening the eyes of young, inexperienced people to the perils of quackery, while drawing attention to how the dreadful dangers in the streets and houses of ill repute can have a lifelong effect...."

Unknown review

"...[Conrad] Veidt portrayed the syphilitic painter. ... He performs with masterly technique and, here, first achieves true expression and simplicity in the death scene. Here, he becomes as mature as the beggar and forgets the onus of his reputation as a great actor; here, the artist triumphs over the poseur...."

Unknown review,
Berlin newspaper — F.S.

"Concerning the plot, Richard Oswald created an interesting and moving work. Syphilis, which is just tragic and not dramatic, is interwoven with the actors into a really exciting film. ... In the leading role, as the thoughtless painter — and, later, depraved sufferer — Conrad Veidt shows the whole spectrum of his abilities. He provides outstanding acting..."

Lichtbildbühne, 7 April 1926

Dürfen wir schweigen? exists in fragmentary form.

Another of Connie's many cinematic "artists," Paul Hartwig. (*Dürfen wir schweigen?*)

"…Conrad Veidt portrays the sick painter, unshakable and deeply afflicted on the road from being a young, life-loving man, to the beggar, obsessed with death. Veidt, who never settles into routine, answers the film's title by the power of his performance with a determined 'NO!'…"

> Unknown review,
> following premiere at
> Alhambra Theater, Berlin

"…What Veidt accomplishes is thrilling and overwhelming. He may be the most impressive actor in Germany today… This film ought to be successful, shown in many cinemas, and I wish for that to happen, but the applause at the premiere, and this should be stressed, was only for Conrad Veidt."

> *Der Film* (Berlin), No. 15;
> 11 April 1926

"…Richard Oswald [has produced] a seven-part drama that is filled with excitement and vivid scenes of the swamp that is city life. It is also filled with hope, as it shows that even the most severe problems can be repaired, when one follows the advice of competent physicians.

"Conrad Veidt gives one of his finest performances…"

> Unknown review,
> 8 April 1926 — Z.

"…This moving film showcases Conrad Veidt, again in command of his powers, who actually ensures the success of the film from the outset. Isn't it the greatest indication of art, that, made up as a ragged old man, he stumbles along Leipziger Street, in the heart of Berlin, unnoticed by thousands of passers-by, of whom perhaps one casts a pitiful look upon [him] as he bends to pick up a cigar butt?"

> *Kreuz-Zeitung*, 11 April 1926

Kreuzzug des Weibes

The Wife's Crusade aka *Unwelcome Children*; *The Cross Women Have to Bear*; Arthur Ziehm-Internationale Film Exchange, Berlin — 1926; Distributed by Arthur Ziehm; Filmed at Staaken, August-September, 1926; *Zensur*: 24 September 1926 — 7 Acts, 2225 meters; Forbidden to adolescents; World premiere: 1 October 1926 Alhambra Kurfürstendamm *and* Primus-Palast, Berlin

CAST: Conrad Veidt *the Prosecutor*; Werner Krauss *the Idiot*; Harry Liedtke *the Doctor*; Maly Delschaft *the Woman*; Andja Zimowa *the Rich Woman*; Ernst Hoffmann *Her Husband*; Aribert Wäscher *their Family Doctor*; Fritz Alberti *the Worker*; Gertrud Arnold *his Wife*; Hedwig Wangel *their Eldest Daughter*; with Simone Vaudry, Dr. Philipp Manning, Iwa Wanja, Hilde Gerdt, Heinrich Schmück

CREDITS: *Producer* Günther Stapenhorst (for Arthur Ziehm), Heinz Sander; *Director* Martin Berger; *Original Music* Friedrich Holländer; *Scenario* Osio Koffler, Martin Berger; *Set Design* Robert A. Dietrich; *Preliminary Sketches* Osio Koffler, R.A. Dietrich; *Photographed by* Sophus Wangoe, A.O. Weitzenberg; *Camera Effects* Paul R. von Knüpfer

Synopsis: Public Law §218 forbids abortion.

The prosecuting attorney (Conrad Veidt) knows that this law often causes a good deal of pain, but he is steadfast in his commitment to uphold it. One day, he must intervene in two cases of forbidden abortion: a rich lady (Andja Zimowa), fearing the loss of her figure, gets rid of the unwanted fetus and bribes her physician (Aribert Wäscher) to testify that her life had been otherwise endangered, the only mitigating circumstance. The prosecutor's hands are tied.

The other case is that of a poor worker (Fritz Alberti) and his wife (Gertrud Arnold). Unable to cope with another mouth to feed, they plead for help from their physician (Harry Liedtke). Fearing the consequences of the law, the doctor declines to help; the woman attempts to perform the abortion herself and dies in the process. Her husband is cited under law §218 and the prosecutor, although aware that this means the children will be without both parents, proceeds with the arrest. His fiancée, a teacher (Maly Delschaft), who feels strongly for the poor worker, is appalled; for the first time, her relationship with her lover is imperiled.

She visits the worker's children and tries to comfort them. In her absence, a basket of delicacies arrives from the prosecutor, who is looking to reconcile. The concierge takes the basket and places it in the teacher's flat. The concierge's feeble-minded son (Werner Krauss) finds the basket and drinks the bottle of champagne he finds therein. Driven by alcohol, he pounces on the teacher when she returns and brutally rapes her. Fearing scandal and shame, the teacher is silent; only her physician learns of the incident, and he pronounces her pregnant. Moved by the woman's situation, the doctor breaks the

law; later, he goes to the prosecutor to turn himself in.

During the doctor's statement, the prosecutor realizes that the woman being described is his fiancée. He rushes to her. At first, he is loath to believe her story. After meeting the feeble-minded man, however, he no longer doubts the teacher's word. The prosecutor is torn between his duty to the law and his love for his fiancée. In the end, he opts for love and steps down from his professional position.

Reviews: "It is sensational, seeing three actors of the caliber of Conrad Veidt, Werner Krauss and Harry Liedtke in one picture... But this delicate subject required the very best actors.

"Director Martin Berger has crafted [this film] well... The characters played by Conrad Veidt and Werner Krauss— the attorney and the idiot — are filled with serious, artistic genius."

Der Kinematograph,
No. 1024; 1926

"A serious attempt at art, a serious attempt at social morality has driven the creator of this work... The ensemble is sufficiently exquisite to assure this film's artistic merit from the very start. Werner Krauss plays an idiot of terrifying ingenuousness; he spares the audience nothing. Conrad Veidt, the attorney, offers an excellent character study and what must be stressed is that he avoids any and all exaggeration or caricature."

Lichtbildbühne, No. 235;
2 October 1926

"Martin Berger breaks with all cinematic conventions. There are no cars driving by, no cigarettes casually smoked, no love scenes. Because of this, the sparse, economical, rational Berger has become a far more interesting creator than the one we've known. He inspires his actors to a

Opposite: Original release poster. (*Kreuzzug des Weibes*)

vivid intensity, as well. He so realistically creates the scene of the brutal rape of the teacher by the idiot that even the censor must be silent…"

Film-Kurier, No. 231;
2 October 1926

NOTES AND QUOTES: Shades of the *Aufklärungsfilme*! This proabortion film was one of a series of sensationalistic "socially aware" films from late '20s, including William Dieterle's *Sex in Fetters* (1928). Per William K. Everson, Veidt "brings power and conviction to the role of an anti-abortion lawyer, with Delschaft as his social-worker fiancée, whose personal circumstances force him to rethink his position; additionally, it is a perverse pleasure to see Liedtke and Werner Krauss respectively as a sympathetic abortion doctor and someone who should have been pre-terminated."

It is interesting to note that, despite its explosive subject, *Kreuzzug des Weibes* was not cut a foot during censorship. This may well have been due to the fact that, although the film dealt with abortion, not once was the word mentioned.

In dealing with this controversial theme, director Martin Berger opted to depict the characters impersonally: no one has a name; all are symbols. The art director, too, has chosen settings closer to those found on the legitimate stage than to film sets. In addition, in an effort to avoid identification with any one locale, the décor is rather sparse and, at times, almost Expressionistic. In the office of the prosecuting attorney, sitting amidst the rectangular furniture, is a chair with a backrest so high that no human being could fill it.

Discussions that would ordinarily require multiple title cards are reduced to the production of simple pictures. When the attorney cites the sixth commandment, the physician counters with a picture of endless rows of graves of soldiers, killed during war. Harry Liedtke does well with the difficult role of the physician, forbidden as he is by the director's vision from depicting any of his character's innate, human goodness. Maly Delschaft is not quite so successful; her doll-like poses do not convey the same, nonpersonal color that Liedtke achieves. Connie is perhaps the only actor who remains a human being while not straying from the symbolic sphere that has been so carefully established. Werner Krauss, whose idiot is enigmatically disturbing (one can neither understand, nor like nor hate him) cops the prize for most impressive performance.

Der Student von Prag

The Student of Prague; aka *The Man Who Cheated Life* (USA); H.R. Sokal-Film GmbH, Berlin — 1926; Distributed by Sokal-Film; Filmed at Staaken, July — September 1926; *Zensur:* 19 October 1926 — 7 Acts, 3173 meters; Forbidden to adolescents; World premiere: 25 October 1926 Capitol, Berlin; Reissued as a part-sound film (music/sound effects) in 1930; Original running time: 117 minutes (24 fps)

CAST: Conrad Veidt *the Student, Balduin* (*Baldwin*); Werner Krauss *Scapinelli*; Elizza La Porta *Lyduschka, a flower girl*; Ferdinand von Alten *Baron Waldis Schwarzeberg*; Fritz Alberti *Count von Schwarzeberg*; Agnes Esterhazy *Countess Marguerite*; with Max Maximilian, Sylvia Torf, Marian Alma, Erich Kober

CREDITS: *Producer* Max Maximilian; *Director* Henrik Galeen; *Asst. Director* Erich Kober; *Scenario* Henrik Galeen, Hanns Heinz Ewers; *Based on* William Wilson *by* Edgar Allen Poe; *Set Designs* Hermann Warm; *Photographed by* Günther Krampf, Erich Nitzschmann; *Theater Music* Willy Schmidt-Gentner

SYNOPSIS: The student Balduin (Conrad Veidt) is the best swordsman in Prague, but he's almost penniless all the time. He meets up with the mysterious Scapinelli (Werner Krauss), who offers his help. The poor student would really like to marry a rich heiress, so Scapinelli irritates the horse of Margit (Agnes Esterhazy), the beautiful daughter of Count Schwarzenberg (Fritz Alberti) during a hunt, so that Balduin can save her. The two fall in love, although Margit is betrothed to her cousin, Baron Waldis-Schwarzenberg (Ferdinand von Alten).

In return for this "favor," Balduin sells his mirror image to Scapinelli for a fortune in gold pieces; the no-longer-poor student can now continue to court the countess. He discovers to his chagrin, however, that not only does he no longer cast a reflection in a looking glass, but that his mirror image has a life of its own and is apparently dedicated to thwarting his every move and devastating his plans.

The gypsy girl Lyduschka (Elizza La Porta), who secretly loves Balduin, informs Baron Waldis-Schwarzenberg of the love affair going on between his fiancée and the student. Furious, the baron challenges his rival to a duel. Balduin arrives late for the duel and encounters his mirror image, bloodied rapier in hand; the doppelgänger has fought the duel for him.

Balduin is expelled from the university and abandoned by his friends. The countess, to whom he has confessed his dealings with Scapinelli, turns away from him. His mirror image follows him everywhere. Before long, the desolate ex-student has had enough, and he shoots his doppelgänger. Once again, he can see himself in the glass, but his shirt is full of blood, for the bullet meant for the phantom has hit him. He dies.

REVIEWS: "No picture of any nationality has been so consistently pictorially well composed as this. The acting is magnificent and the direction masterly...."

"Conrad Veidt gives a performance that, of its kind, is unequalled in screen annals. He fascinates and expresses vividly every emotion during his checkered downfall...."

Kinematograph Weekly, 1926

"Today's version, with Conrad Veidt, is much better, much more demonic [than Wegener's 1913 version] and it doesn't matter that beside the genius of this actor, and that beside a great talent like Werner Krauss, is Elizza La Porta — a novice — or Agnes Esterhazy, who is not very talented."

Der Kinematograph, No. 1028; 31 October 1926

"Sixteen years ago, Wegener was this dark, nihilistic Student of Prague, who surrendered his reflection to the money-lender... Today it is Conrad Veidt. And he is at least as magnificent as his predecessor."

Film-Kurier, 26 October 1926 — W. Haas

"... [*The Man Who Cheated Life*] is a relatively antiquated German production with a modicum of interest due to the plot of the story and, to a certain extent, to Conrad Veidt's careful and intelligent interpretation of the leading role. His acting, however, suffers through the technical weakness of pictures of the time. His movements are often too studied or too accelerated...."

New York Times, 11 February 1929 — Mordaunt Hall

(As *The Man Who Cheated Life*) "To our mind it is [Conrad Veidt's] best performance in any picture of his shown in America. Certainly the final sequence of his vain flight from his ever pursuing image and the life and death climax before the shattered mirror is one of the finest achievements of screen pantomime and camera magic. ... New to and indicative of Mr. Veidt's hitherto inadequately revealed mimetic range is his convincing portrayal of a lover in his scenes with Marguerite."

National Board of Review Magazine, February 1929

NOTES AND QUOTES: The Capitol Theater in Berlin, where the film premiered,

Balduin and his doppelgänger. (*Der Student von Prag*)

sold out daily, and the press compared Veidt's fencing scenes with Douglas Fairbanks' in *The Mark of Zorro*. Even the original scenarist gave it high marks. "In many respects, the second film is much superior to the first... a powerful work of art and proves for the second time that in film, pure art can have great success," Hanns Heinz Ewers wrote in 1930. Echoing this sentiment was Paul Rotha (*The Film Till Now*), who observed that

Expressionist themes and cubist settings, so marked in the first German period, had developed into motives of mysticism and Baroque design, to give place again to the naturalness of the street, the town, and the individual. *The Student of Prague* combined both of these latter two periods. It had open spaciousness and dark psychology, wild poetic beauty and a deeply dramatic theme. Beyond this, it had Conrad Veidt at his best... As a film that relied for its emotional effect on the nature of the material, the lighting and pictorial composition, it was unparalleled.

Der Student von Prag was first produced in 1913 by Apex/Bioscop studios and carried the alternative title *A Bargain with Satan*. Paul Wegener and his wife took the leads, and John Gottowt essayed the role of Scapinelli. The sound remake came in 1935, courtesy of Cine Allianz, with Anton Wohlbrueck (later Walbrook), Dorothea Wieck, and Theodor Loos as the juveniles and the Dark One, respectively.

It's ironic that Wegener's *Student*, Germany's first fantasy film of note, took as its source not the *Niebelungenlied* or other of the Teutonic Ur-legends, but a short story (*William Wilson*) by American writer Edgar Allan Poe.

Die Flucht in die Nacht

The Flight in the Night; aka ***Enrico IV***; ***Die lebende Maske*** (Austria); Nero-Film GmbH, Berlin—1926; Distributed by Domo-Strauss-Film, Rome; *Zensur*: 13 November 1926—6 Acts, 1856 meters; Forbidden to adolescents; World premiere: 13 December 1926 Marmorhaus, Berlin; Released in the USA in 1928 as *The Living Mask*

CAST: Conrad Veidt *Count Heinrich di Favari* (German print), *Count De Nolli* (Italian print); Agnes Esterhazy *Countess Matilde Spine [Matilde de Toscana]*; Henriette Fantis *Her Daughter, as an Adult*; Robert Scholz *Baron Tito Belcredi [Carlo D'Angio]*; Hermann Vallentin *Doctor Genoni*; Paul Biensfeldt *Old Giovanni*; with Angelo Ferrari, Oreste Bilancia, Hertha von Walther, Georg John, John Gottowt, Carl Geppert

CREDITS: *Director* Amleto Palmeri; *Filmed Scenario* Dr. Alfred Schirokauer, Kurt Wesse; *Early Scenario* Amleto Palmeri; *Based on the play* Enrico IV *by* Luigi Pirandello; *Photographed by* Curt Courant, Arpad Viragh; *Set Designs* Hermann Warm

Nota bene: It was possible to screen only a cut Italian print of this picture; hence, the nomenclature in the synopsis is that of *Enrico IV*, not *Die Flucht in die Nacht*.

SYNOPSIS: The fabulously wealthy Count Di Nolli (Conrad Veidt) is hosting an elaborate masquerade, one that encompasses all the vast expanses of his lands. Each of his guests is dressed as a nobleman, an emperor or a prince, from a century of his or her own choosing. Di Nolli is dressed as the Emperor Henry IV; riding alongside him in an elaborate parade of pageantry is the Countess Matilde Spine (Agnes Esterhazy), arrayed as Matilde of Toscana. Galloping behind the pair is the Baron Tito Belcredi (Robert Scholz), who is in love with Matilde and enormously jealous of Di Nolli. Belcredi repeatedly sticks Di Nolli's horse in the hindquarters with his sword, driving the animal into a frenzy. The horse bolts and Di Nolli is soon thrown. He is taken back to the villa posthaste.

Di Nolli regains consciousness shortly thereafter, to the relief of Matilde, her young daughter, and all of the guests save Belcredi. The count, however, takes

Matilde's hand and proceeds haughtily among his assembled guests. At first, the onlookers attribute the count's regal mien to his being a splendid actor; it gradually becomes evident, though, that the fall from the horse has caused the nobleman to believe that he really is Enrico IV.

Years pass. Di Nolli, caught up in his delusion that he is the medieval emperor, has become a recluse. Cared for by his servants (who dress up for the roles they are playing) and basically confined to a small portion of the villa (his "throne room" and his bed chamber), the "emperor" only rarely sees outsiders. In the interim, Matilde has become Belcredi's consort (it is unclear from the print viewed whether the two have actually married), while her daughter (Henriette Fantis), now grown, has a beau of her own. Both women and their admirers meet with Dr. Genoni (Hermann Vallentin), a physician specializing in disorders of the mind.

In order to determine whether Di Nolli can be cured, the doctor must visit with the recluse. Donning the guise of the Bishop of Cluny, Genoni — along with a costumed Matilde and Belcredi — are granted "an audience" with the emperor. As they await Enrico IV in his throne room, Matilde's daughter notices a mural of Matilde di Toscana. The portrait is the spitting image of Matilde Spine (in her youth), and of Matilde's daughter, at this very moment. The emperor appears and greets the "bishop" with humility and gratitude. While he notes (but apparently does not recognize) Matilde, he does react to Belcredi, whom he denounces as Pietro Damiani, "the traitor!"

The three impersonators leave the throne room, pausing on the other side of the door for both a recap of the experience and Genoni's thought on the possibility of a cure. Enrico listens carefully from the other side of the locked door. Turning to his attendants, he astonishes them by re-vealing that he is aware of everything the doctor and his friends are doing! Not long afterwards, Genoni and the others hold a meeting wherein the physician says that a bit of radical action may be necessary to snap Di Nolli out of his delusion. As the portrait of the medieval countess on the wall of the throne room is Matilde's daughter to a "T," the young woman must dress the part, confront Di Nolli, and seek to bring him around. Initially no one is in favor of this plan; as they bicker among themselves, however, Di Nolli, who has been wandering through the "normal" rooms of his villa courtesy of an unlocked door, observes their movements from a staircase. He misunderstands Belcredi's reaching for Matilde; the couple were arguing over Belcredi's treatment of Matilde as a plaything, his slave.

It is finally agreed to go ahead with Genoni's scheme. With Belcredi and Matilde within earshot, Matilde's daughter — dressed in an exact replica of the costume seen in the mural — approaches Enrico. As the emperor's thoughts soon turn to love for his lady, Belcredi is informed by the costumed attendants that Di Nolli recovered his wits some time ago! Belcredi runs into the room and confronts Di Nolli. Matilde looks on incredulously as "Enrico" admits that, somehow, his reason returned suddenly some time earlier. When he saw himself in the mirror, however, and realized that he had spent much of his life in the darkness of the medieval delusion, he decided to remain Enrico IV, and to punish those who had made him miss out on life. Rejecting Matilde for having gone over to his rival, Di Nolli makes for the daughter: in her, he can recapture his youth! The young woman screams and Belcredi lunges for the count. Di Nolli stabs Belcredi, who dies repeating: "You are not crazy! You are not crazy!"

REVIEWS: "Nero-Film has just shot their new film *Enrico IV* in Staaken. They

As Count Heinrich di Favari, aka Count De Nolli, in *Die Flucht in Die Nacht*, aka *Enrico IV*.

have adapted Pirandello's well-known novel [*sic*] about a man who believes himself to be a king… This is an outstanding achievement for Veidt, one that arose under the careful direction of the Italian director, Palmeri. Much praise, too, for the architect, Hermann Warm; we have seldom seen such magnificent period-rich decorum than the throne room and the stairs."

> *Reichsfilmblatt*, No. 1926;
> 26 June 1926

"It seems that no one has ever considered creating an archive for film-acting masterpieces, where outstanding performances are collected and preserved… Many scenes from *Enrico IV*, that are real masterworks of Conrad Veidt, are worth being collected in such an archive. On the whole, unfortunately, the film is a failure…. Besides Conrad Veidt's acting, everything pales into insignificance…"

> *Der Bildwart* (Berlin), No. 2;
> February 1927

NOTES AND QUOTES: Pirandello's play was once heralded (throughout Europe, at least) as "the twentieth-century *Hamlet*," so the film version, which was underwritten jointly by Roman and German companies, was photographed (with an eye to authenticity) on location in the vicinity of Florence. As a phenomenally successful (and profitable) stage production of the play had just closed, the playwright was persuaded to back the film project; the fact that his friend Amleto Palmeri was to direct helped make the decision an easy one.

Veidt does an admirable job shifting backward and forward between feigning the madness he had suffered through (and survived), and enacting the madness he has assumed voluntarily. In Pirandelloish terms, his Di Nolli is a canny lunatic who clings to his madness as a survival strategy. Even though his performance can be experienced only via a washed-out copy of a piecemeal print, one can only marvel at how the actor displays a spectrum of emotion and comprehension with his eyes and facial expressions. It is no exaggeration to state that the other principals, who do breathe life into what are essentially mundane figures, are in a different league altogether when it comes to subtlety and nuance.

Enrico IV has been remade several times since Palmeri's silent feature: twice in Italy (the 1983 color production, starring Marcello Mastroianni and Claudia Cardinale, is still readily available) and once (with substantial rewriting and the introduction of several tenuously related subplots) in France.

The Beloved Rogue

A Feature Production, released through United Artists— World premiere: 12 March 1927 —10 reels (c. 99 minutes)

CAST: Conrad Veidt *Louis XI*; John Barrymore *François Villon*; Marceline Day *Charlotte de Vauxcelles*; Henry Victor *Thibault d'Aussigny*; Lawson Butt *John, Duke of Burgundy*; Mack Swain *Nicholas*; Slim Summerville *Jehan*; Otto Matieson *Olivier, the King's Barber*; Rose Dione *Margot*; Bertram Grassby *Duke of Orleans*; Lucy Beaumont *Villon's Mother*; Angelo Rossitto *Beppo*; Jane Winton *The Abbess*; Martha Franklin *Maid*; Nigel de Brulier *Astrologer*; Dick Sutherland *Tristan l'Hermite*; Dickie Moore *Infant Villon*

CREDITS: *Director* Alan Crosland; *Production Manager* Walter Mayo; *Screenplay by* Paul Bern; *Based on the operetta* The Vagabond King *by* Rudolf Friml; *Titles* Walter Anthony, George Marion, Jr.; *Photographed by* Joe August; *Art Director* William Cameron Menzies; *Editor* Hal C. Kern; *Asst. Director* Gordon Hollingshead; *Wardrobe Manager* Frank Donellan; *Technical Director* Ned Herbert Mann; *Comedy Construction* Bryant Foy

SYNOPSIS: John, the Duke of Burgundy (Lawson Butt), has his eye on the French throne, despite it's being occupied by King Louis XI (Conrad Veidt). The extremely superstitious Louis is putty in the hands of the court astrologer (Nigel de Brulier), who counsels that the king tread lightly and politely where Burgundy is concerned. Thus it is that Louis accedes without hesitation when Burgundy asks that the king's ward, Charlotte de Vauxcelles (Marceline Day), be given over in marriage to the duke's cousin, Thibault d'Aussigny (Henry Victor). The king seemingly pays little heed either to Charlotte's protests or to the fact that the new liege of Vauxcelles will have his foot in Paris.

In the meanwhile, poet and carouser François Villon (John Barrymore) is selected by the Paris mob as king of fools for All Fools' Day. When he makes a witty but unfortunate remark to Burgundy, Louis banishes him from Paris. Accompanied by his sidekicks, Nicholas (Mack Swain) and Jehan (Slim Summerville), Villon conspires to steal a wagon filled with food and to catapult it to the Parisian poor; in the process, he is hurled through an inn window and into the very room where Charlotte is huddled, as she and Thibault wait out a snowstorm. Through bravado and dumb luck, Villon defeats Thibault in an uneven duel, and the poet and the lady — who now realizes that she is in the company of Francois Villon, the poet she reveres (and the man she comes to love) — make their escape.

When (inevitably) captured, Villon plays on the king's superstitions— the poet announces how it is written that his own death will precede the king's by 24 hours—and becomes a favorite at court. Charlotte is then kidnapped by Burgundy's men and Villon, who has made the king realize the duke's innermost plans to seize the throne, follows them and is captured and subjected to torture. Moments before the poet is executed, the disguised Louis, along with his soldiers and a good number of loyal Parisian riffraff, rescues Villon and puts an end to Burgundy's perfidy. Not long after, the moody king consents to the marriage between Villon — surely the brightest of all commoners— and the lovely Charlotte de Vauxcelles.

REVIEWS: "...Conrad Veidt, that competent German character actor, fills the role of the inquisitive and crafty Louis. Mr. Veidt gives a sound performance, making this whimsical ruler perhaps a little too healthy and well nourished in appearance. It is a part in which Fritz Lieber excelled, and while Mr. Veidt's characterization is satisfactory, it does not measure up to Mr. Lieber's brilliant impersonation of the Fox film *If I Were King*."

New York Times, 14 March
1927 — Mordaunt Hall

"...The film is important to us because Conrad Veidt has made the figure of King Louis XI one of his heartfelt creations, one that no one else could play. Veidt's role [however] was trimmed a great deal in comparison with Barrymore's. John Barrymore is not only a charming man, but a great actor, who deserves better scripts than these dishes of ice cream he is served..."

Der Kinematograph, No. 1054;
1 May 1927

Right: Connie's name and image figured prominently in all German advertising. (*The Beloved Rogue*)

Connie's height — apparently something of a surprise to both Barrymore and studio execs — forced him to play Louis XI from the crouch. (*The Beloved Rogue*)

"The picture is sure-fire hokum with Barrymore splendid in a role somewhat out of the ordinary for him, and a production replete with fine sets and lavish display... The picture will undoubtedly merit the decided approval of the fan crowd."

Film Daily, 20 March 1927

"...[John] Barrymore's work is excellent and it will doubtless surprise some of his fans to see him as a screen buffoon engaged in action that in modern short subjects would be labeled as slapstick. ... Conrad Veidt gives a convincing and excellent characterization of the crafty, superstitious monarch...."

Motion Picture World,
2 April 1927

"...[When previewed] the Veidt film *The Beloved Rogue* [contained] few scenes with Veidt.... The film is regarded as a Bar-

rymore film; Conrad Veidt has therefore sunk to the level of a second-class artist.... But now that Barrymore's impact ... is less than had been expected ... what happens? They will cut out more scenes with Veidt, which will weaken the impressive figure of Veidt's Louis XI even more"

Die Filmwoche, No. 17;
27 April 1927

NOTES AND QUOTES: "*The Beloved Rogue* ... might be considered the cornerstone of Hollywood gothic... Almost in spite of himself, Crosland was influenced (as were many directors of the period) by the work of German directors like F.W. Murnau and Fritz Lang. The use of scenery, lighting, and effects in *TBR* do much to enhance the story and Barrymore's performance... Conrad Veidt's interpretation of King Louis [is] thoroughly stylized and Germanic."

John Rogers; laserdisc

liner notes/*The Beloved Rogue*
(Voyager/Killiam Silent Classics)

The German reviews of *The Beloved Rogue* quoted above are representative of the tone taken toward the picture. Germany, which had had a brief affair with *Kostümfilme* (period pictures, heavy on costumes and settings, laced through with historical portent) earlier in the decade, now reacted with the self-righteous indignation of a jilted lover. With regard to commentaries from pre–Nazi days, it is difficult to ascertain whether the vituperation of many of the German critiques of English-language films starring German expatriates reflected personal emotion (anger, frustration, disappointment), professional passion (arrogance, superiority, envy), or both. As various citations peppered throughout this book reveal, few Hollywood productions employing German artists or technicians escaped critiques couched in sarcasm or grounded in condescension.

Following the commercial (if not critical) success of *The Beloved Rogue*, First National set out to sign Veidt for *The Easiest Way*, a social drama based on the eponymous 1909 play by Eugene Walter. Belle Bennett had been tagged to appear opposite the German actor, and Henry King had been assigned to direct. Producer David Fink dropped the project before Connie could be signed, however, as the Hays Office had forewarned First National that the scenario, as proposed, would have more than its fair share of censorship problems. Veidt went over to Universal; so, for the moment, did *The Easiest Way*. Uncle Carl's advisors likewise recommended passing on the property, which was ultimately made — starring Constance (not Belle) Bennett and Adolphe Menjou — by MGM in 1931.

A Man's Past

[LOST] Universal (Super Jewel)—1927—6 reels (6047 feet); World premiere: 13 October 1927, Colony, New York

CAST: Conrad Veidt *Paul La Roche*; Barbara Bedford *Yvonne Fontaine*; Ian Keith *Dr. Paul Fontaine*; Arthur Edmund Carewe *Lieut. Destin*; George Siegmann *Governor of the Prison*; Charles Puffy *Prison Doctor*; Corliss Palmer *Sylvia Cabot*; Edward Reinach *Dr. Renaud*

CREDITS: *Presented by* Carl Laemmle, Sr.; *Director* George Melford; *Based on the play* Diploma *by* Emerich [Imre] Foeldes; *Adaptation* Paul Kohner; *Titles* Tom Reed; *Continuity* Emil Forst; *Photographed by* Gilbert Warrenton; Silent and part sound, with synchronized music and sound effects.

SYNOPSIS: Sentenced to ten years imprisonment at the French garrison on the Isle of St. Noir for extending euthanasia to a patient suffering from an incurable illness, Dr. Paul La Roche (Conrad Veidt) is asked to attend to the Warden [some sources say "a prison official"], after he has been shot by a convict. Lieutenant Destin (Arthur Edmund Carewe), the second-in-command, assures the physician that he will be freed in return for saving the Warden's life. Once recovered, however, the Warden does not honor the bargain, and La Roche escapes to the mainland, where he meets Dr. Paul Fontaine (Ian Keith), his childhood friend, and Fontaine's beautiful sister, Yvonne (Barbara Bedford). As Fontaine is going blind, La Roche performs several operations for him, gaining an enviable reputation for his surgical skills. When Fontaine, La Roche (posing as Fontaine), and Yvonne move to Algiers, La Roche also attracts the attention of Dr. Renaud (Edward Reinach), who offers him a position. La Roche reveals his love for Yvonne during an excursion to a Bedouin camp, but Lieutenant Destin, fresh from the prison, arrives and threatens La Roche with exposure unless he surrenders the hand of Yvonne. During a chess game with

As Paul La Roche in *A Man's Past*, the actor's only lost American film.

Fontaine, the blind doctor shoots the extortionist. La Roche saves Destin with an operation and wins a full pardon.

REVIEWS: "Conrad Veidt is the gent John Barrymore brought back from Europe and announced as quite an actor. ... Veidt is primarily an actor.... Like [Emil] Jannings and Lon Chaney, this newcomer to Hollywood is practically devoid of sex appeal; and in his first American picture he registers less forcefully than his two confreres....

"Veidt's work, without comparing it to that of contemporaries, may be called good acting. The s.a. [sex appeal] is blotto...."

Variety, 5 October 1927

"...[At] the head of the cast is Conrad Veidt, the brilliant German actor who triumphed through his excellent work in *The Cabinet of Dr. Caligari*, and in this, his first American screen adventure, Mr. Veidt does more than anyone else to make it interesting. But even he, occasionally, has been forced to do a little strained acting...."

New York Times, 4 October 1927 — Mordaunt Hall

"Unusually fine dramatic theme that is certain to be enthusiastically received where they appreciate an attempt to get away from dumb frivolity... The story is unusual, strong in dramatic situations, and forcefully told. Unfortunately, *A Man's Past* is one of those infrequent worthwhile affairs that probably won't make the box-office grade... because there aren't enough people to appreciate it...."

Film Daily, 11 September 1927

"Mr. Veidt has never done anything as good as his convict surgeon in *A Man's Past*... Mr. Veidt is a magnificent actor and what he cannot say with his eyes doesn't need to be said. He probably will set a new style in screen lovers..."

New York Herald-Tribune, 4 October 1927 — Harriette Underhill

"The story as worked out is so full of absurdities and obvious studio expedients that it is not worth consideration other than as providing a cut-to-the-pattern vehicle for Mr. Veidt's acting, and Mr. Veidt can certainly act..."

World, 5 October 1927

"Universal solemnly tried to make this a strong picture and succeeded too well. The story gets very heavy before the end and just goes on and on. Conrad Veidt enacts a convict-surgeon who, through mistaken identity, escapes prison to save lives and win hearts in the desert. Not too convincing and Veidt, though a good actor, is unromantic. Try this only on a night you're bored with comedies."

Photoplay, October 1927

"This is a good melodrama although it is somewhat disjointed in the telling, and the direction fails to give full effect to some strong situations. For the same reason, the efforts of a strong company fail in effect. ... Conrad Veidt has little chance to exploit his strong personality and undoubted talent. He fails to make the part of La Roche anything more than a theatrical figure."

Bioscope (England), 22 September 1927

"Veidt remains unique, strange, extraordinary. His eyes—a mediocre photographer can only distort them — are so deeply opalescent that no American can water them down. Nevertheless, although Hollywood has the proven Veidt goods, he's come not so much for the experience as to show off his demons. And someone must stop all of his flirting; he must seem so handsome that even the teenagers are falling for him. Conny Valentino..."

Film-Kurier, 11 August 1928 — E. Jäger

NOTES AND QUOTES: *A Man's Past* may well have been "a superficial melodrama" (as Jerry C. Allen tagged the film in his *Conrad Veidt: From* Caligari *to* Casablanca) — God knows, it didn't set the critical world on fire — but it was a Universal Super Jewel, nonetheless, and that meant that big bucks had been spent to assure that "superficial" didn't necessarily mean mediocre. While it was, de facto, the first film in Connie's multiple-picture deal with

Universal, things hadn't started out that way.

Signed at $1500 a week, Veidt had chosen to work on the pseudo–Devil's Island melodrama with George Melford — an amiable helmsman who had been sitting in the director's chair since 1914 — only after the actor had been removed from *The Chinese Parrot*, a mystery thriller about to be directed by his old friend Paul Leni. Connie had originally been tapped by Uncle Carl Laemmle to play the part of Charlie Chan, and had actually concocted a make-up treatment for the role. The 12 March 1927 *Universal Weekly* reveals that he had "been photographed in the Freulich studio with enough clever portraiture to fill all the art magazines in the United States with his celestial competency [*sic*]." Heeding the advice of his executives and technicians, though (almost everyone else in Universal City thought it strange that the studio was wasting the great actor in a "Chinese role"), Laemmle took Veidt off the project and announced that the actor would instead portray the rabbi in the up-and-coming film version of *Lea Lyon*, Alexander Brody's drama from 1915. *Lea Lyon* was subsequently released as *Surrender*, with Nigel De Brulier enacting Rabbi Mendel. The celebrated Japanese actor Kamiyama Sojin stepped into Chan's empty shoes, and Connie was made ready for the part of Paul La Roche in *A Man's Past*.

A week prior to the premiere of *A Man's Past* at the Colony in Manhattan, the Fulton Theater presented the American stage opening of *Dracula*, with Bela Lugosi in the title role. The Hungarian would enact the part for some 33 weeks on Broadway before he — and the play — moved to the Coast. When the news broke that Universal was looking to film *Dracula*, Lugosi began a fervent campaign to land the role he had introduced to American audiences. Ultimately, Bela won what would prove to

be a Pyrrhic victory: typecast as Dracula, he found his film career taking a continuous nosedive thereafter. Before he was awarded the role, however, he found himself in line behind both Veidt (Uncle Carl Laemmle's only real choice for Stoker's vampire) and Connie's costar from *A Man's Past*, Ian Keith.

"Conrad Veidt carries the brunt of the action, but it is impossible to adequately express how admirably he is supported by Arthur Edmund Carewe, Ian Keith, George Siegmann and Edward Reinach. Barbara Bedford has little to do, but she does it in a manner which is a fitting corollary to the magnificent efforts of Conrad Veidt and his supporters. After seeing this film one can safely place Conrad Veidt amongst the world's first half dozen tragedians."

Pressbook, *A Man's Past*

The Man Who Laughs

Universal (Super Jewel) — New York premiere 27 April 1928 — 10 reels; Recalled and released nationally with synchronized musical score and effects, 4 November 1928. Also released as a silent.

CAST: Conrad Veidt *Lord Clancharlie/ Gwynplaine*; Mary Philbin *Dea*; Olga Baclanova *Duchess Josiana*; Josephine Crowell *Queen Anne*; George Siegmann *Dr. Hardquannone*; Brandon Hurst *Barkilphedro*; Sam De Grasse *King James*; Stuart Holmes *Lord Dirry-Noir*; Cesare Gravina *Ursus*; Nick De Ruiz *Wapentake*; Torben Meyer *The Spy*; Edgar Norton *Lord High Chancellor*; Julius Molnar, Jr. *Gwynplaine, as a Child*; Charles Puffy *Innkeeper*; Frank Puglia, Jack Goodrich *Clowns*; Carmen Costello *Dea's Mother*; Zimbo *Homo, the Wolf*

CREDITS: *Presented by* Carl Laemmle, Sr.; *Production Supervisor* Paul Kohner; *Director* Paul Leni; *Story Supervisor* Dr. Bela Sekely; *Scenario* J. Grubb Alexander (*and, uncredited,* Charles Whittaker, Marion Ward, May McLean); *Based on the novel* L'Homme qui rit *by* Victor Hugo; *Art and Technical Directors* Charles D. Hall, Joseph Wright, Thomas F. O'Neill; *Photographed by* Gilbert Warrenton; *Film Editors* Maurice Pivar, Edward Cahn; *Cos-*

tumes David Cox, Vera West; *Production Staff* John M. Voshell, Jay Marchant, Louis Friedlander (aka Lew Landers); *Technical Research* Prof. R.H. Newlands

MUSIC: Song "When Loves Comes Stealing" by Walter Hirsch, Lew Pollack, Erno Rapee

SYNOPSIS: Son of Lord Clancharlie (Conrad Veidt), a political enemy of King James II (Sam de Grasse), young Gwynplaine (Julius Molnar, Jr.) has his mouth carved into a permanent smile by the bizarre Comprachicos as part of the punishment meted out to his father. Abandoned by the mutilators, the boy stumbles across the snowy reaches of England, before coming across the body of a woman who has frozen to death shielding her infant daughter. Gwynplaine rescues the baby, who is found to be blind, and luck brings the two to the wagon of Ursus (Cesare Gravina), a "philosopher" who works at village fairs. When they reach adulthood, Gwynplaine (Conrad Veidt) and Dea (Mary Philbin) are members of a troupe of traveling clowns: Gwynplaine is renowned as "The Laughing Man."

At a performance, the beautiful Duchess Josiana (Olga Baclanova) is intrigued by this "laughing man," and arranges that he come to meet her. Unknown to the duchess, Barkilphedro (Brandon Hurst) — once jester to King James, now a thoroughly evil toady of Queen Anne — has discovered that Gwynplaine is the legitimate heir to the property Josiana occupies. Barkilphedro informs her majesty (Josephine Crowell) of the situation, and the queen — looking for some way to keep Josiana (who is her half sister) in line — arranges that the duchess marry the new peer of the realm: the Laughing Man. At the convening of the House of Lords, Gwynplaine refuses to enter the "hated marriage" and escapes to find Dea and Ursus, who have been banished from England. He is pursued by soldiers as he heads for the docks, but the townspeople

help him along the way. At the waterfront, Gwynplaine's pet wolf, Homo, tears out the throat of the treacherous Barkilphedro, and the Man Who Laughs makes it safely to the ship on which Dea and Ursus are set to sail.

REVIEWS: "...[Conrad Veidt's] acting virtuosity is both blinding, yet simple and plain at the same time... The direction is in Paul Leni's hands, and this is more than enough to assure that the beauty, richness and novelty of the original would be seen... *The Man Who Laughs* is a high point, possibly the turning point in the history of film, and therefore, of the history of our time."

Mein Film (Vienna), No. 160;
18 January 1929 —
Julius Siegfried Seidenstein

"...[The title] part is portrayed with astounding cleverness by Conrad Veidt.... Part of the time he covers his abnormal mouth, but on other occasions, through wearing huge false teeth, Mr. Veidt sends a chill down one's spine. His affection for Dea, the blind girl, is disquieting, but at the same time he elicits a great deal of sympathy...."

New York Times, 28 April
1928 — Mordaunt Hall

"This picture may get by in Europe under the name of Art, but in this country it will have little interest. Dragged into a super-production by extremely slow action, it loses the dramatic value of a story which might have succeeded under the name of 'something different.' Conrad Veidt does a splendid piece of acting."

Photoplay, Vol. 33, No. 6;
May 1928

"Conrad Veidt triumphs in *The Man Who Laughs*, which last night began a limited engagement at the Columbia Theater before a very large audience...."

"Veidt ... uses his eyes superbly, con-

Der
Mann, der lacht

MIT CONRAD VEIDT UND MARY PHILBIN
REGIE: PAUL LENI

veying the emotions and passions of the man through them.

"Between the first and second parts last night, Veidt made his appearance in a box and was introduced to the audience. He said nothing, but was vigorously applauded."

San Francisco Chronicle, 2 July 1928 — George C. Warren

"...The picture is undeniably better than *The Hunchback of Notre Dame*....

"Mr. Conrad Veidt's impersonation of the laughing man is at least as good as anything Lon Chaney ever did with the aid of makeup. Baclanova's portrayal of the loose duchess is without parallel in the *Hunchback* and burns holes in the screen...."

Motion Picture World, 13 October 1928 — T.O. Service

"...Above a laughing set of teeth, Veidt's deep eyes. Why did they have his smile so distorted? It would not make any of the audience laugh (in the film itself, it is laughed about)... For Veidt, the director should have invented a devilishly funny laugh. As it is, the audience becomes enormously sad, a psychological mistake.

"The whole Veidt-role is an absurd but entrancing mistake...."

Film-Kurier, 2 March 1929 — Ernst Jäger

"...The grin makes it difficult for Conrad Veidt to do much acting. Glycerine tears do not quite succeed in conveying soul torture nor [sic] in creating romantic illusion.

"*Man Who Laughs* will appeal to the Lon Chaney mob and to those who like quasi-morbid plot themes. To others it will seem fairly interesting, a trifle unpleasant, and intermittently tedious...."

Variety, 2 May 1928 — Land

NOTES AND QUOTES: "The film as a whole shares the vaguely populist sentiments found whenever Hollywood can safely distance political disputes to a remote and unthreatening past: the court and the nobility are corrupt, scheming, promiscuous, cruel and selfish; while the poor are, for the most part, picturesquely squalid, grotesque and comical, though they rally round the persecuted hero at the end to thwart the soldiers who are pursuing him and give him a chance to escape to safety... The focus is on the fate of a few individuals rather than on any serious discussion of social inequities and injustices, and the fulfillment or destruction of a love relationship becomes more important than any political crisis."

Graham Petrie, *Hollywood Destinies*, p. 202.

The Man Who Laughs premiered — as a silent — at a trade show at the London Pavilion Theatre in Piccadilly on 4 May 1928. Despite adverse conditions ("two hours of the hottest weather London has experienced for months," per the *Universal Weekly*), the reaction to the film was sensational. Upon general release — opening at the Rialto Theatre in the West End barely a week later — the picture played to packed houses for over three months. On 4 February 1929, *The Man Who Laughs* revisited the Rialto — with synchronized score, effects, and the song *When Love Comes Stealing* — and the theater did land-office business once again.

"To play Gwynplaine was the dream of my boyhood. I have been fascinated by this character ever since I read Victor Hugo's novel in high school. One has to feel pity for Gwynplaine, as he is mutilated, but the result of that mutilation — the laughing, grotesque face — looks

Opposite: Original German-language release one-sheet, courtesy of Rubin Sherman. (*The Man Who Laughs*)

In addition to playing Gwynplaine, Connie also portrayed his father, the doomed Lord Clancharlie. (*The Man Who Laughs*)

funny. For a film actor, that presents an artistic challenge that could hardly be more complicated. So what did I have left as my main means of communication? The eyes!"

Conrad Veidt in *Filmphotos wie noch nie*, Giessen, 1929

Victor-Marie Hugo (1802–1885), who stood at the forefront of the Romantic literary movement in his native France, is best known in Great Britain and the United States for his novels (especially *Notre Dame de Paris* [aka *The Hunchback of Notre Dame*, 1831] and *Les Misérables* [1862]). Interestingly, Hugo is celebrated in France nowadays chiefly for his poetry, while, during his lifetime, his plays brought him his greatest fame. *L'Homme Qui Rit*, which has always been regarded as one of the author's lesser works, was penned in 1869.

Still, despite its relative lack of celebrity, the story was filmed twice prior to the 1927/28 Universal Super-Jewel: adapted in France in 1909, it was subsequently reworked (as *Das grinsende Geschicht*) by Austria's Olympic-Film in 1921. (Quasimodo had beaten Gwynplaine to the screen by some three years, however, with Gaumont's production of *Esmeralda* [1906].) In 1966, Cipra and Sanson Film collaborated to produce *L'Uomo che Ride*, a French/Italian effort that shifted Angelo (nee Gwynplaine) from the 17th century England of James II to the 16th century Italy of the Borgias. Critiques of the film — which are scant — dismiss it as unpleasant and unfaithful both to its source novel and the 1927/28 "original."

Per Philip J. Riley (*The Making of "The Phantom of the Opera."* Absecon [New Jersey]: MagicImage Filmbooks, 1999; pp. 39–41.), Universal had considered filming *L'Homme Qui Rit* (retaining the original French title had worked admirably in the case of a celluloid version of *Les Misérables*) — starring Lon Chaney as Gwynplaine — as early as April 1924. Contract negotiations faltered, however, when it was discovered that no one had thought to obtain the rights to the property from the *Société Générale de Films*, and, by the time the smoke had cleared, the "Man of a Thousand Faces" had signed on for *The Phantom of the Opera* at a significantly higher salary.

Phantom players Mary Philbin and Cesare Gravina were reunited in *The Man Who Laughs*. As the blind Dea, Miss Philbin was spared the dramatics of another unmasking scene. The lovely young actress went on to appear opposite Veidt shortly thereafter in Paul Fejos' *The Last Performance* and only Connie's being replaced as the rabbi in *Surrender* (1927) had prevented the pair from costarring in a *third* Universal-Jewel. In the full-blown featured role of Ursus, the traveling "philosopher," Mr. Gravina enjoyed something of a promotion; he had had only a bit as the retiring opera house manager in the 1925 Chaney feature.

Veidt, himself, had the briefest of ties to the Opera Ghost. The 27 October 1928 issues of *Moving Picture World* and *Exhibitors Herald* advised that:

> Universal will make a picture to sequel *The Phantom of the Opera*. It will be called *The Return of the Phantom* and will be directed by Paul Leni. Carl Laemmle, Jr. is the supervisor and Conrad Veidt is the logical man for the big role. It was Chaney who had the "Phantom" role in the other.

Rather than shooting a sequel, Universal opted to reissue *The Phantom of the Opera* with synchronized sound effects and music and limited dialogue. Lon Chaney, under contract to MGM at the time, did not participate in the reworking, and advertisements for the hybrid feature alerted audiences to the fact that the phantom remained a silent figure.

As is evident from the selection of reviews cited above, *The Man Who Laughs* wasn't unanimously and unconditionally celebrated at home. Reports indicate that the European export versions (replete with the synchronized music and effects track, and target-language title cards) enjoyed greater approbation than the domestic original, if only (arguably) because the source novel and the film's director and lead actor were all from the Old World. Nonetheless, if film historian Thomas J. Saunders (*Hollywood in Berlin: American Cinema and Weimar Germany.* Berkeley [California]: University of California Press, 1994.) is dead on, in Germany — where *Der Mann, der lacht* premiered at Berlin's Universum am Lehninger Platz on 2 March 1929 — they were having none of it.

The scenario left much to be desired, avers Saunders, so far as the contemporary German palate was concerned. In the course of adapting the macabre and rather downbeat story for the consumption of avid moviegoers everywhere, Universal had inserted a lengthy but breathtaking chase sequence into the picture, which was then capped off with a happy ending. Most Americans found the ending cathartic (if a tad predictable), as the popular domestic consensus was that the pathetic Gwynplaine deserved to sail off into the horizon with his lady fair after 10 reels of humiliation and abuse. German critics (and ticket buyers), however, spurned the scripted uplift as typical Hollywood pap, and in spite of Leni's vision and Veidt's presence, the film did only middling business in the Fatherland. Perhaps Maxim Ziese's declaration, as quoted by Saunders, illustrates best how it was once maintained that only Übermenschen could produce "Überkino":

> Somewhere in the film ruins of Neubabelsberg we store the seal of superior film art; such a secret is not exportable. The great directors and performers must leave it here when they go to America and go after the dollar. Certainly we don't intend to cry over them because Hollywood has changed them, made their works and achievements more marketable. But we will admit that they were different here, that they were better here — even if they create more profit over there. [Ibid. p. 196.]

The passage of time, thankfully, has brought with it a bit of mellowing in the critical temperament. Thus, while Robert Klepper's statement that "Of all of Leni's films in Germany and in the United States, [*The Man Who Laughs*] is widely acclaimed as his crowning achievement" (*Silent Films, 1877–1996.* Jefferson [North Carolina]: McFarland & Company, 1999; p. 474.) may be every bit as dogmatic as was Ziese's manifesto, it lends itself to more polite and enjoyable debate.

Die Filmstadt Hollywood

aka **Wir in Hollywood** (*We in Hollywood*); Max Goldschmidt, Berlin; World premiere: 18 November 1928 Capitol, Berlin (as a "Sondervorführung," a "special performance"); General release: 29 November 1928 Mozartsaal, Berlin

CAST: Conrad Veidt *as himself*; Charles Chaplin, Ernst Lubitsch, Greta Garbo, Emil Jannings, Dolores del Rio, Arnold Höllriegel

CREDITS: *Director* Arnold Höllriegel, Max Goldschmidt

Feature-length documentary on the German film stars and technicians who had immigrated to Southern California. Connie is seen in his swimming pool and playing ping-pong.

1931: released as a 16mm cutdown, retitled *Hollywoodstars in ihrem Heim* (*Hollywood Stars at Home*)

The Last Performance

aka in Germany as *Illusion*; Universal (Jewel)—7 reels (72/80 minutes); World premiere: 13 October 1929; New York premiere: 2 November 1929 Little Carnegie Playhouse

CAST: Conrad Veidt *Erik Goff*; Mary Philbin *Julie Fergeron*; Leslie Fenton *Buffo*; Fred Mackaye *Mark Royce*; Gustav Partos *European Theater Manager*; Eddie Boland *American Theater Manager*; William H. Turner *Booking Agent*; Anders Randolf *Judge*; Sam De Grasse *District Attorney*; George Irving *Defense Attorney*

CREDITS: *Presented by* Carl Laemmle; *Supervised by* Carl Laemmle, Jr; *Director* Paul Fejos; *Titles* Walter Anthony, Tom Reed; *Story/Scenario* James Ashmore Creelman; *Photographed by* Hal Mohr; *Film Editors* Edward Cahn, Robert Carlisle, Robert Jahns

WORKING TITLES: **The Play Goes On** and **Erik the Great**

SYNOPSIS: Celebrated stage conjurer Erik Goff (Conrad Veidt) tours the European theater circuit along with his troupe, which consists of Julie Fergeron (Mary Philbin) and Buffo (Leslie Fenton). It transpires that Erik is hopelessly smitten with the much younger Julie, who has begun to resign herself, out of a sense of obligation, to life (and possibly marriage) with the magician. Buffo, who is also enamored of Julie, has contempt for Erik.

One night, in the Royal Hotel in Budapest, Erik surprises a young man, Mark Royce (Fred Mackaye), who has entered the magician's rooms surreptitiously in search of food. When Julie and Buffo arrive on the scene, the young woman asks Erik to forgive the starving Mark and to hire him as another assistant. Unable to deny his lovely charge anything, Erik agrees. As time passes and the troupe prepares for a tour of America, Buffo notices that Erik is unaware that his young assistants are spending more and more time together.

In New York, Erik arranges for a banquet, at which he plans to make public his engagement to Julie. Moments before the big announcement, however, Buffo leads Erik into the penthouse garden, where Mark and Julie are found to be holding hands. Stunned, Erik leads the two back into the ballroom, where he announces that Julie is to marry... Mark! Later, back in the garden, Julie assures Mark: "He understands. I know he will forgive us."

Some time later, Erik, Mark, and Buffo are busy practicing an illusion where a man, apparently skewered by swords thrust through a trunk, is revealed to be unharmed. During a subsequent performance of the illusion, Mark handles the swords under Erik's watchful eye. Buffo is in the trunk. As the swords are withdrawn, the last is seen to be covered with blood! Erik opens the trunk and pulls Buffo's lifeless body into view. Mark is charged with murder.

The trial appears to be a formality; almost everyone in the courtroom believes Mark to be guilty. Nearly hysterical, Julie turns to Erik and pleads that he somehow save her love. Powerless to resist her, Erik confesses to having arranged Buffo's death himself. The blood on the sword was Erik's own. He had used a magician's trick to rid himself of the fiercely disloyal Buffo and his romantic rival, Mark, at the same time. Having confessed all, Erik stabs himself and dies in front of the astonished spectators.

REVIEWS: "This is Conrad Veidt and Mary Philbin's swan song for Universal, contracts of neither being renewed....

"Besides being very slowly paced there isn't a great deal of action. ... [The] picture can't rely on originality, if there is any here. There doesn't seem to be the least...."

Variety, 3 November 1929

"*Illusion*. The last film of Veidt's American period, the last film of his 'demonic' period. They roped Conny in the American way over there; the story of the aging illusionist in love with his young assistant is American, with all its various bits and pieces. ... Veidt is impressive in the makeup and gestures of the illusionist Goff, but the unfolding of the plot does not allow him to show his true art of acting...."

Der Kinematograph, No. 131; 7 June 1930

"It seems to us little short of appalling that two such men [as Emil Jannings and Conrad Veidt], so far beyond anything this country has yet produced in vivid, imaginative dramatic power and technique, should be denied to the [American] public because they cannot speak the right language.

"[In his final film in the U.S., *The Last Performance*,] Conrad Veidt is a master of subtle and convincing pantomime, his gestures are eloquent in their stark simplicity and his face is one of the most interesting and expressive we have ever seen...."

Boston Herald, 28 October 1929 — Elinor Hughes

"Paul Fejos directed. *Illusion* has been created dark and mysterious.... Often, however, the direction comes dangerously close to kitsch, sometimes using suspect means, but there are thrills, and the end justifies the means...

"Conrad Veidt is Goff. The character is not new to him. The mysterious piano player, Orlac, was the same, only 10 years earlier, and thrilling again today..."

Film-Kurier, 7 May 1930

"After a promising beginning, it levels off a bit, but at the end the story is exceedingly thrilling once again. Unfortunately, some clarity is lost in the attempt at effecting charm and achieving surprise. Veidt's acting achievement surpasses the excellent ensemble, the direction is precise, the sets and photography, excellent."

Paimanns Filmlisten (Vienna), No. 702; 20 September 1929

"...[*The Last Performance*] was made some time ago by Dr. Paul Fejos at the Universal studio, was probably Conrad Veidt's last performance before returning to work in Germany.

"...Due to the fantastic nature of the story, the occasional glimpses of the way in which the magician, Erik the Great, deceives the eyes of his audiences, Mr. Veidt's clever acting and Mary Philbin's captivating charm, this picture holds one's attention...."

New York Times, 4 November 1929 — Mordaunt Hall

NOTES AND QUOTES: The picture was released in Austria, as a silent, more than a half-year before its debut in Germany. For reasons that remain unclear, the Austrian title was *Dr. Gift* (*Dr. Poison*)!

"Veidt was a fine actor, and it was a good cast, but it wasn't much of a story." — Hal Mohr, taken from an interview in *Film Comment*, Sept/Oct 1974. Adding to the air of repressed resignation, director Paul Fejos (as related by Graham Petrie in *Hol-*

Original herald. (*The Last Performance*)

lywood Destinies) "claimed… that he had little interest in making the film beyond the opportunity it gave him to work with Conrad Veidt" (p. 165).

"*Eric the Great* [*sic*] opens with a bravura display of technique… A quick series of dissolves brings us inside the theatre where Eric, a magician and hypnotist, is about to perform onstage; multiple images of the legs of chorus girls and the faces of spectators flash across the screen; another series of rapid dissolves shows the preparations for raising the curtain, and Eric himself appears onstage, the lighting throwing his shadow, hugely enlarged, on the backcloth.

"Once the highly melodramatic plot gets underway, however… Fejos seems to lose interest and contents himself with creating a few striking scenes and images.

"A trial scene, in which Mark is wrongly accused of murdering Buffo, is presented entirely without titles, Fejos manipulating the evidence through rapid superimposed flashbacks of earlier scenes, and a shot of a spectator drawing a picture of the judge and a gallows indicating the inevitable verdict.

"*Eric the Great*, in fact, is interesting mostly as an example of how efficiently and succinctly silent film language could be employed to create, entirely by means of images, relatively complex emotions and relationships and to carry through an intricate and potentially very confusing narrative. As usual, Fejos avoided titles as far

A BROADWAY THRILLER

Starring the "John Barrymore of Europe"

CONRAD VEIDT

CONRAD VEIDT plays Count Cagliostro, a self-styled mystic whom men despised and women fawned upon. The play is "The Charlatan," by Ernest Pascal and Leonard Praskins. Its mystery on the stage held New York playgoers in a vise-like grip. The Count, at a seance, puts a woman in a cabinet. Then he learns it is his former wife—and dreads exposure. With the climax comes the solution of the mystery—held to the end. A real thrill.

Another project discussed for Connie ended up being filmed with Holmes Herbert.

as possible... Lighting, shadows, close-ups, superimpositions, flashbacks, camera movements, all contain, and convey, codes that guide the spectator smoothly through the story though ... the codes of this film are essentially narrative ones and carry few reverberations beyond this."

"Paul Fejos in America"
by Graham Petrie. *Film Quarterly*, Vol. 32, No. 2, Winter 1978-79; p. 34.

In his *The Making of The Phantom of the Opera*, Philip J. Riley quotes actress

Mary Philbin's recollection of *The Last Performance*: "It was the greatest thrill of my life when I heard my voice from the screen in my first talking picture. It was too good to be true" (p. 16). Alas! It was almost just that. Unless she was present in either Boston or San Diego for the part-talkie version's extremely limited run, Miss Philbin heard her voice at a studio preview. Although absent an "official" studio announcement of same, the film was withdrawn following the "coastal premieres," the talkie reel was replaced with its mute equivalent, and the picture went into general release as a silent with the first New York showing on the 2 November.

Universal had blueprinted *only* last reel dialogue (as both the *Variety* and *Boston Herald* reviews indicate), so the existing footage clearly shows that virtually *all* of the lines (apart from some breathless pleading from Mary Philbin) would have gone to Veidt, as Erik's summary and confession take up most of the reel. Because a decent portion of the confession is rendered via flashback, Veidt need only have provided a *voice-over*, rather than have attempted to synchronize his speaking voice with his lip movements. Likewise, most of his other "speeches" within the scene are delivered with his back to the camera (again obviating the need for meticulous match work), leaving only one or two brief snippets where a bit of patience and a knack with cut-and-paste might have produced admirable results.

(A scenario that depicts Connie recording English-language dialogue from the Ufa sound studios via transatlantic telephone has been reported, as if either Universal's own dialogue tracks were unacceptable from the get-go, or the studio had not considered making a "part-talkie" until after its star had left the country. Neither road is without its bumps. The complete lack of mention of this anomaly in the contemporary press can lead nowhere except to the conclusion that the recording session, if ever actually held, was an unqualified, immediate failure.)

Within these parameters, the notion of a German, Hungarian, or French-language talkie version (*L'Illusioniste* was released in Paris in the last half of 1931) may well have been tenable. Yet, with the American "original" ultimately bereft of dialogue, would it therefore have made sense to take extraordinary measures in order to assure that the export versions of the film were part talkies? Undated program notes, issued in conjunction with a

screening of the extant footage by Britain's National Film Theatre, aver that...

> The studio developed the script in June and July 1928, with added dialogue scenes submitted in January 1929... As was the custom at the time, foreign language versions were produced simultaneously: a German version and a Hungarian version. (Fejos was Hungarian.) But again, none of these part-talkie versions seemed to have survived; only the silent version is known to exist. Although apparently produced before *Broadway*, this film did not appear until several months later, sneaking into release, and oblivion, on October 13, 1929.

Nonetheless, surviving documentation (in the form of programs and souvenir booklets issued for the film's sundry export editions) indicates that neither the German nor the French foreign-language version was a part talkie. Both were apparently released as silent, with target-language title cards. (The research I've conducted for this volume has turned up several bits of evidence that Universal at least jump-started the machinery for a Hungarian-language part-talkie, but I am not yet convinced that said production ever saw general release. [Cf. *Of Gods and Monsters: A Critical Guide to Universal Studios' Science Fiction, Horror and Mystery Films, 1929–1939* (pp. 60–62).])

The *Illustrierter Film-Kurier*, for example, printed its program for *Illusion* (the German release title) in December 1930 — the film had premiered at Berlin's Schauberg Theater on June 6th — and nowhere does the magazine indicate that the picture had any sort of dialogue track that had been translated — even in part — into German. The *Der Kinematograph* review, dated the day after the Berlin premiere and cited above, also stresses that the film is to be found "wherever silent films are still shown." Hence, either there *was* no dialogue soundtrack, or, as film historian Thomas J. Saunders argues,

Some dozen German language talkies, produced either in the United States or at a studio outside Paris, provoked little interest even though released within a relatively short time span from late 1930 through 1931. [*Hollywood in Berlin: American Cinema and Weimar Germany*. p. 239.]

This observation loses some steam, however, when Saunders goes on to add that, with respect to these imports, "Casts and production values were almost uniformly second class," and that "Hollywood employed lesser directors and performers whose departure meant scant loss to the German industry." [Ibid.] Dulling the force of these arguments are the facts that: a) *The Last Performance* was a Universal "Jewel," a designation connoting a substantial investment in production values on the part of Universal Studios. b) Paul Fejos was already on his way to international renown because of his features *Lonesome* (1928) and *Broadway* (1929), both of which were released in both domestic and export versions before *Illusion* saw the carbon arc in Germany. c) The film starred Conrad Veidt, who, far from being "expendable to the German film industry," was one of a select cadre that — in Saunders' words — read "almost as a who's who of Weimar production." [Ibid. p. 197.]

In addition to their being completely silent, the extant prints of *The Last Performance* (usually retitled *The Magician*) have been edited to exclude any mention of Erik Goff's talents as a mesmerist. Scarcely any photographic evidence of this plot wrinkle remains, aside from the brief sequence wherein Buffo tries unsuccessfully to pack his bag and flee. Graham Petrie (cited above) recalls another scene of Goff's hypnotic power which has not, it appears, survived the years: "In the course of his act, Eric demonstrates his hypnotic control of his assistant, Julie, and also his power over the audience, in a series of short cuts of his eyes and the faces of the audience, and

then swirling images of the city, with Eric's face looming in superimposition over it all."

Why or when this editing was done is at present unknown.

Das Land ohne Frauen

[LOST] *The Land without Women* or *La Terra Senza Donne*; aka **Die Braut Nr. 68** (*Bride Number 68*); F.P.S.-Film GmbH, Berlin/Tonbild-Syndikat AG (Tobis), Berlin; A Tobis (Licht- und Nadleton) Sound Picture; Filmed at Ufa Studios, Tempelhof *and* at D.L.S. Studios, Staaken bei Berlin; Distributed by F.P.S.-Film GmbH, Berlin; Censored (silent film): 8 August 1929 — 9 Acts, 3220 meters; Forbidden to adolescents; Registered (silent film) as an "Artistic" picture: 27 August 1929; Censored (sound film): 24 September 1929 — 9 Acts, 3220 meters; Forbidden to adolescents; Registered (sound film) as an "Artistic" picture: 10 November 1929; World premiere: 30 September 1929 Capitol, Berlin; Austrian premiere: 7 November 1929 Wien

CAST: Conrad Veidt *Dick Ashton*; Elga Brink *Evelyne Narnheim*; Grete Berger *Ashton's Mother*; Mathias Wieman *American Doctor in Coolgardie*; Clifford McLaglen *Steve Parker, Gold-miner in Coolgardie*; Ernst Verebes *O'Donegan, Gold-miner in Coolgardie*; Erwin Faber *Jimmy Sleigh, Gold-miner in Albany*; Carla Bartheel *Mary Dawson*; Boris de Fas *Captain of the "Hastings"*; Kurt Vespermann *Joe Smith, Chief Steward of the "Hastings"*; Karl Huszar-Puffy *Filthy Man*; Philipp Manning *Fat Gold-miner in Coolgardie*; Kurt Katsch *Scrawny Gold-miner in Coolgardie*; with Arthur von Klein-Ehrenwalten

CREDITS: *Producer* Alfred Schmidt; *Director* Carmine Gallone; *Production Supervisors* Emmerich Pressburger, Hermann Fellner; *Scenario* Ladislaus Vajda; *Based on the novel* Die Braut Nr. 68 by Peter Bolt; *Photographed by* Otto Kanturek, Bruno Timm; *Asst. Director* Géza von Cziffra; *Set Design* Hans Sohnle, Otto Erdmann; *Musical Score* Wolfgang Zeller; *Orchestra* Tobis-Orchester; *Conductor* Wolfgang Zeller; *Sound* Karl Brodmerkel, Adolf Jansen; *Sound Mix* Hans Oser; *Sound Cameraman* Max Brink; *Still Photographer* Rudolf Brix

MUSICAL SELECTION: Gold-miner Song (Ich ging in die Fremde/I left my home)

Predominantly shot silent (albeit with synchronized music) and then postdubbed. (DIF)

SYNOPSIS: Australia, at the end of the 19th century. Many adventurers and gold-miners lack one thing: a woman at their side. The few who have been lucky enough to have their wives with them protect them fiercely, and anyone caught chasing after a married woman is hanged.

An appeal is sent back to England, inviting young unmarried women to journey Down Under for the express purpose of marrying the men they find there. Four hundred thirteen hopeful young women accept the invitation, and 413 Australian men are at the dock to meet the ship. Each of the women has been assigned a number, and she will be matched up to the man holding the same number.

However, one of the women dies during the journey. The officers aboard the ship decide to make this circumstance into a game. Rather than have the man whose number matches that of the dead girl remain "womanless," they draw lots to find the loser. It is number 68. Hence, bride number 68 is now matched with the man whose woman had died onboard ship, while man number 68 is to remain alone.

When the ship docks, man number 68, Dick Ashton (Conrad Veidt), learns that the officers' game has sent his intended bride, Evelyne Bernheim (Elga Brink), along with goldminer Steve Parker (Clifford McLaglen) to Coolgardie. Dick is blind with rage, but he returns to the telegraph office where he works.

In Coolgardie, Steve must head out to stake a claim, so his new bride awaits his return in their house. Dick finds this out via a telegram that Steve has sent to a friend. Dick travels to Coolgardie at once so that he can at least have a look at the woman who had once been his. When he sneaks into the house, Evelyne cries out, and a crowd quickly gathers to have a

lynching. Before they can get hold of him, Dick tells Evelyne of the cruel game the officers played, and she persuades the crowd not to hang the telegraph man. Beaten badly, but alive, Dick returns home.

Meanwhile, Steve and his partner are lost in the desert. They determine that the only way to summon help is to tear down a telegraph pole, thus triggering the alarm in the closest telegraph office. They do so, but Dick ignores the alarm, knowing full well that to do so means death to his rival. When Dick has gone home at the end of his shift, the worker on the next shift receives a call from another telegraph office, asking if anything has been done about the earlier alert. Although the worker can't find any sign or note of any such alert, he dispatches a rescue team to the desert. Steve's partner has already died of thirst, but Steve himself is rescued at the last moment.

Coming to his senses, Dick is appalled; his jealousy has caused the death of an innocent man. Disconsolate, he runs out into the night and throws himself under a train. Steve Parker returns to his Evelyne.

REVIEWS: "...Conrad Veidt, who plays Ashton, gives a sterling exhibition of the high-strung fellow, but it takes too long... Mr. Veidt's work is as good as anything he has done, a little slow sometimes, but nonetheless painstaking and earnest. The director, however, gives over too much time to Mr. Veidt's reactions without considering what's happening to the other characters...."

New York Times, 15 April 1930 — Mordaunt Hall

"...The scenarist and the director have avoided overindulging in sound, having recognized clearly that in this *Land ohne Frauen*, not too much talking should be done... It has to be mentioned that Elga Brink is about ninety percent effective as a 'talker,' and that Connie, the leading man,

There may have been few women in the outback, but who knew there were so many camels? (*Das land ohne Frauen*)

has reached the degree of film talk perfection that is not only enough but he is already capable of creating strong artistic effects [with his voice]..."

Unknown review

"I don't know how often it has been announced in the past one-and-a-half years, but here, finally, is the first full-length German talking movie. It's turned out remarkably well...

The acting takes a step back in favor of the acoustical effects. The actor's glance, his step, his most subtle gesture... are wan compared to sound. But Conrad Veidt comes through anyway... Director Carmine Gallone ... proves himself imaginative, technically..."

Film-Kurier, 1 October 1929

NOTES AND QUOTES: Nineteen twenty-nine's *Das Land ohne Frauen* was Connie's first German "talkie," and the production was cursed by poor sound mixing, lack of attention to levels, and the sort of general technical incompetence that was demonstrated far too frequently everywhere during sound's initial appearance upon the scene. The picture was predominantly shot silent (albeit with synchronized music) and then postdubbed.

As Veidt later opined for a fan magazine interview: "Bad machinery can make the most beautiful voice in the world into a squeaking horror. My first talkie was not at all perfect. The talk and the silence were all mixed up."

Bride Number 68— English-language version —1929

Distributed by Woolf & Friedman Film Service Ltd., London; A Tobis (Nadelton) Sound Picture; World Premiere: 8 April 1930 New Gallery Theatre, London
CAST and CREDITS: as above

Die letzte Kompagnie

The Last Company aka *13 Men and a Girl*; Universum-Film AG (Ufa), Berlin 1929/30; A Klangfilm; Filmed at Ufa-Studios, Neubabelsberg; Distributed by Universum-Filmverleih GmbH, Berlin; Censored: 7 March 1930 — 9 Acts, 2167 meters; World premiere: 14 March 1930 Ufa-Pavillon am Nollendorfplatz, Berlin; Austrian premiere: 7 April 1930 Ufa-Tonkino Taborstasse, Wien; Censored: 7 August 1930 — 6 Acts, 2263 meters

CAST: Conrad Veidt *Captain Burk*; Karin Evans *Dore*; Paul Henckels *Pitsch*; Erwin Kaiser *The Miller*; Else Heller *The Miller's Wife*; Maria Pederson *The Maid*; Heinrich Gretler *Pelle*; Ferdinand Asper *Götzel*; Martin Herzberg *Heller*; Werner Schott *Biese*; Alexander Granach *Haberling*; *Max Wilhelm Hiller* Machnow; Ferdinand Hart *Klotz*; Albert Karchow *Wernicke*; Horst von Harbou *Stibbe*; Dr. Phillipp Manning *Mollman*; with Gustav Püttjer

CREDITS: *Producer* Joe May; *Director* Kurt Bernhardt; *Production Supervisor* Joe May; *Asst. Director* Erich von Neusser; *Executive Producer* Eduard Kubat; *Scenario* Ludwig von Wohl, Heinz Goldberg, Hans J. Rehfisch; *Based on an idea by* Hans Wilhelm and Hermann Kosterlitz; *Photographed by* Günther Krampf; *Set Decorations* Andrej Andrejew; *Production Supervisor* Joe May; *Music* Ralph Benatzky, Franz Grothe; *Costumes* Alexander Arnstam; *Make-up* Hermann Rosenthal, Friedrich Havenstein, Karl Holek; *Editor* Carl Winston; *Sound* Gerhard Goldbaum, Erich Schmidt

MUSICAL SELECTIONS: *Ballade von der letzten Kompagnie*; *Wir sind dreizehn Grenadiere*; *Die letzte Kompagnie* (Grothe); *Es war einmal ein Soldate...*; *Gibt's ein schöneres Leben*; *Wir dreizehn Mann*; Music Publishing House Ufaton-Verlags GmbH, Berlin

Shot in both silent and sound versions for Germany.

SYNOPSIS: It is 1806. After the Battle of Jena (during the Napoleonic wars), a small Prussian company — of which only 12 soldiers and the captain are left — is ordered to defend a strategically located mill in order to protect their retreating comrades. Until all the troops cross the Saale River and the bridge is blown up, it is the company's duty to hold off the French.

The miller (Erwin Kaiser) and his wife (Else Heller) and daughter (Karin Dor) are evacuated, but the girl returns to be with the captain (Conrad Veidt), as she has fallen in love with him. The Prussian army does make it across the river, but at the cost of every man in the company, and the girl, as well. When the victorious French general enters the mill, he finds only corpses, and is moved to doff his hat in a gesture of respect for such bravery in the face of overwhelming odds.

REVIEWS: "…What interests principally is the characterization of the captain and his various soldiers, each of whom is made a human being with individualized personality. In some the humorous is uppermost, in others the tragic.

"Conrad Veidt as the captain underlines the sense of duty which underlies his every action. Only when the girl asks him to stay with him [*sic*] does he soften…."
Variety, 2 April 1930

"…There are thrills in *Die letzte Kompagnie*, the talking picture that arrived at the Little Carnegie Playhouse yesterday…

"Conrad Veidt is fine as the best type of old Prussian officer and Fräulein Evans makes an appealing country maiden. Nevertheless, her presence does not add to the value of the picture and the dragging in of 'love interest' is quite uncalled for…."
New York Times,
26 August 1932 — H.T.S.
(German-language version)

"…Conrad Veidt has the part of the Captain and Karin Evans that of the girl. In the original, Ufa, production, it is possible the film was fair enough entertainment. Some of the scenes are good. But after the soldiers have finished their vocal salutations, the whole drops down into that unhappy mire which is bathos."
New York Times,
17 August 1931— L.N.
(English-language version)

The Byronic Veidt. (*Die letzte Kompagnie*)

"…brilliant acting. Above all is Conrad Veidt, the captain. One can see how this strong, subtle, sensitive actor was 'murdered' artistically in the United States. Still, it's easily seen how German directors—apart from Joe May and Kurt Bernhardt—erred is assuming that Conny is the decadent type. In this film, he is the ideal man of steel, who sees duty above all else. [Veidt is] an actor-personality of fascinating charisma."

Der Kinematograph,
No. 63; 1930

NOTES AND QUOTES: *Der letzte Kompagnie*—Veidt's second talkie for Ufa—provided a bonanza at the box office. Apparently the sound problems that had plagued the German cinematic crowd for some little while (cf. *Das Land ohne Frauen*) had been overcome with satisfaction and finality. As film companies worldwide were anxious to preserve—if not expand—their international markets, they found themselves challenged by replacing easily concocted silent title cards with synchronized soundtracks in any number of target languages. One could opt to finance a second production for export—replete with appealing target-language speakers or polyglots—or one could choose to have the original dialogue dubbed into the target language by actors with an ear for idiom and an eye for on-screen lip movement. Ufa went this latter route with *Die letzte Kompagnie*, and—sadly—it is only the English-dubbed version that has survived the intervening decades.

"The film was criticized at the time for glossing over 'the contradiction between enraptured submission to a leader/cause and the human horror of the results of war.' German film historian Herbert Holba has attributed the film's glorification of endurance ('A command is a command…and…heroic death is the only way for a man to prove his love for the father-

land') to the politics of the Ufa chairman. Ironically, the film is the work of several men who left their 'fatherland,' either voluntarily or by force: director Bernhardt, co-writer Hermann Kosterlitz (Henry Koster), cinematographer Guenther Krampf and actor Conrad Veidt."

PFA Filmnotes,
21 September 1984—
William K. Everson

If nothing else, *Die letzte Kompagnie* marked a shift in Veidt's roles: from here on in—until he was subsumed by the British/American Nazi cycle—he would enact heroic types, rather than bizarre, off-kilter losers.

The Last Company

English-language version—1930; Universum-Film A-G, Berlin; Tonsystem/Klangfilm; Filmed at Ufa Studios, Neubabelsberg; Distributed by Wardour Films, Ltd., London; World premiere: 27 September 1930 Regal Theater, London

CAST and CREDITS: as above—dubbed into English

Die grosse Sehnsucht

The Great Yearning; aka *Achtung! Aufnahme!*; *Im weissen Licht*; Cicero-Film GmbH, Berlin—1930; Tobis Tonfilm (Licht- und Nadelton) ; Photographed at Efa Studios, Berlin; Distributed by Deutsche Universal-Film A-G, Berlin, and Cinéma Film-Vertriebs GmbH, Berlin; Censored: 19 August 1930—9 Acts, 2400 meters; Admissible to adolescents; World premiere: 25 August 1930 Capitol, Berlin; Austrian premiere: 6 November 1930 Tuchlauben-Kino, Wien; Censored: 16 February 1931—9 Acts, 2482 meters; Admissible to adolescents

CAST: Conrad Veidt *Himself*; Camilla Horn *Eva von Loe, Extra*; Paul Henckels *Klieht, the Producer*; Paul Kemp *Mopp, the Assistant Director*; Theodor Loos *Hall, a Director*; Berthe Ostyn *Carla Marventa, Actress*; Irma Godau *Mary, Eva's Friend*; Harry Frank *Paul Wessel,*

Extra; Anna Müller-Lincke *Frau Bluhmann, Wardrobe Mistress*; Erwin van Roy *Berg, a Director*; Ferdinand Bonn *Cornelius*; Walter Steinbeck *Film Director*; with Otto Fassel, Alfred Braun, Jenny Jugo, Ivan Petrovich, Maria Corda, Victor Varconi, Ludwig von Wohl

Guest Artists (playing themselves): Betty Amann, Elga Brink, Lil Dagover, Liane Haid, Camilla von Hollay, Charlotte Susa, Olga Tschechowa, Adele Sandrock, Wilhelmine Sandrock, Maria Paudler, Anny Ondra, Gustav Diessl, Paul Heidemann, Fritz Kortner, Walter Janssen, Karl Huszar-Puffy, Hans Adalbert Schlettow, Fritz Rasp, Franz Lederer, Harry Liedtke, Walter Rilla, Luis Trenker, Jack Trevor, Ernst Verebes, Hans H. Zerlett

CREDITS: *Producer* Eugen Tuscherer; *Director* Stefan (Istvan) Szekely; *Production Supervisors* Joe Pasternak, Eugen Tuscherer; *Asst. Director* Laslo Benedek; *Executive Producer* Hans Landsmann; *Dialogue Director* Paul Henckels; *Artistic Supervision* Kurt Bernhardt; *Photographed by* Mutz Greenbaum; *Musical Score* Friedrich Höllander, Joe Alex, Frank Strip; *Musical Director* Paul Dessau; *Text* Friedrich Höllander, Karl Brüll, Rudolf Eisner, Erwin W. Spahn; *Set Design* Hans Sohle, Otto Erdmann; *Costumes* Tichomar [Tihamér] Varady; *Make-up* Alfred Lehmann, Adolf Arnold; *Sound* Alfred Norkus; *Sound Recording Supervisor* Victor Behrens; *Editor* Willy Zeunert; *Radio Advertising* Alfred Braun; *Still Photographer* Otto Stein

MUSICAL SELECTIONS: *Alles, was schön ist, hört einmal auf* (Höllander/Höllander); *Bleibe bei mir!* (Höllander/Höllander); *Das Mädel hat sex appeal* (Alex/Brüll, Spahn); *Ich wunsch' mir was* (Höllander/Höllander); *Lou-Lou* (Strip/Brüll, Eisner); Music Publishing House Edition Karl Brüll, Berlin

SYNOPSIS: During lunch break at the movie studio, the extras rush to the canteen. Hans Adalbert von Schlettow, Maria Paudler and Luis Trenker are chatting at a table. Eva von Loe (Camilla Horn)—a beautiful young extra—rushes past; she is looking for her fiancé, Paul Wassel (Harry Frank), who is also an extra. She has to return to the set where the famous director Hall (Theodor Loos) is shooting a scene. He is dissatisfied with his star, Carla Marventa (Berthe Ostyn), who is wrong for the cabaret scene he must photograph. Hall notices Eva, but laughs at her desire to replace Marventa.

At that moment, Conrad Veidt comes on the scene; he assumes that Eva is the star, and the extra—embarrassed at the situation—runs off as Hall informs Veidt of his mistake. Later, instead of attending a birthday party in Anny Ondra's dressing room, Hall pores over a number of photos, looking—unsuccessfully—for a replacement for Marventa. In the end, the director sends the script and an invitation to test for the part to Eva.

In their modest apartment, Eva and Paul are thrilled at the news. They rehearse the scene with zest. The next morning, Eva is engaged to play the role, opposite Fritz Kortner. From that moment on, Eva moves farther and farther away from Paul; her work, her duties as a rising star keep her busy day and night. A terrible argument ensues.

Eva really loves Paul, though, and during a reception Hall is throwing for some of his stars (like Lil Dagover and Olga Tschechowa), she has a nervous breakdown. Hall helps her recuperate, however, and soon Eva is celebrated throughout the country. One day, an extra announces rather loudly that the only reason Eva made it big was her having an affair with Hall. Paul, nearby, overhears and punches the slanderous extra. Paul rushes to Eva and announces that they are through forever. Eva wants to rush out after her true love, but Hall holds her back. When he sees how miserable his star is, the director asks Eva whether she wants to postpone shooting in order to get herself in order. At that moment, Eva decides in favor of her career and is wildly applauded at the studio when she appears to film her big revue scene.

REVIEW: "...Many artists play themselves, and it's amusing to discover that sometimes film actors don't know how to play film actors in a true-to-life manner.

But it's quite charming when Liane Haid shows Camilla how to put on her makeup, and it's sweet how Connie Veidt supports his little colleague.

"…The principal and supporting actors were there in person and could hardly manage the crowds of youngsters keen on getting autographs."

Der Kinematograph (Berlin),
No. 198; 26 August 1930

NOTES AND QUOTES: Released in both sound and silent formats.

Franz Lederer later gained fame as the international leading man Francis Lederer.

Menschen im Käfig

[LOST] *People in a Cage*; aka *Kap der Verlorenen*; *Kap Forlorn*; *Leuchtfeuer*; *Der Leuchtturm*; British International Pictures, Ltd.— 1930; An RCA-Photophone Sound Film; Filmed at Elstree Studios, London; Distributed by Süd-Film A-G, Berlin; Censored: 20 November 1930—11 Acts, 2336 meters; World premiere: 21 November 1930 Gloria-Palast, Berlin

CAST: Conrad Veidt *Gordon Kingsley*; Fritz Kortner *William Kell*; Tala Birell *Eileen Kell*; Julius Brandt *Parsons*; Heinrich George *Cass*

CREDITS: *Producer* John Harlow; *Director* E.A. Dupont; *Scenario* E.A. Dupont, Victor Kendall; *Based on the play* Cape Forlorn *by* Frank Harvey; *Photographed by* Claude Friese-Greene, Walter Blakeley, Hal Young; *Set Design* Alfred Junge; *Sound* Alec Murray; *Editor* A.C. Hammond; *Production Supervisor* E.A. Dupont

SYNOPSIS: Scene: "Cape Forlorn," a lighthouse in the open sea, far off the coast of New Zealand. Two men are stationed there: "Captain" Kell, the ward (Fritz Kortner), and Cass, the helper (Heinrich George).

One day, Kell returns from shore leave to the lighthouse with a bride, Eileen (Tala Birell), who is young and beautiful. She soon discovers she doesn't fit in the "tower of men" and becomes depressed by her life there. Smitten by the young

woman, Cass tells her that Cape Forlorn will become even drearier once the bad weather strikes. He piques her interest when he reveals that he has saved quite a sum of money and is waiting for the right circumstances so that he can leave the lighthouse and have a better life ashore. Wanting to believe Cass, Eileen sneaks into his room.

Suddenly there is an alarm, and Eileen rushes back into her own room before her husband can sense anything is amiss. A man lies injured on the rocks, the victim of a shipwreck. The stranger—Gordon Kingsley (Conrad Veidt) he calls himself—is taken back to the lighthouse where his wounds are dressed. Kingsley is concerned about his missing jacket; when it is found and returned to him, his relief is as apparent as the thick bundle of banknotes therein. Eileen notices something else in his jacket—a revolver—and she takes it.

Cass is furious, as Eileen has forgotten him now that Kingsley is there. He watches every move the woman and the newcomer make. Eileen calms him and promises to visit his room again. When she is with Kingsley, however, all such promises are forgotten.

That night, Cass is on watch, where he listens to the radio. The big news is that the director of the "Otago Insurance Company"—whose description fits Kingsley—has embezzled the company's assets and disappeared. Making matters worse, Captain Kell invested all his money in Otago! Cass confronts Kingsley with his information, but Kingsley refuses to flee the lighthouse and leave Eileen behind. A fight breaks out. Eileen arrives just as Kingsley is about to be beaten by the brutish Cass; she blindly shoots the revolver, and Cass is mortally wounded.

Kell runs in and is aghast at seeing a gun in his wife's hands. Thinking quickly, Kingsley says that Eileen fired in self-defense, in order to protect herself against

From the original program. Left to right: Connie, H. George, F. Kortner, Tara Birell (*Menschen im Käfig*)

Cass's advances. Kell first extinguishes the beacon—the sign to send help from shore—then he takes Eileen aside, to question her. It's not long before Kell has obtained a complete confession from her about her adultery with Kingsley. A police boat arrives, and Kingsley is arrested. Having learned that the man he saved stole not only his wife but his life savings as well, Kell sends Eileen ashore on the police boat; he remains behind, a broken man.

Years pass. Kell runs into Eileen in a dance hall, where she is a paid hostess. She tells her ex-husband that she is waiting for Kingsley, whose sentence will soon be over. She talks about her life on Cape Forlorn, about the many nights, about that one night. But when she looks up to glance at the white-haired man who was her husband, she finds that she is alone.

REVIEWS: "The 'ballad' is shown from all sides with a great deal of artisanship by director Dupont. It is, for example, very nice just to hear a slap without having to see it in an adjoining scene... One may well guess at the speech by the mimicry of the speaker... There is a great deal to admire in the film..."

Das Tagebuch, Vol. 11, No. 48; 29 November 1930

"When E.A. Dupont makes a film with Heinrich George, Fritz Kortner and Conrad Veidt, that is an event worthy of all the attention it gets...

"The problem is three men [focused on] one woman. ... Perhaps E.A. Dupont couldn't find an actress who was a worthy partner for the three stars. He cast Tala Birell, a newcomer who cannot match her partners. That ... means that Dupont has concentrated the picture around the three men..."

Film-Kurier, 22 November 1930

"If there were unfavorable reports by the Berlin press about this picture, they were not unfounded. Its action is too heavy, too broad, and the experienced visitor will know in advance what is going to happen; he reads the names of four men and one woman and knows enough...."

"...Conrad Veidt still has much of the demon whom the little girls once upon a time used to adore, [and is] therefore unreal and posing...."

Variety, 16 December 1930—Magnus.

NOTES AND QUOTES: *Menschen im Käfig* was "Eine Mehrsprachenproduktion" (a polyglot production).

Although by 1930 the process of dubbing a soundtrack for export was well on the road to being perfected, the filming of separate, target-language versions of a motion picture would continue for several years to come. The presence of a Harry Baur or a Conrad Veidt would work far more potent box-office magic in France or Germany than merely dialogue *dans le Francais* or *auf Deutsch* tumbling haphazardly from the lips of a British contract player. The *Variety* review, quoted above, was wired to that paper from Germany; hence, its ungainly English translation.

Ironically, *Menschen im Käfig*—Connie's first picture to emerge from a British studio—was a German talkie, while the first film he ever appeared in while speaking English (*The Congress Dances*) was shot in Germany.

Cape Forlorn— English-language version—1930

aka ***Love Storm*** (USA release title); British International Pictures, Ltd.; An RCA-Photophone Sound Film; Photographed at Elstree Studios, London; Distributed by Wardour Films Ltd., London; World premiere: 9 January 1931, Regal Theatre, London; Original British running time: 86 minutes

CAST: Frank Harvey *William Kell*; Fay Compton *Eileen Kell*; Ian Hunter *Gordon Kingsley*; Edmund Willard *Henry Cass*; Donald Calthrop *Parsons*

CREDITS: *Producer/Director* E.A. Dupont

Le cap perdu— French-language version —1930

British International Pictures, Ltd.; An RCA-Photophone Sound Film; Photographed at Elstree Studios, London; World premiere: 4 April 1931, Aubert-Palace, Paris

CAST: Harry Baur *Captain Kell*; Marcelle Romée *Hélène*; Jean Max *Cass*; Henri Bosc *Kingsley*

CREDITS: *Director* E.A. Dupont; *French Translation/Dialogue (Scenario)* Jean Sarment

Der Mann, der den Mord beging

The Man Who Murdered; aka **Nächte am Bosporus**; Terra-Film AG, Berlin—1930; A Klangfilm; Filmed at Ufa-Atelier, Neubabelsberg; Distributed by Terra-United Artists, Berlin, and G.P.-Films GmbH, Berlin; Censored: 16 January 1931— 2537 meters; Shortened and recensored: 10 Acts, 2474 meters; Forbidden to adolescents; World premiere: 23 January 1931 Gloria-Palast, Berlin; 9 February 1931 Schweden-King, Vienna (Austria)

CAST: Conrad Veidt *Colonel Marquis de Sevigné*; Heinrich George *Lord Edward Falkland*; Trudy von Molo *Lady Mary Falkland*; Rolf Drucker *Georg*; Frieda Richard *Lady Foult*; Friedrich Kayssler *Mehmed Pasha*; Erich Ponto *French Ambassador Boucher*; Friedl Haerlin *Lady Edith*; Gregori Chmara *Stanislaus Cernuwicz*; Hans Joachim Moebis *Terrail, a Dancer*; Yvette Rodin *Mme. Terrail, a Dancer*; with Bruno Ziener

CREDITS: *Producers* Curt Meinitz, Ralph Scotoni; *Director* Kurt Bernhardt; *Asst. Director* Laslo Benedek; *Production Supervisor* Eugen Tuscherer; *Production Manager* Viktor Skutetzky; *Executive Producers* Kurt Heinz, Otto Lehmann; *Scenario* Heinz Goldberg, Harry Kahn, Hermann Kosterlitz, Carl Mayer; *Based on the novel* L'Homme qui assassina *by* Claude Farrère, *and the stage play of the same name by* Pierre Frondaie; *Photographed by* Curt Courant; *Dramatic Advisor* Carl Mayer; *Music* Hans J. Salter; *Costumes* Alexander Arnstam; *Make-up* Franz Siebert, Ilse Siebert; *Set Designs* Hermann Warm, Arno Richter; *Artistic Director* Alexander Arnstam; *Editor* Laslo Benedek; *Sound* Gerhardt Goldbaum

SYNOPSIS: Constantinople, the dawn of the 20th century:

Colonel Sevigné (Conrad Veidt) is the new instructor of the Turkish army. Brought in from France, he meets Lord Falkland (Heinrich George)—a man of enormous influence, but hard, egotistical and unscrupulous—and Stanislaus Cernuwicz, the Russian attaché, a weak toady. Mehmed Pasha (Friedrich Kayssler) befriends Sevigné and warns him to watch Falkland and Cernuwicz.

On several occasions, the Frenchman comes in contact with Lord Falkland's wife, Lady Mary (Trude von Molo), who is suffering through a loveless marriage. She is a tender, cultivated and beautiful woman, and many men adore her, including Cernuwicz. Sevigné also falls under her spell and tries to persuade her to divorce her husband. She refuses, however, knowing full well Falkland would never let her leave with Georg, his only son.

For his part, Sevigné decides to accompany Falkland on his nightly jaunt through bars and clubs, hoping to get evidence of disgraceful behavior that might make the subject of divorce more appealing to Lady Mary. Meanwhile, things get worse at the Falkland manse. After a loud squabble with Falkland's cousin Edith (Friedl Haerlin), Mary moves into the garden house where she's caught by her husband while having an innocent tête-à-tête with Cernuwicz. Falkland forces his wife to sign a paper saying that she is the guilty party in the matter of divorce and that she will cede their son to him. Sevigné, who has followed Mary out of fear for her safety and has overheard everything, shoots Falkland after his wife has left the scene.

Mehmed Pasha investigates the murder, and finds evidence of Cernuwicz having been at the scene of the crime. The Turkish officer also determines Mary was an accomplice to the crime. Sevigné cannot stand by and watch Lady Falkland be found guilty of something she did not do. Admitting his guilt to Mehmed Pasha, the Frenchman is banished forever from Turkey. He will never again see the woman he adores.

REVIEWS: "...[*Der Mann, der den Mord beging* is a] waste of the fragile intensity of Trude von Molo, of the fine reserve of Conrad Veidt, of the surging power of Heinrich George. And this was the first talker scenario by Carl Mayer, who gave us *Caligari* and *The Last Man*. Has speech on the screen cut him off from us?"

New York Times, 22 February
1931— C. Hooper Trask

"*Der Mann, der den Mord beging* is a very excellent Conrad Veidt film. ... Veidt, at last, *is* the man who committed the murder; one of his best and most beautiful roles ever. [He is] secure and elegant in his every action... avoiding excesses... One must be grateful that the director understood that Veidt had to be what he so seldom is allowed to be: a human being."

Die Filmwoche, No. 6;
4 February 1931

NOTES AND QUOTES: *Der Mann, der den Mord beging* was "Eine Mehrsprachen-produktion," a polyglot production.

Although Trudy von Molo's long-suffering heroine is the pivot upon which the plot turns, Veidt's Marquis de Sevigné and Heinrich George's Lord Falkland share the honors as the twin focal points upon which the viewer's attention is riveted. George's monocled, crew-cut, barrel-chested Teutonic bull is quite acceptable as the egocentric English peer, as the actor — like his American counterpart, Louis Wolheim — was possessed of a talent that transcended the brutish roles that normally fell his way. Falkland's slow, deliberate movements follow all too transparent bouts with heavy thinking, but the burly nobleman proves to be as insightful as he is stolid; his ambiguous glances at his

If not a murderer, Connie, a mercy killer ... certainly not a demon. (*Der Mann, der den Mord beging*)

"friend" Sevigné speak volumes although his dialogue is usually restricted to grunts, epithets, or brief pronouncements.

Connie underplays beautifully as the French expatriate who finds an *affaire du coeur* while seeking a career challenge in Constantinople. Although more plentiful and diverse than George's, Veidt's dialogue is not especially memorable, so Connie works his wonderfully expressive face overtime. The result is a textbook illustration of how predictable, even banal dialogue can occasionally be perceived as *bons mots* when delivered with panache.

El hombre que asesinó— Spanish-language version—1931

Paramount British Productions; Filmed at British and Dominion Studios, Elstree; Original Spanish running time: c. 69 minutes

CAST: Rosita Moreno *Lady Maria Falkland*, Ricardo Puga *Lord Archibald Falkland*, Carlos San Martín *Coronel De Sevigné*; with Gabriel Algara

CREDITS: *Directors* Dimitri Buchowetzki, Carlos de Battle

Stamboul — English-language version — 1931

Paramount British Productions; Filmed at British and Dominion Studios, Elstree; Original British running time: 75 minutes; World premiere: October 1931, London

CAST: Warwick Ward *Col. André de Sévigne*; Henry Hewitt *Baron von Strick*; Rosita Moreno *Baroness von Strick*; Margot Grahame *Countess Elsa Talven*; Abraham Sofaer *Mahmed Pascha*; Garry Marsh *Prince Cernuwicz*; Alan Napier *Bouchier*; Stella Arbenina *Madame Bouchier*

CREDITS: *Producer* Walter Morosco; *Director* Dimitri Buchowetzki; *Scenario* Reginald Denham

L'Homme qui assassina — French-language version — 1931

Terra-Film A-G, Berlin; Filmed at Ufa-Atelier, Neubabelsberg; Distributed by Etablissements Braunberger-Ricchebé, Paris; World premiere: 21 January 1931 Marivaux Theater; Pathé–Victor Hugo, Paris

CAST: Jean Angelo *Marquis de Sévegné*; Gabriel Gabrio *Sir Archibald Falkland*; Marie Bell *Lady Falkland*; Edith Méra *Lady Edith*; Max Maxudian *Mehmed Pascha*; Abel Jacquin *Prince Chernuwicz*

CREDITS: *Directors* Kurt Bernhardt, Jean Tarride

Die Nacht der Entscheidung

[LOST] *The Night of Decision*; aka **Der General**; Paramount Publix Corporation — 1931; A Western Electric Sound Film; Photographed at Paramount Studios, Joinville; Censored: 7/4/31 — 8 Acts, 2082 minutes; World premiere (and potential exhibitors' screening) 8/5/31 Gloria-Palast, Berlin; General release: 9/17/31 U.T. Kurfürstendamm, Berlin

CAST: Conrad Veidt *General Platoff*; Peter Voss *Lieut. Sablin*; Olga Tschechowa *Marya Fedorowna, his Wife*; Trude Hesterberg *Madame Alexandra*; Erik Werntgen *Colonel Prokoff*; Emil Ritter *Velajeff*; Frédéric Mariotti *Jegor*; Alfons Fryland *Spoliansky*

CREDITS: *Director* Dimitri Buchowetzki; *Scenario* Brenno Vigny, Martin Brown, Louise Long; *Based on* **The General** *by* Lajos Zihaly; *Photographed by* Philipp Tanura

SYNOPSIS: Marya Ivanovna (Olga Tschechowa), a wealthy and beautiful Russian girl, agrees to marry Lieut. Victor Sablin (Peter Voss), a young medical student, though she is unconvinced of her love. When war is declared, Sablin, a reserve officer, is taken from his bacteriological research, and Marya goes to Platoff (Conrad Veidt), a stern and unyielding general, to plead for his exemption, but this favor is curtly refused. Sablin proves to be a poor soldier in the accepted sense, and maddened by Platoff's sarcasm, he berates the general for refusing him a transfer to the medical corps. Later, Platoff has him arrested and sentenced to death for sedition. Hoping to sway the general, Marya bribes her way into a brothel, causing him to fall in love with her, but he harshly refuses her request that he spare her husband. Later, however, he pardons Sablin and restores him to duty. Learning how his life has been "bought," Sablin plots to kill the general, who, for a second time, saves his life in action. Realizing that Marya sincerely loves the general, Sablin returns to St. Petersburg and gives her liberty. She is reunited with Platoff.

REVIEWS: "…Such romantic yearnings [as are featured in *Die Nacht der Entscheidung*] don't ask for logical motives or artistic methods — a pity, really, because films like this one wouldn't [then] be produced anymore, and Conrad Veidt and Olga Tschechowa would have been spared roles like these. Nonetheless, Veidt has some very strong moments courtesy of his wonderfully decent style, and Olga Tschechowa is charming and tries to show some depth of humanity…"

Die Filmwoche, No. 40;
1 October 1931

"…The picture will interest its audience because Conrad Veidt, an actor whose

General Platoff (Connie) is pitching woo, and Marya Federowna (Olga Tschechowa) is taking all the way. (*Die Nacht der Entscheidung*)

popularity is rarely seen, plays the leading part. Veidt gives this role substance, whereby he helps the audience breach one or two holes in the plot. He is a man of integrity, believable in his every action…"
Film-Kurier, 18 September 1931

NOTES AND QUOTES: *Die Nacht der Entscheidung* was "Eine Mehrsprachenproduktion" (a polyglot production).

Le Rebelle— French-language version —1931

Photographed at Paramount Studios, Joinville; A Western Electric Sound Film
CAST: Thomy Bourdelle *General Platoff*; Pierre Batcheff *Boris Sablin*; Suzy Vernon *Maria Ivanovna*; Paule Andral *Madame Alexandra*
CREDITS: *Director* Adelqui Millar; *French Translation/Dialogue (Scenario)* Benno Vigny

Generalen— Swedish-language version —1931

Photographed at Paramount Studios, Joinville; A Western Electric Sound Film
CAST: Edvin Adolphson *General Platoff*; Inga Tidblad *Maria Sabline*; Paul van der Osten *Viktor Sabline*; Karin Swanström *Alexandra*
CREDITS: *Director* Gustaf Bergman; *Swedish Translation/Dialogue (Scenario)* Gustaf Bergman

All three were foreign-language versions of:

The Virtuous Sin— Paramount-Publix Corp.— 24 October 1930

A Western Electric Movietone Sound Film
CAST: Walter Huston *General Platoff*; Kay Francis *Marya Ivanovna*; Kenneth MacKenna *Lieut. Victor Sabline*; Jobyna Howland *Alexandra*
CREDITS: *Directors* George Cukor, Louis Gasnier; *Scenario* Martin Brown, Louise Long; *Photographed by* David Abel

Der Kongress tanzt

Erich Pommer-Produktion der Universum-Film AG (Ufa), Berlin; A Klangfilm; Photographed at Ufa Studios, Neubabelsberg; Censored: 28 September 1931—10 Acts, 2763.60 meters; World premiere: 29 September 1931 Scala, Vienna (Austria) ; Censored: 9 October 1931: 10 Acts, 2768 meters; German premiere: 23 October 1931 Ufa-Palast am Zoo, Berlin; Original running time — Germany — 85 minutes

CAST: Conrad Veidt *Prince Metternich*; Lilian Harvey *Christel Weinzinger*; Willy Fritsch *Czar Alexander and Uralsky, his Double*; Lil Dagover *the Countess*; Alfred Abel *King of Saxony*; Paul Hörbiger *Heurigen Singer*; Adele Sandrock *the Princess*; Otto Wallburg *Bibicoff, Adjutant to the Czar*; Carl-Heinz Schroth *Pepi, Metternich's Private Secretary*; Eugen Rex *the Saxon Envoy*; Alfred Gerasch *the French Envoy*; Margarete Kupfer the *Countess*; Julius Falkenstein *Minister of Finance*, Boris Romanoff *Dancer*; Max Gülstorff *Burgomaster*; Ernst Stahl-Nachbaur *Napoleon*; Sergius Sax *Russian Servant*; with Hermann Blass, Trude Brionne, Franz Nicklisch

CREDITS: *Producer* Erich Pommer; *Director* Erik Charell; *Production Supervisor* Erich Pommer; *Asst. Directors* Paul Martin, Basil Ruminow, Kurt Hoffmann [uncredited]; *Executive Producer* Eberhard Klagemann, Eduard Kubat; *Screenplay* Norbert Falk, Robert Liebmann; *Photographed by* Carl Hoffmann; *Special Effects Photography* Theodor Nischwitz; *Original Music* Werner Richard Heymann; *Musical Director* Werner Richard Heymann; *Text* Robert Gilbert; *Set Designs* Walter Röhrig, Robert Herlth; *Editor* Viktor Gertler; *Costumes* Ernst Stern; *Make-up* Emil Neumann, Maria Jamitzky, Oscar Schmidt; *Dances* Boris Romanoff; *Sound* Fritz Thiery; *Editor* Viktor Gertler

SYNOPSIS: Vienna, 1815: Napoleon has been banished to the isle of Elba. The remaining European monarchs come together in Vienna both to attend the congress and to negotiate their conflicting claims. Christel, a Viennese glove-seller (Lilian Harvey), greets each visiting head of state with a little bouquet of flowers, in which she has hidden a notice about her glove shop. Pepi (Carl-Heinz Schroth), who is in love with Christel, is sent by his master, Prince Metternich (Conrad Veidt), to warn Christel not to give flowers to Czar Alexander of Russia, who is expected the next day. Christel tosses a bunch of flowers at the Czar (Willy Fritsch) and, when they hit him, she is seized, arrested as an anarchist, and taken to prison.

When he hears the particulars of Christel's dilemma, Alexander has her released. Smitten by her beauty, he takes her to a beer-garden, and then sets her up in a villa of her own. In the meantime, Metternich has persuaded a lovely countess (Lil Dagover) to seduce the Czar, hoping to distract Alexander from political matters with an *affaire du coeur*.

Alexander is nobody's fool, and has Uralsky (Willy Fritsch) — his double — take his place. As Uralsky has been specifically instructed to be cautious, Christel is disconcerted by the "Czar's" sudden coldness. Likewise, it is Uralsky whom Metternich's countess meets at the opera; she regards her turning the "Czar's" head as a *succès d'estime*.

As the dances at the congress grow more and more exuberant, Alexander heads back to the beer garden with Christel. Just as the young woman is beginning to enjoy the Czar's attention once again, Adjutant Bibicoff (Otto Wallburg) appears with the unsettling news that Napoleon has escaped his island prison and has returned to France. The Czar must return home at once.

Like Cinderella at the stroke of midnight, Christel is once again what she was at the outset of the congress: a young glove seller. She is, however, very happy to be left with memories of her romance "as congress dances."

REVIEWS: "The Johann Strauss Theater in Vienna has been transformed into a sound film palace that could not be more beautiful [were it] in Berlin. For the opening night, the UFA contributed its great film, *Der Kongress tanzt*, so that for the first

Connie and Lil Dagover, frozen in time. (*Der Kongress tantzt*)

time in UFA's history, a premiere did not take place in Berlin... The film, a masterpiece of the UFA, received tumultuous applause..."

Der Kinematograph (Berlin), No. 226; 30 September 1931

"This film shows us two different things: fabulous technique and the miserable cultural level of the film industry nowadays. A critic from 'Scherl' wrote—like he supposedly knows—that director Herr Charell spent money like water on this film. Well, if one forks over such money in these times of poverty, it should be for a thing well worth it. Not according to UFA; no, UFA doesn't follow these new artistic ways... The Jew Charell has made kitsch of this subject; he has trivialized it, has rendered it banal. He has reduced it to the status of a revue, to a revue that we are

sick of today... But how—for heaven's sake—did Herr Löwenberg [Charell's real name] (Sorry, Charell) fritter away so much money? Apparently, for extras and for costumes. This is disastrous Jewish megalomania: to direct the masses, with a staff of sub-vice-assistant directors and the heroic waving of arms...

"If Löwenberg/Charell did not have that excellent photographer, Hoffmann, the film would be absolute rubbish. Hence, it is—from a photographic viewpoint, at least—an artistic masterpiece. UFA has thrown itself at the mercy of revue-director Charell. As for the excellent actors, Willi Fritsch best resists the Löwenberg tomfoolery, while Conrad Veidt already gives in too much...

"A historic film? That's what you think! Löwenberg/Charell uses a topic concocted by a Jewish 'Ullstein' author, in which everything becomes tomfoolery and lark, kitsch and sugar icing. Metternich (Veidt) becomes a comic Dr. Mabuse in a children's magazine format, Tsar Alexander (Fritsch) a mere postcard beauty, and the glove-seller (Harvey), a joint-shaking marionette who would be unbearable if we did not know she is a real artist. Löwenberg/Charell damned her — out of a hatred for everything female? — to be a panty-showing soubrette. Oh my God! The lovely money! Poor UFA…"

Angriff, 28 October 1931
[Angriff was the paper of the NSDAP, the Nazi party.]

NOTES AND QUOTES: *Der Kongress tantzt* was "Eine Mehrsprachenproduktion" (a polyglot production).

Klaus Kreimeier reports that "Of the 137 German sound films of the 1930-1931 season, more than a third, most of them Ufa products, were released in several languages" (*The Ufa Story*. New York: Hill and Wang, 1996; pp. 195–96).

"This is a film in its original, true sense of the word. The script is only a rough frame… When one accepts that Metternich is a funny role (which is played charmingly and lovably by Conrad Veidt), and that all historical facts are meaningless and only private moments are important, then the film has some terrific scenes."

Von Reinhardt bis Brecht III
1930–1932 — Herbert Ihering

Congress Dances

Aka *Old Vienna*—English-language version; Universum-Film AG (Ufa), Berlin; A Klangfilm; Photographed at Ufa Studios, Neubabelsberg; Distributed by Gaumont-British; World premiere: 30 November 1931 Trade Show, London; Official premiere: 31 November 1931 Tivoli, London; General release: 11 April 1932; Original British running time: 92 minutes

CAST: Conrad Veidt *Prince Metternich*; as above, save Henri Garat *Tsar Alexander and Uralsky, his Double*; Gibb McLaughlin *Bibikoff*; Reginald Purdell *Pepi*; Philip Manning *King of Saxony*; Humberston Wright *Duke of Wellington*; Helen Haye *The Princess*; Spencer Trevor *Finance Minister*; Tarquini d'Or *Heurige Singer*

CREDITS: *Producer* Erich Pommer; *Directors* Erik Charell, Carl Winston; *Scenario* Rowland V. Lee; *Based on a Story by* Norbert Falk, Robert Liebmann; *Production Supervisor* Erich Pommer; *Asst. Directors* Paul Martin, Basil Ruminow; *Executive Producer* Eberhard Klagemann; *Original Music* Werner Richard Heymann; *Musical Director* Werner Richard Heymann; *Set Design* Robert Herlth, Walter Röhrig; *Costumes* Ernst Stern; *Sound* Fritz Thiery; *Editor* Viktor Gertler

SYNOPSIS: As above.

REVIEWS: "…There is a potpourri of tongues in this film, what with Miss Harvey's English, M. Garat's French accent, Herr Veidt's deep German enunciation; likewise Lil Dagover's agreeable manner of speaking English, and several British players. Mr. Veidt is quite effective in his part…."

New York Times, 12 May
1932 — Mordaunt Hall

"…Conrad Veidt speaks a trifle carefully and precisely, but every word's understandable, and this deliberateness is not ill suited to the diplomatic deliberateness of the statesman Metternich, whom he is interpreting…."

"Notes of the Berlin Screen"
in the New York Times,
15 November 1931

"Certainly one of the most brilliant films since talkies broke the great silence….

"Conrad Veidt, that greatest of German stage and screen actors, is brilliant as Prince Metternich…."

Picturegoer Weekly,
9 April 1932

"Sparkling, captivating romance, set in Vienna of 1815, between the Tsar of Russia and a little glove-seller. Tuneful, lilting

One of the Ufa's all-time most popular productions, *Der Kongress tantzt* was ultimately condemned by the Nazis for "too much Jewish participation."

music, delightful comedy, touches of fantasy are blended with superb skill, while the photography and settings are exceptional, and the acting excellent. A picture that should on no account be missed."

Picture Show, 15 April 1932

"…The outstanding performance is by Conrad Veidt as Metternich who betrays an unexpectedly incisive wit; Lil Dagover is elegantly ironic as the Countess, but Willy Fritsch's approach to a gay romantic style is not, now, without its ludicrous side. Lilian Harvey, reminiscent at times of the early Anna Neagle, is at least lively and determinedly coquettish."

Monthly Film Bulletin,
Vol. 22, No. 260;
September 1955 — J.M.

NOTES AND QUOTES: This— CV's first English language talkie — was made in Germany.

Le Congrès s'amuse

Aka *Le Congrès qui danse*— French-language version —1931; Universum-Film A-G, Berlin; A Klangfilm; Photographed at Ufa Studios, Neubabelsberg; Distributed by Alliance Cinématographique Europèenne, Paris and Universum-Film A-G, Berlin; French premiere: 30 October 1931 Miracles Theater, Paris; Original French running time: 93 minutes

CAST: as above, save Armand Bernard *Bibikoff*; Pierre Magnier *Prince Metternich*; Robert Arnoux *Pepi*; Odette Talazac *the Princess*; Jean Dax *Talleyrand*; Sinöel *Minister of Finance*; Paul Olivier *Burgomeister*

CREDITS: as above, save *Directors* Eric Charell, Jean Boyer; *French Translation/Dialogue (Scenario)* Jean Boyer; *Song Text* Jean Boyer

OVERVIEW: "In their own way Ufa's revue and operetta films orchestrated and illustrated an unprecedented contemporary tragedy: the death throes and demise of Germany's first democracy. Economic crisis and self-inflicted political impotence on the one hand, and *Liebeswalzer* (*Waltz of Love*), *Bomben auf Monte Carlo* (*Monte Carlo Madness*), and *Der Kongress Tanzt* on the other. It seemed as if the Weimar Republic was dancing its way toward the abyss with reckless musical abandon" (Kreimeier, p. 186).

On March 28, 1933, Joseph Goebbels, as Minister for National Education and Propaganda, met with film industry executives at Berlin's Kaiserhof Hotel. The notes of the meeting, which were circulated the following day, reported that:

> As a result of the national revolution taking place in Germany, the question of continuing the employment of Jewish staff members in Ufa has become pressing. It will henceforth be our policy, where possible, to terminate contracts with Jewish employees. Further, we shall take immediate steps to terminate the contracts of people affected by this policy...

Further to this, Kreimeier relates how "In October 1937 the [Nazi] censorship office retroactively banned the most successful sound film of the 1931-32 season, Erik Charell's *The Congress Dances*, because too many Jewish, emigrated, and politically undesirable artists were listed in its credits. Film criticism worthy of the name no longer existed" (p. 256).

A color remake of the film was shot in Austria in 1955 and was released in the States through Republic Pictures the following year. Directed by Franz Antel, the picture starred Johanna Matz as Cristal, and featured Karl Schönböck in the role of Count Metternich.

Der Kongress tanzt was subsequently reworked for radio broadcast; Connie and Lilian Harvey repeated their roles.

Die andere Seite

The Other Side; Candofilm Produktion GmbH, Berlin; A Tobis-Klangfilm; Filmed at Jofa Studios, Berlin-Johannisthal; Distributed by Candofilm Sales and Distribution; GmbH, Berlin, and Richard Goldstaub, Sound Film Distributors, Frankfurt/Main; Censored: 8 October 1931—11 Acts, 2933 meters; World premiere: 29 October 1931 Atrium, Berlin

CAST: Conrad Veidt *Captain Stanhope*; Theodor Loos *Lieut. Osborne*; Friedrich Ettel *Lieut. Trotter*; Viktor de Kowa *Lieut. Hibbert*; Paul Otto *the Colonel*; Wolfgang Liebeneiner *Lieut. Raleigh*; Jack Mylong-Münz *Captain Hardy*; Willy Trenk-Trebitsch *the Cook*; Reinhold Berndt *the Sergeant*

CREDITS: *Producer* Joseph Candolini; *Director* Heinz Paul; *Production Supervisor* Joseph Candolini; *Scenario* Hans Reisiger, Hella Moja; *Based on the play* Journey's End *by* R.C. Sherriff; *Photographed by* Viktor Gluck; *Asst. Cameraman* Wolfgang Hofmann; *Music* Ernst Erich Bauder; *Text* Fred Barny; *Set Design* Robert Dietrich; *Costumes* Willi Ernst; *Make-up* Willi Wollschläger; *Sound* Karl Brodmerkel, Carl Erich Kroschke; *Sound Editor* Max Brenner; *Executive Producer* Harry Dettmann; *Still Photographer* Paul Rischke

SYNOPSIS: March 18, 1918 — three days before the big battles of Arras and La Fère:

A small group of British soldiers under the command of Captain Stanhope (Conrad Veidt) await the German offensive. The five men have been stripped of all their illusions, have lost all their pretensions: they have been at the front for three years. Lieut. Osborne (Theodor Loos)—called "Uncle" for his calm nature and avuncular advice — is young Captain Stanhope's best friend. The captain has seen too much war. His soldiers adore him — to them, he is a legend — but all that time at the front has all but broken him. What only Osborne knows is that for Stanhope to continue to lead his men, for him to continue to appear the fearless soldier, who knows only duty, the officer must drink.

Lieutenant Trotter (Friedrich Ettel) is a fatalist: he obeys his every order without

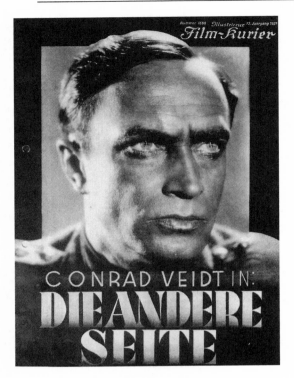

Connie as Captain Stanhope. (Colin Clive essayed the role in the English-language "original.") (*Die andere Seite*)

asking why or wherefore. Lieutenant Hibbert (Viktor de Kowa) is just the opposite, and he would do anything to leave the front.

Three days before the anticipated offensive, a new face appears in the trenches: Lieutenant Raleigh (Wolfgang Liebeneiner), fresh from officers' training school and filled with enthusiasm. Stanhope is appalled. Raleigh is his fiancée's brother, and he doesn't want the new officer (who adores him) to see how the war has ruined him. The thought that Raleigh might write to his sister that her lover is a drunken coward is too much for him. When the colonel (Paul Otto) orders a move against the German front in order to capture someone with information about the offensive, Stanhope declines to volunteer anyone, as it is too tempting to send Raleigh. The colonel decides for him, how-

ever, and it is Raleigh (and Osborne) who are chosen for the assignment.

The move is successful; a capture is made, but Osborne is killed. Raleigh cannot handle the pressure of the situation, and is aghast at how Stanhope and the others drink and laugh at death. He accuses the captain of being heartless and says that he isn't the same man Raleigh came to know and admire three years earlier. Realizing that he cannot do otherwise, Stanhope pours out the feelings he had suppressed for so long in his effort to appear a model soldier still. Raleigh understands.

Comes the morning of the offensive, Raleigh is the first to leave the trenches. He is hit almost immediately and dies in Stanhope's arms. Moments later, the trench suffers a direct hit from a bomb, and everyone is killed.

REVIEWS: "...Conrad Veidt is an experience... A true man, even in his contradictions: a leader in front of his men, a despair-filled character in private. He reveals uniquely wonderful flashes of humanity. Here, he is even surer of his powers than in *Die letzte Kompagnie.*"

Film-Kurier, 30 October
1931— Ernst Jäger

"...Conrad Veidt plays Captain Stanhope. We again have — as we did in *Die letzte Kompagnie*— marvelous acting which demonstrates emotion, movement, compassion, and adoration...

"The picture was received at the premiere in the Atrium Theater with gratitude and warm applause. The principal actors and the director enjoyed several curtain calls and basked in the affectionate applause of the audience."

Der Kinematograph, No. 252;
30 October 1931

"As we've already said ... this is the most noble war film to date, because we have no battles, no brutal slaughter of entire companies here; everything is suggested. ... Veidt [shows] impressive strength, a wonderful Stanhope, a broken man — one who does not think of himself as a hero, but who is one in spite of everything. Commendable direction by Heinz Paul...."

Die Filmwoche, No. 46;
11 November 1931— Paul Ickes

Rasputin

aka *Der Dämon der Frauen; Rasputin, Der Dämon der Frauen*; *Der Ungekrönte Zar*; Gottschalk Tonfilm-Produktions GmbH, Berlin; A Tobis-Klangfilm; Filmed at Efa Studios, Berlin-Halensee, and Terra-Conservatory, Berlin-Marienfelde; Distributed by Fundus-Film GmbH, Berlin; Praesens-Film GmbH, Berlin; Gloria-Film GmbH, Düsseldorf; Union-Film GmbH, München; Filmhaus Nietzsche A-G, Leipzig; Censored: 12 February 1932 (Condensation) 1 Act, 106 meters; Forbidden to adolescents; Censored: 19 February 1932 — 9 Acts, 2419 meters; Forbidden to adolescents; World premiere: 19 February 1932 Capitol, Berlin

CAST: Conrad Veidt *Grigori Rasputin*; Alexandra Sorina *Anna Wyroubova*; Paul Otto *Tsar Nicholas II*; Hermine Sterler *Tsarina Alexandra*; Kenneth Rive *the Tsarevich*; Karl Ludwig Diehl *Prince Youssoupoff*; Brigitte Horney *Luscha*; Bernhard Goetzke *Luscha's Father*; Theodor Loos *the Pope*; Franziska Kinz *Dunja*; Ida Perry *Countess Ignatiev*; Theo Shall *Lieutenant Suschkoff*; Charlotte Ander *Musja, his Bride*; Elza Temary *Nina*; William Trenk-Trebitsch *Ossipowitsch*; Marion Chevalier, Franz Spira *Aristocrats*; Heinrich Heilinger *Petroff*; Edith Meinhard *his Beloved*; Magnus Stifter *Bishop of Tobolsk*; Ernst Reicher *Home Secretary*; Werner Hollmann *Police Chief*; Friedrich Gnass *Dr. Derevenko*; Paul Henckels *V.M. Pourischkevik*; Alexander Murski *Sergeant-Major*; with Gerhard Bienert

CREDITS: *Producer* Ludwig Gottschalk; *Director* Adolf Trotz; *Production Supervisor* Ludwig Gottschalk; *Asst. Directors* Hans Davidson, Leo de Laforgue; *Screenplay* Conrad Linz, Adolf Lantz; *Based on a Manuscript by* Ossip Dymow, Adolf Lantz; *Photographed by* Curt Courant; *Asst. Cameraman* Georg Leschke; *Executive*

Producer Rolf Baum; *Set Designs* Walter Reimann, Gustav A. Knauer; *Original Music* Wladimir Metzl, Fritz Wenneis; *Costumes* Leopold Verch; *Costume Consultant* Alexander Arnstam; *Make-up* Alfred Lehmann, Adolf Arnold, Adolf Doelle; *Wardrobe* Josef Kempler; *Sound* Alfred Norkus; *Editor* Géza Pollatscek; *Artistic Advisor* Alexander Arnstam; *Still Photography* Walter Lichtenstein

SYNOPSIS: Russia, at the beginning of the 20th century.

In the village of Pokrowskoje lives one Grigori Rasputin (Conrad Veidt), a rather worldly monk. He is said to have the mystical power of healing. Women are attracted to him, the sick and infirm seek him out, but he is hated by the men of the village and regarded with contempt by the Church.

As his renown spreads throughout Russia, an official delegation is sent to investigate. Inspector Petroff (Heinrich Heilinger) is impressed with the monk's way with the poor and the sick, and he brings Rasputin back to St. Petersburg. There, with the help of Petroff's fiancée (Edith Meinhard), Rasputin's renown spreads throughout polite society. Soon, word reaches the court, where Tsar Nicholas (Paul Otto) and Tsarina Alexandra (Hermine Sterler) fear for their only son (Kenneth Rive), who is seriously ill. Rasputin is invited to court and is able to heal the tsarevich. His grateful parents present the monk with money and a flat near the palace. Before long, women of all backgrounds are queuing up in front of Rasputin's door.

Both holy man and roué, Rasputin begins to enjoy the good life, which includes drinking to excess and the nonstop seduction of the women who flock to his flat. In addition — exploiting his influence with the royal family — he now has a voice in political decisions, even to the point of suggesting certain men for ministerial appointments.

This newfound influence troubles the St. Petersburg nobility who see nothing but a coarse, immoral peasant in Rasputin. The secret police keep his flat under observation, seeking to collect proof of his wild lifestyle. Lieutenant Suschkoff (Theo Shall) and Prince Yousoupoff (Ludwig Diehl) especially loathe the monk, for the lieutenant's fiancée, Musja (Charlotte Ander), has fallen under his spell, and Yousoupoff has lost out on a ministerial post because of him. With the help of other nobles, and buoyed by the evidence collected by the secret police, the men succeed in having Nicholas banish Rasputin from St. Petersburg.

Back in his village, Rasputin continues his life of debauchery, but errs in seducing Luscha (Brigitte Horney), the daughter of the village innkeeper (Bernhard Goetzke). Luscha's father attacks the monk, seriously hurting him. Taken to the hospital, Rasputin learns that Nicholas is mobilizing his armies. Desperately, the wounded man tries to warn the tsar against this war — in his visions, he sees the ultimate destruction of Mother Russia — but in vain. Rasputin rushes back to St. Petersburg. Nicholas, now uncertain about the future, begins to heed the holy man once again; soon, Rasputin's influence is stronger than ever.

The alliance headed by Suschkoff and Yousoupoff decides to act: assassination is the only solution to an intolerable situation. The monk is lured to Yousoupoff's home, where he is plied with poisoned food and drink. Astoundingly, the poison appears to have no effect! It takes a half-dozen pointblank shots from two pistols before Rasputin succumbs.

REVIEWS: "The exceptional success that this film — [made] under the skilled direction of Adolf Trotz — enjoyed is mainly due to the excellent acting of Conrad Veidt in the title role..."

Der Kinematograph,
23 February 1932

"...Conrad Veidt's portrayal is masterly, and he completely dominates the picture, although the rest of the cast is exceptionally good. The final scene of his death must live as one of the finest we have seen on the screen...."

Picturegoer Weekly,
14 January 1933 —
Lionel Collier

"...Conrad Veidt and the mighty bull of Pokrowskoje cannot be reduced to a common denominator. The two differ [from each other] like the nuance of a perfumed cigarette and the smell of the earth from the Russian steppe. But still... [there are] moments of poetic profundity, touching and moving, as when the murderer sings to his victim, or when the deadly ill Tsarevich is brought back to life by the wondrous monk...."

Lichtbildbühne,
20 February 1932

"...A strange aspect to the performance of the leading characters is clearly noticeable, and Veidt demonstrates it as well. He tries to surrender his prominence in closeups and blends into the ensemble... Still, a pensive Veidt towers head and shoulders above his fellow cast members. At the end, fighting against death, [he's] very simple..."

Film-Kurier, 20 February 1932

NOTES AND QUOTES: A great deal of publicity was generated by Prince Yousoupoff's legal action against M-G-M's production of *Rasputin and the Empress* (aka *Rasputin the Mad Monk*, 1933), starring the three Barrymores. As Sir David Napley relates, the German motion picture, released about a year earlier than the Barrymore epic, had also (albeit briefly) been targeted by the outraged royal:

Sir William Jowitt: Have you brought libel actions in respect to other of the Rasputin films?

An intriguing publicity photograph of Connie as the mad monk. (*Rasputin*)

Prince Yousoupoff: I did one where Conrad Veidt was playing in Germany.

SWJ: Did you start proceedings there and then give them up?

PY: Yes... I signed papers and sent them to Berlin and I really did not interest myself very much about that because I had a lot of work to do at that moment. Then suddenly I read in a paper that the lawyer who was chosen in Berlin settled for me; they were going to pay me quite a big sum of money, but they were not going to get out of the film the part which compromised me. So I cancelled the whole thing because I could not take the money because the film would not be cut. That is the whole story.

SWJ: So you abandoned your action?

PY: I gave up my action.

SWJ: Do you tell me that you refused to accept a sum of money?

PY: Yes, I did.

Rasputin in Hollywood,
London: Weidenfeld &
Nicolson, 1990; pp 134–35.

It is difficult to follow this logically. Was it Yousoupoff's position that, unless *both* of his conditions (a monetary settlement *and* an edit of the film) were met, he saw no reason for legal action? Did he in fact drop his suit against the German company because they would *not* edit out the passages Yousoupoff felt were "compromising," even though they *would* pay him "quite a big sum of money?"

The story of the "Mad Monk" and his influence on the Czarina Alexandra had fueled cinematic fires since 1917, only months after Rasputin had been (with some difficulty) slain by the prince. At the virtual outset of his film career, British character actor Montagu Love impersonated the randy mystic in Peerless/World Film's *Rasputin, the Black Monk*, which opened in Manhattan on 17 September 1917. Perhaps with an eye to avoiding litigation, the scenario (by E. Richard Schayer, who went on to head the screenplay department of Universal Pictures under the Laemmles) changed many of the character names extensively. Iliodor Pictures' *The Fall of the Romanoffs* (with Edward Connelly as Rasputin) also opened in New York the following week, although the picture didn't go into general release until January of the following year. The AFI Film Catalog relates that this presence of one too many films on the "Mad Monk" in the downtown area at the same time prompted a fistfight between the films' respective producers.

November 1917 also first saw Germany move to record the saga on its own terms. The succinctly titled *Rasputin* was filmed in five acts for Saturn-Film AG, Berlin, by a director identified by the DFI only as "Arno." In 1928, director Martin Berger helmed *Rasputins Liebesabenteuer* for his own company, as new techniques and heightened cinematic sophistication demanded another look at the theme, and around the same time (sources disagree, citing variously 1927, 1928 and 1929), Max Neufeld directed his version of *Rasputin* for Piscatorbühne GmbH, Berlin. Not to be outdone, the Russians recorded their "definitive" *Rasputin* under Nikolai Larin in 1929. There is no record that Prince Yousoupoff brought suit against any of these productions.

On 27 April 1933, this film — which had earlier been awarded with the certification "artistically valuable" — was forbidden by Goebbels throughout Germany. All prints and all advertising materials were ordered delivered to be destroyed. The original pictorial and soundtrack negatives were spirited into Austria by director Adolf Trotz and hidden in a farmhouse.

… "My Rasputin will by no means be a frightening bogeyman, but, hopefully, a very human and full-of-life personality. That the well-known Russian author Ossip Dymow who knew Rasputin and the people around him personally, is writing the script will guarantee for that along.…

Mein Film, No. 39, November
1931 — Conrad Veidt

Der schwarze Husar

The Black Hussar; Universum-Film AG (Ufa), Berlin; A Tobis-Klangfilm; Filmed at Ufa Studios, Neubabelsberg; Distributed by Universum-Filmverleih GmbH, Berlin; Censored: 4 October 1932 — 9 Acts, 2585 meters; World premiere: 12 October 1932 Ufa-Palast am Zoo, Berlin

CAST: Conrad Veidt *Captain Hansgeorg von Hochberg*; Wolf Albach-Retty *Lieut. Aribert von Blome*; Mady Christians *Marie Luise*; Ursula Grabley *Brigitte*; Otto Wallburg *Governor Darmont*; Günther Hadank *Captain Fachon, his Aide*; Gregori Chmara *Prince Potovski*; Bernhard Goetzke *Duke Friedrich Wilhelm von Braunschweig*; Herbert von Meyerinck *the Governor's Cook*; Fritz Greiner *the Corporal*; Franz Stein *the Spy*; with Lutz Altschul, Ernst Behmer, Rudolf Biebrach, Gerhard Dammann, Karl Hannemann, Ernst Pröckl, Berthold Reissig

CREDITS: *Producer* Eduard Kubat; *Production Supervisor* Bruno Duday; *Director* Gerhard Lamprecht; *Photographed by* Franz Planer; *Asst. Cameraman* Bruno Stephan; *Scenario* Curt Johannes Braun, Philipp Lothar Mayring; *Based on an idea by* Leo Lenz; *Set Designs* Robert Herlth, Walter Röhrig; *Music* Eduard Künneke; *Text* Friedrich Günther; *Costumes* Leopold Verch; *Make-up* Waldemar Jabs; *Wardrobe* Eduard Weinert, Berta Grützmacher; *Still Photographer* Günther Pilz

SYNOPSIS: Prussia is occupied by French troops. Captain von Hochberg (Conrad Veidt) and Lieutenant Von Blome (Wolf Albrech-Retty) of the "Totenkophusaren" (Prussian Death's Head Hussars) lead the resistance against Napoleon's armies. The men are commissioned to rescue Princess Marie Louise of Baden (Mady Christians) from a forced marriage with Prince Potovsky (Gregori Chmara) and deliver her to her official fiancé, the Duke of Braunschweig (Bernhard

Der schwarze Husar was produced with an eye to raising German audiences' awareness of their national heritage.

Goetzke). They succeed in catching the prince while he is en route to the princess; he is hidden and his clothes are appropriated. In disguise, the Hussars seek out the princess and flee together.

Marie Louise recognizes von Hochberg, who has saved her previously and with whom she is in love. The captain realizes that the woman he loves is betrothed to Duke Friedrich Wilhelm and resolves not to let his personal feelings stand in the way of his doing his duty. In the end, the duke renounces his claim to her hand.

REVIEWS: "...The central figure [in *Der schwarze Husar*] is not an actual historical character, but Conrad Veidt as a dashing Captain of the famous Prussian Death head Hussar Regiment.

"...Herr Veidt and Frau Christians are excellent and their supporters are competent. The direction is fair."

New York Times,
23 December 1932 — H.T.S.

"Lamprecht is not the sort of man who falls for a sort of 'Hooray for Patriotism!' He is meticulous with lofty words, such as 'God' and 'Fatherland.' ... Conrad Veidt needs few gestures or words to express what takes others long-winded sentences: he is a man who gets the job done and who fears nothing, not even the devil. This role is one of Veidt's best accomplishments."

Film-Kurier, 13 October
1932 — Georg Herzberg

"A film with the highest marks in acting. An epic, that offers Conrad Veidt a superb role, one that will bring this actor numerous friends once more."

Der Kinematograph,
13 October 1932

"A galloping romance of the Napoleonic period is *Der schwarze Husar*, that had its premiere at the Little Carnegie playhouse last night. *The Black Hussar* is the skillful and dashing Conrad Veidt in a role that he plays superbly.

"*Der schwarze Husar* is another of the semihistoric, semiromantic pictures Germany has been producing in considerable numbers recently. Some are good and some are only fair; this is one of the very good ones...."

New York Sun,
23 December 1932 — W.B.

"...Conrad Veidt's name has never meant anything at the American box office....

"Veidt is one of Germany's finest actors with an important history going back to the days of *Caligari*. But he's one of those lads who just love to flourish his arms and heave his chest. Director here lets him run loose with disastrous results...."

Variety, 3 January 1933 — Kauf.

NOTES AND QUOTES: *Der schwarze Husar* was only one of eight "fatherland" films premiered in 1931-1932, and Ufa produced and brought out through its own distributors two: *Husar* and Gustav Ucickny's *Yorck* (1931). The so-called "fatherland" films were meant to restore national pride in the German filmgoer by highlighting moments in German history (mythic or otherwise) for the dual purposes of entertainment and edification.

Rome Express

Gaumont-British Pictures Corporation Ltd., London; World premiere: 12 November 1932 Trade show, London; General release: 3 February 1933; USA premiere: 16 February 1933 (released through Universal) ; Reissued by Gaumont in 1940; 94 minutes

CAST: Conrad Veidt *Zurta*; Esther Ralston *Asta Marvelle*; Joan Barry *Mrs. Maxted*; Harold Huth *George Grant*; Gordon Harker *Tom Bishop*; Cedric Hardwicke *Alastair McBane*; Donald Calthrop *Poole*; Hugh Williams *Tony*; Frank Vosper *Inspector Jolif*; Muriel Aked *Spinster*; Eliot Makeham *Mills*; Finlay Currie *Sam, Asta's Publicist*

CREDITS: *Producer* Michael Balcon; *Asst. Producer* Philip Samuel; *Director* Walter Forde; *Asst. Director* W.J. Dodds; *Screenplay* Clifford Grey; *Dialogue* Frank Vosper, Ralph Stock; *Additional Dialogue* Sidney Gilliat; *Photographed by* Günther Krampf; *Art Director* Andrew Mazzei; *Editor* Frederick Y. Smith; *Costumes* Gordon Conway; *Sound Recording* British Acoustic Film; *Sound Supervisor* George Gunn

SYNOPSIS: As the Rome Express leaves the City of Lights, her passenger list includes a number of people whose lives will shortly be changed: millionaire philanthropist Alastair McBane (Cedric Hardwicke) and his put-upon secretary, Mills (Eliot Makeham); American film star Asta Marvelle (Esther Ralston) and her publicist, Sam (Finlay Currie); George Grant (Harold Huth), arm in arm with Mrs. Maxted (Joan Barry); Mr. Poole (Donald Calthrop) and his briefcase; Monsieur Jolif (Frank Vosper) with his bottled beetles; the overwhelmingly affable Tom Bishop (Gordon Harker); and two men — Zurta (Conrad Veidt) and Tony (Hugh Williams) — who have to board the moving train on the run. It's not long before compartments —

and plans — are changed. Upon discovering that the talkative bug collector in his compartment is also the head of the Sûreté, Mr. Poole packs up and heads for the dining car. He joins Grant and Mrs. Maxted at their table, as does Bishop, Grant's neighbor at home; this proves exceedingly awkward for the couple, who were hoping for a private romantic fling so that they might forget their respective spouses for a while. Grant tells the gregarious Bishop that he is traveling with Poole on business, and that the two men are sharing a compartment. After the meal, Grant quietly tells Mrs. Maxted that they should separate for a while — with her finding another compartment to share — until he can straighten everything out.

Zurta and Tony are looking for a man who stole from them the Van Dyke painting the two had stolen from a private collection. While strolling through the train — hoping to spot the "double crosser" — Tony bumps into Asta, whom he had known in New York some four years previously. The two had been involved in a theft in the shop where the actress had worked, and neither is anxious to have the past dug up and reexamined. Tony admits he's still walking the crooked road, and Asta encourages him to change his ways. After clearing customs at the Italian border, Zurta and Tony have a drink in the dining car. They're joined by Bishop, who invites them to play poker with him and a couple of his friends. When they agree, Bishop goes off and returns with Grant and Poole. Zurta's face lights up; Poole is the man he's been looking for.

The men begin to play poker, and Poole has exceptional luck, winning every hand. During the game, Bane's secretary, Mills, comes in and sits at the table behind the card players. He puts his briefcase on the floor, next to Poole's. The cases are virtually identical and, when Mills gets up to leave, the wrong case goes with him. At the end of the session, Poole and Grant head back to the compartment they "share." Despite the agreement they had made earlier, Poole refuses to leave the compartment; it's worth his life. Angry, and aware that Mrs. Maxted will be showing up at any moment, Grant tries to throw Poole out physically. The men struggle and Poole knocks Grant unconscious with a water bottle. Zurta enters, demanding the Van Dyke. Poole discovers that the bags were switched and, desperate, tries to stab Zurta. Zurta kills Poole with his own knife, but before Zurta and Tony can heave Poole's body out the window, they notice the train is pulling into a station. They leave the corpse in the compartment with the unconscious Grant. Grant revives after Mrs. Maxted arrives and they find Poole's body. When a night porter — seeking to help Mrs. Maxted free her dress from the compartment door — also sees the body, the jig is up. He calls the *chef de train*, who enlists Monsieur Jolif in his official capacity. The head of the Sûreté begins his interrogation of the passengers.

Zurta is found ransacking McBane's compartment, and the millionaire — who has hidden the Van Dyke behind a mirror — brings the furious thief to M. Jolif at gunpoint. When told that his story is but a tissue of lies, Zurta reaches behind him, pulls open the train door, and falls to his death.

Once the train arrives in Rome, the passengers — most of whom are sadder, but wiser, for their experiences — pick up with their lives.

REVIEWS: "...Michael Balcon, chief of the executive department of Gaumont-British, got together an all-star cast of British actors and reinforced them with Conrad Veidt and Esther Ralston to play the roles of an international crook of presumably German extraction and an American film star...."

New York Times, 18 December 1932 — Ernest Marshall

"...Casting is superb and the players all excellent. Esther Ralston, Conrad Veidt, Cedric Hardwick [sic], Frank Vosper, Donald Calthrop, Gordon Harker, and Joan Barry are exceptionally well spotted and each turns in an outstanding performance. Miss Ralston's name may help sell the film in America, although she has the smallest assignment of the lot"."

Variety, 28 February 1933 — Kauf.

"...This current feature has a very capable cast, which includes ... Conrad Veidt, that excellent German actor, who left Hollywood after talking pictures came into vogue....

"It is not disclosing anything to say that Zurta, played by Mr. Veidt, is one of the lawless persons. ... Mr. Veidt gives a quiet, but impressive portrait of Zurta."

New York Times, 27 February 1933 — Mordaunt Hall

NOTES AND QUOTES: *Rome Express* marked a number of firsts: it was producer Michael Balcon's first production at Gaumont-British; it was the first picture to be filmed at G-B's expanded Lime Grove studios; it marked the first time screenwriter Sidney Gilliat (who had been crafting scenarios and punching up dialogue since 1928) received on-screen credit; and it marked Conrad Veidt's first British movie. The film was directed by Walter Forde, a veteran helmsman who had broken into show business as a piano player and comedian in music hall. Forde moved quickly to film and came to be regarded as one of Britain's best comics during the early silent period. In the early '20s — some years before Veidt was invited over by John Barrymore — Forde went to Hollywood, where he worked for Universal. Returning home before the end of the decade, he soon won renown as the director of some of England's most popular comedies and thrillers.

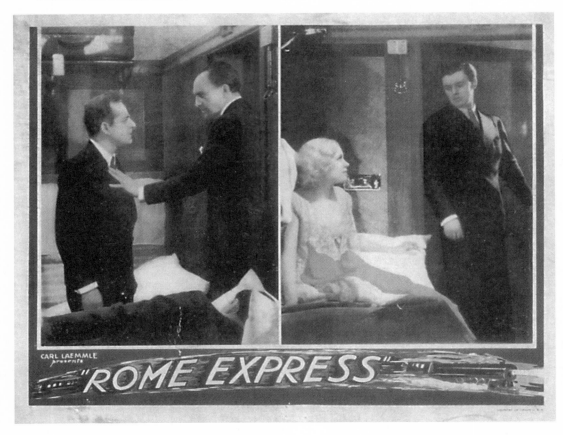

Universal was noted for its "montage" lobby cards in the early '30s. That's Connie getting pushy over on the left. (*Rome Express*)

Connie's presence in *Rome Express* was a key element in Michael Balcon's calculated scheme to give the film box-office potential outside of Britain's borders. Importing Veidt, beautiful Esther Ralston and Austrian cinematographer Günther Krampf did much to give the project a truly international air, as did sprinkling "foreign types"— Teutonic villain, American film star, French policeman — among the stalwart British cast. (It really mattered little that Sam, the New York publicity hack, was enacted by Scottish character man Finlay Currie, or that Monsieur Jolif's Gallic sagacity was intoned by Londoner Frank Vosper, whose early death would interrupt an amazingly varied career. For countless ticket buyers, Fox's Charlie Chan

was flawlessly Chinese, and all the thanks went to the Swedish Warner Oland. Almost no one cared how things *were* in the movies; what really mattered was how they *appeared*.)

Rome Express was remade as *Sleeping Car to Trieste* by Two Cities Films in 1948. Finlay Currie, who had stolen every scene he was in as Sam, the publicist, in the 1932 original, was "promoted" to the role of Alastair McBain in the retread.

"We were off to a good start at Lime Grove for *Rome Express*, the first film made there, certainly justified the jamboree at the opening of the studio. It was quite a coup to persuade Conrad Veidt to play in his first British film. 'Connie' had established a big reputation in Europe with what can only be called the *avant-garde* films of the time… He had made a film or two in Hollywood, but, curiously enough, despite a growing international reputation, he was not as 'box office' in Germany as Hans Albers. This created a curious situation in some of our Anglo-German films, when we opted for Conrad Veidt, believing that his performance would be common to both English and German versions, only to find the UFA would play Albers in their version."

Michael Balcon in
Michael Balcon presents…
A Lifetime of Films.
London: Hutchinson of
London, 1969; p. 63

F.P. 1

English-language version of **F.P. 1 Antwortet Nicht**; Universum-Film AG (Ufa), Berlin/Gaumont-British Picture Corporation Ltd., London; Original Release: 93 minutes; World premiere: 3 April 1933 Trade show, London; General release: 2 October 1933; Reissued in 1938 as **Secrets of F.P. 1**

CAST: Conrad Veidt *Ellissen*; Leslie Fenton *Droste*; Jill Esmond *Claire Lennartz*; George Merritt *Lubin*, ; Donald Calthrop *Sunshine, the Photographer*; Nicholas Hannen *Matthias Lennartz*; William Freshman *Conrad Lennartz*; Warwick Ward *Officer*; Alexander Field *Sailor*; Francis L. Sullivan *Sailor*

CREDITS: *Producer* Erich Pommer; *Director* Karl Hartl; *Production Supervisor* Eberhard Klagermann; *Screenplay* Kurt Siodmak, Walter Reisch; *English Translation/Dialogue* Robert Stevenson, Peter Macfarlane; *Set Designs* Erich Kettelhut; *Based on the novel* **F.P. 1 Antwortet Nicht** by Kurt Siodmak; *Music* Allan Gray; *Musical Direction* Hans-Otto Borgmann; *Orchestra* Ufa-Jazz-Orchestra; *Technical Assistance* A.B. Henninger; *Sound* Fritz Thiery; *Film Editor* Willy Zeyn, Junior; *Sound Editor* Rudolf Schaad; *Flying Sequences* Deutsche Verkersfliegerschule

SYNOPSIS: Renowned aviator Major Ellissen (Conrad Veidt) intrigues Claire Lennartz (Jill Esmond) when he sneaks into the shipyards she and her brothers own, and moves a set of plans from one floor to another. The plans—for a huge floating platform to be used for refueling planes flying across the Atlantic—are designed by his friend Droste (Leslie Fenton), and Ellissen hopes that his little escapade will bring "F.P. 1" to the attention of some "Captains of Industry." The Lennartzes agree to build the platform, and Claire is taken with Ellissen. On the verge of responding in kind, Ellissen chooses rather to be the first man to fly nonstop around the world, and he leaves Claire in Droste's hands.

Two years pass. Ellissen has vanished from sight, F.P. 1 is poised to take on its first airplane, and Claire and Droste have found each other. With Droste out on the platform, however, Claire and her brothers are startled by the sudden reappearance of Ellissen, whose nonstop flight "errrr … stopped." The aviator is all for chucking his adventuresome ways and taking up at the point he and Claire were at the last time he was in town. Claire asks for time to consider.

Meanwhile, there are problems on F.P. 1. Lubin (George Merritt), a saboteur working for a nameless international cartel, has arranged for the platform to sink, having first shot Droste and gassed the rest of the complement. The Lennartzes hear the gun battle over the wireless, but can't raise Droste or the others minutes later. "F.P. 1 does not answer," their wireless operator informs them. As her brothers fear that a well-publicized S.O.S. will result in adverse publicity for their expensive project, Claire asks Ellissen to fly her to the platform to see what's happening.

Ellissen's plane is disabled during the landing on the floating strip, and both he and Claire work feverishly to revive the unconscious men. The aviator notes Claire's affectionate concern for the fallen Droste, and—having ascertained that the

An excellent study of Major Ellissen. (*F.P. 1*)

platform will sink within 24-hours unless oil to turn the diesel engines is somehow acquired — he becomes embittered and fatalistic. The crew panics and flees F.P. 1 via motorboats. Droste discovers that Lubin has damaged the planes aboard and he and the several loyal officers remaining aboard work through the night to make one functional aircraft out of the three available to them. Claire speaks briefly to Ellissen and, with the coming of dawn, the aviator flies off the platform in search of a ship. In the nick of time one is found; oil to power the diesels is delivered, the platform is saved, and Droste and Claire get about all of the business at hand. Ellissen remains aboard the ship he has discovered, choosing to re-embark on his life of adventure.

REVIEW: "An impressively staged melodrama, with a decidedly original theme, is the present tenant of the Seventh Avenue Roxy's screen....

"Leslie Fenton acts Droste in the mood demanded by the melodrama. Conrad Veidt portrays Ellissen in a generally effective fashion. Jill Esmond is satisfactory as Claire. It is, however, a film in which the mechanical, rather than the human element, is the mainstay."

New York Times, 16 September 1933 — Mordaunt Hall

NOTES AND QUOTES: The "science-fiction" element of *F.P. 1 Antwortet Nicht* (Kurt Siodmak's 1931 source novel for all three versions of the film under discussion) was passé *years* before the book was printed. The USS *Langley*— the first operational aircraft carrier in the United States Navy — had reported for duty in November 1924, and biplanes had taken off from and landed on experimental battle cruisers as much as two years prior to that. When one stops to consider that Lindbergh had made his nonstop flight across the Atlantic on May 20-21, 1927, the fanatical concerns of that "nameless international cartel" become really hard to understand. Nonetheless, if one had little interest in real life technology or simply wanted a rudimentary exercise in the suspension of disbelief, the Ufa/Gaumont-British/Fox coproductions were just the ticket.

According to PFA program notes by film historian William K. Everson, some of the difference in running time between the German- and English-language versions was due to a "rousing air force opening" that the British opted to forego. This, plus a "diminution" of the role of Foto-Jonny (the German print featured the increasingly popular Peter Lorre as the photographer) — who was retagged "Sunshine" for British audiences— removed some 15 minutes from the "original" screenplay. When the picture was shipped across the Pond by Gaumont-British for nationwide distribution by Fox, another 20-odd minutes hit the cutting room floor. Thus, the "American" version timed out at 70 minutes long.

"In May 1932, it was announced that Gaumont would be making a series of quality versions of selected Ufa super-productions: 'A number of wonderful Ufa productions have been barred to British-speaking [*sic*] audiences by language difficulties, and the idea is to make English-speaking versions of such pictures.'"

Still, none of the Ufa/Gaumont productions could be registered as a "British film," which inevitably made them less attractive to exhibitors since they did not qualify for quota purposes. *F.P. 1* did not qualify as British, either, nor could it realistically be regarded as a product of the British film industry."

> "A Film League of Nations"
> by Andrew Higson. *Gainsborough Pictures*, edited by Pam Cook.
> London: Cassell, 1997; pp. 72–73.

"The film was shot in three languages—German, English and French—more or less simultaneously, with the character of Ellissen being portrayed by Hans Albers in the German version, Charles Boyer in the French, and Veidt in the English. When the German Ellissen discovers the reason the woman he loves (but who loves another) has bid him fly halfway across the ocean for her, he exclaims, '*Aha! Also deshalb musste ich herfliegen!*' ('Aha! That's why I had to fly here!') The Gallic Ellissen was a bit terser ('*Ah, c'est pourquoi*'), while Connie's flyer let loose with a succinct '*Hmmmmph!*'

Watching the different casts at work, Hans Albers approached director Karl Hartl, smiling. 'You know, dear Hartl,' the German actor observed, 'if this dialogue shortens automatically with every version, the Spanish Ellissen wouldn't say anything at all. A Chinese Ellissen would then surely not even appear in the film!'"

> Dr. Oskar Kalbus.
> *Vom Werden deutscher Filmkunst—der Tonfilm*, 1935.

FP 1 Antwortet Nicht— German-language version—1932

Universum-Film A-G, Berlin (Ufa); A Tobis-Klangfilm; Filmed at Ufa Studios, Neubabelsberg; Distributed by Universum-Film A-G, Berlin; Premiere: 22 December 1932 Ufa-Palast am Zoo, Berlin; 114 minutes/111 minutes

CAST: Hans Albers *Ellissen*; Sybille Schmitz *Claire Lennartz*; Paul Hartmann *Droste*; Peter Lorre *Photographer "Foto-Jonny"*; Hermann Speelmans *Chief Engineer Damsky*; Arthur Peiser *Man with Toothache*; Gustav Püttjer *Man with Falsetto Voice*; Georg August Koch, Hans Schneider *Officers*; with Paul Westermeier

CREDITS: *Producer* Erich Pommer; *Director* Karl Hartl; *Scenario* Kurt Siodmak, Walter Reisch; *Photography* Günther Rittau, Konstantin Irmen-Tschet, Otto Baecker; *Assistant Cameramen* Karl Plintzner, Ekkehard Kyrath; *Set Designs* Erich Kettelhut; *Sound Supervision* Alexander Desnitzky; *Sound Technician* Fritz Thiery; *Production Supervisor* Eberhard Klagemann; *Music* Allan Gray; *Music Supervision* Hans-Otto Borgmann; *Editor* Willy Zehn

Note: *FP 1 Antwortet Nicht* was "Eine Mehrsprachenproduktion" (a polyglot production). The German version was considered the "parent" production.

I.F. 1 ne répond plus—French-language version—1932

Universum-Film A-G, Berlin (Ufa); A Tobis-Klangfilm; Filmed at Ufa Studios, Neubabelsberg; Distributed by Alliance Cinématographique Européenne, Paris, and Universum-Film A-G, Berlin

CAST: Charles Boyer *Ellissen*; Danièle Parola *Nora*; Pierre Brasseur *Georges*; Ernest Ferny *Mathieu*; Marcel Vallée *Damski*; Pierre Piérade *Photographer*; with Jean Muratoste, Marcel Merminod, André Saint-Germain, Théo Tony, Willy Leardy, Marcel Barnault, André Siméon, Louis Zellas, Frédéric Mariotti, Gérard Paulette, Georges Gauthier, Jacques Ehrem

CREDITS: as above, save *French Translation/Dialogue* André Beucler

Ich und die Kaiserin

I and the Kaiserin; aka *Der Handschuh der Kaiserin*; *Das Strumpfband der Kaiserin* (*The Kaiserin's Glove*; *The Kaiserin's Garter*); *Die Kaiserin und Ich*; Erich Pommer Produktion der Universum-Film AG (Ufa), Berlin; A Tobis-Klangfilm — 1932/33; Filmed at Ufa Studios, Neubabelsberg; Distributed by Universum-Filmverlieh GmbH, Berlin; Censored: 22 February 1933 — 9 Acts, 2434 meters; Original running time: 82 minutes; World premiere — 22 February 1933 Gloria-Palast, Berlin

CAST: Conrad Veidt *Marquis von Pontignac*; Mady Christians *Kaiserin Eugenie von Frankreich*; Lilian Harvey *Juliette, her maid*; Heinz Rühmann *Didier*; Hubert von Meyerinck *Aide-de-Camp*; Friedel Schuster *Arabella*; Hans Hermann Schaufuss *Medical Officer*; Julius Falkenstein *Jacques Offenbach*; Kate Kühl *Marianne*; Paul Morgan *Bicycle Inventor*; Heinrich Gretler *Medical Orderly*; Eugen Rex *Etienne, Manservant to the Marquis*; Hans Nowack *Telephone Inventor*; with Hans Deppe

CREDITS: *Producer* Erich Pommer; *Director* Friedrich Holländer; *Production Supervisors* Erich Pommer, Fritz Wechsler; *Scenario* Walter Reisch, Robert Liebmann; *Based on an idea by* Felix Salten; *Photographed by* Friedl Behn-Grund; *Asst. Cameramen* Franz von Klepacki, Gerhard Brieger; *Musical Score* Friedrich Holländer, Franz Wachsmann [Waxman], *based on melodies by* Jacques Offenbach, Charles Lecocq, *and* Edmond Audran; *Text* Robert Gilbert, Walter Reisch, Robert Liebmann; *Sung by* Friedel Schuster; *Orchestra* Ufa Jazz-Orchester; *Musical Director* Franz Wachsmann; *Set Designs* Robert Herlth, Walter Röhrig; *Costumes* Robert Herlth; *Makeup* Emil Neumann, Hermann Rosenthal, Maria Jamitzky; *Wardrobe* Max König, Adolf Kempler; *Sound* Gerhard Goldbaum; *Executive Producer* Otto Lehmann; *Still Photographer* Willi Klitzke; *Editors* Heinz Janson, René Metain

MUSICAL SELECTIONS: *Das Lied* Holländer/Holländer; *Die Grossherzogin von Gerolstein* Offenbach; *Die schöne Helena* Offenbach; *Lied der Kaiserin: Aber kaum sind wir entre nous* [Franz] Wachsmann, after Audran and Leibmann/Reisch; *Mir is heut' so millionär zu Mut* Wachsmann after Lecocq/Gilbert; *Wie hab' ich nur leben können ohne Dich* Holländer/Holländer; Music Publishing House Ufaton-Verlags GmbH, Berlin

SYNOPSIS: During a hunt, the Marquis de Pontignac (Conrad Veidt) finds a garter that has been lost by Juliette (Lilian Harvey), maid to the Empress Eugenie (Mady Christians). As he bends to retrieve it, his horse shies and the marquis is thrown, hurting himself badly. When he is taken to a nearby barracks, the regimental doctor pronounces his injuries to be fatal. Asked if he has a last request, the marquis answers that he would like to see the love of his youth — the singer Marianne (Kate Kühl) — one last time. Meanwhile, Juliette has arrived at the barracks; she is searching for the garter she borrowed from the empress. Mistaken for Marianne, she is led to the marquis, who cannot see her, as his eyes have been bandaged. She sings to oblige the wounded man. When he falls asleep, she kisses him, takes the garter, and leaves.

Contrary to the pronouncement of the doctor — but to the surprise of his friends (and his lover, the actress Arabella [Friedel Schuster) — the marquis recovers. Disgusted by the tactless behavior of the "mourners," he turns his back on them and thanks Marianne, who has arrived in the meantime, for the song. Marianne says she had not sung for him, and no one knows the identity of the beautiful and mysterious singer.

De Pontignac begins his search for the young woman who saved his life. He turns to Didier (Heinz Rühmann), assistant to composer Jacques Offenbach, and asks for help in tracing the notes of that special song, hoping — in turn — to identify the song and its singer. Then, he's off to the palace for an audience with the emperor. Meanwhile, Juliette returns to the castle where, while doing the empress's hair, she begins to sing that song, which was specially composed for her by Didier, who is her sweetheart. The marquis, waiting for his audience in an anteroom, hears the song and makes for the empress's room. Taking no notice of her maid, he presumes

Lilian Harvey and Connie amid the cluttered contrivances of romantic operetta. The Ufa's orchestra fiddled while "old Germany" burned. (*Ich und die Kaiserin*)

it was the empress singing. Torn between joy that he has found the woman who saved him and sadness that nothing can come of the relationship, he returns home, where Didier awaits him. After humming a few notes of "the song," the marquis tells Didier that he has discovered that the singer was the empress. Without saying a word to the contrary, Didier leaves the marquis.

Still believing the empress to be his mystery singer, de Pontignac attends a soirée at the palace. Juliette, who has fallen in love with the marquis, looks to explain matters to him, but fails; he believes that the letter she has written to him is from the empress who, coincidentally, appears at the appointed place at the appointed moment. The marquis, convinced that Eu-

genie is the woman, dares to suggest a tête-à-tête the next evening. The empress, in turn indignant, amused and flattered, doesn't answer. As the time for the assignation draws near, Juliette convinces the empress that it would be best for everyone if she — Juliette — took the monarch's place. *Finally*, de Pontignac realizes who his mystery singer is, and he takes Juliette into his arms.

REVIEWS: "The direction is correct in every instance: all is cultivated, lovable, slightly ironic... Conrad Veidt has poise and noblesse..."

Berliner Morgenpost,
23 February 1933

"As the director, Holländer is still first and foremost a musician. ... He recognizes the natural line of visuals surprisingly well for a debutant [, however]....

"Under his direction, Conrad Veidt and Lilian Harvey are shallower than usual; mind you, their performances are good in themselves, just not as good as earlier ones."

Der Film, No. 9;
25 February 1933

NOTES AND QUOTES: *Ich und die Kaiserin* was "Eine Mehrsprachenproduktion" (a polyglot production).

"The script, which our dear Lilian never read all the way to the end, had her hairdresser getting together with the charming [Heinz] Rühmann. And this ending was good and it felt right...

Imagine what our dear Lilian did when we finally reached that scene... She couldn't believe her ears, and when we showed her the script, she didn't believe her eyes. 'What!?' she cried. 'I get Rühmann? He is a young actor! A Harvey can *flirt* with him, but she doesn't *marry* him! I am the star, so I have to get the star!'

'That's impossible,' I said. 'The plot leads straight that way! The hairdresser and the marquis? No one will believe that.'

'*I* believe it!' she answered.

The discussion continued in the offices of Corell, the general manager...

Lilian asked calmly, 'You see for yourself, no, Herr Direktor?'

He nodded; he saw for himself. The issue was decided. Lilian got her Connie. Did you doubt it?"

Friedrich Holländer,
Von Kopf bis Fuss (autobiography).
Munich, 1965

The Only Girl — English-language version — Ufa — 1933

Photographed at Ufa Studios, Neubabelsberg; Distributed by Gaumont-British — May, 1933 — 84 minutes; Released in the USA as *Heart Song*
CAST: as above, save Charles Boyer *the Duke* [*Marquis von Pontignac* in the German

original]; Ernest Thesiger *Aide-de-Camp*; Maurice Evans *Didier*; Huntley Wright *Medical Officer*; Reginald Smith *Medical Orderly*; Ruth Maitland *Marianne*; O.B. Clarence *Etienne*
CREDITS: as above, plus *English Translation/Dialogue* Robert Stevenson, John Heygate

Moi et L'Imperatrice — French-language version — Ufa — 1933

Photographed at Ufa Studios, Neubabelsberg; Distributed by Alliance Cinématographie Européenne, Paris
CAST: as above, save Daniele Brégis *Kaiserin Eugénie von Frankreich*; Pierre Brasseur *Didier*; Renée Devilder *Arabella*; Julien Carette *Medical Officer*; Pierre Stephen *the Kaiser*; Nilda Duplessy *Marianne*; Michel Duran *Medical Orderly*; with Jacques Ehrem, Fernand Frey, Willy Leardy, Verly
CREDITS: as above, save *Directors* Friedrich Holländer, Paul Martin; *French Translation/Dialogue* Bernard Zimmer

I Was a Spy

Gaumont-British Picture Corporation Ltd., London; Distributed through Woolf and Freedman Film Service; World premiere: 26 July 1933 Trade show, London; General release: 20 November 1933 — 83 minutes (British print); Reissued in 1939 by General Film Distributors; Released in USA by Fox Film Corporation; USA premiere: 15 December 1933 — 75 minutes (American print)
CAST: Conrad Veidt *Commandant Oberaertz*; Madeleine Carroll *Marthe Cnockhaert*; Herbert Marshall *Stephan*; Gerald du Maurier *Doctor*; Edmund Gwenn *Burgomaster*; Donald Calthrop *Cnockhaert*; May Agate *Mme. Cnockhaert*; Eva Moore *Canteen Ma*; Martita Hunt *Aunt Lucille*; Nigel Bruce *Scotty*; George Merritt *Reichmann*; Anthony Bushell *Otto*; Cyril Smith *Officer*; Eliot Makeham *Pharmacist*
CREDITS: *Producers* Ian Dalrymple, Angus McPhail, Louis Levy, George Gunn; *Director* Victor Saville; *Asst. Director* Herbert Mason; *Screenplay and Dialogue* W.P. Lipscomb; *Additional Dialogue* Ian Hay, J.H. Beith; *Contract Writer* Jerry Horwin; *Based on the novel by* Marthe Cnockhaert McKenna; *Photographed by* Charles Van Enger; *Art Director* Alfred Junge; *Film Editor* Frederick Y. Smith; *Costumes*

Gordon Conway; *Sound* William Salter; *Unit Manager* William J. Dodds

SYNOPSIS: In 1915, while Belgium is occupied by the Germans, Marthe Cnockhaert (Madeleine Carroll) becomes a volunteer nurse at a military hospital in Roulers, treating both Germans and captured allied soldiers. At the prodding of her Aunt Lucille (Martita Hunt), she becomes a spy for the allies; soon after, she is given a code name — Laura — by another of the Belgian underground, Canteen Ma (Eva Moore). Marthe finds she can obtain valuable information both at the hospital and at the Café Carillon, which is owned by her parents.

At the hospital, Marthe comes under the scrutiny of German orderly Stephan (Herbert Marshall), who also turns out to be working undercover for the allies. When she and Stephan realize that the Germans have been stockpiling chlorine gas in town, they blow up the stockpile, causing the commandant (Conrad Veidt) to warn the burgomaster (Edmund Gwenn) that acts of sabotage by the locals will be punished by death. After a succession of adventures (including a selfless act of bravery in which she tends to scores of wounded German soldiers, for which she is awarded the Iron Cross), Marthe is found out and captured. She is convicted by the German court and ordered to be shot, but Stephan — with whom Marthe is in love — turns himself in so that she will not be killed. The valorous young woman is imprisoned for the rest of the war.

When Roulers is finally liberated by a regiment of Scottish troops, Marthe weeps for joy that the sacrifices she and Stephan had made have contributed to the liberation of Belgium.

REVIEWS: "...The picture can well boast of its cast, for among the players are Madeleine Carroll, Herbert Marshall, Conrad Veidt, Sir Gerald du Maurier, Edmund Gwenn and Donald Calthrop...

Miss Carroll is both beautiful and convincing in her acting. ... Herbert Marshall is splendid as Stephan and Mr. Veidt is sufficiently convincing as the German commandant."

New York Times, 15 January 1934 — Mordaunt Hall

"The most splendid film produced in this country."

Daily Mail (London), 21 November 1933

"...The acting honors go to Madeleine Carroll as the fine-spirited young girl. Veidt as the head of the German troops looked his part; Edmund Gwenn made a realistic burgomaster; and Herbert Marshall was a first-rate Herbert Marshall...."

Variety, 19 September 1933 — Jolo.

"A film equal to Hollywood's best."
Daily Dispatch (London), 21 November 1933

NOTES AND QUOTES: Time may heal all wounds, but the passage of some seven decades may likewise cause a film's inherent creaking to become exacerbated. Thus, it's difficult for a Millennium-Age viewer to appreciate the examples of British critical overstatement cited above. When viewed nowadays, *I Was a Spy* strikes one less as a film "equal to Hollywood's best" — no matter *which* era we're contemplating — than as a frenetic, episodic and not terribly well-wrought treatment of the exigencies confronted by the Belgian populace during the outset of the Great War. Many scenes are but short sequences in which characters or plot wrinkles are introduced rather breathlessly before being bypassed in favor of some other personage or situation that has popped up, again with a sense of urgency. Then, following a montage of grasping hands, sidelong looks and whispered instructions — and yet another

As Commandant Oberaertz. This was the image of Connie most fans had during the last decade of his career. (*I Was a Spy*)

lengthy shot of tunicked Huns on parade — those earlier commodities are shuffled back into the hand just dealt. In one of "Hollywood's best" efforts, this kind of leaping back and forth would not only have demonstrated meticulous precision, but would also have focused the audience's attention on the unfolding drama. Here, the strategy seems lackluster and confusing, with some inserts too brief to register clearly on a first viewing, and others too protracted to impact effectively.

Also, in seeking to relate the undeniably noble actions of Mlle. Cnockhaert, scenarist W.P. Lipscomb and director Victor Saville create a Roulers wherein our heroic damsel is but one cog in a citywide machine of sabotage and intrigue. Within the first five minutes, the audience is led to believe that, with the exception of all those smartly attired Prussian troops, virtually

everyone else in town is involved up to their shabbily collared necks in undermining the Kaiser's efforts to subjugate Europe. When wooden-visaged but British-cadenced German orderly Stephan No-Last-Name is subsequently shown to have the resistance movement's two-safety-pin high sign secured to the underside of *his* uniform, it seems that even the Germans are torn this way and that over the Teutonic drive to rule the world.

Madeleine Carroll is gorgeous and does a nice job as the nurse who finds herself decorated variously by the King of Württemberg for service to Germany and by the King of England for service to the British Crown. Miss Carroll's character does tend to wring her hands incessantly, though, and she screws her lovely face into an unflattering mass of worry lines so frequently that, even in a town solely populated by soldiers and spies, she ought to attract *someone's* attention more quickly than she does here. A small quibble, however. If I risk offending the shade of Mordaunt Hall by maintaining that Herbert Marshall is just awful as Stephan, so be it. Marshall marches through the part with an expressionless map and a quintessentially disinterested British delivery of any and all of his lines, regardless of whether he's spewing venom, barking out instructions, or confessing his love.

The disjointed unfolding of the narrative sees Conrad Veidt pop up — for mere moments at a time — for better than half the picture. Connie manages to imbue these brief glimpses of Commandant Oberaertz with flashes of personality: if nothing else, the officer appears more balanced and cerebral than the contemporary stereotype. (Nonetheless, later scenes show Oberaertz succumbing to the sort of genetic lustful urges shared by all uniformed Germans.) Connie does what he can with the sketchy role, but there's not much meat on this bone.

Film historian Roy Armes (*A Critical History of British Cinema*. New York: Oxford University Press, 1978, p.79.) saw *I Was a Spy* and such as a reactive move by UK production companies:

> British film makers [of the '30s] attempting to rival Hollywood turned their backs on the everyday reality of British life and offered little more than a liberal helping of Alexander Korda spectaculars, Jessie Matthews musicals, Conrad Veidt spy melodramas and Will Hay, Gracie Fields or George Formby comedies.

While the fuss the English trade press made over the film is hard to understand in this day and age, the perceived importance of the production must have been reassuring to Veidt. The expatriate actor had ongoing concerns over non–German perceptions of his status as a gifted actor and the quality of his film career.

The Wandering Jew

Twickenham Film Studios Ltd., Twickenham — 1933; Distributed by Gaumont-British Picture Corp., Ltd.; World premiere: 20 November 1933 Trade show AND Tivoli, London; 111 minutes; General release: 26 February 1934; Released in USA by Olympic Pictures (1935) — 80 minutes

CAST: Conrad Veidt *Matathias*. Phase I: Cicely Oates *Rachel*; Marie Ney *Judith*; Basil Gill *Pontius Pilate*. Phase II: Dennis Hoey *de Beaudricourt*; Anne Grey *Joanne de Beaudricourt*; Bertram Wallis *Prince Boemund*; Jack Livesey *Duke Godfrey*; Hector Abras *Isekah*. Phase III: Joan Maude *Gianella*; John Stuart *Pietro Morelli*; Arnold Lucy *Andrea Michelotti*. Phase IV: Peggy Ashcroft *Olalla Quintana*; Felix Aylmer *Ferara, Lay Inquisitor*; Francis L. Sullivan *Juan de Texada*; Ivor Bernard *Castro*; Abraham Sofaer *Zapportas*

CREDITS: *Producer* Julius Hagen; *Director* Maurice Elvey; *Based on the eponymous play by* E. Temple Thurston; *Adapted by* H. Fowler Mear; *Photographed by* Sydney Blythe; *Music* Hugo Riesenfeld

SYNOPSIS:

FOREWORD

Out of the unrecorded past come many tales that have been told long before books were written, passing from mouth to mouth, through many languages and lands, firing artists' imaginations, and filling poems and stories. Some of them have grown out of man's eternal questioning of life and death, wondering what it would be like to live forever — to be so blessed or so cursed. No one knows their ancient sources; for the most part our only record lies in the contradictory documents of the Middle Ages. It is here we find the strangest tale of all, the story of THE WANDERING JEW.

Matathias (Conrad Veidt), a haughty aristocrat of Judea, seeks out Christ, hoping that He will heal Judith (Marie Ney), Matathias' consort, who is at the point of death. "Return the woman to her husband," answers Jesus, "and she will be cured." Unwilling to do so, and angered that the crowd laughed at those words to him, Matathias later spits on the Nazarene as he is en route to being crucified. Christ tells Matathias, "I will not wait for you, but you shall wait for me until I come again." Judith dies soon after; distraught, Matathias tries to stab himself, only to see the blade snap off at the handle. He realizes that Christ's words were a curse: he is alone, unable to die.

Thirteen hundred years later, Jerusalem is in the hands of the Moslem infidels. In the midst of the crusaders is the Unknown Knight, who has bested the others at the joust: it is Matathias, who appears not a year older than he had been in Judea. Prince Boemund (Bertram Wallis) has old Izekah (Hector Abras) tell the knights that he believes the invulnerable newcomer to be the Wandering Jew. Joanne de Beaudricourt (Anne Grey) is asked to find out more about this mysterious warrior, so, after the day's joust, she and Matathias arrange an assignation for later that night.

Matathias (Connie), cursed by Christ to live indefinitely. (*The Wandering Jew*)

As the crusaders prepare for Mass that evening, she arrives at Matathias's tent. Matathias arms his servant with a sword, warning him "Should the husband follow, I would not like even his death to disturb me." While Mass is sung, Matathias embraces Joanne passionately, but the moment quickly passes. Appalled by what she has done, the woman cries out: "To think that mine have touched those lips that spat on Christ!" Releasing her, Matathias stands transfixed; outside, Joanne finds the lifeless body of her husband (Dennis Hoey), who indeed followed her at his peril.

Two centuries later, Matathias has become Matteu, a Sicilian merchant. While he bargains for a jewel-encrusted cross, Matteu is presented with the body of his small son, who is near death after having been bitten by an adder. When the child dies, Matteu seeks solace in his work, but his wife, Gianella (Joan Maude), turns

to God. With the guidance of the priest Pietro Morelli (John Stuart), Gianella joins the convent. Stunned at discovering this, the merchant holds a knife at his wife's back, but he allows her her freedom when she avows "If you were to kill me now, I still should be with Him." Once again, the presence of Christ has left the Wandering Jew alone in the world.

Time passes: the scene is Seville, during the days of the Spanish Inquisition. Olalla Quintana (Peggy Ashcroft), a beautiful woman of the streets, is injured when the wheel of a carriage passes over her ankle. She is cared for by the physician Mathias, who comes to her home without passing judgment on her. As proclamations are read, urging all good Christians to denounce heretics and Jews, the physician not only heals Olalla's foot, but also helps her realize her basic human worth. "What hope have I when Christ shall claim his own?" she worries. Mathias, grown tolerant and wise over his centuries of unnatural life, consoles her: "It would go hard with Christ to know his own if he should come again."

Olalla is questioned by a pair of inquisitors and, innocently, she reveals Mathias's comment about Christ. The physician is brought before the board of inquisition, but Juan de Texada (Francis L. Sullivan), knowing of both the man's popularity and the good he has done, says they must proceed carefully. Ferara (Felix Aylmer), a lay inquisitor, opts for loosening Mathias's tongue by threatening to execute Olalla. Mathias confesses to being a Jew and to saying those fateful words. He renounces the inquisitors and refuses the opportunity to convert to Christianity.

The following dawn, he is led to a cruciform stake. The sky darkens and the flames die down. The populace is terrified as a light descends from the heavens. A look of extreme peace on his face, Mathias, the Wandering Jew, acknowledges:

Matathias, the Wandering Jew (Connie), finally finds death and redemption — on a cross. (*The Wandering Jew*)

"Thou hast come to me... again," before dying.

REVIEWS: "...Conrad Veidt's moving portrayal of the Jew, perfectly attuned to each of the four phases of his wandering and conveying, by delicate implication, the changes in the character during the intervening centuries, is the life and essence of this film. He is supported by a generally competent cast, with special praise for the work of Peggy Ashcroft...."

New York Times, 14 January 1935 — Frank S. Nugent

"...Though like many long lost films it doesn't quite live up to expectations, it is so constructed that it grows stronger as it progresses, and the climactic sequence contains a powerful concentration of thespic talent, including a remarkable film debut by Peggy Ashcroft. Conrad Veidt's performance is quite outstanding."

PSA Filmseries Program Notes, 27 January 1988 — William K. Everson

NOTES AND QUOTES: *The Wandering Jew* was a sound remake of the 1923 Stoll silent feature that had also been directed by Maurice Elvey. Popular British character actor Matheson Lang had essayed the title role. As noted by William K. Everson (and quoted above), the theme has been filmed widely and fairly often, and there were innumerable theatrical renditions before the legend was recorded on nitrate stock for the first time in 1904 by master magician and showman George Méliès.

The Twickenham production made it over to the States in 1935, on the coattails of an American-made version that had been shot in Yiddish and released with English subtitles. In the can by late summer 1933, *Der Vanderer Yid* was one of the first projects of the Jewish American Film Arts Company, and it did decent enough business in big cities to warrant a reissue (following a substantial edit) as *A Jew in Exile* in 1937. (With a finger on the pulse of current events and an eye to profitability, the film was reissued twice more: in 1939, as *Nazi Terror* [!] and in 1941, as *The Jew in Germany*.)

Regarding Elvey's second take on the renowned myth, the majority opinion of both British and American reviewers held that Connie did a marvelous job in sustaining Matathias' underlying personality throughout the picture, while demonstrating his spiritual growth and maturation. Most of these same critics, however, found the fantasy a tad facile and overlong. Veidt regarded the picture — and his demanding role — with affection.

Wilhelm Tell [Das Freiheitsdrama eines Volkes]

Terra-Film AG, Berlin/Schweizer-Produktion der Terra-Film AG, Zurich/Film-Finanzierungs-AG, Zurich, 1933; Censored: 21 December 1933; Censored (abridged version): 3 January 1934 — 1 Act, 101 meters; Forbidden to adolescents; Recensored (abridgement): 13 January 1934 — 1 Act, 102 meters; Admissible to adolescents; Censored (feature film length): 12 January 1934 — 2715 meters; Shortened/recensored: 27 January 1934 — 9 Acts, 2711.60 meters; Admissible to adolescents; World premiere: 12 January 1934 Ufa-Palast am Zoo, Berlin; Swiss premiere: 17 January 1934 Apollo, Zurich

CAST: Conrad Veidt *Hermann Gessler*; Hans Marr *Wilhelm Tell*; Emmy Sonnemann *Hedwig, his Wife*; Olaf Bach *Heinrich von Melchthal*; Fritz Hofbauer *Walter Fürst*; Franziska Kinz *Gertrud Stauffacher*; Detlef Willecke *Walter, Tell's Son*; Carl de Vogt *Konrad Baumgarten*; Maly Delschaft *Barbara von Melchthal*; Käte Haack *Frau Baumgarten*; Eugen Klöpfer *Arnold von Melchthal*; Theodor Loos *Werner Stauffacher*; Wolfdieter Hollender *Little William, Tell's Son*; Paul Bildt *Mayor of Luzern*; Herma Clement *Armgard*; Friedrich Ettel *Prefect Wolfenschiess*; Josef Peterhans *Pastor Rösselmann*; Georg Heinrich Schnell *Imperial Governor*; Werner Schott *Prefect Landenberg*; Heinrich Schroth *Imperial Chancellor*; Max Hochstetter *First Imperial Captain*; Willem Haardt *Second Imperial Captain*

CREDITS: *Producer* Ralph Scotoni; *Production Supervisor* Conrad Arthur Schlaepfer, Max Huske; *Director* Heinz Paul; *Asst. Director* Harry Dettmann; *Photographed by* Sepp Allgeier, Franz Weihmyer, Hans Karl Gottschalk, Josef Dahinden; *Asst. Cameraman* Sepp Ketterer; *Director of Photography* Conny Carstennsen; *Scenario* Hanns Johst, Heinz Paul, Hans Curjel, Wilhelm Stöppler; *Based on the eponymous drama by* Friedrich Schiller, *the Chronicle of* Aegidius Tschudi, *and the novel* Der Knabe des Tellen *by* Gottfried Keller; *Musical Score* Herbert Windt; *Musical Supervision* Franz R. Friedl; *Artistic Director* Hanns Johst; *Historical Advisors* Linus Birchler, Robert Durrer, Eduard Achilles Gessler, Paul Lang, Eduard Probst; *Set Design* Robert Dietrich, Bruno Lutz; *Costumes* Alfred Bader; *Properties* Alfred Bader; *Sound* Emil Specht, Fritz Seeger; *Editors* Paul Ostermayr, Lena Neumann; *Military Advisor* Heinrich Danioth; *Still Photographer* Niedecken

SYNOPSIS: Under the heavy hand of the Holy Roman Emperor, Switzerland is in danger of losing its national spirit, and the Swiss, their freedom. Hermann Gessler (Conrad Veidt), latest in a series of oppressive governors, leads a body of Austrian soldiers into the heartland. His mission: to enslave the populace, to confiscate their goods, and to exploit the country's resources.

The Swiss come to feel that, if they could only put aside their petty differences, they could put up a united front and end Gessler's tyranny. At the instigation of

Walter Fürst (Fritz Hofbauer), the men begin to talk of using their cunning to defeat their oppressors' cruelty. Barbara von Melchthal (Maly Delschaft) is retained as a servant by Prefect Landenberg (Werner Schott), but the young woman hears more of Gessler's plans than the Austrians realize.

Slowly coming around to the realization that the Swiss must battle their way back to freedom is William Tell (Hanns Marr), a crack shot with a crossbow. With his son, Walter (Detlef Willecke), he rows across the lake in order to plead for cooperation with the town counsel at Lucerne, only to return in disappointment.

As a series of outrages inflame the Swiss, Heinrich von Melchthal (Olaf Bach)—Barbara's husband—assumes de facto command of his countrymen. When his father, Arnold (Eugen Klöpfer), is blinded by Landenberg as punishment for not betraying his son's whereabouts, Heinrich calls a crucial meeting. En route to the meeting, Tell is arrested for not paying the proper respect to Gessler's helmet, which is mounted on a pole. Moments later, Gessler himself appears; the governor orders Tell to shoot an apple from his son Walter's head with his crossbow. The Swiss patriot does so, revealing afterwards that he kept a second arrow with which to slay Gessler had Walter been harmed. Tell is arrested and packed off to Gessler's waiting boat.

As the boat crosses the lake, a storm arises suddenly, and Tell is untied and instructed to navigate the craft to safety. He brings the ship close to shore before snatching up his crossbow and fleeing over the rocks to freedom. A bit later, as Gessler leads his men up the mountainside in pursuit, Tell kills him with a well-aimed arrow.

Landenberg and the Austrians begin to burn the chalets in the area, and the Swiss have had enough. United in the face of their common enemy, the men storm the fortress and defeat the soldiers. Heinrich strangles Landenberg with his bare hands. As the Austrian colors are burned, and the Swiss flag is hoisted high, William Tell and Walter look forward to a life of freedom.

REVIEWS: "…Conrad Veidt's Gessler shows what these hostilities are about in the clearest way. His thin yet noble face, furrowed with passion, depicts vileness, hatred, despotism, arrogance… Every movement, every glance, every word is right… Many scenes show the secure hand of Heinz Paul, the director. He is to be thanked for the reserve of his actors, for the economy of their gestures…."

Film-Kurier, 13 January 1934

"…The main character in the picture is not Wilhelm Tell, but Gessler, because Conrad Veidt presents him in a fashion that goes beyond the limits of the story… Veidt does not play Gessler, HE IS Gessler, and whether one agrees with his interpretation or not, it seems to me that he has found the style that the film, on the whole, lacks: a grand, sharp cornered, hardwood engraving style."

Die Filmwoche, 24 January 1934

Guillaume Tell—French-language version

Terra-Film AG, Berlin—1934

CAST: as above

Credits (as above): *French adaptation* Claude Allain, Max Maxudian; *Musical Score* Marceau Van Hoorebeke, Jean Yatove, Gioacchino Rossini

SYNOPSIS: as above

Records intimate a Spanish-language version, as well. No other information available.

The Legend of William Tell

Released by Terra-Film AG, Berlin, 1935 (Tobis-Klangfilm), 90 minutes; Distributed by General Foreign Sales Corporation; U.S. Premiere: 30 September, 1935 — 55th Street Playhouse, New York

CAST: Conrad Veidt *Hermann Gessler*; Hans Marr *William Tell*; Emmy Sonnemann *Hedwig, his Wife*; Eugen Klöpfer *Arnold von Melchthal*; Charles Collum *Heinrich von Melchthal*; Maly Delschaft *Barbara von Melchthal*; Dennis Aubrey *Werner Stauffacher*; Franziska Kinz *Gertrud Stauffacher*; Carl de Vogt *Konrad Baumgarten*; Käte Haack *Frau Baumgarten*; Edmund Willard *Walter Fürst*; Detlef Willecke *Walter, Tell's Son*; Wolfdieter Hollender *Little William, Tell's Son*; Werner Schott *Prefect Landenberg*; Friedrich Ettel *Prefect Wolfenschiess*; Josef Peterhans *Pastor Rösselmann*; Herma Clement *Armgard*; Paul Bildt *Mayor of Lucerne*; Willem Haardt, Max Hochstetter *Imperial Captains*; George Heinrich Schnell *Imperial Governor*; Heinrich Schroth *Imperial Chancellor*

CREDITS: *Producer* Ralph Scotoni; *Production Supervisor* Conrad Arthur Schlaepfer, Max Hüske; *Director* Heinz Paul; *Asst. Directors* Harry Dettmann, Georg von Hülsen; *English Supervision* Manning Haynes; *Scenario* Hanns Johst, Heinz Paul, Hans Curjel, Wilhelm Stöppler; *Based on the eponymous drama by* Friedrich Schiller, *the Chronicle of* Aegidius Tschudi, *and the novel* Der Knabe des Tellen *by Gottfried Keller*; *Photographed by* Sepp Allgeier, Franz Weihmayr, Hans Karl Gottschalk, Josef Dahinden; *Asst. Cameraman* Sepp Ketterer; *Director of Photography* Conny Carstennsen; *Musical Score* Herbert Windt; *Musical Supervision* Franz R. Friedl; *Artistic Director* Hanns Johst; *Historical Advisors* Linus Birchler, Robert Durrer, Eduard Achilles Gessler, Paul Lang, Eduard Probst; *Set Design* Robert Dietrich, Bruno Lutz; *Costumes* Alfred Bader; *Properties Manager* Alfred Bader; *Make-up* Richard Timm, Ilse Siebert, Willy Wollschläger; *Wardrobe* Hans Kothe, Friedrich Wilhelm Grossmann, Anny Loretto; *Properties* Walter Dettmann, Otto Garden; *Sound* Emil Specht, Fritz Seeger; *Editor* Paul Ostermayr; *Military Advisor* Heinrich Danioth; *Still Photographer* Josef Höfer

SYNOPSIS: as above

REVIEW: "...Conrad Veidt, best-known member of the cast on this side of the Atlantic, has little opportunity to make of Gessler anything more than a rubber-stamp despot. Hans Marr is soberly heroic as Tell and Emmy Sonnemann and young Detlef Willecke perform capably as the wife and son. But it is the photography, not the drama or the acting, that rates the applause.

New York Times, 2 October 1935 — Frank S. Nugent

NOTES AND QUOTES: *The Legend of William Tell*, in any and all of its myriad sound versions, was basically a remake of the 1923 Althoff-Ambos-Film production. The one element missing from the earlier picture was the tedious and drearily formulaic business about the lovely Bertha von Bruneck and the effect she had on both Gessler and Ulrich von Kudenz; in fact, neither Bertha nor Ulrich is present in the sound version at all. The picture was shot on location in the Swiss Alps and the cantons of Schwyz, Uri, and Wallis, where the logistics of filming almost every scene outdoors overwhelmed the Tobis sound system. Interiors, as well as studio-shot inserts (which were *supposed* to be taking place among the Alpen crags), fared better and were more representative of a typical Tobis-Klangfilm. In an effort to cooperate with the overtaxed sound technology, director Heinz Paul laid the story out as a lengthy series of extremely brief sequences; this enabled him to capture most of the expository dialogue succinctly in closeups or two-shots, while handling the equally short action sequences in long shots. Veidt, whose English had been steadily improving since his return from Hollywood and the Laemmles, delivered his lines in both export languages, plus his native German. Most of the other principals were more at home in French than English, and several sequences of profound Austrian plotting (in *Legend*) border on the ludicrous to

"Okay… You see this apple?" Gessler (Connie, right) makes Wilhelm Tell (Hans Marr, left) an offer he can't refuse. (*Wilhelm Tell*)

modern viewers because of almost comically thick German accents.

Despite the brevity of its individual scenes, the picture offers little in the way of mobility until the climactic rebellion. Most of the Swiss plod along at a funereal pace no matter whether they're joyous or downtrodden, and the Austrian soldiers seem both self-conscious and uncomfortable in their armor. Watching Hans Marr stomping none too agilely about the rocky countryside does nothing to reinforce either the character's relevance to the story or the actor's suitability to the role. Marr, who was a tad shy of *60* years old when production closed on *Wilhelm Tell*, presents the audience with an aging, corpulent, balding hero, an image that many Ameri-

can ticket buyers must have found incongruous and less than reassuring. The few lines that fall to him are spit out in a disinterested *basso profondo*, and he seems physically sapped for most of the picture.

In addition, Heinz Paul so blatantly mishandles Tell's two big crossbow incidents that neither the character of Tell nor the dramatic thrust of the story enjoys much catharsis. Neither flight of arrow is photographed in long shot; rather, both feats are recorded via a series of cuts that work against the drama (and credibility) of the situation. Hence, Walter's apple adventure seems nothing more than the quick shuffling of still photographs, while Gessler's murder — effected from a concealed niche some distance from the governor—can be viewed as really nothing less than a cowardly assassination.

Besides Marr and Veidt, only two actors appeared in both versions of *Wilhelm Tell*: lovely Käthe Haack was promoted from Bertha von Bruneck's female companion to the role of Mrs. Baumgartner, and Josef Peterhans—the villainous Landenberger in 1923—jumped over to the side of the angels as Pastor Rösselmann in the remake.

Connie takes the golden apple, acting wise, but that's not saying much. Granted, he's wearing an empty quiver, as far as memorable speeches are concerned: Gessler's dialogue is just a collection of villainous bromides designed to keep the audience members hooting from their seats and the Swiss yodelers clutching at their throats. Nor has he an awful lot to do, other than glower ominously at the rabble or narrow his eyes, mid-scheme. As he had with Marr's marksmanship displays, director Paul manages to muck up Veidt's death scene: "It ... was ... Tell..." the skewered heavy reveals with three last breaths—each of which has been meticulously punctuated by a measured degree of physical collapse—as if the search party had fully expected that the bolt had been fired by some *other* crack-shot fugitive hidden not 15 yards from where Tell had bounded from the boat. (Still, the botched death scene does set into motion that last-reel, freedom-winning fracas from which Switzerland's crossbow champion will be conspicuously absent.) Gessler's big moment, of course, centers on Tell, the boy and the apple, but, as every schoolchild is aware of the outcome before the scene gets under way, there is no possibility to build any much-needed dramatic tension.

Fräulein Emmy Sonnemann, by the way, quit the movies following *Wilhelm Tell*. She had caught the eye of one of the higher-ups in the ever-more-popular Third Reich and was soon answering mail addressed to Emmy Göring.

While *Wilhelm Tell* was in production, Veidt received an offer from British-Gaumont Pictures to star in a picture based on Leon Füchtwanger's best-selling novel, *Jud Süss*. (The actor and the author had been friends for several years and shared a growing unease about the spread of Nazism throughout Germany. Füchtwanger, a Jew, would shortly be forced to flee to France to avoid internment; he arrived in the States in 1940.) Veidt telegraphed his acceptance of the part, agreeing to report to the British studios upon completion of his work in Germany. In the interest of "national security," copies of all telegrams entering of leaving the Fatherland were passed on to the authorities; there is no reason to suppose that actors' and artists' communiqués were exempted from this policy. Thus it was that *Wilhelm Tell* wrapped and, for all intents and purposes, Veidt disappeared.

It devolved that the actor had been forbidden to leave the country on the order of Josef Goebbels, Nazi minister of propaganda. Cognizant that Füchtwanger's novel depicted 18th-century Germany as a hotbed of anti–Semitism, the diminutive Reichsminister—angered that a Berlin-born patrician would even *consider* casting cinematic aspersions on his national forebears—held Veidt incommunicado. A frantic Lily Veidt appealed to Gaumont-British to investigate. The studios were subsequently informed that Herr Veidt had taken ill and was just then recuperating; he was, of course, unable to travel. A letter—purportedly from Veidt himself—arrived at Gaumont-British shortly thereafter. Although in the actor's distinctive handwriting, the letter's text and grammatical construction made it obvious to anyone familiar with Conrad Veidt that he had merely penned what he had been instructed to write.

At length, the studios and the British Foreign Office arranged to have an English physician sent to conduct an independent physical examination of the actor; not surprisingly, he was found to be in perfect health and able — even anxious— to travel. It would take a great deal of legal wrangling — in a milieu in which the foundations of law were becoming more and more unstable — to effect Conrad Veidt's release from his native land. In the end, probably due more to a desire on the Nazis' part to avoid what would have been a scandalously embarrassing incident than to a triumph of the international legal system, Veidt was reunited with his wife on English soil.

Jew Süss

USA: *Power*; Gaumont-British Picture Corporation Ltd., London; World premiere: 4 November 1934 Tivoli Theatre (London) and Radio City Music Hall (New York) AND Canadian general release, which started this same day in Toronto) ; London opening: October 1934 — 110 minutes (British print) ; New York opening: week of 4 October 1934 — 105 minutes; (American print); General release (Britain): 1 July 1935 [per DIF]; Released in the USA by Gaumont-British Picture Corporation of America

CAST: Conrad Veidt *Joseph (Jew Süss) Oppenheimer*; Paul Graetz *Landauer*; Campbell Gullan *Thurne-Taxis*; Cedric Hardwicke *Rabbi Gabriel*; Dennis Hoey *Dieterle*; Benita Hume *Marie Auguste*; Sam Livesey *Harprech*; Pamela [Mason] Ostrer *Naomi Oppenheimer*; Joan Maude *Magdalene Sibylle*; Gibb McLaughlin *Pancorgo*; George Merritt *Bilfinger*; Eva Moore *Jantje*; Percy Parsons *Pflug*; Hay Plumb *Pfaeffle*; James Raglan *Lord Suffolk*; Francis L. Sullivan *Remchingen*; Frank Vosper *Duke Karl Alexander*; Haidee Wright *Michele*; Gerald du Maurier *Wessensee*; Mary Clare *Countess Wurben*; with Randle Ayrton, Michael Brantford, Frank Cellier, Jane Cornell, Selma Vaz Dias, Victor Fairley, Helen Ferrers, Henry Hallett, Henry Hewitt, Glennis Lorimer, Robert Nainby, Kynaston Reeves, Robert Rietty, Marcelle Rogez, Percy Walsh

CREDITS: *Producer* Michael Balcon; *Director* Lothar Mendes; *Scenario and Dialogue* A.R. Rawlinson; *Based on the novel* Jud Süss *by* Leon Füchtwanger; *Adaptation* Dorothy Farnum; *Original Music* Louis Levy; *Photographed by* Bernard Knowles, Günther Krampf; *Editor* Otto Ludwig; *Costumes/Period Advisor* Herbert Norris; *Sound* W. Salter; *Art Direction* Alfred Junge; *Unit Production* Manager Graham Cutts

SYNOPSIS:
Prologue:

Würtemberg in the 18th century was a small independent State, ruled by an hereditary duke.

It was a time of brutality and universal intolerance and the Jews above all suffered oppression and boycott. At last there rose up a man who, by sacrificing all to securing political power, resolved to bring prestige to the State and to break down, once and for all, the barriers of the ghetto.

Joseph Süss Oppenheimer was a man of human frailty. His work remained unfinished — his story lives.

Würtemberg, 1730: Joseph Süss Oppenheimer (Conrad Veidt) and his friend Landauer (Paul Graetz) have a chance encounter with lovely courtier Marie Auguste (Benita Hume), when their respective carriages come within inches of grazing each other. The noblewoman's coachman drives off in disgust, however, after informing Marie Auguste that the occupants of the other carriage are Jews. Later, at an inn, Süss provides Karl Alexander (Frank Vosper), an impecunious nobleman in line for the ducal throne, with a costume for the fancy dress ball that evening. At the ball, Karl tells Marie Auguste — who is even now considering his proposal of marriage — that he will have some fun with this Jew, Süss. Confronting Süss, however, Karl is swayed by the man's charm and wit; when Süss bankrolls him at the gaming tables and then promises to support him with vast financial resources, Karl names the Jew the "Keeper of the Privy Purse." All seems to be going Süss's way: his plan is to forswear everything — friendship, sorrow, pity, or even love — in

**Connie as Joseph (Jew Süss) Oppenheimer.
(*Jew Süss*)**

order to win real power and thus help Jewry.

Rabbi Gabriel (Cedric Hardwicke) appears and informs Süss that his daughter, Naomi (Pamela Ostrer), has reached the age of 15 years without knowing her father. The rabbi will arrange for father to meet daughter in a house in the countryside. Süss is initially hesitant at this, not wanting to introduce a variable — even if it is his own flesh and blood — into his scheme at this point; reluctantly, he agrees. Karl enters, overbearing and not a little drunk, and demands that the rabbi read his palm. Gabriel reveals that a ducal crown is in the nobleman's future. Karl laughs that his cousin, the duke, is still very much alive and that both he and his son stand in Karl's way regarding that crown.

The following day, news of the duke's death — he broke his back in a fall from his horse — greets Karl Alexander. Within two weeks, the duke's son has died as well; Karl is now to be crowned duke and Marie Auguste will be his duchess. The new duke begins his reign by quarreling with his ministers over the cost of increasing the size of the army. Süss puts into play a plan he has whereby the army will grow without any additional taxation of the citizenry; the duke is happy with the help he receives from "his Jew."

Meanwhile, Süss has finally met with his daughter, Naomi, a beautiful yet sheltered young woman. While leaving to return to the court, Süss meets Magdalene Sybille (Joan Maude), the comely daughter of Count Wessensee (Gerald du Maurier), one of the duke's ministers. Attracted to the young woman, he has her invited to the ball he is holding the following week. Come the ball, however, he abandons Fraulein Wessensee to the lecherous duke. Calling on the young woman the next day to apologize for his unspeakable behavior, Süss tells her of his philosophy of allowing no emotion to interfere with his ambitions.

A crisis arises when a merchant in the marketplace — jealous of the number of sales made by Seligmann, a Jewish competitor — riles the crowd into an anti–Semitic frenzy and then accidentally kills his wife when she reproaches him as a bully. The merchant hides his wife's body in Seligmann's cart and later, when the market has closed and he has "found" blood near his stall, the vendor leads the crowd to the home of the Jew. The body, likewise, is "found" and Seligmann is seized by the mob and dragged from his house. Landauer pleads with Süss to intercede on the Jew's behalf with the duke, but it is only when Naomi questions her father's reticence on the subject that he does speak out.

The inhabitants of the Jewish ghetto applaud Süss's carriage as he arrives to visit with his mother. During the visit, Süss is astounded to learn that his father was German field marshall von Heidersdorf: he is not Jewish, after all. "All my slaving and scheming and suffering … unnecessary!" Meanwhile, the duke has been led by Count Wessensee to the house where Naomi lives. Upon seeing the beautiful girl, Karl's lechery gets the better of his common sense, and he pursues Naomi to the rooftop. Rather than submit, the girl throws herself to her death. When Süss arrives, Naomi's body is already in state; the distraught nobleman collapses. The duke passes the entire incident off as a joke, and orders Süss to bury his daughter and hurry back to Stuttgart.

Süss concocts a scheme whereby to get revenge. He convinces Karl to tear up the constitution and declare himself king! No one will stand in his way after all the members of the constitutional committee have been arrested by General Remchingen (Francis L. Sullivan). The duke, keen on being king but even more set on being rid of "his Jew," writes Oppenheimer's name on the list of those to be arrested. Süss becomes aware of this double cross when Magdalene Sybille, out of love for him, brings him the list before it is published. At his hunting lodge, where Karl awaits word of his coup d'état, he is called out to meet with a messenger; it is Süss. The duke is informed that no one has been arrested, save for General Remchingen; the people have prevailed. The duke has a heart attack and dies. To prevent the state from being plunged into chaos, Süss offers himself up for arrest.

Unable to convict the Jew under any current statute, the chief judge sentences him to hang for having flouted a law that is over 200 years old: under penalty of death, no Jew may have carnal knowledge of a gentile. When Süss mocks the judge ("You can't hang me higher than the gallows, can you?"), he is hanged in a special cage that lifts him above the scaffold. At the moment of death, Süss prays loudly in Hebrew: "Hear, o Israel." He remains a Jew to the bitter end.

REVIEWS: "…What effectiveness there is in this pageant … must be credited to Conrad Veidt. His portrait of the Jewish apostate … is a stimulating performance to watch. The Faust-like conflict of soul which he expresses so admirably manages to give meaning and importance to the role. Thus Mr. Veidt stands out as almost the sole merit of a photoplay which is muddy in its development and ornately uninspired in its general arrangement…."

New York Times, 5 October
1934 — Andre Sennwald

"In some cinemas in Vienna there have been demonstrations, even scenes of revolt against the film *Jew Süss*…. The demonstrations [were in reaction to] the depicting of all Aryan persons in the film derisively and the picture obviously serves the end of Jewish propaganda. The director, a Polish Jew who emigrated to England, did not shy away from showing all non–Jews as morally inferior or even being degenerate human beings…"

Deutsche Zeitung,
19 October 1934

"…The Vienna authorities have finally forbidden the showing of the film, *Jew Süss*….

"At this point, we may point out that the seat of Jewish film propaganda has moved from Hollywood to London. British-Gaumont is particularly at its disposal, and, unfortunately, they are even able to engage German actors…"

Deutsche Zeitung,
24 October 1934

"…Conrad Veidt, within the limits prescribed by some starched dialogue, relies mainly on facial expression and on gesture to draw a dour portrait of Süss…. The photography is consistently workmanlike

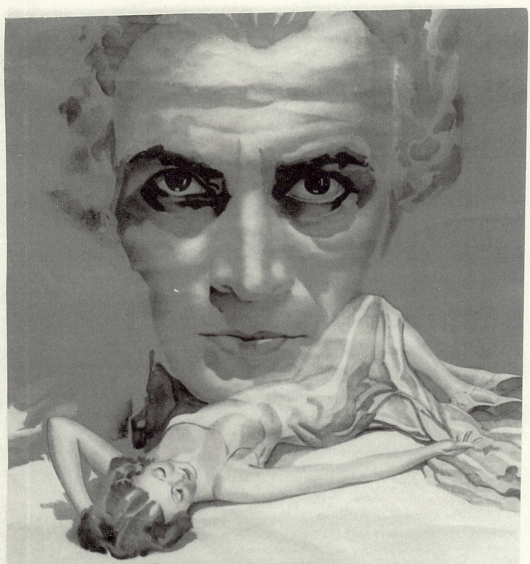

GAUMONT BRITISH *presents*

POWER

Based on the celebrated novel by LION FEUCHTWANGER

CONRAD VEIDT

BENITA HUME   GERALD du MAURIER
FRANK VOSPER   CEDRIC HARDWICKE

Directed by
LOTHAR MENDES

and, indeed, some of the dialogue might with advantage [have] been left to the camera.

"A fine, awe-inspiring and timely production with an idea behind it."

Monthly Film Bulletin,
Vol. 1, No. 9; October
1934 — D.F.R.

"Much care and money have been spent on the elaborate settings, which are excellent, but the characterization has been simplified almost out of recognition. Jew Süss, as the saviour of his people, makes a picturesque part for Conrad Veidt....

"As a piece of screen work, the film was a very impressive reconstruction of the period."

Monthly Film Bulletin,
Vol. 1, No. 9; October
1934 — Y.M.R.

"It is well known that England's Jewish film companies have produced two spectacular pictures for Jewish propaganda purposes... *The Wandering Jew* and *Jew Süss*... Conrad Veidt was rewarded for this treason to his country with the praise of the Jewish people. Because of this, not only is he no longer worthy of a jot of human feeling, but not one finger should be lifted in praise of him in Germany."

Völkischer Beobachter,
23 November 1934

NOTES AND QUOTES: Josef Goebbels and the Third Reich lodged numerous protests with British-Gaumont studios and the British government during the production and release of *Jew Süss*, claiming — with no little justification — that the picture was a virtual indictment of the gentile members of the German citizenry. With the wholesale condemnation of the Nazi philosophy a given then even as now,

A.W. Rawlinson's adaptation of the Füchtwanger original *did* reduce everyone within the Württemberg borders (and, by extension, within the national boundaries, as well) to easily-led, bigoted puppets. Twice in the film, in fact, the only match needed to ignite the fiery crowd is the loud mouth of an ignorant man. The jealous merchant's cry of "Down with the Jew" is all it takes to turn a group of townspeople — to that point, as happy as clams with Seligmann and his merchandise — into a slavering mob, bent on condemnation and, in the end, murder. As the screenplay did nothing at all to indicate that the populace was under any kind of psychological or physical impetus that forced it to act in this way, the only logical conclusion was that die Deutschen were of their very essence anti–Semitic, vengeful and bloodthirsty. The film never played in Germany, but was the object of some intense controversy in Austria (see: *Deutsche Zeitung* reviews, above).

Although Veidt does a wonderful job of fleshing out this Jew Süss, he is given little in the way of help from the screenplay. With Lothar Mendes apparently more concerned with establishing Karl Alexander's many exercises in infidelity than with Joseph Oppenheimer's sundry charities, the viewer is left only with Süss's *word* that he has been acting for all Jewry. The sole instance in which the ambitious Süss is shown doing anything for anybody involves his getting Seligmann off the hook for a murder he did not commit, and it takes the combined exhortations of half of the principal cast to force him to do *that*. Again, the instances in which Süss allows himself — whether actively or passively — to become a procurer for the duke may strengthen his credo regarding commitment to power above all loyalties, but it

Opposite: The striking — if somewhat misleading — American one-sheet from *Jew Süss. Courtesy of Rubin Sherman.*

does nothing to make the character sympathetic or admirable. In addition, the blather about not being able to be hanged higher than the gallows: a quotable sequence, to be sure, but a sequence which ultimately leads to nothing save a bit of pointless dramatic excess.

Still, Veidt's genius as an actor allowed him to transcend such moments of scripted inadequacy or dramatic superfluity. There *is* a certain theatricality to his portrayal of Süss—it has been suggested that several of Veidt's overly elaborate gestures hark back to the days of silent film — an occasional flamboyance that exceeds the then cinematic "norms." Whether this extravagance of technique was purposeful or unconscious, the resulting portrait is the richer for it: a man who essentially denounces his human condition in order to achieve material greatness is forced to act larger than life, if the emotions he is suppressing are to be evident in any way at all.

In contrast, not many of Veidt's colleagues were able to weave much more than a shadow or a caricature from the sides they had been given. Cedric Hardwicke, for example, is positively golemlike as Rabbi Gabriel, droning his every plot-advancing line in a stentorian monotone while casting a baleful eye hither and yon. When the exigencies of the script reduce him to playing fortune-teller to Karl Alexander, they unveil a dramatic quandary: Gabriel sees *two* events, but reveals only the second. Füchtwanger himself would have admitted that Shakespeare handled the second event — warm bodies standing between a throne and an aspirant — much more competently than he in *Macbeth*, but how could the rest of the story unfold without that first event ever coming to light? And why, in God's name, is Gabriel incapable of referring to Naomi as "your daughter" instead of "*the child*?"

Frank Vosper's Karl Alexander is *supposed* to be uncouth, lecherous, drunken, loud, irresponsible, and obnoxious, and Vosper is magnificently successful in peddling the duke's many vices to the audience. Paul Graetz's Landauer is trotted out every couple of reels or so to breathe some humor (he calls Karl Alexander a *schnorrer*, or mooch) into the increasingly portentous proceedings, but he and Veidt later share a marvelous, more serious moment together, when they square off at each other through a set of candlesticks over Süss's inaction regarding Seligmann. Graetz and Veidt were the only two cast members with a German accent (the men had worked together in Berlin's Deutsches Theater years earlier), and this might have been a natural way of setting the Jews apart from the gentiles, were it not for the fact that the rest of the denizens of the ghetto spoke the king's English like … errr … the king.

It's intriguing that a number of contemporary reviews of the film singled out Pamela Ostrer for praise. Miss Ostrer, who would go on to a decent enough film career after marrying James Mason, was the daughter of the chairman of the board of British-Gaumont studios, Isidor Ostrer. The young woman [who *was* scarcely 15 years old during the filming] enacted her few and brief sequences in a fashion that *still* recalls silent film technique.

Jew Süss was the most expensive picture ever to be produced by a British company to that date. Costing in excess of £100,000 (the costumes alone set British-Gaumont back some £20,000), the film was cut by some 15 minutes upon release in order to pass standards set by the Motion Picture Producers and Distributors Association. The scenario had already been pared by some three reels during production, and sequences depicting a casual love affair of Süss's and Naomi's funeral were dropped in the interest of economy and continuity.

Following a theatrical premiere designed to rival the best Hollywood could offer, the film almost immediately began to suffer from adverse word of mouth. British-Gaumont, stung by charges that its picture was ponderous, overly talkative, and "lacking in humanity," orchestrated a print campaign to battle back and win over undecided ticket-buyers to the cause. In the 5 January 1935 edition of *Film Journal* (for example), the gauntlet was hurled:

> There is no need to welcome this film. There is no need to like it. *Only the challenge is that you cannot ignore it.* You cannot dismiss it with the remark that it is dull and slow and boring. Or, if you do then I say you are losing the best in a film which should remain in your minds as an experience as well as an entertainment [p. 23].

The challenge was, for the most part, ignored. Evidently the appeal was greeted with the same casual indifference as had the picture. *Jew Süss* did not make back its costs during its initial domestic release, and records do not indicate that the film was subsequently rereleased theatrically.

In the United States, the picture was set to open at New York City's Radio City Music Hall. For some strange reason, there were difficulties with the appreciation of the picture on this side of the Atlantic, as well. Michael Balcon(*Michael Balcon presents... A Lifetime of Films*. London: Hutchinson, 1969; p. 86.) remembered:

> Rumours began to get around New York that our film might prove objectionable to the Jewish community. This was not only gravely disturbing to [Gaumount executive] Michael Ostrer and to me for obvious personal reasons but the suggestion of a possible Jewish boycott was an alarming one for the theatre owners and could have been financially disastrous for them.
>
> It fell to me to try to get the approval of Albert Einstein, then at Princeton, where he had a house just outside the college campus. I drove out from New York and when we drew up to the door, Einstein appeared with his arms outstretched... Einstein walked past me and embraced the driver of my

hired car. "He was my chauffeur when I was driven around New York in the first days after my arrival from Germany. He is a good friend..." We went to the University cinema and screened the film. Later that night I returned to New York with a written endorsement of *Jew Süss* from the great man [p. 86].

In 1940, as a perverse reaction to Conrad Veidt's more elegant portrayal of Leon Füchtwanger's tragic protagonist, Veit Harlan put a Nazi spin on the source novel and directed a 98-minute feature version for the edification of the Third Reich. *Jud Süss* was thus viewed as an "answer film" to the 1934 British picture that had caused so much embarrassment to Josef Goebbels and the Ministry of Propaganda. Working with an almost unlimited budget and the advantages of on-location shooting, Harlan created a masterpiece of anti–Semitism. Sadly, the cast list reads like a Who's Who from Conrad Veidt's German silent period: Heinrich George, Bernhard Goetzke, Willi Kaiser-Heyl, Theodor Loos, Erna Morena and... Werner Krauss. Postwar critics and commentators found the inclusion of this last name particularly disturbing.

Writing from London (whither he had fled Hitler's Germany a decade earlier) in 1948, Dr. H.H. Wollenberg —former editor of Berlin's leading professional cinematic journal, the *Lichtbildbühne*— warmed to the subject of Krauss's special place (*Fifty Years of German Film*. London: The Falcon Press, 1948; pp. 45–46.) in the Nazi film industry:

> The greatest of all German film actors was Werner Krauss. Without his very real histrionic genius the most important works of the classic German school could hardly be imagined... That he should sign away his genius to Nazi propaganda, degrading himself by acting in a film of the type of *Jew Süss*, is something of a puzzle. Possibly a belief in Nazism was deeply rooted in his innermost being... It may well be that the

Werner Krauss in Veit Harlan's *Jud Süss*.

irrational side of the Nazi myth struck a
chord in Werner Krauss... It is possible that
Krauss, the Doctor Caligari of the early days
of German film, had been born a Nazi without knowing it. An inherent race-hatred was
carefully hidden so long as he sold his art to
Max Reinhardt, Lupu Pick and others; his
true face was only shown in *Jew Süss* in its
horrible, frightening lines; of such an orgy
of anti-semitism only a born Nazi could be
capable."

A more recent German reassessment
of *Jew Süss*:

"...What makes the picture so re-

markable is the acting of Conrad Veidt,
who embodies this elevated yet beaten
creature with the whole nobility of his appearance. ... 'You have a face torn by suffering; you have a Jewish face,' an old rabbi
tells Jew Süss in Füchtwanger's novel. And
all that haughtiness and pride, that pain
and grief, all come together in Conrad
Veidt's physiognomy...."

Tagesspiegel (Berlin),
20 October 1973 —
Volker Baer

Bella Donna

Twickenham Film Studios Ltd., Twickenham; Released through Gaumont-British Picture Corp., Ltd.; World premiere: August 1934, London; 84/89/91 minutes

CAST: Conrad Veidt *Mahmoud Baroudi*; Mary Ellis *Mona Chepstowe*; Cedric Hardwicke *Dr. Isaacson*; John Stuart *Nigel Armine*; Jeanne Stuart *Lady Harwich*; Michael Shepley *Dr. Hartley*; Rodney Millington *Ibrahim*; Eve *Native Dancer*

CREDITS: *Producer* Julius Hagen; *Director* Robert Milton; *Based on the play by* James Bernard Fagan *and the novel by* Robert Smythe Hichens; *Adapted for the screen by* Vera Allinson and H. Fowler Mear; *Photography Supervised by* Sydney Blythe; *Assisted by* Ernest Palmer and William Luff; *Art Direction* James A. Carter; *Egyptian Scenes* William Blakeley; *Coiffure* Charles; *Film Editor* Jack Harris; *Recording* Baynham Honri; *Assistant Direction* Fred V. Merrick; *Musical Direction and Original Compositions* W.L. Trytel; Released in the USA by Olympic Pictures, 1935

SYNOPSIS: Famed nerve specialist Dr. Isaacson (Cedric Hardwicke) smiles enigmatically when Lady Harwich (Jeanne Stuart) informs him that a certain Mrs. Mona Chepstow (Mary Ellis) has set her sights on Nigel Armine (John Stuart), Lady Harwich's brother-in-law and Dr. Isaacson's friend. It is felt that the woman, known to many as "Bella Donna," wants to marry Nigel merely because he is—for the nonce—heir to the Harwich title.

Later that day, Mrs. Chepstow visits Isaacson, not for a medical consultation but rather to feel the doctor out. She asks that he forget their meeting and that night, when Nigel "introduces" Isaacson to Mona Chepstow, the doctor goes along with the charade. Nigel marries Mona despite his family's disapproval, and the two move to Egypt, as Nigel has important work in the Fayoum district. The couple meets Mahmoud Baroudi (Conrad Veidt), a wealthy Egyptian who owns a good part of the district, and it is not long before Mona and Baroudi are attracted to each other. Ba-

roudi gets rid of Nigel by hiring him to oversee a plantation on the Nile owned by the Egyptian. In her husband's absence, Mona falls completely in love with the cunning Baroudi.

When Nigel returns to collect Mona (he must return to his duties in the Fayoum district) they receive news that Lady Harwich has given birth to twin boys. Mona's hopes of becoming a titled lady are dashed, and she becomes despondent. Baroudi's servant, Ibrahim (Rodney Millington), advises the woman that his master has relocated to the Fayoum district. Mona runs to him and is too distracted to take much notice when Baroudi cruelly introduces his beautiful Egyptian wife. Still intrigued by the white woman, the Egyptian plans to do away with her husband without causing scandal.

In the interim, Isaacson has made his way to Egypt; he and Lady Harwich have been worrying about Nigel's mental and physical health. Mona insists that her husband is suffering only from sunstroke and that he is being well looked after by Dr. Hartley (Michael Shepley). Isaccson confers with Hartley, who defers to the famous specialist; Nigel comes under his old friend's care and is aghast when Isaacson tells him that he has been systematically poisoned by his wife. Infuriated, Nigel sends Isaacson away and then confronts Mona. Mona coldly admits to the deed, confessing her love of Baroudi to Nigel.

Running to Baroudi, Mona says that she is now his—forever. Baroudi turns her out of his house; he cannot be touched by scandal of any kind. Near collapse, Mona wanders back to her villa, where she discovers that Nigel and Isaacson have once again joined forces. Isaacson bars the door to "Bella Donna," who is now a stranger in a strange land ... and completely alone.

REVIEWS: "...By far the best performance is that of Cedric Hardwicke as Dr. Isaacson, closely followed by Conrad

Veidt's portrayal of Baroudi. Mary Ellis is not altogether convincing as Mrs. Chepstow (or Mrs. Armine), whose nickname of 'Bella Donna' is variously interpreted as meaning a beautiful woman, or a poison."

New York Times, 26 February 1935 — Frank S. Nugent

"It were better for prospective viewers of this photoplay to brush up on their memory of this modern classic, for the soundtrack of this production can be heard only with difficulty. Add to this the fact that the only familiar voice in the whole thing belongs to Mary Ellis and you get the general idea that *Bella Donna* for all its dramatic value is hard to take."

Daily News (New York), 26 February 1935 — Wanda Hale

"[*Bella Donna*] is very well done, but has not a very strong dramatic grip, probably due to the fact that there is a redundancy of detail which tends to obscure the main thrust of the plot. Mary Ellis is quite good as the woman who falls under the spell of the Egyptian, Mahmoud Baroudi. As Baroudi, Conrad Veidt is well typed, but is not at his best."

Picturegoer, 19 January 1935

"…Conrad Veidt deserves something better than his part in this film as a wealthy, degenerate Egyptian.

"Only a certain seriousness in the direction and acting lift this film out of the common run."

Monthly Film Bulletin, Vol. 1, No. 7; August 1934 — E.H.L.

Original release title card. The three blokes across the top are (left to right) John Stuart, Rodney Millington, and Cedric Hardwicke. (*Bella Donna*)

"With a plot revolving around romantic infatuation, murder and Eastern exotica, the caddish Veidt, here playing an Egyptian and as charismatic as ever, woos his English lover into poisoning her husband. Studio-bound it may be, but the performances, including that of Cedric Hardwicke, lift it well out of the rut."

National Film Theatre
Programme Notes,
London, 1999

NOTES AND QUOTES: The first film adaptation of Robert Smythe Hichens' eponymous novel was produced by Famous Players-Lasky Corporation in 1923. Adapting the story to the screen for the silent Paramount release was Ouida Bergère, who later was to divorce George Fitzmaurice, the director of the sound version of *Bella Donna*, in order to marry British character man Basil Rathbone. Conway Tearle had Connie's role in the silent version, while Conrad Nagel played Armine, and Pola Negri — at the height of her popularity — essayed the title character.

Long thought lost, a print of the Twickenham *Bella Donna* was discovered several years ago in the Czech Republic, whence the British Film Institute obtained a copy. The extant print runs nearly 82 minutes, and a screening of same reveals haphazard jump cuts and more than a handful of clipped lines of dialogue. While we must be grateful to the BFI for acquiring and conserving this print of the otherwise lost feature, the fact that almost 10 minutes of footage is still missing makes cogent commentary difficult.

As has often been the judgment when lost or desperately difficult to find pictures have resurfaced, *Bella Donna* has not aged well. It is, in fact, a bit of a trial for modern audiences, who have grown accustomed to tales of love and intrigue and attempted murder peppered with earthy prose, pulse-pounding music and demonstrations of almost superhuman physical prowess. Although it deals with sexual passion, promiscuity, infidelity, and attempted murder, *Bella Donna*'s dialogue — little of which is noteworthy and none of which could have ever, under any circumstances, been considered earthy — is (for the most part) delivered in the flat, understated fashion that was far better suited to early British sound pictures devoted to the hobbies of the royal family or the economics of sheep-raising than to early British sound pictures touching on sexual passion, promiscuity, infidelity, and attempted murder. Despite his having been apportioned a brace of potentially powerful dramatic exchanges, Cedric Hardwicke seems not to have the energy to raise his eyebrows, let alone his voice, while John Stuart plays Nigel Armine as a poor fellow whose every emotion is channeled directly from his heart to his listener via his nasal passages.

While the music is not pulse-pounding, however, neither is it an amalgam of dreary themes purloined from the stock library. The original mélange was the responsibility of W.L. (Bill) Trytel, whose journeyman efforts also underscored Arthur Wontner (*The Triumph of Sherlock Holmes*, 1935), Seymour Hicks (*Scrooge*, also 1935) and Boris Karloff (*Juggernaut*, 1936). Publicity puffs aver that Trytel incorporated genuine "old Egyptian" work songs into the *Bella Donna* mosaic; their presence is far more rewarding to the ears than are James A. Carter's claustrophobic, warrenlike "Egyptian" sets to the eyes. These slave dirges apart, though, the score's chief feature is its innocuousness; the music seldom complements the attendant action and never hits the kind of melodic stride that has the listener yearning for more. Ironically, this blandest of accompaniments is also rather intrusive, as, with most of the actors consistently underplaying their scenes, the background music is *louder* than the dialogue. Had this feature been ground out in 1929/1930, soundman Baynham Honri might have bought himself a bye. With a release date in the latter half of 1934, however...

The film is also quite deficient in terms of action, and we're not for a moment referring just to "physical prowess." Highlights in the first half of the film include a couple of butlers maneuvering their respective tea services and Cedric Hardwicke's turning a trifle awkwardly to siphon off some soda into a tumbler full of whisky. Adding to the frisson is the fact that, as was the cinematic convention back then, most of the principals light cigarettes continuously, with little concern for their personal safety. A few minutes before the fade, John Stuart climactically grits his teeth to convey passionate displeasure. Mary Ellis (as the titular poisoner) seduces, ensnares and later abandons poor Nigel with little more than a solitary kiss, but she does flare her nostrils regularly, and she widens and narrows her eyes as the mood suits her; surely this counts for something. She also gets lots of headaches. The print's missing footage may have contained other examples of dramatis personae in motion; we may never know.

If partly by default, Veidt's Mahmoud Baroudi is far and away the most interesting character in this dull little tale. Heir to most of the screenplay's paucity of ironic or sarcastic lines, Connie rolls them over with relish and serves them up neat from the most expressive face in the crowd. Watching that face, though, makes the viewer conscious of the fact that Veidt's makeup changes with virtually every camera setup; in some scenes, the actor appears nearly to be in blackface. Still, by dint of his personality, Connie's roué remains a strong figure despite the lethargic performances of the other players and the weaknesses of the screenplay, and that's no mean feat. At one point, Mona demands to

be taken to a den of iniquity frequented by Baroudi, and Ibrahim (Rodney Millington), her ubiquitous Egyptian servant, is nearly beside himself in his attempts to dissuade her. Any hopes for a jot of erotica or a little gratuitous salaciousness are dashed moments later, however, when the audience realizes that the denizens of this hellish hideaway include a belly dancer, a quartet of acrobats, and a ragtag boy, who's feeding a couple of goats. "Making love" meant clever conversation in pre–'60s British motion pictures, where — as here — exotica was usually substituted for erotica, to little notice and with little complaint.

Connie's Egyptian is supposed to be irresistible to the lovely Mona, but let's face it: almost anyone would be after we've a good look at Nigel. There is little romantic tension to be had in contrasting a debonair catalyst with a flaccid protagonist, and when it has also been established *ab initio* that the woman in question is no lady, there isn't any measurable dramatic tension, either. The poison business might have been counted on to add a little oomph to the proceedings, but a) most of the footage that introduces the subplot is missing, and b) the dastardliness is revealed in the same measured monotone that marks the rest of the picture. Hardwicke's Dr. Isaacson shatters Nigel's world with much the same force and urgency he might use in directing his man to have another go at pressing his cuffs.

Claude Rains' observation that "The trouble with the British is that they're so very British" might very well be a capsule commentary on *Bella Donna*. No point in getting worked up, is there, old man? The film trots out the skeleton of the eternal triangle, drapes it cheaply (and, worse, dully) in exotic trappings, and prods it along to its all too predictable end amid wheezes and murmurs and half-hearted sighs; there's not a *Harrruumph!* to be had. Connie's succession of brief appearances provides whatever spice the picture has. *Bella Donna*— despite its decades-long elusiveness— is otherwise not worth the time.

The Passing of the Third Floor Back

Gaumont-British Picture Corporation Ltd., London; World premiere: 9/11/35 Trade show AND Adelphi, London; General release: 1/17/36; American release: 12/15/35 — 90 minutes

Cast: Conrad Veidt *the Stranger*; Rene Ray *Stasia*; Frank Cellier *Mr. Wright*; Anna Lee *Vivian*; John Turnbull *Major Tompkin*; Cathleen Nesbitt *Mrs. Tompkin*; Ronald Ward *Chris Penny*; Jack Livesey *Larkcom*; Beatrix Lehmann *Miss Kite*; Sara Allgood *Mrs. de Hooley*; Mary Clare *Mrs. Sharpe*; Barbara Everest *Cook*; Alex-

ander Sarner *Gramophone Man*; with Philip Merivale

Credits: *Producer* Michael Balcon; *Director* Berthold Viertel; *Associate Producer* Ivor Montagu; *Screenplay* Michael Hogan, Alma Reville; *Based on the eponymous play by* Jerome K. Jerome; *Photographed by* Curt Courant; *Editor* Derek Twist; *Original Music* Hubert Bath; *Musical Director* Louis Levy; *Art Director* Oscar Friedrich Werndorff; *Sound Recordist* F. McNally; *Costume Designer* Marianne

Synopsis: Behind its staid and somewhat scruffy facade, a London rooming house is the scene of unrest, as each of the boarders *and* the staff seems possessed by inner turmoil. Into the midst of it all enters the Stranger (Conrad Veidt), and with him — gradually — comes a sense of peace and understanding. Lecherous businessman Mr. Wright (Frank Cellier), however,

Behind the scenes at *The Passing* (seated, left to right) Cathleen Nesbitt, Anna Lee, Sara Allgood, Mary Clare, Rene Ray. (At rear, left to right) John Turnbull, Ronald Ward, Jack Livesey, Beatrix Lehmann, Berthold Viertel, and Connie. (*The Passing of the Third Floor Back*)

denied the pleasures of a forced marriage to the beautiful Vivian Tompkin (Anna Lee), seems very much disposed to keeping the old tensions and suspicions alive, and he does what he can to frustrate the Stranger's efforts. "I'll give you best tonight," he concedes to the Stranger, following an eventful day's activities aboard a Thames steamer; "My turn's in the morning."

Sure enough, any ground that had been gained the night before is lost with the coming of daylight. As the hours pass, tempers grow shorter and old wounds are reopened. Just as it appears that housemaid Stasia (Rene Ray) is going to succumb to Wright's advances, a prowler accidentally causes Wright's death. In the aftermath, the occupants of the building once again come to an understanding among themselves, and the Stranger departs, as suddenly as he first came.

REVIEWS: "...In telling this fable, the producers have been fortunate in their possession of a cast which etched character clearly, yet did not so blindly follow the allegorical pattern as to become caricature. In the days when Sir Johnston Forbes-Robertson was playing the role of the Stranger, the play probably was considered his. Now, even with Conrad Veidt's sensitive and restrained performance, *The Passing of the Third Floor Back* is not a one-man show...."

New York Times, 29 April 1936 — Frank S. Nugent

"Conrad Veidt's accent is now barely noticeable and only perceptible for one who watches [sic] for it. His voice is soft and almost limpid, but it is the spiritual expressions on his face that make the character genuinely moving....

"...Drawing power of the book, the play, the picturization [sic] and the star should, on form, be invincible."

Variety, 25 September 1935

"...Conrad Veidt cuts an impressive figure as the Stranger as he suddenly appears out of the night to take the room on the third floor back in a London rooming house where hatred, chicanery, pettiness, cruelty, frustrated ambition, etc., run rife. His efforts to straighten out those tangled lives and the curious crosscurrents of human behavior that confront him account for heaps of adroitly pitched emotion...."

Variety, 6 May 1936 — Odec.

"...Conrad Veidt is, on the whole, effective as the Stranger, though his initial suitability for the part is questionable.

"Some of the lighting and photography is excellent and full of atmosphere, and there is a powerfully composed scene between Conrad Veidt and Frank Cellier — Good pleading with Evil — which is especially good...."

Monthly Film Bulletin, Vol. 2, No. 20; September 1935 — A.V.

NOTES AND QUOTES: Jerome Klapka Jerome had been a novelist of note as early as 1886, when his *The Idle Thoughts of an Idle Fellow* first saw print. When it and *Three Men in a Boat* (1889) were subsequently translated into over a dozen languages, Jerome was assured of international fame. In 1892, he (with Robert Barr and George Brown Burgin) founded *The Idler*, a monthly literary magazine that would come to feature works by (among others) Bret Harte and Mark Twain, in the course of a 20-year run. With *The Passing of the Third Floor Back* (1908), Jerome's talents as playwright were widely hailed, and classical actor Johnston Forbes-Robertson went on to make his impersonation of the Stranger one of his signature roles.

This working class fantasy of Good versus Evil was first filmed under the direction of Herbert Brenon in 1917. Adapted for the screen by Brenon and George Edwardes-Hall, *Passing* had not only Forbes-Robertson's fabled portrayal of the Stranger, but also (per film historian William K. Everson) "Brenon's own taste and sensitivity" to recommend it.

The highlights of the 1935 Gaumont-British production have to be the confrontation scenes between Veidt and Frank Cellier. In the first (and briefer) of the two sequences—at nighttime, aboard the Thames steamer—the adversaries parry and thrust in almost hushed, conversational tones. The ironically named Mr. Wright recognizes the Stranger for who he is, and not merely for the course of action he takes. In return, Wright is represented as being something more than just a petty little man, pursuing noisome ends. The second round begins the following day, and both men spar with gloves off. Wright knows fully well the Stranger's goals ("You want to change all their natures, but you want them to do it themselves...") and modus operandi ("You mustn't interfere; whatever happens, you must not interfere!"). The Stranger, in turn, tries mightily to talk the self-made man off the road to perdition, and ultimately finds himself afraid... *for* Wright!

These sequences focus the sundry examples of sin, repentance and forgiveness that surround them, and Veidt and Cellier do a terrific job incarnating the diametrically opposed cosmic forces. Cellier's death is a tad too convenient, and the subsequent wrap is likewise a bit too neat ("It's like seeing for the first time!"), but the year was 1935 and no one needed to be reminded that following the paths of righteousness was a constant struggle.

By the way, the scenario for *Passing* was the product of Michael Hogan and Alma Reville, Mrs. Alfred Hitchcock.

"Evil can be strong and powerful, but it can never take the place of good. I felt this deeply at another time when playing the Christ-like character of the Stranger in the London film production of *The Passing of the Third Floor Back*. My one aim was to play him as a man who wanted to give the world a lift, just as now the world so sadly needs a lift. The Stranger was the most difficult role I ever undertook. There was ever the danger of going too far. If for an instant it were made insincere, the part would fall to pieces.

"Another delicate question was that of appearance. I don't want to be blasphemous, but I played him as a well-dressed man. Forbes Robertson, you may recall, played him in a long, black coat. My one precaution in this respect was to keep the Stranger from any possibility of seeming theatrical. It struck me that those boarding-house people to whom he came might readily think of him as a traveler, even a traveling salesman, and so I had him wear a gray suit and carry a suitcase. His hair was well groomed, though white. But his face was not old. I tried to make him ageless.

"No mysterious light came or went with him. But when he was shown in his dingy room he took a flower from his coat and put it into a glass of water, then opened the blind and let in a gleam of sunlight. It was the simplicity of beauty you can make out of nothing. Of course, there was far more than that, something not quite of this world. The Stranger, like the Wandering Jew played by me earlier, was fantastic in a spiritual way."

Connie, interviewed by Charles Darnton, in the *New York Herald Tribune*, 1 February 1942

King of the Damned

Gaumont-British Picture Corporation Ltd., London—1935; World premiere: 24 December 1935 Trade show, London; General release: 30 March 1936; Distributed in USA by Gaumont-British Picture Corp. of America—USA premiere: 30 December 1935; 76, 81, or 90 minutes

CAST: Conrad Veidt *Convict 83*; Helen Vinson *Anna*; Noah Beery *Mooche*; Cecil Ramage *Ramón*; Edmund Willard *The Greek*; Percy Parsons *Lumberjack*; Peter Croft *Boy Convict*; Raymond Lovell *Capt. Torres*; C.M. Hallard *Commandant*; Allan Jeayes *Dr. Prada*; Percy Walsh *Capt. Pérez*; Gibson Glowland Priest

CREDITS: *Producer* Michael Balcon; *Director* Walter Forde; *Screenplay* Charles Bennett, Sidney Gilliat; *Based on the eponymous play by* John Chancellor; *Adapted by* A.R. Rawlinson; *Additional Dialogue* Noel Langley; *Designs* Oscar Werndorff; *Costumes* Schiaparelli; *Photographed by* Bernard Knowles; *Editor* Otto Ludwig, Cyril Randell; *Sound* A.F. Birch; *Art Director* O. Werndorff; *Music Direction* Louis Levy

SYNOPSIS: Anna (Helen Vinson), daughter of the commandant of the convict island of Santa Maria and fiancée to his second-in-command, Captain Ramón (Cecil Ramage), flies to the island on hearing that her father (C.M. Hallard) is ill. She is attracted to Convict 83, who acts as orderly. An educated man, 83 is planning a revolt of the convicts, whose dissatisfaction is brought to a head by the action of Ramón, who—bribed by a concessionaire—is sending large contingents of prisoners to a road-making squad in the jungle. Ramón, discovering 83 in conversation with Anna, orders him to the road gang, as well.

The uprising is planned to take place when a large number of troops are on a distant expedition, but it breaks out prematurely and is quelled. Mooche (Noah Beery), drunken but faithful ally of 83, is condemned to be executed for killing an informer. Although advised that he will be pardoned, Convict 83 asks permission to parade with the others on the square on the day of execution.

Moments before Mooche is executed, the convicts break rank and rush upon their guards. A secretly assembled machine gun, fired from the hospital window, assures their success. The officers are locked up and, with Mooche's help, 83 begins to

organize the island. The men demonstrate how, under fair conditions, the convicts can accomplish ten times what was done when they were treated as slaves.

Anna surreptitiously sends a message that brings a cruiser to the island. When the officers land, they are welcomed as usual by Ramón and his colleagues, who have been coerced by threats to Anna into pretending that everything is normal. The disclosure by the cruiser captain that his guns are trained on the barracks leads Ramón to tell the truth; the cruiser is signaled and begins to shell the island. Supported by Anna, 83 persuades the captain to promise a fair trial on the mainland to the mutineers.

REVIEWS: "…Its appeal … rests almost entirely on the exceptional realism of its details and the strength of the revolt and execution scenes, reinforced by the fact that it [is] an indictment of the system of punitive settlements. The acting of Conrad Veidt and Helen Vinson is adequate, but the strong part is that of Noah Beery as the heroic blackguard, Mooche."

Motion Picture Herald,
25 January 1936 — Allan

"At the Roxy this week is *King of the Damned*, another picture dealing with the brutalities of insular penal settlements…. A Gaumont-British production, full of unmistakably authentic accents, it is nevertheless a set of rather depressingly dull variations on an originally rather exciting Hollywood theme."

New York Times,
1 February 1936 — B.R.C.

"…Conrad Veidt makes the superior convict as impressive as possible, Noah Beery as his rough but faithful companion supports him well….

"Skillful treatment might conceivably have raised this story to a higher level; as it stands, however, it is never more than stock melodrama — sometimes fairly ex-

Anna (Helen Vinson) looks for Convict 83 (Connie) (right) to help her ill old dad (C.M. Hallard). Dad just happens to be the commandant of the godforsaken island hell where Convict 83 is a guest. (*King of the Damned*)

citing, but sometimes just dull, and occasionally merely brutal."

Monthly Film Bulletin,
Vol. 3, No. 25;
January 1936 — A.V.

"Although the story may strain ... credibility ... the steamy tropical setting is successfully conveyed, despite never actually venturing outside Shepherd's Bush, and the big-budget production, especially the uprising scene, is put over in a style worthy of Hollywood."

Film Notes— National
Film Theatre; London, 1999

NOTES AND QUOTES: *King of the Damned* is a variation on the "remote is-

land-prison" theme that spawned something of a subgenre from the '20s to the '40s. While one might roll one's eyes at the love business— it's as awkward and contrived as it is inevitable — it was a departure from the romance that usually framed the story (while the gritty remote island-prison stuff was endured in flashback). The "forbidden love" motif struck one reviewer as owing a debt to *Romeo and Juliet*; the other critics felt the relationship left the film in the audience's debt. Charles Bennett's screenplay had Connie — who had already taken a shot at the theme and the locale in Universal's *A Man's Past*— a full-fledged romantic action hero, and the actor took the adjustments in stride, although the boy-girl subplot ultimately proved to be less than memorable.

Likewise, while the picture was ostensibly condemning the inhumane conditions that existed in penal colonies like Santa Maria, no one left the theater looking to write a letter to the appropriate authorities, or even to fork over a few coins earmarked for prison reform. In the end, the picture went into the black as a gritty melodrama, carried into profitability on Veidt's and Noah Beery's shoulders.

Dark Journey

Victor Saville Productions, London, for London Film; Productions, London; World premiere: 29 January 1937 Trade show; 30 January 1937 Piccadilly, London; General release: 2 April 1937; USA premiere: (United Artists) 2 July 1937; 72, 77, 80, 82 minutes; Reissued 1943, 1953; 1953 reissue title: **The Anxious Years**

CAST: Conrad Veidt *Baron Karl Von Marwitz*; Vivien Leigh *Madeleine Goddard*; Joan Gardner *Lupita*; Anthony Bushell *Bob Carter*; Ursula Jeans *Gertrude*; Margery Pickard *Colette*; Eliot Makeham *Anatole Bergen*; Austin Trevor *Dr. Muller*; Sam Livesey *Schaffer*; Edmund Willard *Chief of German Intelligence*; Charles Carson *Head of Fifth Bureau*; Phil Ray *Faber*; Henry Oscar *Swedish Magistrate*; Lawrence Hanray *Cottin*; Cecil Parker *Captain of Q-Boat*; Reginald Tate *Mate of Q-Boat*; Percy Walsh *Captain of Swedish Packet*; Robert Newton *Officer of Q-Boat*; William Dewhurst *The Killer*; Laidman Browne *Rugge*; M. Martin Harvey *Bohlau*; Anthony Holles *Dutchman*

CREDITS: *Presented by* Alexander Korda; *Produced and Directed by* Victor Saville; *Based on a play by* Lajos Biro; *Screenplay and Dialogue* Arthur Wimperis; *Photographed by* Georges Perinal and Harry Stradling; *Special Effects* Ned Mann; *SP FX Assistants* Eddie Cohen, Lawrence Butler; *Sets* Andre Andrejew, Ferdinand Bellan;

Vivien and Connie have eyes only for each other. (*Dark Journey*)

Film Editors Hugh Stewart, Lionel Hoare; *Supervising Film Editor* William Hornbeck; *Costumes* Rene Hubert; *Music Director* Muir Mathieson; *Music* Richard Addinsell; *Sound Director* A.W. Watkins; *Sound Recording* Charles Tasto; *Technical Advisor* L. Stackell

SYNOPSIS: In 1918, Swiss fashion designer Madeleine Goddard (Vivien Leigh) is apparently spying for the Germans, traveling back and forth between Paris and Stockholm — where she has her shop — with news of Allied troop movements hidden in the clothing samples she carries. Actually, Madeleine is a French counterspy, and her latest assignment is to discover the identity of the new head of the German secret service. One night, while she is at a nightclub with Bob Carter (Anthony Bushell), an English secret service agent, she meets Baron Karl Von Marwitz (Conrad Veidt), who is rumored to be a deserter from the German Navy.

In a short while, Madeleine and Karl have become quite enamored of each other. When her employee Anatole Bergen (Eliot Makeham) is found murdered, Madeleine is informed by Dr. Muller (Austin Trevor) — who has been sent by Berlin to reorganize the spy front in Stockholm — that the latest information she provided was wrong, with disastrous results for the Germans. She is sent off to Paris to check on her sources; there, she is decorated for her service to her country before returning to Sweden. Karl then reveals to her that he is the new head of the German secret service, and that he knows that she is a French spy; all pretense is dropped. With the help of Bob, Madeleine is "arrested" by the Swedish police and sentenced to deportation, thus outmaneuvering Karl. Once her ship has left Swedish waters, however, a German U-boat blocks its way; Karl boards the ship and arrests Madeleine for being a spy. Out of nowhere, however, comes a British destroyer, which engages the U-boat in battle. The German submarine is sunk, and Karl is captured; he is to be interned for the duration of the hostilities. The lovers wave their goodbyes, tacitly promising to meet up again after the war.

REVIEWS: "With a tsk-tsk over the fact that the Britons are apparently still fighting the World War, let it be reported that Central's *Dark Journey*, a British-made spy melodrama centering around England's most charming screen actress, Vivien Leigh, and that bulwark of villainy, Conrad Veidt, is a swift, colorful and engagingly tangled cinema matter of virtually no importance whatsoever...."

New York Times, 23 August 1937 — J.T.M.

"Spy melodrama originally reviewed in *The Cinema* of February 1, 1937, relating exciting tale of French girl's espionage adventures in pretending to work for Germans. Outstanding British production of its ay still appeals powerfully on colourful espionage exchanges, poignant romance involving French girl and German enemy, and tingling drama of lovers' battle of wits by which each seeks to destroy the other. Lavish production qualities.... Expert direction, first-rate co-starring portrayal, admirable technical treatment. Excellent general entertainment.

"The film has a tremendous asset in its first-rate acting, with Vivien Leigh and Conrad Veidt carrying off the honours as rival spies for whom the war means a denial of their love."

To-Day's Cinema, 31 August 1943 — C.A.W. (reissue)

NOTES AND QUOTES: "Lajos Biro and Arthur Wimperis had tailor-made this improbable and naïve tale of French and German espionage and counter-espionage for Conrad Veidt, the intelligent German actor who had just signed a contract with Korda and for whom Alex had difficulty in finding suitable and acceptable roles. (He was typecast here, as in the later *The Spy in Black* [1939], as the German spy for whom duty always, or almost always, comes first.)"

> Karol Kulik. *Alexander Korda: The Man Who Could Work Miracles.* New Rochelle, NY: Arlington House Publishers, 1975, p. 208

One of the films Korda had announced for Veidt was *Gloriana*, a period epic centered upon romantic and political intrigue in the days of Elizabeth, the Virgin Queen, and Philip II. The project, which went into production almost concurrently with *Dark Journey*, was ultimately released (without Veidt) as *Fire over England*, the name of A.E.W. Mason's source novel.

Dark Journey was the first of the WWI/lowering-clouds-over-Europe subgenre features that allowed the "warrior ethic" to transcend the traditional generalization of the bellicose Hun. This was more a nod to Veidt's own integrity than an attempt at sanitizing Great War operations. The details of Connie's prolonged, involuntary stay in Germany prior to his filming *Jew Süss* had been made public, and the man's resolve to do the right thing, coupled with his mature good looks, made a film centered on honor and commitment in the worst of times a lead-pipe cinch at the box office. Determined to attract the legions of distaff ticket buyers (at whom the testosterone-laden, despairing war dramas of the beginning of the decade had *not* been targeted), Korda sought to envelope Veidt and Vivien Leigh in the star-crossed trappings of *Romeo and Juliet*.

Under the Red Robe

New World Pictures Ltd., London — World premiere: May 1937, London; Original British

running time: 80 minutes; Released in the USA by 20th Century–Fox in 5/21/37 — 82 minutes

CAST: Conrad Veidt *Gil de Berault*; Annabella *Lady Marguerite*; Raymond Massey *Cardinal Richilieu*; Romney Brent *Marius*; Sophie Stewart *Elise, Duchess of Foix*; F. Wyndham Goldie *Edmund, Duke of Foix*; Lawrence Grant *Father Joseph*; Baliol Holloway *Clon, a Servant*; Shayle Gardner *Louis, a Servant*; Frank Damer *Pierre, a Servant*; James Regan *Jean, a Servant*; Edie Martin *Marie*; Haddon Mason *Count Rossignac*; J. Fisher White *Baron Breteuil*; Ben Soutten *Leval*; Anthony Eustrel *Lieut. Brissac*; Desmond Roberts *Capt. Rivarolle*; Ralph Truman *Captain of the Castle*; Eric Hales *Lieutenant of the Castle*

CREDITS: *Producer* Robert T. Kane; *Director* Victor Seastrom; *Dialogue Director* Romney Brent; *Asst. Director* Edward Baird; *Screenplay* Lajos Biro, Philip Lindsay, and J.L. Hodson (Alexander Korda, uncredited); *Based on the eponymous novel by* Stanley Weyman *and the play,* Under the Red Robe, *by* Edward E. Rose; *Adaptation* Arthur Wimperis; *Photographed by* James Wong Howe, Georges Perinal, Ted Pahle; *Special Effects* Ned Mann; *Art Director* Frank Wells; *Film Editor* James B. Clark; *Costumes* Rene Hubert; *Musical Director* Muir Mathieson; *Musical Score* Arthur Benjamin; *Production Manager* Leslie F. Baker; *Sound Recording* A.W. Watkins, T. Coller; *Annabella's Diction Coach*— Flossie Freedman

SYNOPSIS: France, 1622: Gil de Berault (Conrad Veidt), a notorious swordsman referred to as the "Black Death," is warned by Cardinal Richelieu (Raymond Massey) that dueling has been declared illegal and that to duel means to hang. Despite this, Gil is arrested some time later for dueling in a tavern. He is confident that the cardinal will pardon him, but he is actually en route to the gallows before the word does come down. The pardon has strings attached: Gil must infiltrate the household of one of Richelieu's most despised enemies— Edmund, the Duke of Foix (F. Wyndham Goldie)— and seize the duke. Gil is given a manservant, Marius (Romney Brent), a pickpocket whose loyalty is to the cardinal.

By a subterfuge, Gil gains entry to the

Some absolutely glorious artwork from a less than well-received costume epic. (*Under the Red Robe*)

duke's castle, but he mistakes the duke's sister, Marguerite (Annabella), for Elise, the duchess (Sophie Stewart). The very next day, Marguerite meets with Count Rossignac (Haddon Mason) and Baron Breteuil (J. Fisher White), friends of the duke who have come for jewels with which to pay Edmond's soldiers. The king's soldiers show up unexpectedly, forcing the two noblemen to escape; they fail to notice that Marius has relieved them of the jew-

els. Breteuil returns to advise Marguerite of the missing gems and, in the course of a search, the young noblewoman confronts Gil, whom she accuses of being a spy.

Gil returns the jewels — he maintains that he "found" them — but is arrested when the king's soldiers reappear. In the ensuing confusion, he escapes, but Marguerite, hearing the soldiers firing their muskets, fears he has been killed; she reveals to Elise that she loves de Berault.

Once the soldiers depart, Gil returns; discovering at last who Marguerite is, he declares his love for her. The couple spends an idyllic few days together, until Edmund returns and Gil arrests him. The next day, though, while en route to Paris, Gil frees Marguerite and Edmund. Gil explains that once he arrested her brother, he satisfied his promise to Richelieu; still, he must return to Paris to satisfy his honor.

Marguerite arrives in Paris ahead of Gil and begs Richelieu to spare the swordsman; she is arrested. At the same time, at a tavern on the road to Paris, Marius advises Gil to hold off on confronting Richelieu; the cardinal is currently out of favor with the king and will soon be bereft of all power. Nonetheless, Gil is determined to go, and go he does. Before he arrives, however, Richelieu has received a letter of commendation from the king, who is quite pleased that Edmund has been grievously discommoded. The cardinal, realizing that his return to favor is due to Gil's intervention, pardons both the swordsman and Marguerite, and gives them leave to return to Edmond's castle.

REVIEWS: "...Romney Brent ... gives an admirable comedy performance as Gil's unscrupulous servant. Annabella suffers from too many close-ups, and Raymond Massey from a farcical make-up as Richelieu. Conrad Veidt, as Gil, at any rate *looks* impressive.

"Although not convincing from an adult point of view, the film would probably be found quite exciting and entertaining by children."

Monthly Film Bulletin,
Vol. 4, No. 44; 31 August
1937 — A.V.

"My chief objection to the Little Carnegie's *Under the Red Robe* is its selection of Conrad Veidt for the dashing, romantic role of Gil de Berault. Mr. Veidt is an excellent actor ... but I very much doubt that any beauteous Lady Marguerite ever could fall in love with him at first sight...."

"...Mr. Brent's Marius ... serves to relieve the dour monotony of Mr. Veidt's performance and gives the film its much-needed comic relief...."

New York Times, 1 June 1937
— Frank S. Nugent

"...Our own too-seldom seen Conrad Veidt, who in this picture looks like a blend of John Bunny and Douglas Fairbanks, is disappointing. It was for something more worthy of that commanding figure and of those incisive tones that we have been waiting."

Punch ("At the Pictures"),
25 August 1937 — E.Y.

NOTES AND QUOTES: Stanley Weyman's 1894 novel had been filmed twice prior to the New World release of July 1937. Wilfred Noy had directed the first effort, a 1915 (British) Gaumont feature headlining Jackson Wilcox as the cardinal and Owen Roughwood as Gil de Berault. William Randolph Hearst's Cosmopolitan Corporation produced the second version in 1923. With Alan Crosland at the helm, the 10-reeler starred John Charles Thomas as de Berault, Robert B. Mantell as Richelieu and Alma Rubens (and not, surprisingly, Marion Davies) as Renée.

Under the Red Robe's chief claim to fame lay in its being the last picture to be helmed by Victor Seastrom (nee Sjöström; his name was Americanized when he moved to the States in 1923). Originally an actor, Seastrom was most proficient behind the camera during the silent era. In his native Sweden, he directed some 40 films before immigrating to Hollywood, where he guided Lon Chaney and Norma Shearer through the first ever MGM production, an adaptation of Leonid Andreyev's *He Who Gets Slapped.* Seastrom eventually returned to Sweden (and to acting).

The film was well-served by Seastrom's veteran hand, as well as by the genius of cinematographer James Wong Howe, who was just then enjoying enormous acclaim from European filmmakers. As biographer Todd Rainsberger (*James Wong Howe: Cinematographer*. NY: A.S. Barnes & Company, Inc., 1981, p. 20.) avers:

> By the mid–1930s, James Wong Howe was the best known cameraman in the world... At this stage in his career, most of the American articles about Howe dealt with his race and personality. When he got to Britain, the European critics took a serious look at his work. He became a celebrity in England, receiving as much attention from the press as the stars did. He shot *Fire Over England*, *Farewell Again*, and *Under the Red Robe* for Korda before returning to the United States at the request of David O. Selznick.

Whether due to some rather obvious miscasting or poor writing, *Under the Red Robe* was neither a critical nor a popular success. *Robe* was shuffled into the deck of possible pictures when an earlier project — *I Serve* (the story of the 1903 assassination of King Alexander and Queen Draga of Serbia) — had to be abandoned after King Alexander of Yugoslavia was assassinated in Marseilles in the autumn of 1934. Veidt was aware that his many fans had been disappointed both by this costume saga and by *Dark Journey*, which, despite his presence and that of heartthrob Vivien Leigh, had been cited as predictable and not terribly well-crafted. Connie took advantage of a *Film Weekly* (UK) article to answer some criticism from that publication and to buoy up the hopes of just those fans.

> Some of my recent characterizations have been very poor, and it is an effort to "stop the rot" that I have decided to prepare a half dozen scenarios myself... My recent lapse is not just an isolated affair but is, in a sense, the outcome of a much wider influence — namely the deterioration of the British film industry in general. On several occasions in the past I have started work on a picture knowing nothing about the ultimate delineation of the character I was about to play, and relying on vague promises that the role would suit me... [12 March 1938, p. 28].

None of the scenarios to which Connie referred — a study about a Freudian disciple on Harley Street, an attempt to "capture the mentality of a British agent at work in Germany," a film biography of Franz Liszt, a "sort of Svengali story about an impresario of ballet," and screen biographies about Nobel (the inventor of dynamite) and Dunant (the founder of the Red Cross) — came to fruition. A two-picture contract with Alexander Korda led to *The Spy in Black* (which had nothing to do with Veidt's original idea) and *The Thief of Bagdad*. John Barrymore had pretty much done the definitive takes on both Svengali (in Warners' eponymous hit in 1931) and Svengalilike ballet "impresarios" (*The Mad Genius*; same company, six months later). In addition, there would be no more screen biographies in the actor's future.

Despite the raft of naysaying, the picture was profitably reissued in 1943, 1945 and 1948.

Tempête sur l'Asie

[LOST] (*Storm over Asia*); Rio Film, Paris; Released by Les Films Jacques Séfert; Production: December 1937 — January 1938; World premiere: 20 April 1938 Théâtre Normandie, Paris; Running Time: 100 minutes (French-language version); 90 minutes (German-language version)

CAST: Conrad Veidt *Erich Keith*; Raymond Aimos *Pierre, a Pickpocket*; Paul Azaïs *Jonny, the Pianist*; Habib Benglia *Washington-Napoleon Brown*; Roger Duchesne *Dr. Henri Leclerc*; Serge Grave *Jimmy*; Sessue Hayakawa *Prince Ling*; Robert Le Vigan *Sir Richard Thomas*; Alexandre Mihalesco *The Fool*; Madeleine Robinson *Suzanne Vernier*; Michiko Tanaka *Princess Shô*; Lucas Gridoux *Jack Murphy*; with Teddy Michaud

A lost film, the French-made feature — with its Berlin-born star — was a box-office smash in Mexico, where it was released as *The Tyrant of Tibet*. (*Tempête sur l'Asie*)

CREDITS: *Producers* Richard Oswald, Friedrich Brunn; *Director* Richard Oswald; *Asst. Directors* Boris des Aubrys, Georges Fronval, Gerd Oswald (uncredited); *Production Supervisor* Friedrich Brunn; *Scenario* Arnold Lipp[schitz], Théodore H. Robert, Richard Oswald; *Dialogue* Jacques Natanson; *Photographed by* Theodore J. Pahle; *Camera Operator* Jacques Mercanton; *Camera Assistant* J. Barrer; *Still Photographs* Soulié; *Set Design* Claude Bouxin, Raymond Gabutti; *Editor* M. Brenner; *Asst. Editor* Claude Ibéria; *Sound* R. Bugnon; *Asst. Sound Engineer* Boris des Aubrys, Georges Fronval; *Original Music* Ralph Erwin, Paul Saegel, Roger Fernay

SYNOPSIS: Adventurer Erich Keith (Conrad Veidt) persuades English oil baron Sir Richard Thomas (Robert Le Vigan) to finance a hunt for black gold in Mongolia. Keith readies the expedition and brings along his mistress, Suzanne Vernier (Made-leine Robinson), while forbidding other men of his team the pleasure of female company. Once in Mongolia, Keith becomes power-mad, going so far as to enslave the natives. Dr. Henri Leclerq (Roger Duchesne) is appalled by Keith's attitude and attracted to Keith's mistress; the young physician and Miss Vernier soon fall in love.

Prince Ling (Sessue Hayakawa), leader of the native population, is discovered plotting to do away with Keith; Ling is whipped to within an inch of his life. Outraged, the natives surround the members of the expedition, and offer to let the innocent ones go free, unharmed, in exchange for their villainous leader. Keith refuses their demand, and is shot before he can machine-gun the members of his own expedition for surrendering him.

REVIEW: "A moderately good adventure drama, *Tempête sur l'Asie* is set for some success in this country [France] because of Conrad Veidt. It's almost a one-man film and Veidt makes all there is to be made out of a story that sometimes is fantastic enough to seem ludicrous...."

Variety (Paris), 23 May 1938 — Hugo

NOTES AND QUOTES: *Tempête sur l'Asie*, Conrad Veidt's only sound picture for Richard Oswald, marked the last time the actor and producer-director would work together. It was at Oswald's insistence that Connie got the part of Erich Keith; Rio Films, which had already signed Erich von Stroheim for the role, acceded before principal photography got under way.

Le Joueur d'Échecs

(*The Chess Player*) aka **The Devil Is an Empress**—1938; Compagnie Francaise Cinématographique (Sirius Véga), Paris; World premiere: 25 November 1938 Madeleine, Paris; USA distributor (1939): Columbia Pictures; Running time: 90 minutes (France)/85 minutes (UK); 70 minutes (USA)

CAST: Conrad Veidt *Baron de Kempelen*; Françoise Rosay *Catherine II*; Paul Cambo *Prince Boleslas Vorowsky*; Bernard Lancret *Prince Serge Oblonsky*; Micheline Francey *Sonia Vorowska*; Edmonde Guy *Wanda Zalewska, a dancer*; Jacques Gretillat *Prince Potemkine*; Gaston Modot *Major Nicolaieff*; Jean Témerson *Stanislaus, King of Poland*; Delphin *Yegor, the buffoon*; with Manuel Gary, Maurice Morlot, Jacques Vitry, Dagmar Boline

CREDITS: *Director* Jean Dréville; *Scenario* Albert Guyot; *Based on the novel* The Chess Player of Vilna *by* Henri Dupuy-Mazuel; *Dialogue* André Dodoret, Roger Vitrac, Bernard Zimmer; *Production Supervisor* Jean Rossi; *Director of Photography* René Gaveau; *Camera Operator* André Thomas; *Camera Assistant* C. Gaveau; *Automatons* G. Decamps; *Sound Engineer* Robert Ivonnet; *Musical Score* Jean Lenoir; *Set Designs* Lucien Aguettand, Marcel Magniez; *Costumes* Georges Kugelmann Benda, J. Muelle, Ollier; *Asst. Directors* Maurice Merlot, Jacques Vitry, Dagmar Boline; *Editor* Raymond Leboursier

SYNOPSIS: Empress Catherine of Russia (Francoise Rosay) and Prince Potemkine (Jacques Gretillat) are angered and annoyed at the constant friction that exists between the Crown and some of the Poles under Russian rule. The band of rebels, united under Sonia Vorowska (Micheline Francey), is seeking to replace Stanislaus, the figurehead King of Poland (Jean Témerson), with Prince Boleslas Vorowski (Paul Cambo), whom everyone regards as rightful heir to the throne. The empress is aware that Russian prince Serge Oblonsky (Bernard Lancret) is in love with Sonia, but does nothing to discourage him, believing that, ultimately, he would regard his duty to Mother Russia as a higher priority than any affection he felt for the young Polish woman. In the meanwhile, Catherine summons the Baron de Kempelen (Conrad Veidt), an eccentric inventor of mechanical figures. While commissioning an automaton for an up-and-coming court celebration, Catherine broaches the subject of Sonia and the Poles with the baron, who is also a foreigner living in Russia; she is interested in knowing where the expatriate sympathies lie. The empress also orders Major Nicolaieff (Gaston Modot) to keep an eye on all the performers in the political drama that is unfolding.

Sonia is in love with Boleslas and, when he is injured in a fight between some Russians and Poles, she drops all notions of rebellion in favor of returning the prince safely to his homeland. In conjunction with this, she visits de Kempelen, who shows her some of his creations. Sympathetic to Sonia and the Polish cause, the baron suggests that the wounded prince could be concealed in the figure of the chess player and spirited out of Russia thus. Boleslas is made to practice sitting in the figure — a tedious and exhausting situation — a bit longer with each passing day.

King Stansislaus demands some entertainment from de Kempelen and his array of robots, and the baron and Sonia decide to use the chess player (with Boleslas inside) as the acid test. The king is impressed with the automaton and, looking to ingratiate himself with the empress, commands de Kempelen to use the chess player at the court celebration in St. Petersburg! Forced to accede to Stanislaus's directive, the baron tells Sonia to disguise herself as a peasant and remain nearby, ready to take flight at the end of the charade; de Kempelen is certain he and Boleslas will be able to succeed. Through his network of spies, however, Nicolaieff gets wind of the scheme and informs Catherine that she will have Boleslas right where she wants him. Amused by it all, Catherine decides to play along. She tells Nicolaieff to ransack de Kempelen's home while the baron is at court; she wants names of accomplices, so that there will be hangings to discourage other rebels.

The crucial evening arrives and Catherine the Great begins to play chess against the mechanical figure. When Potemkine rushes in to announce that the disguised Sonia has been captured, the chess player seemingly malfunctions, its arms seizing all the pieces on the board. De Kempelen asks for some time for repairs. Catherine laughingly grants him whatever time he needs, telling him that when he has finished, she intends to have the automaton placed before the firing squad! The figure is carried to a basement chamber under guard, and Boleslas emerges from the back, ready to surrender himself to the empress. The only soldier present is Prince Oblonsky, who insists that he is truly Boleslas's friend and that Sonia is in love with him — Boleslas — and not with the Russian prince. Sonia rushes in to prove Oblonsky right, and the little group ponders how to deal with the incipient firing squad.

Back at de Kempelen's home, Nico-

laieff has pulled one ring and chain too many in the course of ransacking the place, and finds himself encircled by a ring of mechanical soldiers, each moving inexorably forward, jabbing with its bayonet. The empress's spy is impaled over and again, and soon lies lifeless on the floor.

At court, the empress, Sonia, and the courtiers assemble at the wall, and the chess player is positioned for execution. Shots are fired and, while everyone's attention is turned to the extraction of a dying man from the recesses of the mechanical figure, Sonia is quickly led away to flee from the city. It is de Kempelen who has been mortally wounded, but the mechanical genius — assured in hushed tones by Oblonsky that the lovers are now safe — expires with a sense of accomplishment.

REVIEWS: "...Despite good acting by the two principals — support is weak — film falters due to poor continuity. Court scenes have been reconstructed rather lavishly with photography of good standard, too.

"Conrad Veidt, as the count, and Françoise Rosay, as Catherine, are excellent. But patriot, as portrayed by Paul Cambo, is flat, and Micheline Francey, as the love angle, slides in many scenes."

Variety (Paris), 27 December 1938 — Hugo

"'The Baron de Kempelen is a bizarre personage' is the refrain chanted by one of the baron's life-sized mechanical puppets. So he was, and is, very effectively played by CV....

"CV seems quite at home in French and his performance is quite distinguished. Françoise Rosay ... gives a magnificent sketch of Catherine, her lewdness, brutality, power and robust wit."

Film Weekly, 4 March 1939

"...The mechanical-minded Baron Kempelen, with his hordes of automa-

Baron de Kempelen (Connie) hopes that the canny Catherine the Great (Françoise Rosay) doesn't see through his robotic chess player. (*Le Joueur d'Échecs*)

tons—a company of whom execute his worst enemy in a delightfully long-drawn-out sequence—could hardly be in better or more experienced hands than those of Conrad Veidt...."

New York Times, 4 December 1939

"In the hands of Mr. Conrad Veidt, Kempelen is a bizarre character who seems to have stepped out of the silent world of *Dr. Caligari* and *The Student of Prague*. Veidt's performance has all the magnetism and subtlety we expect of him, but the film cannot quite succeed in making us take the Baron's contraptions seriously..."

New Statesman, 18 March 1939

"A visually opulent production through both its settings and costumes,

with Veidt giving one of his most accomplished performances."

Programme Notes—National Film Theatre; London 1999

NOTES AND QUOTES: Henri Dupuy-Mazuel's novel had first been filmed in 1927 as a silent for La Société des Films Historique, with Pierre Blanchar in the role of de Kempelen.

Under Jean Dréville's direction, Veidt won excellent notices and the film itself took the prize for best foreign film at the Venice Film Festival.

In an article published in Britain's *Film Weekly* (12 March 1938), the actor revealed to the public that

I am going back [to France] in April to make another film, entitled *The Chess*

Player, about a scientist who invents a robot. The scenario, which I have read, is not treated horrifically, like a Karloff thriller, but is a delightful mixture of fantasy and humor...

The resulting film — a costume picture set in the Russia of Catherine the Great — admirably interwove elements of political intrigue, subterfuge and betrayal with the ersatz science of the Baron de Kempelen, whose home/workshop is populated with *scores* of robots. It's interesting to note how these automatons advance the narrative in various and distinct ways: the crude, hammer-pounding devices that open the film, to the bayonet-wielding mechanical soldiers who dispatch Major Nicolaieff, to the eponymous chess player itself, upon which turns the plot wheel. Still, it is the sight of motionless figures, swathed in cloth and seemingly deposited helter-skelter throughout the baron's lair, that succeeds in raising a few hackles, despite Veidt's protests to the contrary.

Le Joueur d'Échecs is a quirky little film, opening as it does on a scene of possible sexual role reversal: Catherine is dressed in male military garb, while the eye-patched Potemkine wears a nightgown, a flowing robe and a feminine, turbanlike hair covering. The empress's fabled sexual side is constantly alluded to — via word, gesture and nuance — and the dramatic denouement, wherein Oblonsky turns himself in for execution for his part in the debacle, has Catherine take the handsome young royal up to her chambers, where she has him help her disrobe! Françoise Rosay won splendid notices for her portrayal of the Russian ruler, and watching the veteran actress metamorphose from jingoistic virago to feminine tease to bespectacled, tea-pouring housewife leaves little doubt that the praise was well-deserved.

Veidt, likewise, is superlative as de Kempelen, that "bizarre personage." Done

up in his powdered wig and finery, his baron moves easily among the soldiers and courtiers. At home, however, he is garbed in the sort of skullcap and cloak that foreshadow the raiment of that other master of trickery and manipulation: Jaffar, the evil vizier in *The Thief of Bagdad*. His baron also moves easily among his numerous creations, which range from delightful, Rube Goldbergesque blacksmithing humanoids to fully articulated mannequins. In some instances, these latter figures are actual artificial constructs of considerable charm. More frequently, they are impersonated by immobile actors, and, in these instances, the end result is neither as picturesque nor as successful as the wax and cloth models.

While the character of the baron might well have been played with broader, more eccentric touches, director Jean Dréville and Veidt conspired to make de Kempelen an artisan of depth, rather than a mere eccentric. In the baron's rather terse reaction to the revelation that Sonia is not a disloyal Russian but rather a disgruntled Pole, for example, the actor manages to convey the character's political naïveté, personal philosophy, and intellectual curiosity. Not bad for a dozen or so words in a second language.

Apart from a few instances in which Jean Lenoir's score appears to have been composed in direct counterpoint to the action it accompanies, the music serves the narrative well. *Le Joeuer d'Échecs* does have a throwback moment or two to silent film technique (a couple of reaction shots appear to have been purloined directly from Gustav von Seyffertitz in *Sparrows*), and Bernard Lancret's Boleslas *is* something of a dud, but nonetheless the film must be regarded as the showcase for one of the most enjoyable performances in the Veidt canon.

The Spy in Black

USA release title: *U-Boat 29*; Harefield Productions, Ltd., London; World premiere: 15 March 1939 Trade show, London; 82 minutes; General release: 12 August 1939; USA release (Columbia Pictures Corp.): 7 October 1939; 77 minutes

CAST: Conrad Veidt *Captain Ernst Hardt*; Sebastian Shaw *Lieut. Ashington (Cdr. Davis Blacklock)*; Valerie Hobson *Joan, the School Mistress*; Marius Goring *Lieut. Schuster*; June Duprez *Anne Burnett*; Athole Stewart *Rev. Hector Matthews*; Agnes Laughlan *Mrs. Matthews*; Helen Haye *Mrs. Sedley*; Cyril Raymond *Rev. John Harris*; George Summers *Captain Ratter*; Hay Petrie *Engineer*; Grant Sutherland *Bob Bratt*; Robert Rendel *Admiral*; Mary Morris *Edwards, the Chauffeuse*; Margaret Moffatt *Kate*; Kenneth Warrington *Commander Denis*; Torin Thatcher *Submarine Officer*; Skelton Knaggs *Sailor*; Bernard Miles *Hans, the Hotel Receptionist*; Charles Oliver *German Officer*; with Esma Cannon, Diana Sinclair-Hall

CREDITS: *Producers* Irving Asher, Alexander Korda; *Director* Michael Powell; *Screenplay* Emeric Pressburger; *Scenario* Roland Pertwee; *Based on a story by* J. Storer Clouston; *Photographed by* Bernard Browne; *Art Director* Frederick Pusey; *Supervising Art Director* Vincent Korda; *Film Editor* Hugh Stewart; *Asst. Editor* John Guthrie; *Supervising Film Editor* William Hornbeck; *Asst. Director* Patrick Jenkins; *Musical Director* Muir Mathieson; *Music Composed by* Miklós Rózsa; *Sound Director* A.W. Watkins

SYNOPSIS: Captain Hardt (Conrad Veidt), commander of German U-Boat 29, is ordered to the coast of one of the Orkney Islands—the British fleet's home base—during World War I. While he is in transit, Anne Burnett (June Duprez), a schoolmistress en route to her new job and her fiancé, disappears. She has been kidnapped by German spies, and her replacement, Frau Tiel (Valerie Hobson), makes contact with Hardt and orders him to destroy 15 of the British ships. She tells Hardt that specifics will be forthcoming from a certain Lieutenant Ashington (Sebastian Shaw), a "British naval officer with a grudge against the service." Hardt is attracted to the schoolmistress, but has nothing but contempt for Ashington. The turncoat advises the spies of the timetable to move a flotilla of destroyers, thus allowing the Germans to position their U-Boats effectively.

Into their midst walks the Reverend John Harris (Cyril Raymond), who has come to join his fiancée on the island. Harris is promptly trussed up and locked in a spare room.

Later, acting on an amorous impulse, Hardt follows Thiel outside, where he discovers that she is a counterspy, secretly working with Ashington to feed false information to the Germans. Hardt is aghast to learn that the timetables he himself handed over to the submariners will be responsible for the deaths of hundreds of his countrymen. Ashington moves Tiel—who is, in reality, the British officer's wife—onto the steamer, St. Magnus, for safety, before returning with a patrol to arrest Hardt. The German naval man has escaped, however, and, having donned the clerical apparel of Rev. Harris, he leaps aboard the St. Magnus just before she sails.

A handful of German prisoners of war are taken aboard the ship at another island, and Hardt both frees them and commandeers the St. Magnus in short order. Pursued by a number of British destroyers, the St. Magnus makes its way toward Sandwick Bay, where it is fired upon by U-Boat 29. Hardt orders the passengers to the lifeboats and goes down with the ship, as U-Boat 29 is sunk by depth charges from the destroyer flotilla.

REVIEWS: "…The British may not have the *Bremen*, but they still have Conrad Veidt….

"The skulking villain of the piece is the submarine, not Mr. Veidt, who is gallantly made out to be a fine, stout-hearted fellow, though a German."

New York Times, 6 October 1939—B.R.C. (Bosley Crowther)

Valerie Hobson and Connie got close — and stayed close — for two exciting features. (*The Spy in Black*)

"*The Spy in Black* ... should do stellar biz here and is a dual possibility for America.

"[Conrad] Veidt has a strong role for which he's admirably suited. Sebastian Shaw is excellent as the English naval officer. Valerie Hobson, as the other spy, is creditable. Supporting cast is competent.

"Direction and photography are excellent."

> *Variety* (London),
> 18 March 1939 — Jolo.

"...[Conrad] Veidt, [Valerie] Hobson and [Sebastian] Shaw are in the film's only meaty roles and acquit themselves capitally....

"Production is A-1, as is the direction....

"It's to producer Irving Asher's credit that there's a complete lack of phoney [*sic*] barbarism."

> *Variety* 11 October 1939 — Scho.

"...The acting is outstandingly good. Conrad Veidt is brilliant in the lead. He is throughout a tragic, if slightly sinister, figure, and wins respect and sympathy as a patriot with the qualities most admirable and admired in soldier, sailor or airman of any nationality — loyalty, courage, obedience, and steadfast endurance...."

> *Monthly Film Bulletin*,
> Vol. 6, No. 63;
> 31 March 1939 — E.P.

"In spite of its many good points, *The Spy in Black* would not, I think, be much without CONRAD VEIDT. ... With Conrad Veidt it becomes worth consideration.

He it is that makes one take the picture seriously, understanding and respecting [the] German submarine-commander....

"...The German is a far more interesting character [than the hero or heroine]—though, as I implied, he might not be if he were not portrayed by CONRAD VEIDT."

Punch ("At the Pictures"),
23 August 1939

NOTES AND QUOTES: *The Spy in Black* was the second of Columbia's "quota acquisitions" which were produced by Irving Asher, the head of Columbia British production. It was produced just before the start of WWII and marked the first collaboration between Emeric Pressburger and Michael Powell. Although Roland Pertwee received an on-screen writing credit — no film could be considered British under the quota laws unless it had been penned by a British citizen — the potent screenplay was the product of Pressburger's ardent massaging of J. Storer Clouston's original tale.

Valerie Hobson was brought in to replace Vivien Leigh, a cost-effective measure that shaved some £4000 from the budget. Leigh, thus at liberty, proceeded to meet up with David O. Selznick and win the role of Scarlett O'Hara in *Gone with the Wind*. Still, the switch in casting proved to be propitious, as the film made National Board of Review's "10 Best" list for 1939, and Veidt, Hobson, Powell, and Pressburger reteamed for *Contraband* later in 1939.

In the course of his biography of Pressburger (*Emeric Pressburger: The Life and Death of a Screenwriter*. London: Faber and Faber, 1994; pp. 150–151), Kevin MacDonald notes how

> Veidt ... had difficulties pronouncing certain English words, and Hobson light-heartedly ticked him off and corrected him. "But it's not my fault," Veidt would say, "my scriptwriter writes with an accent." Their

personal jibes about pronunciation spilled over into the film, where there is a running joke about Captain Hardt's mispronunciation of "butter..."

As an actor [Veidt] was "extremely professional and easy to work with." The sense of ease with which he spoke belied a long struggle with the language. Like Anton Walbrook, the other great Germanic star of Powell/Pressburger films, he made up for a lack of fluency with an exact control of tone and volume. Robert Morley, at one time Veidt's dialogue director, said, "He was a master at delivering lines... He always spoke them very slowly when everyone else spoke rather fast, and soft when everyone spoke loudly..."

Shooting began in Denham in mid–November. Michael [Powell] tried hard to create a sense of claustrophobia in the small house in which most of the film is set. He opted for a directorial style which often pays direct homage to Veidt's demonic image in such classic expressionist films as *Dr Caligari* and *Der Student von Prag*, with tilted camera angles and striking shadows. To Emeric and Michael, Veidt was almost more of an icon than an actor — "He *was* the great German cinema."

Thanks to Pressburger, Connie was allowed to enliven a character who is *miles* from the stereotypical thuggish Hun. Hardt is presented for inspection as a mélange of soldier, patriot, intellectual, wit, and romantic human being. Although the film's title refers to him (and only for the briefest of sequences, in which he makes his way aboard the St. Magnus in Reverend Harris's slouch hat and greatcoat), he is not a spy; in fact, he insists on wearing his uniform although closeted in the rather small house. If he is shot, he has no desire to be executed for donning mufti in time of war. Veidt also indulges in a few *en passant* snatches of conversation on espionage with Valerie Hobson: he is appalled at the (presumed) murder of the real schoolmistress, and coolly assimilates Hobson's pronouncement that different people serve their country in their own ways.

While *The Spy in Black*'s dramatic milieu is ostensibly laid in World War I Scotland, the drama which enthralled its audiences was very much grounded in a more current war. The picture dared to suggest that an enemy could still demonstrate honor, understanding and mercy, a concept that normally went begging in motion pictures of wartime theme or vintage. From a propaganda standpoint, the portrayal of Hardt as a decent, rational man (he poignantly excludes a babe in arms from a threat to shoot uncooperative bystanders; he allows civilians to abandon the sinking ship before soldiers of either nationality; he elects to go to the bottom with the vessel that has *become* his) may have assuaged fears among the populace that contact with the Germans could lead only to a grisly and barbaric fate.

Contraband

Aka *Blackout* (U.S. Release Title); British National, London; World Premiere: 20 March 1940 Trade show, London; General Release: May 1940; UK running time: 92 minutes; Released in USA by United Artists, 29 November 1940; U.S. running time: 80 minutes

CAST: Conrad Veidt *Captain Anderson*; Valerie Hobson *Mrs. Sorenson*; Hay Petrie *Axel Skold, mate of the SS Helvig/Erik Skold, chef of Three Vikings*; Joss Ambler *Lieut. Commander Ashton*; Raymond Lovell *Van Dyne*; Esmond Knight *Mr. Pidgeon*; Charles Victor *Hendrick*; Phoebe Kershaw *Miss Lang*; Harold Warrender *Lieut. Commander Ellis*; Paddy Browne *Singer in Regency*; Manning Whiley *Manager of Mousetrap*; Stuart Latham, Peter Bull, Leo Genn *Brothers Grimm*; Dennis Arundell *Leimann*; Julien Vedey, Henry Wolston, Sydney Moncton, Hamilton Keen *Danish Waiters*; Mark Daly *Taxi Driver*; John Longden, Eric Maturin *Passport Officers*; Molly Hamley-Clifford *Baroness Hekla*; Toni Gable *Miss Karoly*; Desmond Jeans and Eric Hales *the Karolys*; John Roberts *Hanson*; Eric Berry *Mr. Abo*; Olga Edwards *Mrs. Abo*; Bernard Miles *Man lighting Pipe*; Torin Thatcher *Sailor*; with Frank Allenby, John England, Haddon Mason, Johnnie Schofield,

Townsend Whitling, Ross Duncan, Albert Chevalier

CREDITS: *Producer* John Corfield; *Director* Michael Powell; *Original Story* Emeric Pressburger; *Screenplay* Michael Powell, Brock Williams; *Photography* F.A. (Freddie) Young; *Camera Operator* Skeets Kelly; *Associate Producer* Roland Gillett; *Original Music* Richard Addinsell, John Greenwood; *Film Editors* John Seabourne Sr. and Joseph Sterling; *Art Director* Alfred Junge; *Production Manager* Anthony Nelson Keys; *Sound Engineers* C.C. Stevens, A.W. Watkins; *Asst. Director* William Reidy; *Music* Richard Addinsell; *Musical Director* Muir Mathieson; *Production Secretaries* Betty Curtis, Joan Page

SYNOPSIS: Captain Anderson (Conrad Veidt), master of the Danish freighter *Helvig*, is unwillingly delayed for inspection by a British warship. He's given shore passes for himself and his first officer, only to have them stolen by Mrs. Sorensen (Valerie Hobson) and Mr. Pidgeon (Esmond Knight), two of his passengers. Anderson follows them ashore, and catches up with Mrs. Sorensen as she is en route to London. Gradually warming to each other, the captain and the lady — whose real name is Clayton — make for the Three Vikings Danish restaurant; they head into the London blackout afterwards, hoping to meet up with Mr. Pidgeon.

They are, however, captured by German spies who are headquartered in a Soho cellar flat. Van Dyne (Raymond Lovell), the master spy, has discovered that Miss Clayton — who, along with Mr. Pidgeon, is a British secret agent — has been reporting on German ships posing as neutral vessels. Van Dyne and his accomplice, Miss Lang (Phoebe Kershaw), tie Anderson and Clayton up and leave to pass phony information on to Clayton's contact.

Anderson succeeds in escaping from the hideout via the lift, and he returns with a band of Danes — waiters and cooks from The Three Vikings restaurant — to rescue Clayton as well as Pidgeon, who was seized at the Army and Navy Club. The spy ring is soundly thrashed by the Danes and a group of inebriated British clubmen, and Van Dyne is knocked unconscious by Anderson.

Anderson, Miss Clayton and Pidgeon return to the *Helvig* in time to sail at the appointed time. At breakfast, shortly thereafter, Captain Anderson orders "Mrs. Sorensen" to his quarters, where the two share an embrace and, presumably, the beginning of a life together.

REVIEWS: "...Through it all Conrad Veidt, as the cavalier captain, behaves with his usual marvelous élan and the remaining cast is well chosen...."

"Though *Blackout* ... it is good melodrama ... and if it has been robbed of some of its urgent excitement, the reason ... may lie partly in the fact that the film was made before incendiary bombs lit up the darkened island and war came home to England."

New York Times,
2 December 1940 — T.S.

"This exciting story is dramatically put over and excellently directed. ... Conrad Veidt, as the resourceful, courageous captain, gives a brilliant performance, while Valerie Hobson not only looks charming but acts extremely well as Mrs. Sorenson. Hay Petrie, who plays two parts, provides some excellent comic relief."

Monthly Film Bulletin,
Vol. 7, No. 76;
30 April 1940 — V.G.-S.

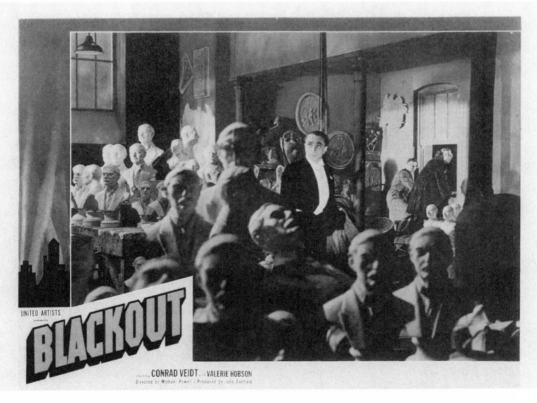

Dozens of plaster busts of Neville Chamberlain — surely one of the "wrongest" statesmen in diplomatic history — allow the forces of righteousness to escape the Nazis. Left to right: Connie, Esmond Knight and Valerie Hobbon. (*Contraband*)

"...Conrad Veidt as the Danish seaman is authentic to the point where it's questionable as to his ease as a lover in the smart company of Valerie Hobson. Her role is handled with aplomb. All of the rest reach for the same standard, particular attention going to Hay Petrie for his comedy work in a dual role...."

Variety (London), 2 April 1940

NOTES AND QUOTES:

(About Veidt:)
We mustn't forget that he was German, and at the time, with the war just starting, it was difficult for him. I think he always felt faintly embarrassed by the fact that he'd been a German star and had a very ripe German accent. Very cleverly Emeric [Pressburger] made him not a German in *Contraband*. He was just as believable being a Dane, and that was charming...

[Emeric] wrote the film around the kind of things that Connie Veidt and I actually did. We used to go out to dinner to this funny restaurant which they actually put into the film as *The Three Vikings*— they copied it almost exactly in the studio... almost to the Hay Petrie character as the dotty chef.

—Valerie Hobson, as quoted by Kevin MacDonald (*Emeric Pressburger: The Life and Death of a Screenwriter*; p. 161)

While in preproduction, Michael Powell and producer John Corfield opted not to hire Hungarian composer Miklós Rózsa (who had written the effective score for *The Spy in Black*), but Brits Richard Addinsell and John Greenwood, instead. To screenwriter Emeric Pressburger, this was more "a simple act of bloody-mindedness" than a patriotic move on the director's part.

As was the custom, a print of the completed feature was sent to Hollywood so that it could be edited for optimum effect on American audiences. Along for the ride went Connie, who had volunteered to publicize the film while drawing attention to the need to support the British war effort. Veidt, who had intended to return to Britain after a short tour of the USA, received an offer to replace Paul Lukas in MGM's *Escape* and thus opted to remain in the States in order to make films. As he had done while in England, the Berlin-born actor donated a portion of his American salary to British war relief. Sadly, he would never return alive to the country of his adopted citizenship.

Contraband proved to be even more popular with American ticket buyers than *The Spy in Black*, although some critics felt the fictional elements of the film suffered in comparison with the occasional documentary clip.

Veidt and Hobson winningly repeated the kernel of the roles they had enacted together earlier that same year: she, the spy, and he, the seafaring man with a sense of honor *and* a sense of humor. There is a significantly lighter tone about *Contraband* than there had been about *The Spy in Black*, however. The picture foreshadowed the élan of 1941's *All Through the Night*, and *Contraband*'s London — populated by a comedic working class that nonetheless regards the war effort with deadly earnest — is the mirror image of Gloves Donahue's New York, where comic thugs and coppers find themselves on the same side of the fight against the Third Reich. Though the thrills are relatively tame — does Van Dyne really think that a hotheaded American freighter captain can precipitate war with England?— the humor of the scenario remains potent. Connie never had a part like Anderson, which enabled him to win laughter from his audience, while allowing him to chuckle at himself. For Veidt aficionados, *Contraband* ranks up there with *A Woman's Face*, *The Thief of Bagdad* and *Das Cabinet des Dr. Caligari* as requisite canon entries.

The Thief of Bagdad

London Film Productions Ltd., London (DIF); Alexander Korda Films, Inc. (AFI); Released in USA by United Artists Corporation; World premiere: 5 December 1940 Radio City Music Hall, NY; UK premiere: 24 December 1940 Trade show, London; General release: 25 December 1940; Running time: 105–106 minutes; Technicolor

CAST: Conrad Veidt *Jaffar*; Sabu *Abu*; June Duprez *Princess*; John Justin *Ahmad*; Rex Ingram *Djinn*; Miles Malleson *Sultan*; Morton Selten *the Old King*; Mary Morris *Halima*; Bruce Winston *Merchant*; Hay Petrie *Astrologer*; Adelaide Hall *Singer*; Roy Emmerton *Jailer*; Allen Jeayes *Story Teller*; Viscount *the Dog*; with Glynis Johns, John Salew, Norman Pierce, Frederick Burtwell, Otto Wallen, Henry Hallett, Cleo Laine.

CREDITS: *Presented by* Alexander Korda; *Producer* Alexander Korda; *Associate Producers* Zoltan Korda, William Cameron Menzies; *Directors* Ludwig Berger, Michael Powell, Tim Whelan (also: Alexander Korda, Zoltan Korda, W.C. Menzies); *Associate Directors* Geoffrey Boothby, Charles David; *2nd Asst. Director* Jack Clayton; *Screenplay & Dialogue* Miles Malleson; *Scenario* Lajos Biro; *Photographer* Georges Perinal; *Special Effects* Lawrence Butler; *Associate Photographer* Osmond Borradaile; *Camera Operator* Robert Crasker; *Technicolor Consultant* Natalie Kalmus; *Color Production Design* Vincent Korda; *Film Editor* Charles Crichton; *Supervising Film Editor* William Hornbeck; *Set Design Associates* Frederick Pusey, Ferdinand Bellan; *Scenic Backgrounds* Percy Day; *Costumes* Oliver Messel, John Armstrong, Marcel Vertes; *Music Direction* Muir Mathieson; *Music Score* Miklós Rósza; *Songs: Since Time Began* Nic Roger, William Kernell; *I Want to Be a Sailor* Miklos Rozsa, R. Denham; *Orchestral Arrangements* Albert Sandrey; *Sound Direction* A.W. Watkins; *Production Manager* David Cunynghame; *Production Assistant* André de Toth

SYNOPSIS: The evil magician Jaffar (Conrad Veidt) arrives in Basra, where he seeks to use his powers to make the beautiful princess (June Duprez) his own. The princess has been entranced and awaits the kiss of her true love, Prince Ahmad of Bagdad (John Justin). The prince, however, is now a blind beggar who wanders about in the company of his dog. Jaffar has Ahmad brought to court, where the blind man regales the palace maidens with his story.

He tells how he *was* the Caliph of Bagdad, but was regarded as cruel, arrogant and unforgiving — all due to the machinations of his vizier, Jaffar. When he decided to travel among his people in disguise, so as to learn what they really thought of him, Jaffar had him seized and thrown into prison, under sentence of death. With the help of a young thief, Abu (Sabu), Ahmad escaped and fled to Basra. Exploring that city, Ahmad espied the beautiful princess and, later, in the recesses of her private garden, he met her and the two fell in love. But Jaffar had likewise come to Basra, hoping to win, if not the princess's love, the Sultan's approval; the magician tempted the old ruler with mechanical wonders. The princess claimed to love another, however, and Jaffar, furious when confronted with Ahmad and the young thief, used his powers to blind the one and transform the other into a mongrel. When she discovered what had happened to her true love, the princess fell into a trancelike sleep, from which even Jaffar's magic was powerless to awaken her.

Not knowing that Jaffar is close at hand, Ahmad kisses (and awakens) the princess, who professes that she still loves him. In a trice, Jaffar kidnaps the princess aboard his ship, where he tells her that only her being in the magician's arms can restore Ahmad's sight. She surrenders to him, but with distaste; fully restored, Ahmad and Abu pursue Jaffar in a small boat. The vizier summons the wind to sink the boat, but Abu finds a bottle containing a djinn (Rex Ingram), which he tricks into granting him three wishes. After a series of adventures — using two of the wishes — Abu is reunited with Ahmad; the pair gaze helplessly into a magical ruby, which reveals to them the treacherous murder of the sultan at the many hands of another of

Jaffar's infernal contraptions. When Ahmad sees that the princess is about to be charmed into forgetting the past — and her love for him — he blames the thief and wishes he were back in Bagdad. "I wish you were, too," echoes Abu, and the third wish is carried out. Fighting desperately, Ahmad is nonetheless overpowered, and he and the princess — who has again refused Jaffar's attentions — are both condemned to death.

Aghast by what he sees, Abu smashes the ruby, which opens a portal into a land of blessing and wonderment. Knowing that Allah will take care of His faithful, Abu steals a flying carpet and a magic crossbow, and makes for Bagdad. Just as Ahmad is to be beheaded, the populace catches sight of the carpet, flying in from the heavens; taking this to be the fulfillment of an old prophecy, the people rise up against Jaffar. The vizier seeks to escape on a wondrous mechanical flying horse, but he is shot by Abu, and he and the horse fall to the ground far below.

Ahmad is once again Caliph of Bagdad, and he and his princess bride plan to look after Abu's education. The young thief has other ideas, however, and prefers to seek more adventures, courtesy of his flying carpet.

REVIEWS: "...[Helping make *The Thief of Bagdad* truly exciting entertainment are] the performances of Sabu, the Indian boy, as the little thief; of Conrad Veidt as the turbaned Grand Vizier with eyes of amazing potency, of John Justin as the handsome prince, June Duprez as the luscious princess and Rex Ingram as the monstrous djinni with the lock of jet black hair. So the least one can do is recommend it as a cinematic delight, and thank Mr. Korda for reaching boldly into a happy world."

New York Times, 6 December 1940 — Bosley Crowther

"...Conrad Veidt is most impressive as the sinister grand vizier, sharing honors with Sabu, who capably carries off the title role. Supporting players are typically English in both their acting and methodical reading of dialog. On both the acting and directing sides, picture is obviously deficient."

Variety, 16 October 1940 — Walt.

NOTES AND QUOTES: *The Thief of Bagdad* enjoyed a lengthy production schedule: several years, in fact. Filming in England was halted by the advent of World War II and, following the brief shoot (some records say 12 days) of the propaganda feature *The Lion Has Wings*, the production of *Thief* resumed in the United States. Dissatisfied with the efforts of Ludwig Berger, his director of record and a specialist in intimate drama, Korda went on to hire Tim Whelan and Michael Powell (without sacking Berger) in an effort to make the film livelier and more spectacular. Before the picture was released to theatres, it would become something of a patchwork quilt, reflecting the styles, not only of these three men, but also of William Cameron Menzies, of Korda, himself, and of his brother, Zoltan; none of this last triumvirate would receive screen credit.

In light of this mélange, Korda biographer Karol Kulik (*Alexander Korda: The Man Who Could Work Miracles.* New Rochelle, NY: Arlington House, 1975; p. 244) opines:

The film fails as much in execution as it does in conception. Static camera placements and a plodding editing style, which precludes any imagination in the scene transitions, are bound to undermine the exotic atmosphere so dependent on action, movement, and fluid or dynamic cutting techniques. It is not coincidental that all the best scenes, especially the opening harbour sequence with its sweeping and rhythmic camera movements and the scene of Sabu's discovery of the djinn on a deserted beach, are directed by Michael Powell, the only one of the five directors whose visual imagination was allowed free reign...

Wonderful behind-the-scenes shot of June Duprez and Connie acting up a ...ummmmm ... storm. (*The Thief of Bagdad*)

The Thief won an Oscar for Special Effects, but many of the sequences are below standard — witness the bad matching of the flying horse sequence and the at times unconvincing use of models.

A perennial criticism of Alexander Korda held that the producer regarded his actors as being secondary to spectacle, effects or art direction. "Only Conrad Veidt and Rex Ingram escape the fate of the rest of the cast," writes Kulik, "who look like puppets being manipulated around a lavish stage. John Justin and June Duprez, as two lovers caught in Jaffar's intrigues, are too inexperienced to stand out against the technical fireworks around them" (p. 243). Veidt and Ingram — screen veterans, both, and men who did not hesitate to speak their mind — were not about to be relegated to the cinematic back shelf by Alexander Korda's vision, William Cameron Menzies' visuals, or anything anyone else could possibly concoct. In an interview with Les Hammer (quoted in the January 2001 issue of *Nocturne*, the journal of the *Conrad Veidt Society*), Justin related his take on the lopsided situation:

> At the time of the making of *The Thief*, it was my very first movie... I didn't know my arse from my elbow and on the production side the picture was a nightmare. Connie saved my sanity. I discovered early on that if I told my trouble to him — he always asked me if things were okay when we had a scene together — it would get seen to as if by magic.

Originally, it had been Douglas Fairbanks and Julianne Johnson who had found love amid the tents and spires of Bagdad in Raoul Walsh's silent version of the Arabian Nights tale. Nonetheless, the 1924 United Artists release bore little resemblance to the 1940 Technicolor epic, although both features were mounted against the panoply of William Cameron Menzies' breathtaking sets. (Presaging Conrad Veidt's villainous Jaffar was the "Mongol Prince," played by Sojin, the Japanese actor who would go on to replace Connie as Charlie Chan in *The Chinese Parrot*.)

The Thief of Bagdad won three Academy Awards (for special effects, color art direction, and color cinematography), more than any other 1940 release. According to several Hollywood trade magazines of the time, another Technicolor fantasy tale, *The Conjuror*, was heralded as the follow-up to *Thief*; nothing came of it.

Escape

M-G-M — 31 October 1940 — 102/104 minutes

CAST: Conrad Veidt *General Kurt von Kolb*; Norma Shearer *Countess Ruby von Treck*; Robert Taylor *Mark Preysing*; Nazimova *Emmy Ritter*; Felix Bressart *Fritz Geller*; Albert Basserman *Dr. Arthur Henning*; Philip Dorn *Dr. Ditten*; Bonita Granville *Ursula*; Edgar Barrier *Commissioner*; Elsa Basserman *Mrs. Henning*; Blanche Yurka *Nurse*; Lisa Golm *Anna*; Marek Windheim *Hotel Clerk*; Gretl Sherk *Hilda Keller*; Lotte Palfi *Julie*; Janet Shaw *Greta*; Marianne Mosner *Maria*; Ann Sheldon *Helene*; Christina Montez *Suzanne*; Adolph Milar *Salesman*; Frederik Vogeding, Hans Joby *Passport Officials*; Erwin Kalser *Bartender*; Helmut Dantine, Frederick Giermann *Porters*; William Yetter *Heinrich*; Ernst Deutsch *Baron von Reiber*; Maria Ray *Baroness*; Kay Deslys *Waitress*; Henry Victor, Hans Schumm *Policemen*; Arno Fey *Commandant*; Winter Hall *Priest*; Thomas Monk *Priest's Assistant*; William Edmunds *Waiter*

CREDITS: *Producer* Lawrence Weingarten; *Director* Mervyn Leroy; *Additional Scenes Directed by* George Cukor; *Asst. Director* Al Shenberg; *Screenplay* Arch Oboler, Marguerite Roberts; *Based on the eponymous novel by* Ethel Vance; *Photographed by* Robert Planck; *Art Director* Cedric Gibbons; *Associate Art Director* Urie McCleary; *Film Editor* George Boemler; *Set Decorations* Edwin B. Willis; *Gowns* Adrian; *Men's Costumes* Gile Steele; *Recording Director* Douglas Shearer; *Technical Advisor* Raul Huldeschinsky; *Make-Up* Jack Dawn; *Miss Shearer's Hair Styles* Sydney Guilaroff; *Technical Expert* Henry Noerdlinger

SYNOPSIS: American Mark Preysing (Robert Taylor) has come to Germany in search of his mother, German-born actress Emmy Ritter (Nazimova). Unaware that his mother is sentenced to be executed in a concentration camp for helping German refugees when back in the States, Preysing faces a wall of fear and arrogance everywhere he turns. Even Emmy's old servant, Fritz Keller (Felix Bressart), puts on a very public display of anger and unconcern. Secretly, however, Fritz meets Mark and swears he will remain faithful.

One day, Mark meets Countess Ruby

von Treck (Norma Shearer), the American widow of a German nobleman, and asks her for help in finding Emmy. Ruby, who operates a finishing school for young girls, is loath to commit herself. Later, when she is told by her lover, General Kurt Von Kolb (Conrad Veidt), that the actress will die on the following Saturday, she is unable to break this news to Mark. Luck has Mark meet Dr. Ditten (Philip Dorn), the concentration camp doctor who has been attending to Emmy. Ditten discreetly gives Mark a letter from Emmy, before telling the American of his mother's impending execution. In danger of being overheard by the ubiquitous Nazis, Ditten arranges to meet Mark at the doctor's flat the following evening. At that time, he informs Mark that he has drugged Emmy, making her appear as if dead; all Mark has to do is remove "the body" from the camp, and then make sure she is kept warm and allowed to rest. Mark telephones Fritz, who agrees to meet him at the White Swan café later that night.

Fritz never shows, however, and Mark — having told a pair of political police that he is waiting for Dr. Ditten — is taken off by them to the concentration camp. Thinking quickly, Ditten gets Mark off the hook, and Fritz and the American remove the casket containing Emmy Ritter right under the noses of the suspicious police. Mark succeeds in reviving Emmy in the back of the truck, but snow and ice block the road, forcing them to seek warmth and shelter at the countess's house. Ruby is extremely hesitant to help them, but she relents when she sees Emmy come around and embrace her son. Von Kolb calls to inquire after a truck he saw pull up to the house as the car left; Ruby tells him it backed up and kept on going.

The next day, Emmy is provided with a passport — courtesy of one of Ruby's girls who has no affection for the Nazis — and everyone, including Ruby, prepares to escape to freedom. Ruby has arranged for the girls to go off skiing, but General Von Kolb — who shows up unexpectedly — is quickly steered onto the topic of Mark Preysing and Emmy Ritter by some comments made by one of the girls. Soon, the jealous Von Kolb insists that the American be telephoned and invited to come skiing with them. Preysing is found at the front door moments later, and Von Kolb warns him to leave the country immediately.

That night, Fritz, Emmy and Mark make ready for their trip to the airport and their subsequent flight out of Germany. Ruby promises to meet Mark on 57th Street in New York City sometime in the future; she remains behind to keep Von Kolb occupied until the plane has taken off. Watching the minutes tick slowly away, Ruby confesses to Von Kolb that she and Mark love each other, and that the general would have to arrest her — the countess — if he insisted on pursuing Emmy Ritter. Von Kolb's temper rises to the taunts, and he has a heart attack. As he lies helpless, sprawled across the desk, he begs Ruby not to leave him. With tears in her eyes, knowing full well that Mark and the others are safely in the air, she agrees to stay on.

REVIEWS: "...Conrad Veidt plays the part of a German general, a friend of the countess, with terrifying malevolence.... Mr. Leroy has permitted the action to drag at certain points but has directed the important scenes with tremendous intensity. The consequence is a picture which crackles with vitality."

New York Times, 1 November 1940 — Bosley Crowther

"...It is excellent, suspenseful material and LeRoy succeeds admirably in sustaining throughout the picture a tense atmosphere of impending danger to the lives and limbs of his actors. In this respect he has most capable assistance from a group

Connie, under the adoring scrutiny of Norma Shearer, wasn't the first choice for the role of General von Kolb. (*Escape*)

of earnest supporting actors, including ... Conrad Veidt...."

Variety, 30 October 1941— Flin.

"The film is adapted from the novel of the same name. The director, who could perhaps have been a little less straightforward and have left more to the imagination of the audience, manages to convey the atmosphere of Nazi Germany where everyone is polite but will only talk on generalities and where every attempt to find something out or the raising of a voice in making a possibly indiscreet remark, immediately raises impenetrable barriers.

"...Norma Shearer plays with restraint the American-born Countess who ... [is] on terms of great friendship with one of the *herrenvolk* in the shape of Conrad Veidt, whose General is as polished a performance as one could wish. The film is also interesting for the return of Nazimova...."

Monthly Film Bulletin,
Vol. 8, No. 85;
January 1941— E.O.

"...The male performances are superb. Robert Taylor gives a fine performance as the distracted young son; Conrad Veidt is properly menacing as the Countess's lover; Felix Bressart is excellent as the frightened but courageous servant and Philip Dorn all but walks away with the picture as the humane camp doctor."

New York Daily News,
1 November 1940 —
Kate Cameron

NOTES AND QUOTES: *Escape* was the debut vehicle for Elsa Basserman, Edgar Barrier and Helmut Dantine.

After the war, it was determined that "Ethel Vance" was the nom de plume of novelist Grace Zaring Stone, whose earlier work *The Bitter Tea of General Yen* had been captured on film by Frank Capra for Columbia Pictures in 1933. As Miss Stone's daughter was living under the occupation at the time of *Escape*'s publication (1939), the novelist opted for the pseudonym to avoid repercussions. *The AFI Catalogue* indicates that none of the picture's musical score was credited on-screen or in reviews and commentaries, again for fear of reprisal against the composers' family members still in Germany.

Director George Cukor had hoped to helm *Escape*, but was removed by producer Lawrence Weingarten, who then offered the picture to Alfred Hitchcock. When Hitch turned it down, the assignment fell into the lap of Mervyn LeRoy. Cukor's involvement in the production would be limited to his shooting some additional scenes (after the initial wrap) in September 1940.

Conrad Veidt wasn't the original choice for Von Kolb. In fact, *Escape* had been in production for about a week when LeRoy summoned him to take over for the Hungarian-born Paul Lukas, whom the director regarded as insufficiently villainous. Veidt immediately arranged that the lion's share of his salary be forwarded to British war relief. For his portrayal of the general, Veidt won — courtesy of the National Board of Review — the only acting honor of his career.

Veidt hasn't much to do in the first half of the picture, other than be absolutely charming both to the girls at the finishing school and to the countess. When his smiles turn to grimaces later on, however — as the general's political suspicions and personal jealousies are brought to the

fore by evidence of Ruby's concern about the handsome American — the actor is every bit as successfully repellant as he had been irresistibly avuncular to that group of adoring girls. In his next-to-last scene, Von Kolb amuses himself by playing cat and mouse with both Mark and Ruby. This is the viewer's first look at the sadistic streak that underlines the general's cold-hearted professionalism, and one finds oneself admiring Veidt for his brilliant technique even while loathing Von Kolb for his despicable behavior.

A Woman's Face

Loew's Incorporated (MGM), Culver City/New York; 105 minutes; World Premiere: 15 May 1941 Capitol, New York; General Release: 23 May 1941

CAST: Conrad Veidt *Torsten Barring*; Joan Crawford *Anna Holm [aka Ingrid Paulson]*; Melvyn Douglas *Dr. Gustav Segert*; Osa Massen *Vera Segert*; Reginald Owen *Bernard Dalvik*; Albert Bassermann *Consul Magnus Barring*; Marjorie Main *Emma Kristiansdotter*; Donald Meek *Herman Rundvik*; Connie Gilchrist *Christina Dalvik*; Richard Nichols *Lars-Erik*; Charles Quigley *Eric*; Gwili Andre *Gusta*; Clifford Brooke *Wickman*; George Zucco *Defense Attorney*; Henry Kolker *Judge*; Robert Warwick, Gilbert Emery *Associate Judges*; Henry Daniell *Public Prosecutor*; Sarah Padden *Police Matron*; William Farnum *Court Attendant*; James Millican *Reporter*

CREDITS: *Producer* Victor Saville; *Director* George Cukor; *Assistant Directors* Edward Worhler, Marvin Stuart; *Screenplay* Donald Ogden Stewart and Elliot Paul; *Based on the play* Il Était une Fois *by* Francis de Croisset; *Director of Photography* Robert Planck; *Art Director* Cedric Gibbons; *Associate Art Director* Wade B. Rubottom; *Film Editor* Frank Sullivan; *Set Decorator* Edwin B. Willis; *Gowns* Adrian; *Men's Wardrobe* Gile Steele; *Music Score* Bronislau Kaper; *Dance Director* Ernst Matray; *Recording Director* Douglas Shearer

SYNOPSIS: Stockholm, Sweden: Anna Holm (Joan Crawford) is on trial for murder. The witnesses at the trial fill in the details.

Anna, whose face was badly scarred due to a fire her drunken father started when she was a child, was a tavern owner and — along with witnesses Herman Rundvik (Donald Meek) and Christina and Bernard Dalvik (Connie Gilchrist, Reginald Owen) — a blackmailer. Among their victims was Vera Segert (Osa Massen), faithless wife of renowned plastic surgeon Gustav Segert (Melvyn Douglas). Anna, in love with playboy Torsten Barring (Conrad Veidt) — who never treated her as less than a woman because of her disfigurement — comes in contact with Dr. Segert while attempting to up the ante on the blackmail terms she has with Vera. Dr. Segert offers to work on Anna's scarred face and, after a series of twelve operations, she emerges from his clinic a supremely beautiful woman.

She searches out Torsten, who is thrilled at her beauty having been restored, and who needs her help. Throwing her lot in with her lover, Anna poses as Ingrid Paulson, governess to four-year-old Lars-Erik, who is due to inherit the accumulated wealth of Torsten's uncle, Consul Magnus Barring (Albert Bassermann); her mission: to murder the boy so that Torsten will inherit everything. Nonetheless, Anna/Ingrid cannot bring herself to harm the boy, despite her being given an ultimatum by Torsten at a party also attended by Dr. Segert. (Dr. Segert testifies that he has come to love Anna, who — despite all her other failings — could not be a murderer.)

At the consul's birthday celebration, Anna and Segert plan to take a sleigh ride with Lars-Erik, but are appalled to see Torsten's sleigh gallop past them, with a terrified Lars-Erik riding with him. As Segert tries to catch up with the other sleigh, Anna confesses everything to him. They do manage to catch Torsten's sleigh, and, to save the child, Anna shoots her ex-lover, who then tumbles into the falls.

As the judges mull over the testimony, Segert turns his back on Vera and proposes to Anna; together, they await the verdict.

REVIEWS: "...[Joan] Crawford ... seems to lack the ability to project more than the superficial harshness of the character of Anna Holm. ... Conrad Veidt, as the demented villain of the piece, again as suavely satanic a figure as ever, [can] cast a spell over an audience, and there are excellent performances by Melvyn Douglas, as the plastic surgeon, and Albert Bassermann as the aged uncle."

New York Times,
16 May 1941 — T.S.

"...Miss Crawford has a strongly dramatic and sympathetic role, despite her hardened attitude, which she handles in topnotch fashion. ... [Melvyn] Douglas switches from his recent run of light characters to a serious characterization, and does well as the plastic surgeon. Veidt portrays the typical suave villain while Albert Bassermann clicks as the kindly old Swedish consul...."

Variety, 7 May 1941 — Walt.

"...Melvyn Douglas and Conrad Veidt, as the two men who influence [Anna Holm's] life, play their parts well: Melvyn Douglas interested in Anna's particular case but trying to help her for her own good; Conrad Veidt trying with all the sinister wiles of which he is capable to use her for his own ends.

"...George Cukor and Victor Saville as director and producer have certainly produced a film of exceptional dramatic quality."

Monthly Film Bulletin, Vol. 8,
No. 92; August 1941 — E.W.

NOTES AND QUOTES: Connie's studied exercise in villainy is an instance where an actor's performance serves to rescue a poorly delineated character from a fate worse than incredulity. Donald Ogden Stewart and Eliot Paul's scenario has

Reginald Owen (right) and Connie flank the shadow of Joan Crawford. *A Woman's Face* was Connie's favorite picture.

Torsten Barring metamorphose a trifle too readily from irresponsible spendthrift with a penchant for easy money to calculating, would-be murderer. Initially, the canny playboy is just one apple in a barrelful of bad apples; excepting Consul Barring, Dr. Segert and Lars-Erik (a painful performance by little Richard Nichols), the rest of the principals with whom he consorts are shallow, dishonest, unfaithful or just plain selfish. It's established right off the bat that Barring lives on a combination of charm and overextended credit, and this leads one to believe that his continued impecuniousness will result in a never-ending succession of cons and scams. The fact that he gets by on other people's money is the given; thus, his looking to move onto Easy Street via another person's *ruthless-*

ness is not an easy segue to accept. Despite meticulously inserted kernels of characterization — the fact that he "loathes" children is carefully introduced, and Dr. Sagert uses the word "ruthless" almost antiphonally when referring to his scarred patient — the jump to murder is less than totally convincing.

Yet Connie and the excellent Joan Crawford — here, miles from the Max Factored gloss of her more normal venue — pull it off. Her ongoing change of heart, much more predictable than his jump-cut transformation, allows the viewer to sense catharsis chugging 'round the bend. His desperation, which leads him to make for the falls himself with Lars-Erik, demonstrates the Barring backbone that earlier footage had successfully, if unwisely, concealed. This being 1941— in real, as well as reel life — there's little doubt that Lars-Erik will inherit everything his grandfather has earmarked for him. That, however, does nothing to lessen the thrill of seeing Anna whip a revolver out of her purse and drill the maniacal Torsten in the back. It's a rewarding ending to an enjoyable picture, and all the subsequent ambiguity about the verdict is merely a transparent sop to the censors; the audience knows damn well that Segert will hereafter always be at the ready to touch up Anna's body and soul.

Veidt and Crawford got along so well together that Connie was invited back by producer Victor Saville for *Above Suspicion* in November 1942. On the 2nd of that month, Connie starred in the Radio UJH broadcast of *A Woman's Face*, along with Ida Lupino and Brian Aherne.

Francis de Croisset's source play, *Il Était une Fois*, had previously been filmed (as *En kvinnas ansikte*) in Sweden in 1938.

Whistling in the Dark

MGM — August 8, 1941— 76-77 minutes

CAST: Conrad Veidt *Joseph Jones*; Red Skelton *Wally Benton*; Ann Rutherford *Carol Lambert*; Virginia Grey *Fran Post*; Rags Ragland *Sylvester*; Henry O'Neill *Philip Post*; Eve Arden *Buzz Baker*; Paul Stanton *Jennings*; Don Douglas *Gordon Thomas*; Don Costello *"Noose" Green*; William Tannen *Robert Graves*; Reed Hadley *Beau Smith*; Mariska Aldrich *Hilda*; Lloyd Corrigan *Upshaw*; George Carleton *Deputy Commissioner O'Neill*; Will Lee *Herman the Druggist*; Ruth Robinson *Mrs. Robinson*; John Picorri *Gatekeeper*; Joe Devlin *Taxi Driver*; John Wald *Announcer's Voice*; Ken Christy *Inspector*; Betty Farrington *Mrs. Moriarity*; Paul Ellis *Captain*; Dora Clement *Mrs. Upshaw*; James Anderson *Attendant*; Inez Cooper *Stewardess*; Emmett Vogan *Producer*; Barbara Bedford *Local Operator*; Lester Dorr *Dispatcher*; Dorothy Adams *Mrs. Farrell*; Billy Bletcher *Effects Man*

CREDITS: *Producer* George Haight; *Director* S. Sylvan Simon; *Asst. Director* Al Raboch;

Screenplay Robert McGonigle, Harry Clork, Albert Mannheimer; *Based on the eponymous play by* Laurence Gross and Edward Childs Carpenter; *Contract Writer* Eddie Moran, Elliott Nugent; *Director of Photography* Sidney Wagner; *Art Director* Cedric Gibbons; *Associate Art Director* Gabriel Scognamillo; *Film Editor* Frank E. Hull; *Set Decorator* Edwin B. Willis; *Gowns* Kalloch; *Musical Score* Bronislau Kaper; *Recording Director* Douglas Shearer

SYNOPSIS: Joseph Jones (Conrad Veidt) heads Silver Haven, a cult headquartered on Long Island and dependent upon the "contributions" bilked from gullible women. When a $1 million estate is left dangling in front of the cult's collective eyes (it devolves onto Silver Haven only after the death of the heir, Upshaw [Lloyd Corrigan]), Jones and his men decide to hoodwink Wally Benton (Red Skelton), radio's premier detective the "Fox," into helping them get rid of Upshaw without their resorting to murder.

Jones visits the radio station just after Benton is told by his agent that, unless he dates the sponsor's daughter, his show will be dropped for lack of patronage. As Wally is engaged to Carol Lambert (Ann Rutherford), this is some rough sledding, but Jones cons Wally into believing him to be a potential sponsor, and they leave together to negotiate a contract. Wally soon discovers the truth and refuses to help the cult-master and his cronies. Jones has had Carol and Fran (Virginia Gray), the sponsor's daughter, kidnapped and brought to Silver Haven, however, and Wally and the two women are left to think things over.

Following a futile attempt at escape and a threat to his distaff companions, Wally agrees to cooperate. His master plan includes a fast-acting, untraceable poison, which he concocts himself. Key to the scheme is the switching of a harmless powder for the poison, but circumstances dash Wally's hopes. Poison in hand, a Jones accomplice boards Upshaw's plane, sits next to the unwary heir, and awaits the right

'Take your choice... help us make a corpse out of this man... or be a corpse!"

Original lobby card from the first — and many say the best — of the "Whistling" series. (Left to right) Connie, Red Skelton, and Ann Rutherford. (*Whistling in the Dark*)

opportunity to do him in. Back at Silver Haven, Wally has managed to rig the radio in the room into a two-way transmitting set and makes contact with his radio station; soon, he is broadcasting all the details of the sordid affair, hoping to warn Upshaw in the process.

Aghast upon hearing the broadcast, Jones returns to the mansion, but is disarmed by Wally and held as the police arrive. The ingenuity of the "Fox" has won the day again.

REVIEWS: "To the cheerfully swelling list of bright new film comedians you may add the rosy name of one Richard (Red) Skelton....

"...Contributing to [*Whistling in the Dark*'s] vivacity are Conrad Veidt as a cold and sibilant villain, Rags Ragland and Don Costello as a couple of thick-headed mugs, Ann Rutherford and Virginia Grey as competing and incidentally complicating pretties and Mr. Skelton, of course."

New York Times, 28 August 1941— Bosley Crowther

"...Although Skelton carries major burden of the picture, he gets major assistance from [Conrad] Veidt, [Ann] Rutherford, [Virginia] Grey, and 'Rags' Ragland. Writing trio of Robert MacGunigle [*sic*], Harry Clork and Albert Mannheimer freshens both dialog and action, and [Sylvan] Simon's direction is smartly paced throughout, with few dull passages."

Variety, 6 August 1941— Walt.

"Wally Benton, the comic hero of the story, is played by MGM's new discovery,

Red Skelton, whose rather crude efforts are made so much the less effective by his having to play opposite the polished villainy of Conrad Veidt as head of the racketeers in religion. Ann Rutherford and Virginia Grey do the best possible with two rather colourless parts...."

> *Monthly Film Bulletin*, Vol. 8, No. 94; 31 October 1941 — E.O.

NOTES AND QUOTES: This was Red Skelton's first starring film, as well as the first of three *Whistling* films (also *Whistling in Dixie*, 1942, and *Whistling in Brooklyn*, 1943; all three directed by S. Sylvan Simon) featuring Skelton, Ann Rutherford, and Rags Ragland as recurring characters. A fourth series film announced — *Whistling in Hollywood* — was never made. MGM had first filmed *Whistling in the Dark* in 1933, starring Ernest Truex, Una Merkel, and Edward Arnold. This earlier version was directed by Elliott Nugent (who was a contract writer for the 1941 feature) and Charles Riesner (after Nugent became ill).

Although *Contraband* had featured Connie playing opposite British comic Hay Petrie (who enjoyed a dual role), *Whistling in the Dark* was Veidt's first American comedy-thriller. The MGM scenario kept the Berlin-born actor at arms length from Skelton's hi-jinks, but it did allow him — as would *All Through the Night* — the opportunity to indulge in a bit of sardonic humor. One can only speculate whether — had Death not called on Veidt prematurely — the end of the Second World War might not have given him the chance to shine in films noir and comedies.

The Men in Her Life

Columbia Pictures — November 1941 — 89 minutes

CAST: Conrad Veidt *Stanislas Rosing*; Loretta Young *Lina Varasvina aka Polly Varley*; Dean Jagger *David Gibson*; Eugenie Leontovich *Marie*; John Shepperd *Sir Roger Chevis*; Otto Kruger *Victor*; Paul Baratoff *Manilov*; Billy Rayes *Nurdo*; Ludmilla Toretzka *Madame Tatiana Olenkova*; Tom Ladd *Lina's Dancing Partner*; Cherry Hardy *Mrs. Purdy*; Bonnie Dane *Rose at age 3*; Sandra Lee Richards *Rose at age 7*; with Ann Todd

CREDITS: *Producer* Gregory Ratoff; *Director* Gregory Ratoff; *Assistant Directors* Harold Godsoe and Henry Brill; *Dialogue Director* Serge Bertensson; *Screenplay* Frederick Kohner, Michael Wilson and Paul Trivers; *Based on the novel* Ballerina *by* Lady Eleanor Smith; *Directors of Photography* Harry Stradling, Arthur Martinelli; *Cinematographer* Philip Tannura; *Production Designer* Nicholai Remisoff; *Art Directors* Nicholai Remisoff, Ralph Berger; *Film Editor* Francis D. Lyon; *Set Dresser* Earl Wooden; *Costumes* Bridgehouse; *Miss Young's Costumes* Charles Le Maire; *Miss Young's Hats and Accessories* Lilly Dache; *Musical Director* David Raskin; *Orchestral Conductor* Constantine Bakaleinikoff; *Dance Director* Adolph Bolm; *Assistant to the Producer* Gordon Griffith; *Continuity* Barbara Keon

SYNOPSIS: As part of her long-range plan to become an internationally renowned ballerina, Polly Varley (Loretta Young) becomes a bareback rider in a circus. There, she is approached by Stanislas Rosing (Conrad Veidt) — himself a famed dancer — who is taken by the young woman's grace. Later, Polly shows up at Rosing's estate where she convinces the retired dancer to teach her his art. Rosing warns Polly that study with him will be long and arduous, and then changes her name to Lina Varsavina.

Several years later, Lina meets Sir Roger Chevis (John Shepperd) while out riding, and she becomes infatuated with him. Rosing warns her that a true artist has no time for romance. After further study, Lina is permitted to dance for Tatiana Olenkova (Ludmilla Toretzka), a retired prima ballerina. She dances magnificently and is soon set to debut in Paris, courtesy of Rosing. Her Parisian performance is likewise flawless, and, while celebrating af-

Lina (Loretta Young) may be exchanging glances with Sir Roger (John Shepperd), but she'll soon be exchanging vows with Stanislaus Rosing (Connie, right). (*The Men in Her Life*)

terwards with Rosing and friends, Lina is joined by Roger. The young ballerina is overjoyed when Roger declares his love for her and astonished to discover that Rosing, too, wishes her for his own. Lina agrees to marry Rosing, and their wedding is followed by an extensive tour throughout Europe, to end in New York.

En route to New York, Lina meets American David Gibson (Dean Jagger), a wealthy shipbuilder. While she is performing "The White Rose Dance," a special piece that her husband choreographed for her, Rosing dies suddenly. Feeling that their arduous schedule and the lengthy sea voyage contributed to Rosing's death, Lina turns to Gibson for sympathy. The American soon proposes, but Lina turns him down, preferring to embark on another

European tour. In London, she sees Roger, only to find that he has become engaged to another woman. Again, Lina turns to Gibson, and agrees to give up her career to be his wife.

Shortly after their honeymoon, however, Lina leaves Gibson, who has forbidden her to dance in a special memorial concert for Stanislas' Rosing. She heads for Paris where, unbeknownst to her husband, she gives birth to their daughter, Rose, before resuming her career. The public enthusiastically welcomes her back, and it is in London that Roger appears once again to reveal that he has broken his engagement in hope of winning Lina. Soon after, Gibson comes to London; learning that he has sired a daughter, he demands custody of Rose. In exchange for custody, he agrees to divorce Lina so that she may marry Roger. Lina agrees, but the very evening she has said her final goodbyes to her daughter, the coach carrying Lina to the theater overturns. She is injured and Roger is killed.

Alone in the world, Lina is shattered and her career begins to slip. After several years, she decides to perform again in New York, so that she might see her daughter. When she visits Gibson, though, he refuses to allow her to see Rose. Lina asks that Gibson bring Rose to the theater to see her dance, and he does. Lina dances magnificently and Rose asks to be taken back to meet the lovely ballerina. Backstage, Gibson is moved by Lina's love for their daughter, and the couple reconcile. Not long after, the family intact, Lina begins to teach Rose how to dance.

REVIEWS: "...Miss Young is not a good actress; she poses outrageously and her lack of resemblance to a dancer is almost laughable.... Conrad Veidt as the elder tutor and first husband is excellent for a brief time, and Eugenie Leontovich does nicely as a maid who fades in and out...."
New York Times, 12 December 1941—Bosley Crowther

"...[Loretta] Young, through a sterling performance, does much to maintain interest, aided by strong support from [Conrad] Veidt, [Dean] Jagger, [John] Shepperd, Otto Kruger and Eugenie Leontovich... Ratoff overcomes much of the story immobility through carrying various dramatic episodes to dramatic peaks, and then veering away to the next sequence without holding on [to] the climax...."
Variety, 5 November 1941—Walt.

"...Loretta Young has never done anything better than her performance here as Lina. Conrad Veidt gives a more than sympathetic understanding to the part of

Rosing and there is a first-class piece of characterization from Eugenie Leontovitch as Marie, the housekeeper...."
Monthly Film Bulletin, Vol. 9, No. 103; July 1942—E.R.

"This is essentially a woman's picture, with even-paced and slow action, telling of the struggle of a ballerina to attain success and then the conflict between her career and her love of three men.

"Critics may be expected to applaud the acting...."
Motion Picture Herald, 25 October 1941

NOTES AND QUOTES: Working titles: *Tonight Belongs to Us* and *Woman of Desire*.

The Men in Her Life is not technically a lost movie, as prints are known to exist in private collections; currently it is unavailable for public viewing.

The Men in Her Life was the first independent production of Gregory Ratoff and Harry Goetz. The picture was nominated for the Academy Award for best sound recording.

Note: Eugenie Leontovich was Mrs. Gregory Ratoff.

All Through the Night

Warner Bros.—23 January 1942—107 minutes
CAST: Conrad Veidt *Hall Ebbing*; Humphrey Bogart *Gloves Donahue*; Kaaren Verne *Leda Hamilton*; Jane Darwell *Mrs. Donahue*; Frank McHugh *Barney*; Peter Lorre *Pepi*; Judith Anderson *Madame*; William Demarest *Sunshine*; Jackie C. Gleason *Starchy*; Phil Silvers *Waiter*; Wally Ford *Spats Hunter*; Barton MacLane *Marty Callahan*; Edward Brophy *Joe Denning*; Martin Kosleck *Steindorff*; Jean Ames *Annabelle*; Ludwig Stossel *Mr. Miller*; Irene Seidner *Mrs. Miller*; James Burke *Forbes*; Ben Welden *Smitty*; Hans Schumm *Anton*; Charles Cane *Stage*; Frank Sully *Spence*; Sam McDaniel *Deacon*; Leo White, Billy Wayne *Chefs*; Al Eben *Pastry Chef*; Lottie Williams *Flower Woman*; Louis Arco, Wolfgang Zilzer, John Sinclair,

John Stark, Bob Kimball, Charles Sherlock *Gestapo*; Don Turner, Emory Parnell, Clancy Cooper *Policemen*; Gertrude Carr *Mrs. Novak*; Vera Lewis *Mrs. Fogarty*; Charles Wilson *Lieutenant*; Creighton Hale *Waiter*; Dick Elliott *Husband*; Mira McKinney *Wife*; Philip Van Zandt *Assistant Auctioneer*; Hans Joby, Egon Brecher *Watchmen*; Chester Clute *Hotel Clerk*; Charles Sullivan, Bob Perry, Main Bud Geary, Dutch Hendrian *Henchmen*; Lee Phelps *Jailer*; Eddy Chandler *Sergeant*; Henry Victor, Otto Reichow *Guards*; Frederick Vogeding *Doctor*; Carl Ottmar *Lichtig*; Chester Gan *Chinese Laundryman*; George Meeker, Roland Drew, Ray Montgomery, De Wolfe Hopper, Walter Brooke *Reporters*; with Regina Wallace, Leah Baird, Stuart Holmes, Mary Servoss

CREDITS: *Executive Producer* Hal B. Wallis; *Associate Producer* Jerry Wald; *Director* Vincent Sherman; *Assistant Director* Bill Kissell; *Screenplay* Leonard Spigelgass, Edwin Gilbert; *Story* Leonard Q. Ross, Leonard Spigelgass; *Director of Photography* Sid Hickox, ASC; *Special Effects* Edwin B. DuPar; *Art Director* Max Parker; *Film Editor* Rudi Fehr; *Gowns* Howard Shoup; *Music* Adolph Deutsch; *Musical Director* Leo F. Forbstein; *Orchestrations* Frank Perkins; *Sound* Oliver S. Garretson; *Make-Up* Perc Westmore

SONGS: "All Through the Night," words by Johnny Mercer, music by Arthur Schwartz; "Cheri, I Love You," words and music by Lillian Goodman.

SYNOPSIS: Gloves Donahue (Humphrey Bogart) is saddened by the slaying of Mr. Miller (Ludwig Stossel)—the baker of the only cheesecakes Gloves will eat—and suspicious of a certain Leda Hamilton (Kaaren Verne), a nightclub singer seen snooping around the Miller household just after the murder. Gloves heads over to the club—owned by gruff Marty Callahan (Barton MacLane)—where his interrogation of Leda is cut short by Pepi (Peter Lorre), her accompanist, who ushers her out the club door.

When one of Callahan's hired help is gunned down, Gloves realizes that Leda has been kidnapped. He traces the taxi in which she was abducted to a warehouse, but, in attempting to find the girl, Gloves'

buddy Sunshine (Jackie [C.] Gleason) is spirited away and Gloves is chased out by gunshots. Deducing that the warehouse is somehow affiliated with a nearby auction house, Gloves takes part in one of the auctions, just to get a closer look at things. He's spotted by Pepi and Leda, however, and knocked cold. He comes to, and is tied up next to Sunshine; Leda helps them free themselves, after which the two men make their escape.

Investigating the auction house, Gloves discovers that the enterprise is being run by German spies and Nazi sympathizers, and that Leda's father died in the concentration camp at Dachau. A gun battle ensues when Gloves tries to force Hall Ebbing (Conrad Veidt), the ringleader, to accompany him to the police station, and Gloves and the others make a run for it. Leda tells Gloves that Miller was forced to work for the Nazis against his will and that she, too, must do what they say, or they'll kill her father. When she's told about Dachau, however, she agrees to fight alongside Gloves and his friends.

When Leda tells her tale to the disbelieving police, Gloves determines that he's going to need help from other quarters, and makes contact with Callahan. Soon after, Gloves and Sunshine learn that the Nazis are targeting for destruction a ship docked at the Brooklyn Navy Yard. While Callahan's men are dealing with the spies, Gloves takes off after Ebbing, who has escaped in the melee and aims to blow the ship himself. Ebbing gets the drop on Gloves, though, and forces him to drive a small, explosive-laden boat directly at the ship. Gloves manages to swerve the boat sharply at the last minute, and Ebbing is knocked overboard.

The spies are rounded up, all charges are dropped, and peace once again reigns in New York.

REVIEWS: "…When the Warner gang swings into action, the Nazis don't stand a

Judith Anderson (center) has her doubts about Kaaren Verne (right). Connie (left) usually gave the benefit of the doubt to a pretty face. (*All Through the Night*)

chance, even with Conrad Veidt and Peter Lorre on their side....

"Mr. Bogart as the big shot plays with cool and calculated perfection. Mr. Veidt is equally effective as the brains of the Nazi ring....

"*All Through the Night* is ... a super-duper action picture — mostly duper, when you stop to think."

New York Times, 24 January 1942 — Bosley Crowther

"...Yarn highlights three bad boys, with Humphrey Bogart this time working on the side of the law, order and liberty in trying to clean up a nest of Nazi spies and fifth columnists. Two other toughies are sinister, soft-spoken Peter Lorre and immaculate, iron-fist-in-velvet-glove Nazi agent Veidt, both first rate. Locale is New York City."

Variety, 3 December 1941 — Mori

"A reasonably well produced and directed melodrama. Humphrey Bogart is as good as usual, but there is nothing outstanding in the film."

Monthly Film Bulletin, Vol. 9, No. 103; July 1942

NOTES AND QUOTES: Connie was borrowed from MGM for the part of Ebbing.

Nazi Agent

MGM — Released March 1942 — 82 minutes

CAST: Conrad Veidt *Otto Becker/Baron Hugo Von Detner*; Ann Ayars *Kaaren De Relle*; Frank Reicher *Fritz*; Dorothy Tree *Miss Harper*; Ivan Simpson *Professor Sterling*; William Tannen *Ludwig*; Martin Kosleck *Kurt Richten*; Martin Lawrence *Joe Aiello*; Sidney Blackmer *Arnold Milbar aka Frederick Williams*; Moroni Olsen *Brenner*; Pierre Watkin *Grover Blaine McHenry*; Margaret Bert *Mrs. Dennis*; Mark Daniels, Robert Davis *Taxi Drivers*; Harry B. Stafford *Elderly Man*; Roger Moore *Messenger*; Stuart Crawford *Radio Commentator's Voice*; Hal Cooke *Clerk*; George Noisom *Bellboy*; Roland Varno *Bauer*; William Norton *Bailer Cigar Clerk*; Tim Ryan *Officer*; Tom Stevenson *Headwaiter*; Christian Rub *Mohr*; Hermine Sterler *Mrs. Mohr*; Jeff York *Keeler*; Jessie Arnold *Landlady*; Cliff Danielson *Youth*; James Millican *Operator*; Philip Van Zandt, George Magrill *Thugs*; Brick Sullivan *Radio Operator*; Joe Yule *Barney*; Bernadene Hayes *Rosie*; Art Belasco, Charles Sherlock *Detectives*; William Post, Jr. *Harry's Voice*; Clyde Courtright *Doorman*; Polly Bailey *Overweight Woman*; Joe Gilbert *Sub-radio Person*; Walter Byron *Officer*; Edward Hearn, Jack Daley, Drew Demorest, Wilbur Mack *Reporters*; Baldwin Cooke *Waiter*; Ray Teal *Officer Graves*; Frank Marlowe, Ernie Alexander, Duke York *Sailors*; Russell Simpson, Robert Homans *Captains*; Roy Barcroft *Chief Petty Officer*; Barbara Bedford

CREDITS: *Producer* Irving Asher; *Director* Jules Dassin; *Asst. Director* Tom Andre; *Screenplay* Paul Gangelin and John Meehan, Jr; *Based on an idea by* Lothar Mendes; *Director of Photography* Harry Stradling, ASC; *Art Director* Cedric Gibbons; *Associate Art Director* Stan Rogers; *Film Editor* Frank E. Hull; *Set Decorations* Edwin B. Willis; *Associate Set Decorator* Richard Pefferle; *Gowns* Howard Shoup; *Musical Score* Lennie Hayton; *Recording Director* Douglas Shearer; *Miss Ayars' Hair Styles* Sydney Guilaroff; *Make-Up* Jack Dawn

SYNOPSIS: Kindly Otto Becker (Conrad Veidt), bookseller and philatelist, originally fled from Germany and entered the United States on forged documentation. Holding this over his head — along with the threat of attendant deportation — is Otto's identical twin brother, Baron Hugo Von Detner (Conrad Veidt), who uses this leverage to take over Otto's bookshop as a base for information gathering on the part of Nazi fifth columnists. Otto is permitted to stay on as figurehead at the shop, but his every move is carefully watched by his shop assistant, Miss Harper (Dorothy Tree), one of Von Detner's accomplices. Despite this, he gets a message asking for help off to his old friend Professor Jim Sterling (Ivan Simpson).

Sterling is killed in a bogus car crash and Von Detner, aware of his brother's attempt to notify the authorities, comes to the bookstore to kill Otto. In the struggle between the siblings, a pistol discharges and the baron falls dead. Thinking quickly, Otto shaves off his mustache and beard, dons his twin's clothing and monocle, and — for all intents and purposes — *becomes* Baron Von Detner, the German consul of State City. He succeeds in fooling Miss Harper and the other Nazis waiting below, and it is Hugo's cadaver which is tossed overboard into the sea soon after.

Otto works frantically at familiarizing himself with his brother's hotel rooms, office, staff, contacts and duties. He is helped immeasurably by his valet, Fritz (Frank Reicher), who recognizes Otto by a scar on his shoulder. "From the earliest days," the loyal servant confesses to the disguised Becker, "I belonged with you." Otto manages to relay information on German saboteurs to the police without arousing the suspicion of either Herr Brenner (Pierre Watkin), the local Gestapo chief, or Kurt Richten (Martin Kosleck), Von Detner's secretary. Otto becomes attracted to Mlle. Kaaren De Relle (Ann Ayars); the lovely young woman is clearly acting for the Nazis out of duress. Without knowing of the change in the "baron's" identity, Kaaren soon is moved by what she perceives to be a kind, almost loving streak in the consul.

Working together, Otto and Kaaren

Salute to Courage— aka *Nazi Agent*— was Connie's last dual role.

discover that the Nazis have planted a time bomb aboard a ship that is due to cross through the Panama Canal. The device is set to explode when the ship is in the canal, thus crippling allied naval movement for months to come. A message is sent out to the police and the ship is abandoned while at sea; the Panama Canal has been saved. By this time, the Nazis have determined that it was the baron who was unceremoniously buried at sea, and that Otto Becker has been fouling up their covert operations. Although the police round up the rest of the gang, Kurt Richten holds the trump card: he threatens to reveal Kaaren De Relle's involvement in the spy ring. Aghast, Otto offers himself in trade for the young woman, and Richten accepts.

Without revealing his true identity to Kaaren — or to the U.S. authorities— Otto allows himself to be deported. As the ship carries him past the Statue of Liberty, Becker — the stalwart nationalized American citizen — is moved when he considers the worth of his sacrifice in the fight against Nazi oppression.

REVIEWS: "…A good, tight script, subdued direction….

"It is a simple, straightaway story, told without noise or flourish and nicely performed not only by Mr. Veidt but by everyone in the cast. Keep your hands gloved or pocketed when you go see it, else your fingernails will go."

> *New York Times*, 13 June
> 1942 — Bosley Crowther

"…Veidt gives a fine performance and those around him are exceptionally well cast for the roles they essay…"

> *Variety*, 21 January 1942 —
> Char. (as *Salute to Courage*)

"The plot is exciting and suspense is well sustained throughout, often by the use of trivial details like a bird's song or a glass of milk. Conrad Veidt gives a reserved, dignified performance and maintains the dual role of the twins with practiced ease. Ann Ayars has more than dark good looks to commend her, she has poise and an attractive and definite personality."

> *Monthly Film Bulletin*,
> Vol. 9, No. 103; July 1942

NOTES AND QUOTES: In an interview with the *New York Herald Tribune*'s Charles Darnton (1 February 1942), Connie posited that: "It is the good brother in *Out of the Past* who is the more important to me, especially at this time, when the need of good in the world is so great. We are all poor now inside, with so much that we valued taken out of us, but there will always be love." The actor was using the film's tentative release title; in fact, it had initially borne the working title *House of Spies* and wasn't officially retagged *Nazi Agent* until advance paper hit billboards and theater lobbies the following month. Compounding the felony, the film was reviewed by *Variety* and several other trade papers as *Salute to Courage*.

Veidt had, of course, first done the twin brother business for Karl Grune in *Die Brüder Schellenberg* in 1925-26. Nonetheless, the double role in *Nazi Agent* was a welcome variation on the old tune the actor had been whistling for some time in his films. With few exceptions, the 40s had seen the virulent anti–Nazi playing only Nazis (or ersatz Nazis), and, of the two pictures that were left to him before his untimely death, *Casablanca* would have him in uniform once again. Connie may have rationalized that his catalogue of haughty officers, spies and saboteurs (all of whom were ultimately foiled by the forces of righteousness) offered concerned ticket buyers a look at what would be the inevitable disposition of the Third Reich, and so found some solace in the seemingly endless procession of jackbooted clones. Then again, he might have regarded the rut into which he had fallen as either an irony of cosmic proportion, or a necessary evil. Still, he fared better than costar Martin Kosleck, a Russian character man who was not only frequently cast as a Nazi, but also had something of a second career impersonating Josef Goebbels!

Nazi Agent was the first feature film to be directed by Jules Dassin, a Connecticut-born jack-of-many-trades (including acting and scripting radio shows) who ventured out to Hollywood in 1940. Dassin's forte proved to be films noir (including *Brute Force* [1947] and the classic *The Naked City* [1950]), but these ground to a halt when the director fell afoul of the House Un-American Activities Committee. Dassin fled to France where, following the critically acclaimed *Rififi* (1955), he headed to Greece. There he married Athens-born Melina Mercouri and repeatedly scored bull's-eyes with her in such fare as *Never on Sunday* (1960) and *Topkapi* (1964). Dassin died in 1995.

Casablanca

Warner Bros.— 25 November 1942 (NY Premiere)— 99 minutes

CAST: Conrad Veidt *Major Heinrich Strasser*; Humphrey Bogart *Rick Blaine*; Ingrid Bergman *Ilsa Lund*; Paul Henreid *Victor Laszlo*; Claude Rains *Captain Louis Renault*; Sydney Greenstreet *Señor Ferrari*; Peter Lorre *Ugarte*; S.Z. Sakall *Carl*; Madeleine LeBeau *Yvonne*; Dooley Wilson *Sam*; Joy Page *Annina Brandel*; John Qualen *Berger*; Leonid Kinsky *Sascha*; Helmut Dantine *Jan Brandel*; Curt Bois *Dark European*; Marcel Dalio *Croupier*; Corinna Mura *Andreya*; Ludwig Stossel *Mr. Leuchtag*; Ilka Grüning *Mrs. Leuchtag*; Charles La Torre *Señor Martínez*; Frank Puglia *Arab Vendor*; Dan Seymour *Abdul*; Jean Del Val *Police Officer*; Jamiel Hasson *Muezzin*; Martín Garralaga *Headwaiter*; Hans Twardowski, Henry Rowland *German Officers*; Michael Mark *Vendor*; Olaf Hytten *Prosperous Man*; Leon Belasco *Dealer*; Georges Renavent, Louis Mercier *Conspirators*; Monte Blue, George Carlton *Americans*; Lou Marcelle *Narrator*

CREDITS: *Producer* Hal Wallis; *Director* Michael Curtiz; *Dialogue Director* Hugh MacMullan; *Asst. Director* Lee Katz; *Screenplay* Julius J. Epstein, Philip G. Epstein, Howard Koch; *based on the play* Everybody Goes to Rick's *[unproduced]* by Murray Burnett *and* Joan Alison; *Photographed by* Arthur Edeson; *Montage* Don Siegel, James Leicester; *Director of Special Effects* Lawrence Butler; *Special Effects* Willard Van Enger; *Art Director* Carl Jules Weyl; *Film Editor* Owen Marks; *Set Decorations* George James Hopkins; *Gowns* Orry-Kelly; *Musical Director* Leo F. Forbstein; *Musical Score* Max Steiner; *Orchestral Arrangements* Hugo Friedhofer; *Sound* Francis J. Scheid; *Make-up* Perc Westmore; *Technical Advisor* Robert Aisner; *Unit Manager* Al Alleborn

MUSICAL SELECTIONS: "Avalon," music by Al Jolson and Vincent Rose; "You Must Have Been a Beautiful Baby," music by Harry Warren; "Baby Face," music by Harry Askt; "The Very Thought of You," music by Ray Noble; "One Hour with You," music by Richard A. Whiting and Oscar Straus

SONGS: "Knock on Wood," music by M.K. Jerome, lyrics by Jack Scholl; "It Had to Be You," music by Isham Jones, lyrics by Gus Kahn; "That's Why They Call Me 'Shine,'" music by Ford Dabney, lyrics by Cecil Mack; "As Time Goes By," music and lyrics by Herman Hudfeld; "Tango della rose," music and lyrics by Schreier Bottero; "La Marseillaise," music and lyrics by Claude Joseph Rouget de Lisle; "Die Wacht Am Rhein," music by Karl Wilhelm, lyrics by Max Schneckenburger

SYNOPSIS: Everybody comes to the Café Americain, Casablanca's busiest nightspot, but when beautiful Ilsa Lund (Ingrid Bergman) walks in one evening, owner Rick Blaine (Humphrey Bogart) is beside himself. He and Ilsa were briefly lovers in Paris, just before the Nazi occupation. Although they had planned to flee the country together, a last-minute farewell letter left Rick confused and bitter at the railway station.

Some time has passed since then, and the big news at Rick's place is that two German couriers have been found murdered, their letters of transit — unimpeachable documents assuring safe passage to the bearers — stolen. The news doesn't faze the cynical Rick, but amuses Captain Louis Renault (Claude Rains), Vichy police chief and frequenter of the café. Louis is certain that Victor Laszlo (Paul Henreid), renowned anti–Nazi freedom fighter, is hoping to use those letters of transit to escape from Casablanca.

Also aware of Laszlo's intentions is Gestapo Major Heinrich Strasser (Conrad Veidt), whose sudden arrival on the scene can only mean that Laszlo is not to leave Casablanca alive. Fearing this, Ilsa appeals to Rick to help her get her hands on the letters; she confesses to the stunned Amer-

Two of the screen's undisputed masters of suave villainy: Claude Rains (left) and Connie. (*Casablanca*)

ican that Laszlo is her husband. She ran away from Rick in Paris only because she received word that Laszlo, whom she thought a victim of the Nazis, was still alive. In exchange for Rick's help, Ilsa will stay on in Casablanca with her ex-lover.

Cognizant of Rick's peculiar loyalties, Major Strasser has Renault turn up the heat officially; Louis orders the café closed for illegal gambling. If anything, this only pushes Rick into action all the more quickly. Arranging to sell the place to Signor Ferrari

(Sydney Greenstreet), a black market entrepreneur, Rick offers the documents to the Laszlos and takes them to a waiting plane.

When Major Strasser storms the airport and attempts to detain the couple, he is shot by Rick. A carload of Gestapo goons and Vichy policemen pulls up almost immediately, but, after a tense moment, Louis chooses to side with the angels and sends the Axis agents scurrying off in the wrong direction. Laszlo and Ilsa head for the freedom of Lisbon, and Rick and Louis stroll together into an uncertain future.

REVIEWS: "…The performances of the actors are all of the first order, but especially those of Mr. Bogart and Miss Bergman…. Mr. Veidt plays again a Nazi officer with cold and implacable resolve….

"…*Casablanca* is one of the year's most exciting and trenchant films. It certainly won't make Vichy happy — but that's just another point for it."

New York Times, 27 November 1942 — Bosley Crowther

"*Casablanca* will take the b.o.'s of America just as swiftly and certainly as the AEF took North Africa….

"Superb is the lineup of lesser players … [including] Conrad Veidt, as the usual German officer…."

"…[There are a] variety of moods, action, suspense, comedy and drama that makes *Casablanca* an A-1 entry at the b.o."

Variety, 2 December 1942

NOTES AND QUOTES: First choice for the role of *Captain* Strasser had been Otto Preminger, who was tested on the 27 April 1942. Veidt was subsequently awarded the part without a screen test, receiving a five-week guarantee at $5000 a week.

In an interview held with a studio publicist (as quoted by Aljean Harmetz. *Round Up the Usual Suspects: The Making of Casablanca — Bogart, Bergman, and World War II*. New York: Hyperion, 1992; p. 152) during production, Veidt left no

doubt as to his feeling regarding Strasser in particular and Nazis in general:

"This role epitomizes the cruelty and the criminal instincts and murderous trickery of the typical Nazi. I know this man well. He is the reason I gave up Germany many years ago. He is a man who turned fanatic and betrayed his friends, his homeland, and himself in his lust to be somebody and get something for nothing."

A 1943 *Hollywood Reporter* item noted how Warners was planning a sequel to *Casablanca*. *Brazzaville* was to be set in the African headquarters of the Free French, and was to see Bogart reprise his role as Rick Blaine; Sydney Greenstreet and Geraldine Fitzgerald were to costar.

Above Suspicion

M-G-M — 21 May 1943 — 91 minutes
CAST: Conrad Veidt *Hassert Seidel*; Joan Crawford *Frances Myles, aka Mrs. Edward Smith*; Fred MacMurray *Richard Myles, aka Edward Smith*; Basil Rathbone *Count Sig von Aschenhausen*; Reginald Owen *Dr. Mespelbrunn*; Richard Ainley *Peter Galt*; Cecile Cunningham *Countess von Aschenhausen*; Ann Shoemaker *Aunt Ellen*; Sara Haden *Aunt Hattie*; Felix Bressart *Mr. Werner*; Bruce Lester *Thornley*; Johanna Hofer *Frau Kleist*; Lotta Palfi *Ottilie*; Alex Papana *Man in Paris*; Rex Williams *Gestapo Leader*; Hans von Morhart *Schmidt*; William Yetter *Hauptman*; Steven Geray *Anton*; William "Wee Willie" Davis *Hans*; Lisa Golm *Frau Schultz*; Ludwig Stossel *Herr Schultz*; Ivan Simpson, Arthur Shields *Porters*; Henry Glynn *Chauffeur*; Eily Malyon *Manageress*; Matthew Boulton *Constable Jones*; Marcelle Corday *Maid*; Frank Lackteen *Arab Vendor*; Charles de-Ravenne *Chasseur*; Andre Charlot *Café Manager*; Frank Arnold *Poet*; George Davis *Proprietor*; Jack Chefe Coatroom Attendant; Felix Basche *Guide*; Edit Angold, Irene Seidner *German Women*; Lisl Valetti *Nazi Girl*; Paul Weigel *Elderly Man*; Otto Reichow *Gestapo Voice/Gestapo in Opera Box*; Giselle Werbiseck *Fat Woman*; Frank Reicher *Col. Gerold*; Peter Seal, Nicholas Vehr *Gerold's Aides*; Henry Victor *German Officer*; Egon Brecher *Gestapo Official*;

Walter O. Stahl *Policeman*; John Rice, Hans Furberg, Albert D'Arno, Erno Verebes, Kurt Newman, Henry Guttman *Gestapo*; Steven Muller, Frank Brand, Frederick Bauer *German Boys*; Helen Boice *Fat Dowager*; Max Willenz *Waiter*; Heather Thatcher, Jean Prescott *English Girls*; Sven-Hugo Borg, Walter Bonn, Hans Schumm *German Guards*; Hans Wollenberger *Cook*; Philip Van Zandt *Kurt*; Lionel Royce *Officer at Border*; Joseph deVillard *Italian Sentry*; Gretl Dupont *Barmaid*

CREDITS: *Producer* Victor Saville; *Associate Producer* Leon Gordon; *Director* Richard Thorpe; *Assistant Director* Bert Spurlin; *Screenplay* Keith Winter, Melville Baker, and Patricia Coleman; *Contract Writer* Leonard Lee; *Based on the novel* Above Suspicion *by* Helen McInnes; *Director of Photography* Robert Planck, ASC; *Special Effects* Warren Newcombe; *Art Director* Cedric Gibbons: *Associate Art Director* Randall Duell; *Film Editors* George Hively, James Newcom; *Set Decorations* Edwin B. Willis; *Associate Set Decorator* Hugh Hunt; *Costume Supervision* Irene; *Men's Costumes* Gile Steele; *Music Score* Bronislau Kaper; *Recording Director* Douglas Shearer; *Make-Up* Jack Dawn; *Technical Advisor* Felix Bernstein

MUSIC: Selections from *Piano Concerto No. 1* by Franz Liszt

SONGS: "My Love Is Like a Red, Red Rose," words by Robert Burns, music traditional; "Bird in a Gilded Cage," words by Arthur J. Lamb, music by Harry Von Tilzer

SYNOPSIS: Americans Richard Myles (Fred MacMurray) and his wife, Frances (Joan Crawford), are honeymooning incognito (as Mr. And Mrs. Edward Smith) in England. Richard is approached by an old classmate, now working for the Foreign Office, who asks that he and Frances meet up with a contact in southern Germany to obtain information on a new mine the Germans have invented. They

Above Suspicion was Joan Crawford's swan song at MGM. Tragically, it was Conrad Veidt's last film anywhere.

agree and head for Paris, where Frances buys a hat with a rose, which is to serve as a signal to their contact.

Following a series of involved maneuvers designed to keep them on track and out of harm's way, the couple finally arrive in Salzburg, where Hassert Seidel (Conrad Veidt), a local guide, recommends a certain boarding house to them. Thence, it is on to a Liszt concert, where a Nazi officer is assassinated and Colonel Sig von Aschenhausen (Basil Rathbone), *another* old classmate of Richard's saves them — and their new friend, Thornley (Bruce Lester)—from a Nazi interrogation. All three repair to Sig's mother's estate, where Thornley admits to killing the Nazi as revenge for the torture and death of Thornley's Austrian girlfriend.

Then, the next day, the couple proceeds to a shop in Pertisau, and from the shop to the home of a Dr. Mespelbrunn (Reginald Owen). At the doctor's home, they encounter Sig, who—with his Nazi accomplices—is holding Mespelbrunn captive in his own home. Richard and Frances make their escape into a nearby wood, where they are aided by Hassert Seidel. Seidel helps the couple free Maspelbrunn, and the four make for Innsbruck. The doctor provides Richard with the data on the mine, and Seidel arranges for the Americans to receive disguises and false passports with which to make their escape from a Mr. and Mrs. Schulz. The Gestapo discover the passport photo negatives when they arrest the Schulzes, however, and Frances is arrested before she can re-

unite with her husband. Still, she has managed to have Thornley inform her husband about her arrest, and the men seek out Seidel once again.

That night, Thornley, Richard and Seidel shoot their way into Gestapo headquarters, in order to rescue Frances. Stealing Nazi uniforms and appropriating a command car, they make their escape; Thornley is killed in the process, however. Keeping Frances out of sight, Richard and Seidel drive across the border and into freedom.

REVIEWS: "…The late Conrad Veidt must have enjoyed this sabbatical from his portraits of thin-lipped villainy; here he plays a sort of underground Robin Hood who bobs up in various guises just when the professor needs him most."

New York Times, 6 August 1943 — T.S.

"Both MacMurray and Miss Crawford competently handle their roles, despite drawbacks of script material. The late Conrad Veidt clicks solidly in major supporting spot, along with brief appearances of Basil Rathbone as Gestapo leader. … Richard Thorpe's direction is standard, but he's obviously handicapped by story material provided."

Variety, 28 April 1943 — Walt.

NOTES AND QUOTES: Connie must have been grateful to be supplanted by Basil Rathbone in what had become an evitable role for him.

Conrad Veidt died on 3 April 1943. This was his last film.

Appendix

The following films have been listed in one source or another as featuring Conrad Veidt. Other sources, however, do NOT list Connie as a participant. Hence, this is the inevitable "gray area" that researchers dread.

Der Weg des Todes (*The Road of Death*)— Deutsche Bioscop GmbH, Berlin, 1916; Filmed at Bioscop-Atelier, Neubabelsberg; *Zensur*: January 1917 — 4 Acts, 1538 meters; *Nachzensur*: 21 January 1921— 4 Acts, 1545 meters; Forbidden to adolescents; 1921 rerelease entitled ***Weg des Todes***

CAST: Conrad Veidt ???; Maria Carmi *Maria*; Carl de Vogt *Rolf*; Ewald Brückner *the Count*; Helene Brahm, *the Countess, his Mother*

CREDITS: *Director* Robert Reinert (aka Robt. Dinesen); *Scenario* Robert Reinert; *Set Design* Robert A. Dietrich

SYNOPSIS: The count (Ewald Brückner), happily married to his wife, Maria (Maria Carmi), is followed by a mysterious stranger. Uneasy and looking to be left in peace, the couple move into an old castle, complete with dungeons. Nonetheless, the stranger has followed them; he finally appears at a feast and forces Maria to have an assignation with him. Maria recognizes the stranger to be Rolf (Carl de Vogt), her lover from her former life. (Ten years earlier, before meeting and marrying the count, she

was a prostitute.) She lures Rolf to the castle and locks him up in one of the dungeons. Her guilty conscience drives her to reveal everything to her husband. He wants to forgive her, but she inhales poison gas, frees Rolf, and expires on the castle steps.

REVIEWS: "Fantastic tale with Maria Carmi... Plot very good, photography and settings excellent."

Paimanns Filmliste (Vienna),
No. 76; 13–19 August 1917

NOTES AND QUOTES: Virtually every Veidt filmography published to date has the actor playing Rolf in this picture. An extant advertisement for the film, however, cites Carl de Vogt in this role and does not even mention Connie's name. As there is no way (currently) to cross-check whether the advertisement contained an error (not unheard-of, even today), or whether there might have been two characters with the same name (father/son, perhaps?) in the scenario, I cannot ascertain that *Der Weg des Todes* is a genuine "Conrad Veidt film."

CineGraph has the title leading off its published filmography, thus stating by position, if not by number, that *Todes* is the earliest of the Veidt cinematic canon. If one leans this way, one might possibly theorize that Conrad Veidt was not yet enough of a name to merit inclusion in the advertisement. Herbert Holba's list (in the Summer 1975 *Focus on Film*) cites *Wenn Tote sprechen* as a *possibility* and posits *Der Weg des*

Modernes Theater

Breite Str. 21   Köln   Tel. A 7121

Jeder staunt

über das

fabelhafte Spiel

von

Maria Carmi

und

Carl de Vogt

dem aufgehenden Stern der Deutschen Bioskop
(früher am Schauspielhaus in Köln)

in dem Sensations=Schlager

Der

Weg des Todes

Das Drama einer unglücklichen Frau

in 4 Akten

von Robert Reinert.

Hauptdarsteller:

Der Graf _ _ _ _ _ _ _ _ _ _ _ _ _ _ _ _ Ewald Brückner
Maria _ _ _ _ _ _ _ _ _ _ _ _ _ _ Maria Carmi
Die Gräfin, seine Mutter _ _ _ _ _ _ _ Helene Brahm
Rolf _ _ _ _ _ _ _ _ _ _ _ _ _ _ _ Carl de Vogt

Der letzte und beste Carmi-Schlager
dieser Saison.

Jeder muß lachen über

Albert Paulig

in

Der Freund des Fürsten

Lustspielschlager in   3 Akten   von Georg Kaiser

Personen:

Edda, Prinzessin von Waldenheim (als Gräfin
  Wildheim reisend) _ _ _ _ _ _ _ _ _ _ Sacy von Blondel
Else, Baronesse von Kröner, ihre Freundin—Maria Winterfeld
Bodo IX., Fürst von Helmstadt (als Freiherr
  von Bruck reisend) _ _ _ _ _ _ _ _ Einar Bruun
Fritz Haarich, Damenfriseur _ _ _ _ _ _ *   *

Albert Paulig der beliebte Lustspieldarsteller.

Beginn der Vorstellungen 3 Uhr nachm.

Kassenöffnung ¼ Stunde vorher.

No sign of Conrad Veidt. Or Konrad Veidt. Or Conrad Veith. Or... (Possibilities)

Todes (with Connie as Rolf) in the number 2 spot of definite titles. The newspaper ads reproduced in this volume can at least refute Holba's quarter-century-old theory about *Tote*, but they can do little except cause greater uncertainty about *Todes*. The only other graphic found anywhere on *Todes* is the photograph on page 17 of Wolfgang Jackson's *Conrad Veidt: Lebensbilder,* but, as misidentification of movie stills is a more commonplace occurrence than are sins of omission in movie ads, the scrupulous researcher can no longer accept the photo with its attribution at face value.

Some readers may feel that relegating *Der Weg des Todes* to this appendix on the basis of one newspaper ad is a case of overreacting, but I must to my own self be true. That said, allow me to state that I positively welcome evidence that Herr Veidt did, in fact, grace the screen in *Der Weg des Todes* (or any of these films).

Die Claudi vom Geiserhof—Messter-Film GmbH, Berlin—1917 (per Gerhard Lamprecht, a *Gebirgs-Drama*/Drama of the Highlands; Filmed at Messter-Film-Atelier, Blücherstrasse 32; Originally distributed by Hansa-Film-Verleih GmbH; *Nachzensur*: upon rerelease by Universum-Film-Verleih GmbH, Berlin—15 March 1921—4 Acts, 1387 meters; Forbidden to adolescents

CAST: Conrad Veidt; Henny Porten; Eduard von Winterstein; Paul Hartmann; Lupu Pick; Josef Klein

CREDITS: *Producer* Oskar Messter; *Director* Rudolf Biebrach

The program for *Die Claudi vom Geiserhof* is on file in the Deutsches Filminstitut; the cast list printed therein does not include Veidt.

Die Serenyi— Berliner Film-Manufaktur GmbH, Berlin, 1918; *Nachzensur*: 19 September 1921— 4 Acts, 1115 meters; Forbidden to adolescents

CAST: Conrad Veidt; Lya Mara; Erich Kaiser-Titz

CREDITS: *Director* H. Fredall (Alfred Halm); *Scenario* Otto Erich Hartleben

NOTES AND QUOTES:

"*The Serenyi* (Berliner Film-Manufaktur). Another literary film, with the theme adapted by H. Fredall from Otto Erich Hartleben. It concerns the fate of a little girl, who remains faithful until the final act, despite being suspected of having betrayed her lover. Here we have the choir singer who almost perishes in her quest to become a prima donna [in the world of operetta]. One is reminded of the scandal in the late 80s [1880s!], caused by a certain renowned opera singer, whose fate may well have inspired Hartleben.

Fredell adapted this story to the screen quite well, and directed it himself. Fredell — which is an alias for a well-known theatrical personality — has a style of his own, which is tasteful while still appealing to a broad audience. Lya Mara plays the leading role, with the very best of results. This young artist has a good appearance and knows how to use her excellent dramatic talents. She also has a great supporting cast: Kaiser-Titz and Lupu Pick.

The audience showed unusual empathy."
Der Kinematograph (Düsseldorf),
April 1918

While Connie is not mentioned by name in the review, it may be argued that this means only that he did not *star* in the picture.

Afterword

by Henry Nicolella

Conrad Veidt:
The Last Romantic

It's sad that most moviegoers best remember Conrad Veidt for one of his least interesting roles, the Nazi major in that talkiest of classics, *Casablanca*. The more complex Nazi character Veidt had played in *Escape* had given way to the snarling *Schweinhund* that was the staple of wartime propaganda. The Nazis had courted Veidt and tried to keep him in Germany, but I wonder how clearly they grasped the essence of his movie persona, the tragic romanticism that Goebbels and company would surely have denounced as decadent and defeatist had they been astute enough to recognize it.

Superficially, Veidt exuded the same continental charm as Charles Boyer, Hans Albers or Louis Jouvet — perhaps with a bit of the world-weariness of a Claude Rains thrown in. With Veidt, however, there was an edge of sadness that often cast its melancholy shadow over his performances. "Women fight for Conrad Veidt!" the publicity department proclaimed, but one need only look at his films to see that he seldom got the girl. And if he did, she died.

Or he died. The only major star with a worse track record was Lon Chaney, who also shared with Veidt a penchant for playing dual roles. Of course Chaney always played the perpetual outsider: the criminal or misfit who was usually short an appendage (or two). Veidt was his polar opposite: aristocratic, intellectual, overbearingly handsome; no matter whether soldier, poet or king, he was a sophisticate, assured of and confident in his place in society. Nonetheless, for all their talents, one had the feeling that his characters would not live happily ever after, that their best efforts were futile and that they perhaps knew it.

Veidt could convey that fatalism with a tentative pause, a slight lowering of his voice, a turn of the head. At the end of *Nju*, right after his lover's suicide, he finds the impromptu poem he had written to her among the floor sweepings her landlady is discarding: "I must cut short the words of love." The jest has turned prophetic. Veidt's expression reflects not just sadness and guilt, but also the knowledge that the affair couldn't have ended any other way. It appears as if Baron von Kempelen in *Le Joueur d'Échecs* sacrifices his life so that the lovers may escape, but he's really dying for

319

the woman he loves, a woman long dead. The Wandering Jew must spend century after weary century looking for a redemptive human love that he knows he will never find. In *Das indische Grabmal*, Veidt's Ayan plans a grim fate for his unfaithful wife, but ends up punishing himself when he causes her death. He plays the ruthless maharajah not as a barbarian, but as a victim of his own passion.

As Erik the magician, Veidt commits the perfect crime to win Mary Philbin away from his rival, but then finds he cannot deprive her of the man she really loves. Erik's last, lingering glance at her is heartbreaking. Then, having faithfully played the part that was expected of him, he pronounces the performance ended, and takes his own life. Even his profoundly evil Cesare Borgia perishes for a hopeless — albeit perverse — love. In a moment that is both chilling and pathetic, the fallen Cesare extends his dying hand to the sister who despises him and, in that simple gesture, Veidt gives us a sense of the Heathclifflike obsession that has consumed Borgia so completely. Had Milton's *Paradise Lost* been filmed, Veidt would have made a magnificent Satan, enjoined in a cosmic battle he knows he cannot win and mindful of all that he has lost as a fallen angel, but determined to see the struggle through.

Satanic is certainly the element horror fans look for in Veidt's movies, but this interest distorts his career. He made over 100 pictures but only a few could be described as horror. This misplaced emphasis — yet another thing he has in common with Chaney — stems from his role in *Das Cabinet des Dr. Caligari*, the "first" horror movie, considered to be a classic by genre mavens and film scholars, and a horror by everyone else. Veidt's appearance certainly lent itself to the macabre: his formidable height, thin frame, and domelike forehead, looming over the long features that sometimes gave his face a cadaverous cast (and

which was lost in later years when his face became fuller). His demeanor could even lend an undertone of menace to his courtly bearing, as when he hovers over Elizabeth Bergner's hand (in *Nju*) like some great eagle, perched for the final swoop down onto its prey.

His voice did not seem really suitable for a Gothic fiend, though: sometimes soft and silky, other times pitched a bit higher than one would expect. Perhaps it was no accident that his only horror films were in the silent era. But those eyes…! They could glare imperiously with enough ice to sink the Titanic, or they could almost liquefy into pools of ambiguous charm. The paranoid madness of Ivan the Terrible was conjured up merely by widening those eyes, a simple feat, yet far more effective than all the accompanying Expressionist gestures. While the rest of his face was transfixed by a monstrous grin, Veidt's eyes were his foremost means of expression in *The Man Who Laughs*, and he used them to achieve a poignancy that exceeded even that of Chaney's Quasimodo.

Too, they suggested a heartrending isolation in the most romantic of his horror films, *Der Student von Prag*. The picture's more bizarre scenes fade before the memory of the softness in Balduin's eyes when he first meets the countess, or that hopeless yearning as she rides off. One recalls the resigned disappointment on his face, as he realizes how pitiful are the flowers he has brought to his lady, compared with the huge bouquet offered by her rich suitor. Or that fleeting look of regret when he thinks Scapinelli is going to demand his only precious possession — his dueling sword — in exchange for his services. The face of Balduin's doppelgänger betrays no emotion whatsoever, but his eyes stare out as though this walking reflection knows something too terrible to comprehend.

Veidt's characters often met their pre-

Connie as the Baron de Kempelen; portrait by the renowned photographer Limot. *Courtesy André Limot.*

surable, as though the Black Monk knows that his time will be brief. Veidt is superb as Rasputin weeps while listening to a sentimental ballad sung by the man who will kill him; it's a moment of self recognition as Rasputin recognizes an unattainable love beyond all his power and vices.

"The Jew Mathias is dead," the inquisitor solemnly intoned as the Wandering Jew finally gave up his spirit in a world in which he had never really found a place. And, had death not claimed him so prematurely, what would have been Veidt's place in Hollywood? Perhaps he would have played yet more Nazi villains, or stern Teutonic taskmasters of the sort he essayed in *The Men in Her Life*, all very distant from the wide variety of roles he played in the silent era. The cynical postwar years had little use for fatalistic romance. The mean streets of film noir were full of men foolish enough to think they could realize their petty dreams of easy money and fast women. The film noir hero knows nothing; the Veidt hero, everything. Doomed passion seems especially out of place in the movies today. If anything, it has been relegated to the therapist's couch.

Das Cabinet des Dr. Caligari and *Das indische Grabmal* have been restored and issued on video and DVD, but many of Veidt's silents are either lost or moldering in film archives, accessible only to a few. *The Thief of Bagdad* does turn up on American Movie Classics from time to time and most of Veidt's American films play regularly on Turner Classic Movies, but his British movies are seldom on tele-

destined ends far from contemporary times. He was one of those rare actors who seemed perfectly at home in costume dramas or historical epics, comfortable and natural in a hussar's helmet or a Renaissance doublet. He played any number of real people from the past, including Lord Nelson, Paganini, Cesare Borgia, Don Carlos, and Prince Metternich. He easily outdistanced both Paul Muni — one of his keenest competitors in the field — and the "Man of One Face," George Arliss. Sometimes accused of overacting, Veidt underplayed Rasputin, a role that has pushed many a good actor over the top. His low-key performance gave Rasputin a rather joyless air; thus, the drinking and womanizing seem more compulsive than plea-

vision and most have to be sought out through small, mail-order video outlets or cajoled from other collectors. Film buffs know and admire Conrad Veidt's versatility (although often they have seen only a fraction of his work) but he's virtually unknown to today's moviegoing public. Still, *Casablanca*, another tale of star-crossed lovers, maintains its place in pop movie culture. Ilsa and Rick will always have Paris and, as long as they do, Conrad Veidt will share in their immortality. It's a romantic irony that he — and the charming but tragic men of the world he so often portrayed — would no doubt have appreciated.

Bibliography

Allen, J. C. *Conrad Veidt: From* Caligari *to* Casablanca. Pacific Grove, Cal.: The Boxwood Press, 1987.

The American Film Institute Catalogue: Feature Films 1921–1930; 1931–1940; 1941–1950. Berkeley: University of California Press.

Armes, Roy. *A Critical History of the British Cinema.* New York: Oxford University Press, 1978.

Balcon, Michael. *Michael Balcon Presents ... A Lifetime of Films.* London: Hutchinson of London, 1969.

Barlow, John D. *German Expressionist Film.* Boston: Twayne Publishers, 1982.

Battle, Pat Wilks. "Conrad Veidt" (parts 1–3), in *Films in Review* (magazine). New York, 1993.

Baxter, John. *The Hollywood Exiles.* New York: Taplinger Publishing Company, 1976.

Belach, Helga. *Richard Oswald.* Munich: Cinegraph, 1990.

Bock, Hans-Michael, Wolfgang Jacobsen, and Jörg Schöning, eds. *Reinhold Schünzel.* Munich: Edition Text/Kritik, 1989.

Brown, Geoff and Laurence Kardish. *Michael Balcon: The Pursuit of British Cinema* (brochure). New York: The Museum of Modern Art, 1984.

Bucher, Felix. *Screen Stories: Germany.* New York: A. S. Barnes, 1970.

Casty, Alan. *Development of the Film.* New York: Harcourt, Brace, Jovanovich, 1973.

Christie, Ian. *Arrows of Desire* Boston: Faber and Faber, 1994.

Coates, Paul. *The Gorgon's Gaze: German Cinema, Expressionism, and the Image of Horror.* Cambridge: Cambridge University Press, 1991.

Collier, Jo Leslie. *From Wagner to Murnau: The Transposition of Romanticism from Stage to Screen.* Ann Arbor, Mich.: UMI Research Press, 1996.

Conway, Shirley. *Conrad Veidt (1893–1943): A Tribute to "A Well Grac'd Actor."* Self-published, 1993.

Cook, David A. *A History of Narrative Film.* New York: W. W. Norton and Company, 1981.

Cook, Pam, ed. *Gainsborough Pictures.* London: Cassell, 1997.

Cowie, Peter. *Swedish Cinema.* London: A. Zwemmer Limited, 1966.

Dagover, Lil. *Lil Dagover: Ich war die Dame.* Munich: Franz Schneekluth Verlag, 1979.

Dahlke, Günther and Günter Karl. *Deutsche Spielfilme von den Anfängen bis 1933.* Berlin: Henschel Verlag, 1993.

Dick, Bernard F. *City of Dreams: The Making and Remaking of Universal Pictures.* Lexington (Ky.): The University Press of Kentucky, 1997.

Edmonds, I.G. *Big U: Universal in the Silent Days.* New York: A. S. Barnes, 1977.

Ehrlich, Evelyn. *Cinema of Paradox: French Filmmaking Under the German Occupation.* New York: Columbia University Press, 1985.

Eisner, Lotte H. *The Haunted Screen.* Berkeley: University of California Press, 1969.

_____. *Fritz Lang.* New York: Da Capo, 1976.

_____. *Murnau.* London: Secker and Warburg, 1973.

Everson, William K. *American Silent Film*. New York: Oxford University Press, 1978.

Eyeman, Scott. *The Speed of Sound: Hollywood and the Talkie Revolution; 1926–1930*. New York: Simon and Schuster, 1997.

Friedman, Regin Mihal. *L'Image et Son Juif*. Paris: Payot, 1983.

Goetz, Wolfgang. *Werner Krauss*. Hamburg: Hoffman und Campe Verlag, 1954.

Harmetz, Aljean. *Round Up the Usual Suspects: The Making of Casablanca–Bogart, Bergman, and World War II*. New York: Hyperion, 1992.

Harper, Sue. "Thinking Forward and Up: The British Films of Conrad Veidt" in *The Unknown 1930s: An Alternative History of the British Cinema, 1929–1939*, Jeffrey Richards, editor. London: I.B. Tauris Publishers, 1998.

Ickes, Paul. *Conrad Veidt: Ein Buch vom Wesen und Werden eines Künstlers*. Berlin: Filmschriftenverlag GmbH, 1927.

Jacobsen, Wolfgang. *Conrad Veidt: Lebensbilder*. Berlin: Argon, 1993.

Kasten, Jurgen. *Der expressionistische Film*. Munster: Maks Publikationen Munster, 1990.

Kinnard, Roy. *Horror in Silent Films: A Filmography, 1896–1929*. Jefferson, N.C.: McFarland & Company, 1995.

Klaus, Ulrich J. *Deutsche Tonfilme*. Berlin: Klaus-Archiv, 1995.

Klepper, Robert K. *Silent Films, 1877–1996: A Critical Guide to 643 Movies*. Jefferson, N.C.: McFarland & Company, 1999.

Kracauer, Siegfried. *From Caligari to Hitler: A Psychological History of the German Film*. Princeton, N.J.: Princeton University Press, 1947.

Kreimeier, Klaus. *The UFA Story: A History of Germany's Greatest Film Company, 1918–1945*. New York: Hill and Wang, 1996.

Kulik, Karol. *Alexander Korda: The Man Who Could Work Miracles*. New Rochelle, N.Y.: Arlington House, 1975.

Kurtz, Rudolf. *Expressionismus und Film*. Berlin: Verlag der Lichtbildbühne, 1926.

Lamprecht, Gerhard. *Deutsche Stummfilme*. Berlin: Deutsche Kinemathek, 1969.

Low, Rachael. *The History of British Film*. London: George Allen and Unwin, Ltd., 1971.

MacDonald, Kevin. *Emeric Pressburger: The Life and Death of a Screenwriter*. London: Faber and Faber, 1994.

Manvell, Roger and Heinrich Fränkel. *The German Cinema*. New York: Praeger Publishers, 1971.

_____ and Lewis Jacobs. *The International Encyclopedia of Film*. New York: Crown Publishers, Inc., 1972.

Murray, Bruce. *Film and the German Left in the Weimar Republic: From* Caligari *to* Kuhle Wampe. Austin, Texas: University of Texas Press, 1990.

Napley, Sir David. *Rasputin in Hollywood*. London: George Weidenfeld & Nicholson Limited, 1989.

Nowell-Smith, Geoffrey, ed. *The Oxford History of World Cinema*. Oxford: Oxford University Press, 1997.

Petrie, Graham. *Hollywood Destinies: European Directors in America, 1922–1931*. London: Routledge & Kegan Paul, 1985.

Petro, Patrice. *Joyless Streets*. Princeton, N.J.: Princeton University Press, 1989.

Pratt, George C. *Spellbound in Darkness: A History of the Silent Film*. Greenwich, Conn.: New York Graphic Society, 1966.

Prawer, S. S. *Caligari's Children*. New York: Oxford University Press, 1980.

Rainsberger, Todd *James Wong Howe: Cinematographer*. New York: A. S. Barnes & Company, Inc., 1981.

Robertson, James C. *The Casablanca Man: The Cinema of Michael Curtiz*. London: Routledge, 1993.

Rotha, Paul. *The Film Till Now*. London: Vision Press, 1930.

Saunders, Thomas J. *Hollywood in Berlin: American Cinema and Weimar Germany*. Berkeley: University of California Press, 1994.

Schöning, Jörg, ed. *London Calling: Deutsche in britischen Film der dreissiger Jahre*. Hamburg: Cinegraph, 1993.

Sherman, Vincent. *Studio Affairs: My Life as a Film Director*. Lexington (Ky.): The University Press of Kentucky, 1996.

Soister, John T. *Of Gods and Monsters*. Jefferson, N.C.: McFarland & Company, 1999.

Taylor, John Russell. *Strangers in Paradise: The Hollywood Emigrés, 1933–1950*. New York: Holt, Rinehart and Winston, 1983.

Tegel, Susan. "The Politics of Censorship: Britain's *Jew Süss* (1934) in London, New

York and Vienna" in *Historical Journal of Film, Radio and Television*, Vol. 15, No. 2. Oxford: Journals Oxford Ltd., 1995.

Thompson, David. *A Biographical Dictionary of Film*. New York: Alfred Knopf, 1995.

Vermilye, Jerry. *The Great British Films*. Secaucus, N.J.: The Citadel Press, 1978.

Walker, Alexander. *The Shattered Silents: How the Talkies Came to Stay*. New York: William Morrow and Company, Inc., 1979.

Wollenberg, H. H. *Fifty Years of German Film*. London: The Falcon Press, 1948.

Index

Numbers in **bold** indicate photographs.